पुरातत्त्व
PURĀTATTVA

Bulletin of the Indian Archaeological Society

No. 11 1979-80

Editor
K. N. Dikshit

D.K. Printworld (P) Ltd.
New Delhi

Cataloging in Publication Data — DK
[Courtesy : D.K. Agencies (P) Ltd. <docinfo@dkagencies.com>]

Purātattva : bulletin of the Indian Archaeological Society, no. 11, 1979-80 / editor, K.N. Dikshit.
p. cm.
Includes bibliographical references.
ISBN 8124602875

1. Archaeology — India — Periodicals. 2. India — Antiquities — Periodicals. 3. India — Civilization — Periodicals. I. Dikshit, K.N. II. Indian Archaeological Society.

DDC 934 21

First Published in 1982
First Reprinted in 2005
ISBN 81-246-0287-5
Price for volume 11 (1979-80): Rs. 800 US $ 40

Reprint authorised by
Indian Archaeological Society
New Delhi - 110 016

Purātattva is published annually.

Manuscripts (whether in the form of articles or notes or book reviews) offered for publication should be sent to the Editor, Purātattva, Indian Archaeological Society, B-17, Qutab Institutional Area, New Delhi - 110 016.

Published and printed by:
D.K. Printworld (P) Ltd.
'Srikunj,' F-52, Bali Nagar
New Delhi – 110015
Phone : (011) 2545 3975, 2546 6019 Fax : (011) 2546 5926
E-mail : dkprintworld@vsnl.net
www. dkprintworld.com

CONTENTS

BOOK REVIEWS

EDITORIAL

This is the eleventh issue of *Puratattva,* the Bulletin of the Indian Archaeological Society. As usual it includes articles on Prehistory, Protohistory and Historical Archaeology, but for the first time a good number of papers on art and architecture find place in this issue. Another interesting contribution is the reassessment of the archaeological evidence of Kausambi which happens to be one of the key-sites of the Ganga valley, through a series of three articles. Care has also been taken to incorporate information on the latest conservation techniques including protection of monuments from the air-pollution.

It is heartening to see that the younger generation with their new outlook and interest has shown considerable skill and aptitude in synthesizing and handling of their data. I regret that for want of space it has not been possible to publish in this number all the articles received; however, these will appear in the next issue of the Bulletin.

In this issue all the illustrations be they line drawings or plates, are by the courtesy of the institutions to which respective contributors belong.

I acknowledge with thanks the assistance and cooperation that we have received from the members of the Archaeological Survey in bringing out this issue. It was largely due to the financial grant from the Survey that this publication could be brought out. In this connection I also express my gratitude to Dr. S. P. Gupta of the National Museum, and Dr. Dilip K. Chakrabarti, Delhi University for their help in making this issue an useful reference publication for students and research scholars. Much of the credit for publishing this volume in time goes to my younger colleagues Sarvashri A. K. Sinha, P. K. Trivedi and S. G. Rao of the Society to whom my thanks are due. I will be failing in my duty, if I do not express my sincere thanks to Shrimati Seema Mukherjee of the Sanjay Composers & Printers, New Delhi, but for her involvement, this volume would not have come out.

K.N.D.

OBITUARY

PARESH CHANDRA DASGUPTA (1923-82)

Shri P. C. Dasgupta's contributions to archaeology in West Bengal have been manifold. As the Assistant Curator of the Ashutosh Museum, Calcutta University, he participated in the discovery of large number of early historic sites in lower Bengal. In fact, early historic terracottas of Bengal were his special field of study and he has left behind a number of important publications on the subject. When he became the Director of the newly established Directorate of Archaeology, Government of West Bengal, sometime in the early 1960s he undertook a large-scale programme of prehistoric and protohistoric exploration in the state. This culminated in the excavations at Pandu Rajar Dhibi and Baneshwar Danga and the discovery of the rich prehistoric site of Susunia. It is doubtful if he ever felt at home in prehistoric and protohistoric studies but what matters most in retrospect is that he was able to demonstrate, for the first time, the richness of these remains in West Bengal. He was also an ardent collector of antiquities and the impressive collection of objects in his Directorate has been entirely due to his singular enthusiasm. Archaeology in West Bengal is decidedly poorer without him.

DR SATYA PRAKASH (1914-1982)

The members of the Indian Archaeological Society mourn the untimely death of Dr. Satya Prakash which took place at Jaipur on the 11th May, 1982 only three days after his public felicitation. He was born at Lucknow, and had to his credit a brilliant academic carrier. He was the Director of the Department of Archaeology & Museums, Govt. of Rajasthan from 1948 to 1969 and took charge of the Salar Jung Museum, Hyderabad in 1969 which assignment he accomplished with devotion till 1975. In fact it was his insight and well planned schemes which brought Rajasthan on the Archaeological Map of the country. The Museums of Rajasthan are indebted to his foresightedness and special attention which he paid to them during his tenure. With his long administrative and organizing experience with scholarly temperament he gave his best not only in the reorganization of the gallaries of the Salar Jung Museum on modern scientific lines but also streamlining of the administration. Always an inquisitive researcher, Dr. Satya Prakash was also closely associated with the various universities and learned societies. In his death the country has lost a real worker.

The Banganga-Beas Palaeolithic Industry : A Look-Back

B. B. LAL
Indian Institute of Advanced Study, Simla

In June 1955, the present writer carried out an exploration in the Banganga and Beas valleys and discovered the palaeolithic sites of Guler, Kangra, Dehra-Gopipur and Dhaliara (Lal 1956 : 58-92). Even though no excavation was undertaken and the exploration also was a very brief one, a reasonable number of tools (seventy two) was collected, which brought into focus the fact that the palaeolithic industry from these sites was characterized, on the one hand, by the occurrence in abundance of unifacial choppers and bifacial chopping tools[1] and, on the other, by the absence of handaxes and cleavers. The two specimens of handaxes from Guler, though included in the above mentioned paper because of their general handaxe-like appearance, bore essentially thermal fractures, were badly rolled and were, therefore, regarded as doubtful specimens even at the time of writing the paper (Lal 1956 : 86, f.n.1). The writer had also identified five terraces (T_1 to T_5, from top downwards) of the Banganga at Guler, which stood respectively at the approximate heights of 565 ft (172.2 m), 375 ft (114.3m), 150 ft (45.7 m), 90 ft (27.4m), and 30 ft (9.1 m) above the then water-level of the river.

Much water has flown down the Banganga and Beas since then. During this interval of twenty-seven years many scholars have re-examined these sites and even excavated at two of them. They have also explored many a new site in this very region as well as in other regions of Himachal Pradesh and in the adjacent areas of Jammu, Punjab and Haryana. This work has thrown up a great deal of new material. Besides, lots of theories have been propounded regarding the Banganga-Beas palaeolithic industry, which vary from one end of the scale to the other. It has, therefore, become essential to take stock of the entire situation and find out the emergent picture.

2. FURTHER WORK SINCE 1955

In 1957 a team consisting of H. D. Sankalia, B. Subbarao, R. V. Joshi, K. V. Soundararajan and others visited the Banganga valley in search of more tools and possible evidence of glaciation, while they duly obtained unifacial choppers and bifacial chopping tools, no specimens of the Madras handaxe culture were encountered. These explorers also thought that the ocurrence of huge granite blocks on T_3 constituted 'evidence of the Quaternary glacial movement (*IAR* 1957-58: 43).

In 1961-62, V. D. Krishnaswami discovered chopper-chopping tools in the Sutlej valley near Bilaspur. However, here again no handaxe or cleaver was met with (*IAR* 1961-62: 37-38).

Nearly a decade after his aforementioned work, Joshi again undertook an exploration in which regions around Dehra-Gopipur and Jwalamuki on the south-east and near Nurpur on the north-west —all falling within the Beas drainage—were explored. While the pebble tools were found as usual, the noteworthy outcome of this exploration was the discovery of a few specimens relating to the handaxe-cleaver complex (Joshi 1978 : 96-99). An Assessment of this new evidence, on which lots of theories are being floated, is one of the purposes of the present paper.

The foregoing was followed by the work of a joint Indo-Polish team comprising R. V. Joshi and others on the Indian side and Drs. S. Roziski W. Chmilewski and others on the Polish (*IAR* 1967-68 : 22-23). The efforts were directed primarily towards an examination of the causes of the terrace-formations. While no evidence of direct glacier action in the region was obtained, four distinct 'cone' formations were identified as Sikhov I and II and Kangra I and II, with which, in that order, were correlated the top four terraces, viz. T_1 to T_4 of Guler.

Quite independent of the above work, under a scheme of the Panjab University, G. C. Mohapatra carried out in the early 60's an exploration between Manali and Dehra-Gopipur and located a few palaeolithic sites. These yielded only unifacial choppers and bifacial chopping tools, but no handaxes or cleavers. Encouraged by these results, Mohapatra did further field-work in the area, including excavation on a terrace at Dehra-Gopipur (Mohapatra 1966). Neither in the excavation at Dehra-Gopipur, nor even in the exploration at other sites did he come across any handaxe or cleaver, the choppers and chopping tools being, as if, omnipresent.

Mohapatra (1966 : 221-237) also carried out explorations in the Sirsa valley, Tahsil Nalagarh, Himachal Pradesh, where Olaf Prufer, Y. D. Sharma and D. Sen had worked earlier (cf. Sen 1955). In the late 70's Mohapatra (1979a : 600-602) explored the valley of the Chikni, a tributary of the Sirsa and brought to light about a dozen sites. However, neither the work of Sen *et al* nor even the repeated explorations of Mohapatra led to the discovery of any handaxe or cleaver in this region.

Towards the close of the 60's and in early 70's a region contiguous to Himachal Pradesh on the north-west, viz. that of Jammu was explored by H. M. Saroj. Intensive work in the valleys of the Chenab and its tributary, the Tawi, and in the valleys of the Ravi and its five tributaries, viz. the Devak, Basantar, Ben, Tarnah and Ujh yielded only the chopper-chopping tools, the handaxe-cleaver complex being completely absent (Saroj 1974).

In the mid-70's, a new area in Himachal Pradesh itself was opened up by a joint team of the Deccan College and the Geological Survey of India. The site lies in the famous fossil-park of Saketi in the Markanda valley. Here too only chopper/chopping tools were encountered, there being no handaxes or cleavers (Joshi *et al* 1975 : 464-465).

In recent years intensive exploration has been carried out in the region lying at the foot of the Siwalik range in the Districts of Hoshiarpur and Rupnagar (formerly known as Ropar) in Punjab, in and around the Union Territory of Chandigarh, and in the northern part of Ambala District, Haryana, which has brought to light a large number of Chopper-Chopping tool sites. However, at some sites in this region Acheulian bifaces have been found (Mohapatra 1982 : 28-32; Mohapatra and Singh 1979 b: 65-77; Sharma 1977 : 94-95); which adds a new dimension to the problem. The same will be discussed towards the end of the paper.

3. THE UNIFACIAL 'SUSPECTS'

Before we proceed to discuss the implications of the data obtained from the work referred to above, it may perhaps not be out of place to say a few words about the doubts expressed by certain scholars in regard to the Guler tools, particularly the unifacial ones, as having been made by human agency. During the course of a talk with the present writer in the early 60's, Professor H. D. Sankalia went to the extent of saying, "If they are unifacial they are suspect in my eyes." This very line of thinking is reflected in his book (1974 : 32-33) when he says :

> "While there is not much doubt regarding the character of the bifacially worked choppers, and unifacial choppers which have been extensively worked, other unifacial choppers are really suspect."

In fact the use of the word "*much*" in the above quotation shows that some doubts still persist in Sankalia's mind even "regarding the *character* of the bifacially worked choppers'. One can understand if the objection had been individually in regard to some specimens, but the doubt cast on the *character* of the industry as a whole is really unintelligible.

Similar doubts have been raised by Joshi (1979 : 26) :

"The location of these specimens at Guler is rather interesting. *The majority of them have been found by Lal in the gullies* traversing the slope between the terraces T_1 and T_2. This has been the experience also during the present writer's work in 1966 and 1967. In view of the steep slopes and the fact that the loose pebbles moving down such surface are liable to fracture due to attrition, the high proportion on (perhaps 'of' was intended) *unilaterally flaked pebble tools* at this site may perhaps be attributed to the natural causes of movement of pebbles under gravitational forces. *The human agency may not have any role in the making* of such specimens."

In the first place, the reason why more tools were available to Joshi and the present writer from the rain-gullies in between the terraces is very simple. As is evident, these gullies have been formed by the erosional action of the rain water flowing down from one terrace to another. In the process, the contents of the terraces, which included the tools as well, have been exposed and the latter are available in a relatively heavier concentration in the rain-gullies than on (non-gullied) flat areas.

Now to the more important point about the genuineness of the unifacial tools. While nobody denies that the movement of pebbles down the slopes would have resulted in the removal of flakes from some of the pebbles due to attrition, it is strange to think that such attrition would have resulted in the removal of flakes *only from one side* and not from the other. What was there to prevent the rolling pebbles from being flaked off from the other side as well? In fact one would expect that in the process of the rolling down of the pebbles and of detachment of flakes from them through natural attrition with other pebbles, the flakes would have come out *at random,* from one side or from both sides. But what distinguishes the tools from such naturally flaked off pebbles is the *regularity or systematic pattern* of the flaking in the former and the random nature in the latter. A look at the tools illustrated here on Fig. 1 would convince anyone of the systematic nature of their flaking and, therefore, of their having been made by human agency and not through natural attrition. It is a different matter if a given collection also includes a few odd specimens the flaking on which may be debatable as being human or natural. It is well known that while on the field one tends to collect as much as possible within the short time at one's disposal and thus even some doubtful specimens find their way into the collection-bags. But that does not entitle Sankalia to say what has been quoted above or Joshi to remark in a condescending way : "Granting that the pebble tools from Guler are of human manufacture facture........." (Joshi 1979 : 27). They *are.*

4. THE PROBLEM OF THE MASSIVE GRANITE BLOCKS AND QUARTZITE BOULDERS

Since the present writer is not a geologist, he considers himself incompetent to offer any comments on the formation of the river-terraces at Guler and Kangra. He would, however, like to draw pointed attention to two very important facts. In the first place, it has been observed by all explorers in the area that on these terraces there occur granite blocks which are inordinately large : those occurring on T_3 at Guler are more than 6 metres across. There are no granite bed-rocks in the immediate neighbourhood from which these blocks may have been cut off. It is thus evident that these blocks have been transported over very long distances, from their original home somewhere much further north in the Himalayas. There is also one more point to be noted about these blocks, namely that they are *angular* and not rounded off.

Secondly, on T_1 at Guler there occur very large quartzite boulders bearing 'chatter-marks' (Lal 1956, pl. XIXB). The sources of these quartzite boulders too is not in the neighbourhood. We have thus, seriously to ponder over the correct identification of the agency that could have transported the massive granite blocks as well as the quartzite boulders over such long distances.

Would the following explanation offered by Joshi (1979 :11) sqarely meet the situation?

"It is also possible that *huge lakes* might have been formed due to blocking of the stream channels by the talus at the base of the Dharamsala range, thereby impounding large volumes of water and the subsequent bursting of the same might have caused extensive spread of the sediments. The latter streams have entrenched their beds in this loose material."

Or, in search of the answer we are to dig up once again Medlicott (1865 : 1-187) and Theobald (1874 : 68-98) who opined that the granite erratics and quartzite boulders in the Kangra region had

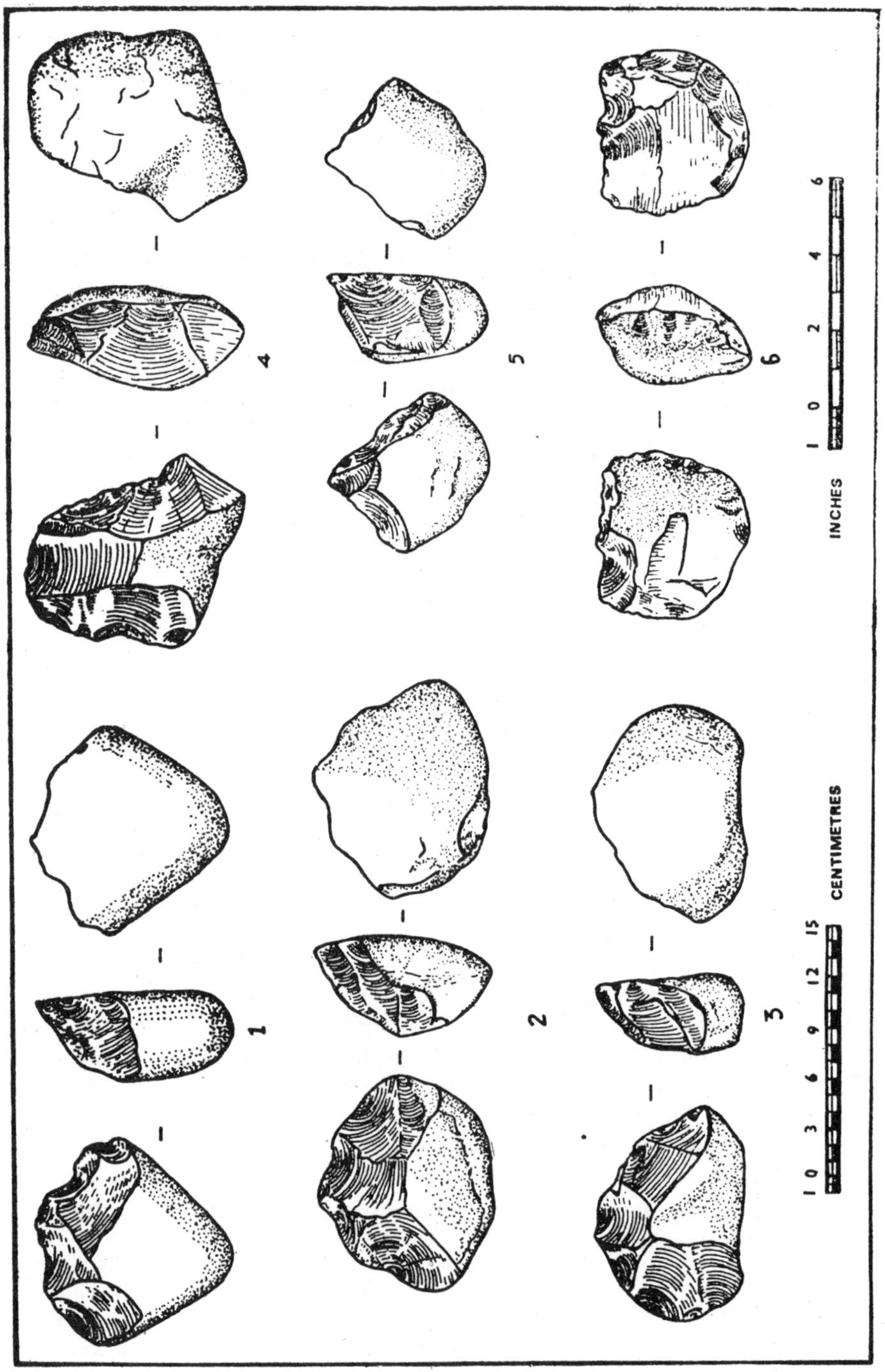

Fig. 1 Pebble tools from Guler: 1—4. Unifacial 'chopper'; 5. Unifacial 'pebble handaxe' and 6. bifacial 'chopping-tool'.

been brought by *floating ice*. Theobald even went to the extent of saying that there were as many as seven glaciations and the one that descended down to the Haripur region (opposite Guler on the Banganga) was the most powerful one. Would this explain more satisfactorily the occurrence of the over 6 m long granite erratics on T_3 at Guler? But positive evidence of glaciation has to be discovered before this explanation can be acceptable.

It is thus obvious that search for the correct answer has to continue.

5. THE REAL IDENTITY OF THE BANGANGA-BEAS PALAEOLITHIC INDUSTRY

The writer has consciously used the geographical term 'Banganga-Beas' to qualify the palaeolithic industry under consideration, instead of using the term the other way about, viz. 'Beas-Banganga'. By giving priority to the Banganga over the Beas, the writer wishes to emphasize that he is referring to that palaeolithic industry which is to be found in the Banganga valley, at sites like Guler,[2] Haripur, etc., and which extends to the Beas valley in the area lying on either side of the confluence of the Banganga with the Beas (cf. fig. 2). In such a consideration, therefore, the collection of tools from the more westerly tributaries of the Beas, such as that from the Sukhardi-Khad (site Panjasaran) has to be examined separately. For thus alone can the real identity of the Banganga-Beas industry be appreciated.

We may now discuss the principal traits of the Banganga-Beas palaeolithic industry. In the first place, let it be admitted that, as matters stand today, there are not sufficient data from excavation which would help us in working out an evolution of this industry from terrace to terrace. Joshi (1979 : 14) got only a few flakes from his excavation of Terrace 1 at Guler. He did not excavate any other terrace. Mohapatra (1966: 225-226) excavated a terrace at Dehra-Gopipur and got quite a few tools therefrom. However, coming as these do from a single terrace, these do not help us in working out an evolutionary sequence. Therefore, in the present state of our knowledge, we are obliged to deal with the Banganga-Beas palaeolithic industry as a whole and find out what characteristic features it betrays. Briefly, these are as follows :

(i) The first thing that strikes any one is that the Banganga-Beas palaeolithic industry is characterized by unifacial choppers and bifacial chopping tools. But this is not all. As would be clear from the accompanying Table, the former far outnumber the latter, the ratio being more than 5 : 1. In fact, it may not be wrong to say that it is essentially a unifacial industry.

(ii) The flakes accompanying this industry have, by and large, a wide angle between the platform and the flake-surface. Rarely is there any evidence of the preparation of the platform prior to the detachment of the flake. This is fully borne out not only by the specimens from surface-collections, but also from those obtained by Joshi (1979) and Mohapatra (1966) from their excavations respectively at Guler and Dehra-Gopipur. The flakes, thus, do not betray Levalloisean traits.

(iii) Though there do occur in this industry a few examples of what have been termed by the present writer as 'pebble-handaxes' (incidently these too are mostly unifacial), there are no true handaxes of the Madrasian (Acheulian) type.

The two specimens collected by the present writer from Guler were even initially regarded as doubtful (Lal 1956: 86 f.n.1). Joshi and Mohapatra too, who carried out further work at this site, did not come across any true handaxe.

Under the heading 'Handaxes', Joshi (1979) deals with three specimens only which are numbered as 22, 23 and 24 and illustrated on Figure 6 and Plate XVII accompanying his paper. A careful examination of the drawings and photographs shows that none of these specimens is really a handaxe in the true sense of the term, as understood in the Madras handaxe-cleaver complex. To discuss the point further. Specimen no 22 "made on small flat pebble of banded cherty shale" "is trimmed along half the margin by step-flaking leaving the rest of the pebble area unworked. On the underside the working is limited to one edge by step technique." In the first place, Joshi himself admits that "the banded nature of the rock, to some extent, imparts step-like flaking and until another specimen is found at the sites yielding cleavers this almond-like tool will have to be taken as an Acheulian tool with caution" (Joshi 1979 : 22). From the drawing and photograph published by Joshi it appears that the tool

TABLE showing the relative occurrence of Unifacial Choppers and Bifacial Chopping Tools

(Note : Only those sites have been included in this table in respect of which actual statistics have been published by the authors)

Sl. No.	Site; and River-Valley	Unifacial Choppers	Bifacial Chopping tools	Reference
1.	Dehra-Gopipur; the Beas	10	x	Lal 1956 : 71
		8	3	Joshi 1979 : 15
2.	Dhaliara; on a left-hand tributary of the Beas	4	x	Lal 1956 : 81
3.	Dhawala; on the Nakehar Khad, a tributary of the Beas	6	x	Joshi 1979 : 16
4.	Guler; the Banganga	24	3	Lal 1956 : 68
		6	3	Joshi 1979 : 14
5.	Haripur; the Banganga	4	x	Joshi 1979 : 15
6.	Jammal; on the Thor Khad, a tributary of the Beas	9	x	Joshi 1979 : 16
7.	Kotla; on the Chumar Nala, a tributary of the Beas	7	3	Joshi 1979 : 17
8.	Panjasaran; on the Sukhardi-Khad, which through another stream joins the Beas south of Pathankot	4	2	Joshi 1979 : 10

may have been a side-scraper. About no 23 too Joshi is doubtful since he refers to it as "a large pebble-butted handaxe (?) from Dhawala which is more like a unifacial chopper of pointed oblate group." This too may have been a scraper. Specimen no 24 is what Joshi himself calls "a huge borer-chopper", "a heavy pebble-butted handaxe." It is similar to what is also available at Guler and called there a 'pebble handax' (Lal 1956 : no 15, fig 8 and pl XXX).

In sum, therefore, there are no true handaxes in this region.

(iv) In the Banganga-Beas valley there are no cleavers either. Neither the present writer nor Mohapatra got any example. However, Joshi lists five specimens of cleavers, one from Kotla (no 17) and four from Panjasaran (no 18-21) The one from Kotla, according to Joshi himself, is 'rolled'—a fact which is also very clear when one compares its drawing and photograph with those from Panjasaran (Joshi 1979 : fig. 5 and pl XVI).

In this context it may be recalled that Panjasaran is *not* in the Banganga-Beas region as defined by the present writer (above, p 5). It is on a much westerly *nala* which, through another stream, joins the Beas south of Pathankot. The implications of this geographical situation will be discussed a little later.

6. DISCUSSION

From the foregoing it would be amply clear that the Banganga-Beas palaeolithic industry, characterized, on the one hand, by the presence of choppers and chopping tools (amongst which the unifacial ones far outnumber the bifacial ones) and high-angled flakes with unfaceted platform, and, on the other, by the absence of the Madrasian handaxe-cleaver complex and true Levalloisean flakes, has its own distinctive personality.

Our trouble is that we have always been looking at this industry wearing the glasses of the Soan (or Sohan) Culture of the Potwar region. Perhaps nobody is to blame for this, for the Soan Culture was discovered as far back as the 1930's, and the Banganga-Beas palaeolithic industry two decades later. Hence, in an assessment of the latter, a back reference to the former is easily understandable, more so since it is the nearest known culture. However, the root cause of the trouble seems to lie in the fact that the Soan Culture itself has not been properly understood by many scholars, may be partly due to the unstratified evidence itself and partly because of the individual's interpretation of it. Thus, it has often been assumed that handaxes and cleavers constitute an integral part of the Early (some scholars have used the term Lower) Soan Culture, of which the Chopper-Chopping tools were the main constituents. For example, Sen (1955 : 181) wrote as follows :

"It is significant that the Abbevillian-Acheulian biface and cleavers which *occur alongside the Early Soan in north-west Punjab as a complex* are so far conspicuous by their absence in Nalagarh in East Punjab."

It may perhaps be argued that this was written way back in 1955 when the clarification given by Paterson and Drummond (1962) was not available (cf. below). But even as the present paper is being written a book has come out which states (Agrawal 1982: 21):

"Later discoveries have shown that both handaxes and the Sohan industries are associated with similar horizons and, therefore, it is difficult to say which industry is earlier—*if they are separate industries at all!*"

The position regarding the Chopper-Chopping Soan Culture *vis-a-vis* the handaxe-cleaver element has been made amply clear by Paterson and Drummond (1962). A reference to the chart published by them as Figure 2 (p 13) of their book categorically shows that: (i) the two are separate entities; and (ii) whereas the Lower Soan, with its characteristic chopper-chopping tools, goes back to Phase m_1 of the Middle Pleistocene, the handaxe-cleaver complex (called by these authors as Middle Stellenbosch because of the African similarity they perceive in the specimens concerned) appears on the scene only later, viz. in Phase m_2 of the Middle Pleistocene. Following this line of argument, the authors, rather dramatically but certainly justifiably, captioned their chapter dealing with the handaxe-cleaver complex as "The Stellenbosch *Invasion*" (*ibid:* 95).

We may now cast off the mantle of the Soan Culture and turn to the Indian side of the border, to which this paper primarily relates. A look at the map (Fig 2) would show that in the Banganga-Beas Valley, from Kangra in the north to Nadaun in the south and from Talwara in the west to Tira Sujanpur in the east, there is not even a single site which has yielded any evidence of the handaxe-cleaver complex. Attention may also be drawn to Bilaspur and its neighbouring area on the Sutlej which too has yielded only the chopper-chopping tools but to handaxes or cleavers. Likewise, in the Saketi area of the Markanda velley in Sirmur District, Himachal Pradesh no element of the handaxe-cleaver complex was encountered, though the choppers and chopping tools were duly found.

To the north-west of Himachal Pradesh, in the Jammu region, about a dozen palaeolithic sites have come to light in the valleys of the Chenab, Ravi and their tributaries. Of these, not even one has yielded any handaxe or cleaver, the chopper-chopping tools, however, being always present.

Thus, there is clearly an area (marked with vertical hatching on the map, fig 2) which is *completely* bereft of the handaxe-cleaver complex and yields only the chopper-chopping tools. Streching from the north-west to south-east, this area, it may be further observed, is essentially hilly and constitutes the *relatively* higher reaches of the rivers concerned, viz. the Chenab, Ravi, Beas, Sutlej and Markanda.

As no large-scale excavation of the terraces of the Banganga or Beas (except the minor operations at Guler and Dehra-Gopipur already referred to above) have been carried out, it is difficult to know whether there was or was not any evolution of the tools from one terrace to another. However, when one comes down to an area like that of the Sirsa valley near Nalagarh (cf. Fig 2) one notes, that, with its proto-Levalloisean and even Levalloisean flakes and smaller and more sophisticated pebble choppers and chopping tools, the palaeolithic industry over here is more evolved than that in the Banganga-Beas valleys (Sen 1955 : 176-184; Mohapatra 1974 : 199-212). But, again because of lack of excavation, we do not have the history of this evolution.

One point, however, ought to be noted that neither Sen nor Mohapatra obtained any handaxe or cleaver from the Sirsa valley, which signifies that *even this area never came under the influence of the handaxe-cleaver complex.*

However, a bit to the south and south-west is the area constituting the foot of the outermost Siwalik range from where the landscape begins to change and the plains emerge. In this area (marked with criss-cross hatching on the map, fig. 2), in the northern parts of Hoshiarpur and Rupnagar Districts of Punjab, in the vicinity of Chandigarh, and in the northern part of Ambala District of Haryana, about eighty sites have yielded palaeolithic assemblages. Of these, about twenty have produced cleavers and handaxes (Mohapatra 1979b) Since no excavation has been done even in this area, it is difficult to be sure of the exact point of time when the handaxe-cleaver element made its appearance in the region. However, on the basis of the available evidence Mohapatra is inclined to assign this element to a period later than that of the chopper-chopping tool complex. Further, the fact that only 25 percent sites have this handaxe-cleaver element shows that it is not likely to have evolved locally. Otherwise, one would have expected the cleavers and handaxes to occur at most of these sites. In fact, Mohapatra informs the writer that two of the sites, viz. Aibarpur and Chandikotla, have only the handaxe-cleaver complex. Therefore, there is a clear case for hypothesizing that the *handaxe-cleaver element is not indigenous to the area but represents an intrusion.* The source and direction of this intrusion, however, still remain to be worked out.

7. THE EMERGENT PICTURE

To sum up. The following picture would appear to emerge in the present state of our knowledge :

(i) The Banganga-Beas palaeolithic industry has a separate identity, characterized by unifacial choppers, bifacial chopping tools (the former far outnumbering the latter), and high-angled flakes with unfaceted platform.

(ii) In this industry there is total absence of handaxes, cleavers and real Levalloisean flakes.

(iii) In its above-mentioned form, the industry occurs mainly in the ralatively upper reaches of the Beas and Sutlej (shown with vertical hatching on the map, fig 2). This area is essentially hilly and constitutes the hinterland as compared to that mentioned at (iv) below.

(iv) In the Siwalik frontal region (shown with criss-cross hatching on the map, fig 2) which is contiguous to the Punjab and Haryana plains, there are certain sites, constituting about 25 percent of the total number of the sites, which have yielded handaxes and cleavers in addition to choppers and chopping tools. Two of these sites have, in fact, yielded cleavers/handaxes only.

(v) From no iv it is self-evident that even in the Siwalik frontal region the handaxe-cleaver complex is an intruder. Had it not been so, and had it evolved in this very area, these tools would have been available at most of the sites in it.

(vi) From exactly where this intrusion took place it is difficult to say in the present state of our knowledge. But certainly it was not from the north or north-east where, the handaxe-cleaver element is altogether wanting. However, located to the south of Punjab and west of Haryana is Rajasthan which is well known for the occurrence of the handaxe-cleaver industry. But much more evidence is needed to determine the migrational route if the intrusion was from that direction.

(vii) To still another question, namely, whether the chopper-chopping tool complex is autochthonous to the Jammu-Himachal region as marked out on the map, or it reached their from somewhere in the north or north-west, no answer can be given at the moment. In a very general way, one may recall the fact that Soviet Central Asia too abounds in chopper-chopping tools, but has yielded no typical handaxes or cleavers (Ranov 1966; Gupta 1979). The situation in China is none too different. What is the significance of these similarities yet remains to be seen.

ACKNOWLEDGEMENTS

The writer would like to express his thanks to : Shri S. K. Srivastava for preparing the map (Fig 2); Shri K. K. Grover for the help in re-assembling the sheet of Fig 1; and Shri S. K. Arora for typing out the script. Dr. G. C. Mohapatra has been kind enough to supply generously information regarding the sites explored by him; and Shrimati Kusum Lal has been of immense help in a number of ways during the course of the preparation of the paper. To them both the author is very grateful.

NOTES

1. In spite of the obvious drawback in using a functional terminology of which no one can be too sure, the present author would like to retain in this paper the above terms and not suddenly switch over to those suggested by Paterson and Drummond (1962). The argument for doing so is that a name that has long been in use should be allowed to continue since it is understood by all scholars at denoting a particular kind of

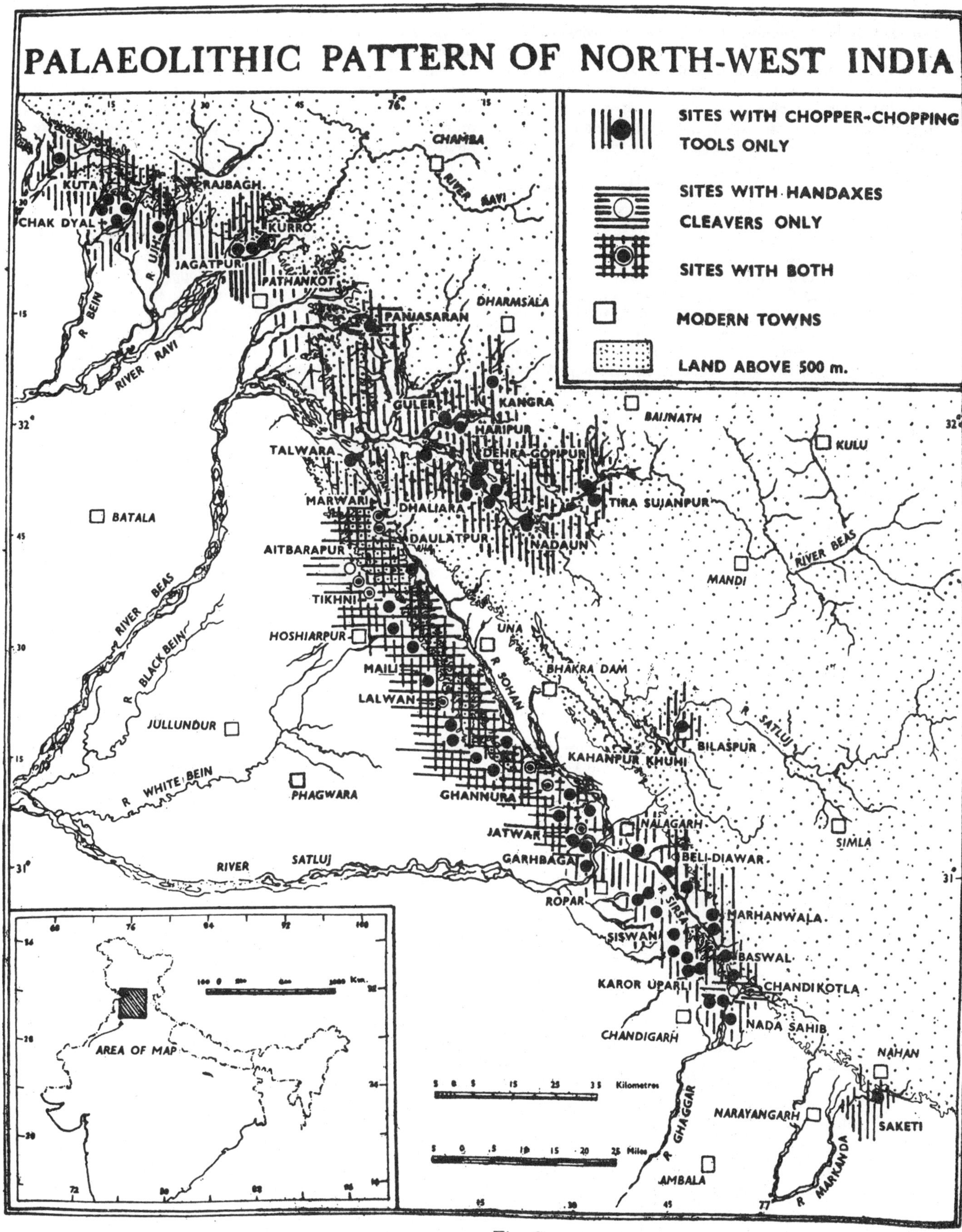
PALAEOLITHIC PATTERN OF NORTH-WEST INDIA
SITES WITH CHOPPER-CHOPPING TOOLS ONLY
SITES WITH HANDAXES CLEAVERS ONLY
SITES WITH BOTH
MODERN TOWNS
LAND ABOVE 500 m.
CHAMBA
RIVER RAVI
KUTA
RAJBAGH
CHAK DYAL
KURRO
JAGATPUR
PATHANKOT
DHARMSALA
PANJASARAN
R BEIN
RIVER RAVI
GULER
KANGRA
BAIJNATH
HARIPUR
KULU
TALWARA
DEHRA GOPIPUR
TIRA SUJANPUR
MARWARI
DHALIARA
BATALA
DAULATPUR
NADAUN
AITBARAPUR
RIVER BEAS
MANDI
RIVER BEAS
TIKHNI
HOSHIARPUR
UNA
R SOHAN
MAILI
BHAKRA DAM
R BLACK BEIN
LALWAN
JULLUNDUR
R SATLUJ
BILASPUR
KAHANPUR KHUHI
R WHITE BEIN
PHAGWARA
GHANNURA
NALAGARH
SIMLA
JATWAR
RIVER
SATLUJ
GARHBAGA
BELI-DIAWAR
ROPAR
R SIRSA
MARHANWALA
SISWAN
BASWAL
KAROR UPARLI
CHANDIKOTLA
NADA SAHIB
CHANDIGARH
NAHAN
AREA OF MAP
Km.
Kilometres
Miles
R GHAGGAR
NARAYANGARH
SAKETI
R MARKANDA
AMBALA

Fig. 2

tool. Let it be remembered that the tool concerned is still called the 'handaxe', even though it is realized by all that it could not have functioned as an axe, nor is it certain that it was used directly with the hands.

2. Joshi had at one stage (1979 : 32) suggested that this industry may be called the 'Guler Industry', but perhaps it may be better to qualify it with the names of the river-valleys rather than with the name of a place. However, if scholars think that the association of Guler with the name of the industry is better, because that site is a typical one, with its well-marked out terraces, the present writer will have no objection to it. All that he wishes is to emphasize the separate identity of this industry.

REFERENCES

Agrawal, D.P. 1982 *The Archaeology of India*, Curzon Press Ltd., London and Malmo.

Cheng Te-Kun 1959 Archaeology of China 1, Cambridge,

De Terra, H. and T.T. Paerson. 1939 Studies on the Ice Age in India and Associated Human Cultures, Carnegie Institute, Washington.

Graziosi, P. 1964 *Prehistoric research in northwestern Punjab*, Scientific reports of Italian Expedtions to the Kara-Korum (K2) and the Hindu Kush, Leiden : Brill.

Gupta, S.P. 1979 *Archaeology of Soviet Central Asia and the Indian Borderlands* 1, B.R. Publishing Corporation, Delhi.

Indian Archaeology-A Review, 1957-58; 1961-62; 1967-68.

Joshi, R.V. 1968 Early Stone Age Discoveries in the Beas-Banganga region, *Cultural Forum* 9(1-2).

1979 Stone Age environment and sequence in the Kangra Valley, Himachal Pradesh, *Prehistory of Himachal Pradesh* (ed) V.C. Ohri, Simla.

S.N. Rajguru, G.L. Badam and P.C. Khanna 1975 Early and Middle Polaeolithic Tools from the River Terraces in the Saketi Area, Markanda Valley, Himachal Pradesh, *Current Science* 44 (13).

Lal, B.B. 1956 Palaeoliths from the Beas and Banganga Valleys, Panjab, *Ancient India 12*.

Medlicott, H.B. 1865 On the geological structure and relations of northern portions of the Himalayan ranges between the River Ganges and Ravee, *Memoir Geological Survey of India* 3 (4).

Mohapatra, G.C. 1966 Preliminary report of the exploration of Stone Age sites in eastern Punjab, *Bulletin Deccan College Research Institute*.

1974 Lithic Industries of Himachal, *Perspectives in Palaeoanthropology : Sen Festschrift* (ed) Asok K. Ghosh, Calcutta.

1981 Acheulian discoveries in the Siwalik Frontal Range, *Current Anthropology* 22 (4),

1982 Acheulian discoveries in the Siswaliks of Punjab, *Indian Archaeology : New Perspectives* (ed) R.K. Sharma, Agam Kala Prakashan, Delhi.

and Mukesh Singh 1979a Prehistoric Investigations in a sub-Himalayan Valley, Himachal Pradesh, India, *Current Anthropology* 20(3).

and Mukesh Singh 1979b Stratified assurrence of lithic artifacts in the Siwalik Frontal Range of Western sub-Himalaya, *Panjab University Research Bulletin* (Arts) 10(1-2).

Movius Jr., H.L. 1948 Lower Palaeolithic cultures of southern and eastern Asia, *Transactions of American Philosophical Society* 38.

Paterson. T.T. ond H.J.H. Drummond 1962 *Soan, the Palaeolithic of Pakistan*, Deptt. of Archaeclogy, Government of Pakistan, Karachi.

Ranov, V.A. 1966 Pebble Tools and their role in the Palaeolith of Central Asia, *Report and Information on Archaeology in USSR*, Moscow.

Sankalia, H.D. 1974 *Prehistory and Protohistory of India and Pakistan*, Deccan College Postgraduate and Research Institute, Poona.

Saroj, H.M. 1974 *Lithic industries of Jammu*, Ph.D. dissertation (unpublished). Panjab University, Chandigarh.

Sen, D. 1955 Nalagarh Palaeolithic Culture, *Man in India* 35 (3).

Sharma, J.C. 1977 Palaeolithic Tools from Pleistocene Deposits in Panjab, India, *Current Anthropology 18(1)*.

Soundararajan, K.V. 1965 Is 'Soan' a Separate Culture? *Indian Prehistory*: 1964 (ed) V.N. Mishra and *M. S. Mate*, Poona. This has observations of other scholars as well.

Theobald, W. 1874 On the Former Extension of Glaciers within the Kangra District, *Rec. G.S.I.* 7(3).

Further Light on Lower Palaeolithic Occupation and Palaeoenvironment in Semi-arid Zone of Rajasthan.

V. N. Misra,[1] S. N. Rajaguru,[1] R. J. Wasson[1], G. Singh[1] and D. P. Agrawal[2]
[1]Deccan College, Pune
[2]Physical Research Laboratory, Ahmedabad

The semi-arid and arid regions of Rajasthan have received considerable attention for prehistoric and palaeoenvironmental research during last two-and-a-half decades. While a large number of sites of Middle Palaeolithic (Misra 1962:85-156, Mohapatra *et al* 1963:205-223, Allchin and Goudei 1974:358-368; Allchin Goudie and Hegde 1978) and Mesolithic (Misra 1973:92-110; Allchin, Goudle and Hegde 1978) have been located, the evidence of Lower Palaeolithic was quite scanty until two years ago and that for Upper Palaeolithic is still so. It is true that the flake-tool culture represented at many sites in the Luni basin had a small component of handaxes and cleavers. But these two types were morphologically diminutive, technologically advanced, and statistically they formed a very small proportion of an industry otherwise dominated by scrapers, points and borers, and were therefore considered to represent an early stage of the Middle Palaeolithic. The only Lower Palaeolithic site west of the Aravallis known for many years was Govindgarh near Ajmer (Misra 1965 : 205-208) where a small number of artefacts were found in a gravel deposit. In recent years Allchin, Goudie and Hegde have reported small assemblages of Lower Palaeolithic tools from Hokra and Savitri Hill west of Ajmer, at Gurha and Mogra south of Jodhpur, and at Marwar Bagra south of Jalor. In 1978 Agrawal, Misra and Rajaguru *(IAR* 1978-79) discovered a small Lower Palaeolithic assemblage from a buried gravel conglomerate at Bhadrajun between Jalor and Pali. All these collections were, however, statistically very small to give a clear typological picture of the Lower Palaeolithic, and they represented at best only scanty human occupation in western Rajasthan during this period.

It was against this background that in January 1979 Misra, Rajaguru and Agrawal following a clue supplied by Bimal Ghose of the Central Arid Zone Research Institute, Jodhpur, discovered an exceptionally rich Lower Palaeolithic site near Jayal (74°11' E, 27°13' N.) in Nagaur district. Here thousands of typical Lower Palaeolithic artefacts lay scattered on the surface of a 15 km long gravel ridge, testifying to the existence of large human populations over a long period of time in that area. The occurrence of tools only to a depth of 0.50 m in the primary gravel and to a depth of several metres in the re-deposited gravel meant that man appeared on the scene only towards the end of the grayel formation but he was witness to the subsequent modification of this formation by erosional forces. The extent of the gravel ridge over a 15 km length, its thickness of over 50 m, the large size of the boulders (up to 50 cm across), considerable rounding of pebbles and boulders all suggest a large and powerful stream system responsible for its deposition. This is the most telling geomorphic evidence for a relatively more humid climate and an active drainage system in the semi-arid zone of Rajasthan. The high degree of cementation of the gravel and the considerable modification of the gravel ridge by erosional forces probably imply a high antiquity for its origin. The gravel ridge is post-Early Tertiary in age and on the basis of sedimentological and geomorphological data it has been tentatively dated to the early Pleistocene (Agrawal *et al* 1980 : 51-56; Misra *et al* 1980 : 19-31).

Even more interesting evidence for early Palaeolithic occupation and contemporary environment was discovered by the present authors in January-February, 1980, in and around Didwana, in Nagaur district. Here an early Acheulian industry was discovered in a calcareous clayey formation (marl). The present paper gives a preliminary account of the stratigraphy, palaeoclimate and the typological nature of this industry.

LOCATION OF THE SITE (Fig 1)

Didwana (74°35' E, 37°24' N) is a small town located 100 km due east of Nagaur town in Nagaur district. The surrounding countryside consists of a flat alluvial plain dotted with linear sand ridge with a SW-NE orientation and with heights of 4-10 m. There is a small cluster of Aravalli hills a few km to the SW of the town, but the main Aravalli hills are about 50 km to the east. The area receives between 40 and 50 cm annual rainfall but there are no drainage channels of any significance. The rain water is absorbed by the sand mantle and finds its way into the saline depression through the sub-surface flow of water.

Immediately south of Didwana there is a large salt lake, a shallow depression oriented SW-NE and 7 km long and 2.5 km wide. It is bounded on the north and south by linear sand ridges with heights of 4 to 11 m and on the west by an artificial embankment over which runs the railway line to Degana. On the eastern side the lake opens to the sand covered alluvial plain. To the southwest of the town and separated from the salt lake by 1.5 km stretch of sand dunes is another large depression known as Singi Talav, 2.5 km long and 0.75 km broad which runs parallel to the Didwana-Nagaur road on its southern side. It is bounded by sand dunes on all sides.

QUATERNARY STRATIGRAPHY

Stratigraphic information was collected from dunes, lime quarries, wells and the Didwana salt lake. There are a number of deep quarries in and around Amarpura village, about 1.5 km west of Didwana railway station. The sequence of formations exposed in these quarries is as follows :

I. AMARPURA QUARRIES

0-165 cm. Aeolian fine sand with brownish top (A horizon) and diffused carbonate below, becoming nodular in yellow sand at a depth of 1 m and below. Sharp sub-horizontal boundary indicating an erosional surface.

165-395 cm. Nodular carbonate in sandy loam including some coarse sand, poorly sorted as compared with dune sand; carbonate nodules 5 to 10 mm in diameter, becoming larger with depth; basal part is clayey and resembles marl.

Several Acheulian tools were collected at different depths from this horizon. A larger number were picked up from the surface where they had been discarded after sieving of the calcareous clay by quarry workers.

395-745 cm. Sandy loam with crude sub-horizontal bedding. Both vertical and lateral variation in texture between clayey loam and silty sand. Well-developed carbonate nodules 2 to 4 cm in diameter. Layer below 045 cm undug.

II. SINGI TALAV

This a flat depression and contains shallow water only during the rainy season. A very large area has been dug for obtaining clay near the southeastern edge of the depression. The section of this pit was as follows:

0-40 cm. Sandy clay.

40-160 cm. White calcareous clay or marl as at Amarpura.

Three artefacts were found *in situ* in this horizon around the quarry where the overlying sandy clay has been removed by the local potters. These tools were sticking to the surface of the marl and could be easily extracted.

III. BANGAD CANAL

Some forty years ago a canal was dug from the hills southwest of the village of Marwar Balia to the Singi Talav depression to divert the run off from the hills into this Talav for meeting the water requirements of Didwana. The canal though now abandoned is well-preserved. The canal is dug into the sandy clay and underlying a marl and the excavated debris is piled up on both banks to form 4-5 m high embankments. In the marl which forms the top of the embankment a large number of artefacts were collected opposite the village of Indola ki Dhani. The horizon of these artefacts is clearly the marl formation.

IV RAILWAY CUTTING SECTION

A deep cut is exposed in the high dune to the south of Singi Talav because of the laying of the railway line through this dune. The stratigraphy of this cutting is as follows (The depths are approximate).

0-200 cm. Brownish fine sand.

200-400 cm. Yellowish fine sand with diffused carbonate.

400-800 cm. Rootcasts and diffused carbonate within the yellowish fine sand. Carbonate becomes better developed and harder with depth but is never more than 10% of the whole.

800-1020 cm. Sharp boundary to well developed nodular carbonate in fine sand, nodules up to 3 cm in diameter in the lower part and 1 cm in the upper part. Carbonate begins to decrease in proportion below 2 m.

V DIDWANA SALT LAKE WELL SECTION

A 7.0 m deep well was dug in the bed of the Didwana salt lake about 200 m away from the Mataji temple on the southwest shore of the lake, to study the stratigraphy and collect samples for sedimentological and radiometric analysis. The stratigraphy of the well consists of following nine formations.

Formation I. 0-38 cm. Four units of yellowish clayey silt, clayey loam, light clay and clayey silt of 7 to 12 cm thickness each. Lamination appears in Unit 4.

Formation II. 38-112 cm. Two units of medium clay with laminations.

Formation III 112-304 cm. Three units of medium to light clays with fine laminations.

Formation IV. 305-340 cm. Medium clay with poorly expressed laminae and with 1 cm thick bed of laminated carbonate at 310 cm depth.

Formation VI. 360-415 cm Light clay with poor lamination; clay laminae separated and disturbed by putative gypsum crystal much.

Formation VII. 415-460 cm. Silty clay with laminations disturbed by authergenic gypsum. The boundary between Form. VII and Form. VIII is very sharp.

Formation VIII. 460-560 cm. Salt crystal dominoted by sheets of crystalline halites up to 8 cm thick and separated by grey light clay bands of maximum 1.5 cm thickness.

Formation IX. 560-750 cm. Grey silty fine sands resembling Formation VII. Could not be examined *in situ* because of the upwelling of water.

On the basis of the correlation of sedimentary units of sections from Amarpura quarry, Singi Talav, Indola ki Dhani, Railway cutting and Did-

Rock unit	*Cultural content*	*Probable Age and Environment*
I. Lacustral saline clays and re-activated dunes	Mesolithic occupation on stable dunes	Late Holocene-Semi-arid
II. Lacustral fresh water clays	Mesolithic occupations on stable dunes surrounding the lake	Early Holocene-Sub-humid
III. Highly saline lacustral clays and evaportes		Late Pleistocene Arid
IV. Dunes (relationship between III & IV is not yet clear)		Late Pleistocene Arid
Long time gap as suggested by sharp junctionwith Unit V.		
V. Alluvial clays and gravels	Acheulian occupation lake shore	Smi-arid to sub-humid?

wana Lake well the following scheme of rock units, cultural content, palaeoenvironment and age can be tentatively reconstructed.

The region under consideration has undergone drastic environmental changes. If we take into consideration the time period involved in such changes, then the Acheulian industry of Didwana appears to be considerably older than the dune and lake sediments of Late Pleistocene Age.

ENVIRONMENT OF ACHEULIAN MAN AROUND DIDWANA

Field characters of fluvial sediments in which extremely fresh Acheulian tools have been discovered at the localities mentioned earlier, suggest that the drainage was sluggish and favoured the development of interchannel shallow pools as indicated by marly beds. Acheulian hunter-gatherers seem to have camped along the banks of sluggish streams or around shallow pools.

Probably while the Acheulian man was still living in the area, the drainage system became totally defunct due to drastic environmental changes. The changes in the hydrology of the area may be in response to climatic changes or tectonic movements or both. Our further work will throw more light on the problem of the disappearance of the drainage system in Didwana area in post-Acheulian times.

Preliminary examinations of the lake sediments down to depth of 7 m show that the lake was carrying fresh water during the early Holocene (*c.* 10,000-*c.* 3,500 B. P.) (Singh *et al* 1974 : 467-501). The lake was predominantly saline, at times hypersaline during the late Pleistocene. Detailed chronological and sedimentological and palynological studies of lake sediments and of the tool-bearing marls in the area will provide multidisciplinary information on the Pleistocene environmental changes which will ultimately help us

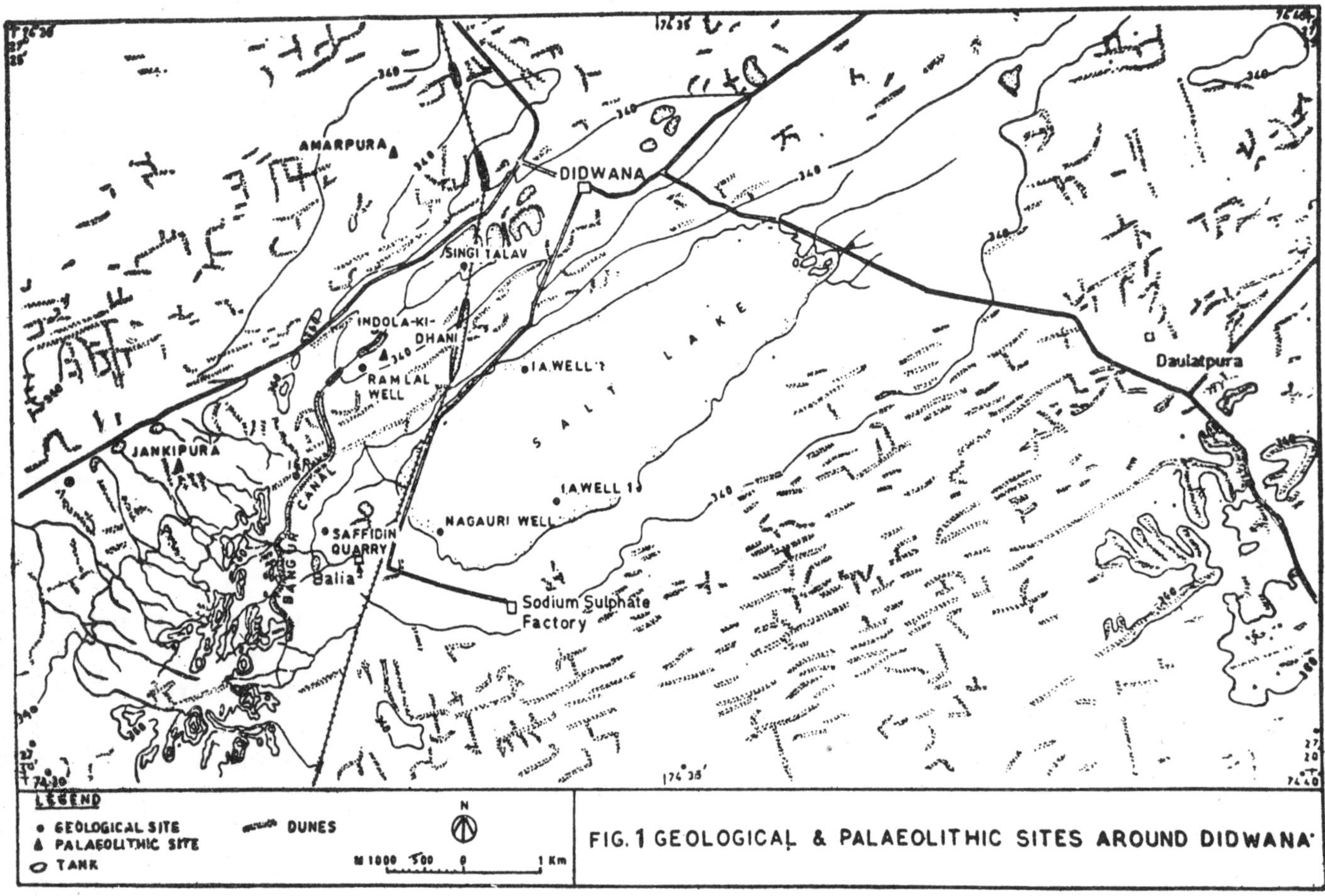

FIG. 1 GEOLOGICAL & PALAEOLITHIC SITES AROUND DIDWANA

in knowing something of the history of palaeohydrology during Acheulian and post-Acheulian times.

THE INDUSTRY

A total of 130 flaked artefacts were collected from the three localities-22 from Singi Talav, 82 from Indola ki Dhani and 26 from Amarpura. Two hammer stones were also found at Singi Talav but these are excluded from frequency analysis presented in Tables 1-2. The assemblages from all the localities are small to be useful for statistical analysis. They can also not be regarded as fully representative of the original composition of the assemblages from the localities because they do not come from controlled situations. The Amarpura collection was mostly picked up from the surface and represents the material discarded after the sieving of the earth by quarry workers. There is no way to find out how many artefacts were thrown away or got removed to other places. The material from Indola ki Dhani is derived from the surface of the marl displaced during canal digging and one does not know what proportion of the artefacts lie buried in the heaped up marl. Only at Singi Talav the artefacts were collected from a limited area and they came either from the section of the quarry or from the surface of the marl in which they were superficially buried. This surface is trampled upon by cattle and other animals as testified by numerous hoof-impressions, and it is likely that smaller artefacts will get buried in the wet clay during monsoon under the impact of the animal feet. The present collections therefore only partially represent the original composition of the assemblages from these localities.

STATE OF PRESERVATION

The artefacts from all the three localities are remarkably fresh, in some cases so much so that they appear to be very recently made. Their edges as well as inter-flake ridges are very sharp. Majority of them bear varying degrees of calcium carbonate encrustation as a result of having lain buried in the carbonate rich clay. There can, however, be no doubt that the artefacts have suffered little or no displacement since they were discarded, and therefore they are more or less in a primary context. The absence of gravel in the marl horizon also show that no heavy material was transported and deposited when the marl was under formation.

RAW MATERIAL

Majority of the artefacts are made of coarse vein quartz of milky white to greyish white colour and some of dark grey quartzite. Quartz is a very intractable material and does not lend itself to good conchoidal fracture. In spite of this inherent limitation several of the handaxes and chopping tools have been shaped to a very symmetrical shape. Except for a few specimens which are made on pebbles, all are made on fresh pieces or rock. The raw material available in plenty in the Aravalli hills a few km south-west of Didwana, and pieces of rock and pebbles may have been picked up from the colluvial wash coming down from these hills.

TYPOLOGY

The typological classification of the assemblages from the three localities of the site is set out in Tables 1 and 2. As will be seen, the assemblages comprise polyhedrons pl IV, handaxes pl I-II, chopping tools pl III, denticulates, choppers, pl III and side scrapers. Cleavers are conspicuous by their absence in all the assemblages. The proportions of finished tools to debitage are 63.64:36.36 at Singi Talav, 45.12 : 54.88 at Indola ki Dhani and 61.54 : 38.46 at Amarpura. The high percentage of finished tools in all the assemblages is probably accounted for by two factors: (1) the assemblages do not come from controlled situations, and it is likely that at Amarpura the smaller artefacts were thrown away or got dispersed from the sieved and discarded stone material, and at Singi Talav and Indola ki Dhani they may be buried in the marl. (2) We are likely to be dealing with situations which are living camp-sites and only partially factory sites. It is likely that a part of the tool kit was manufactured near the source of raw material close to the hills and therefore collections made from those localities are more likely to yield higher proportions of debitage material.

In the three collections taken as a whole poly hedrons account for the highest proportion (35.83%), handaxes come at second place (29.85%) and chopping tools at third (20.90%) among the finished tools. Flake tools, like side snapers and denticulates, from only 9 per cent of the finished tools. All these characters together with the absence of cleavers and Levallois flakes show that the Didwana industry represents a very early stage of the Acheulian culture in India.

METRICAL ANALYSIS OF THE INDUSTRY

All complete specimens of handaxes, polyhedrons, chopping tools, cores and flakes were measured for their length, breadth, thickness and weight. The mean, maximum and minimum values of these four parameters are plotted in Table 3. In the case of handaxes the variation between the mean values on one hand and minimum and maximum value on the other in respect of all the four parameters is very high. This is because of the presence of several truly miniature handaxes in the collection. Found by themselves these miniature handaxes would be attributed to Middle Palaeolithic stage. In the case of chopping tools the mean values are fairly close to minimum values showing that most of the tools belong to the small size bracket. In the case of polyhedrons, cores and flakes, the mean value fall more or less in the centre of the minimum and maximum values showing greater variation in size and weight range. It is significant that the maximum length and width of the flakes are 94 and 71 mm respectively. The absence of larger flakes is probably explained by the raw material employed, namely quartz which inhibits the production of large flakes.

CONCLUSION

While the Acheulian industry of the Jayal graval ridge is quantitatively rich, it is not very clearly defined because of the presence of definitely post-Acheulian tools on the surface of the ridge. This is because in the Jayal area enormous amount of good quality raw material was available on the surface and hunter-gatherers of post-Acheulian age continued to exploit this source for making their tools. At the other few Lower Palaeolithic sites reported in western Rajasthan the assemblages are very small—consisting of 10 to 20 artefacts—and therefore their cultural character is very ill-defined. The Didwana industry is the only Acheulian industry from the semi-arid and arid zone of Rajasthan which occurs in a stratified context, is quantitatively not very small, is typologically homogeneous and free from contamination with later lithic material. Because of the high proportion of chopping tools, polyhedrons and choppers and the absence of cleavers and Leval-

Table 1 *Classification of Palaeoliths from Singi Talav, Indola ki Dhani and Amarpura Localities of Didwana site*

Site locality / Artefact type	Singi Talav		Indola ki Dhani		Amarpura		Total	
	no	%	no	%	no	%	no	%
1. Handaxe	12	54.55	7	8.54	1	3.85	20	15.38
2. Chopper	—		3	3.66	—		3	2.31
3. Chopping tool	—		7	8.54	7	26.92	14	10.77
4. Polyhedron	2	9.09	14	17.07	8	30.77	24	18.46
5. Side Scraper	—		2	2.44	—		2	1.54
6. End scraper	—		—		—		—	
7. Denticulate	—		—	4.88	—		4	3.08
Total	14	63.64	37	45.13	16	61.54	67	51.54
8. Side Flake	2	9.09	2	2.44	—		4	3.08
9. End Flake	2	9.09	14	17.07	2	7.69	18	13.85
10. Indeterminate Flake	—		—		3	11.54	3	2.31
11. Blade	—		2	2.44	—		2	1.54
12. Chip	1	4.54	2	2.44	—		3	2.31
13. Bifacial core	3	13.64	5	6.10	3	11.54	11	8.46
14. Amorphous core	—		7	8.54	2	7.69	9	6.92
15. Debitage	—		13	15.85	—		13	10.00
Total	8	36.36	45	54.88	10	38.46	63	48.47
*16. Hammer Stone	2		—		—		2	
Total	22	100.00	82	100.00	26	100.00	130	100.00

*excluded from the Total

lois flakes it certainly represents a very early stage in the evolution of Acheulian Culture in India. In conjunction with the evidence from Jayal area the new evidence from Didwana conclusively proves that Acheulian man had colonized the territory at least in the immediate vicinity of the Aravalli hills in western Rajasthan.

The archaeological evidence together with that of the sedimentary characters of the implement bearing formation also shows that climatic conditions during the Acheulian period were not only conducive to human occupation but they were also markedly different from those obtaining in the area at present.

In the Indian sub-continent majority of the Acheulian sites have been located in high energy channel environment and are therefore in secondary context. Surface sites, even when of a primary nature, have limited value in interpreting chronology and palaeoecology. The Acheulian sites of Didwana are not only primary but also stratified in a low energy fluvial formation. It therefore offers unique opportunity for palaeo-environmental and cultural studies in the Indian subcontinent. Probably this is for the first time in India that an Acheulian occupation site has been discovered in the context of defunct fluvial system, stabilished dunes and fluctuating lake regime. Future multidisciplinary investigations in this area are planned to unravel the mystery of man-land relationship during Acheulian times in the semi-arid core of western Rajasthan.

Table 2 *Classification of Palaeoliths from Singi Talav, Indola ki Dhani and Amarpura localities of Didwana site.*

Locality Artefact type	Singi Talav		Indola ki Dhani		Amarpura		Total	
	no	%	no	%	no	%	no	%
I *Tools...*								
1. Handaxe	12	85.71	7	18.92	1	6.25	20	29.85
2. Chopper	—		3	8.11	—		3	4.48
3. Chopping Tool	—		7	18.92	7	43.75	14	20.90
4. Polyhedron	2	14.29	14	37.84	8	50.00	24	35.83
5. Side Scraper	—		2	5.41	—		2	2.98
6. End Scraper	—		—		—		—	
7. Denticulate	—		4	10.81	—		4	5.97
Total	14	100.00	37	100.00	16	100.00	67	100.00
II *Debitage*								
1. Side Flake	2	25.00	2	4.44	—		4	6.35
2. End Flake	2	25.00	14	31.11	2	20.00	18	28.57
3. Indeterminate Flake	—		—		3	30.00	3	4.76
4. Blade	—		2	4.44	—		2	3.17
5. Chip	1	12.50	2	4.44	—		3	4.76
6. Bifacial Core	3	37.50	5	11.11	3	30.00	11	17.46
7. Amorphous Core	—		7	15.56	2	20.00	9	14.29
Other Debitage	—		13	28.89	—		13	20.63
Total	8	100.00	45	99.99	10	100.00	63	99.99
III. Hammer Stone	*2		—		—		*2	
Sum Total	22		82		26		130	
%Tools to Debitage	63.64 : 36.36		45.12 : 54.88		61.54 : 38.46		51.54 : 48.46	

*excluded from the Total

Table 3 *Metrical Analysis of Lower Palaeolithic artefacts from Didwana*

Artefact type		Length (in mm)	Breadth (in gms)	Thickness (in mm)	Weight (in mm)
Handaxe (No 20)	Mean	101	65	37	299
	Maximum	224	102	68	1370
	Minimum	48	27	14	20
Chopping Tool (No 13)	Mean	63	57	43	341
	Maximum	104	97	76	522
	Minimum	69	60	38	200
Polyhedron (No. 30)	Mean	79	70	56	313
	Maximum	139	98	71	637
	Minimum	43	36	19	27
Core (No 17)	Mean	66	63	38	165
	Maximum	97	96	56	420
	Minimum	42	35	18	25
Flake (No 19)	Mean	69	48	22	69
	Maximum	94	71	38	225
	Minimum	31	30	14	20

REFERENCES

Agrawal, D.P., P.S. Dutta, S. Husain, R.V. Krishnamurty, V.N. Misra, S.N. Rajaguru and P.K. Thomas 1980 Palaeoclimate, stratigraphy and Prehistory in north and west Rajasthan, *Proceedings of Indian Academy of Sciences* 89(1).

Allchin. B., and A. Goudie 1974 Pushkar : Prehistory and climatic change in western India. *World Archaeology 5 (3).*

Indian Archaeology 1978-79. A Review

Misra, V.N. 1962 Palaeolithic cultures of Western Rajputana. *Bulletin of the Deccan College Research Institute* 21.

1965 Govindgarh, a Palaeolithic site in western Rajasthan. *Journal of the Asiatic Society of Bengal* 38.

1973 Bagor-a Late Mesolithic settlement in NW India. *World Archaelogy 5* (1).

Misra, V.N., S.N. Rajaguru, D.P. Agrawal, P.K. Thomas, Z. Husain, and P.S. Dutta 1980 Prehistory and Palaeoenvironment of Jayal, western Rajasthan. *Man and Environment* 4.

Mohapatra, G.C., S.B. Bhatia, and B.K. Sahu 1963 The Discovery of a Stone Age site in the Indian Desert, *Research Bulletin (N.S.) of the Panjab University* 14 (3 and 4).

Singh, G., R. D. Joshi, S.K. Chopra, and A.B. Singh 1974 Late Quaternary history of vegetation and climate of the Rajasthan Desert, India, Philosophical *Transactions of the Royal Society* 267B.

Excavations at Gufkral-1981

A. K. SHARMA
Archaeological Survey of India, Nagpur

Gufkral (literally *Guf*-cave, *Kral*-potter)—a site inhabited by potters who are utilising the caves cut into the Karewa—was excavated by the Prehistory Branch of the Archaeological Survey of India in 1981. On the slopes of the 35m high mound, there are a number of caves, both single and multi-chambered with pillars, some occupied by krals and some deserted.

The site (lat. 35°54′ N, long. 75°60′ E) is situated 41 km to the south-east of Srinagar, near Tahsil town of Tral in District Pulwama of Jammu and Kashmir state. It is located on an extensive deposit of upper Karewa, adjacent to village Ban-Mir in between two *nullahs* that join the Jhelum nearly 10 km to the west. At the top the mound measures 400 m north-south and 75 m east-west. Maximum height of the mound from the road level on the western side is 35m.

On the eastern edge of the mound, almost at the centre, are found a number of menhirs on the slope. None of them, however, is in its original and upright position.

CULTURE-SEQUENCE

The site was explored in 1962-63 by the Archaeological Survey of India. The aim of this season's dig being to ascertain the culture sequence of the site, the excavation was restricted almost to the centre of the mound, where 3.10 m of habitational deposit was encountered over the natural soil. Some scrapings which revealed oval and rectangular pits were also made in the rain gullies.

One of the excavated quadrants was near one of the menhirs. Three main cultural periods of occupation (Fig. 1), were brought to light. They are:

Period IA—Aceramic Neolithic
Period IB—Early-Neolithic
Period IC—Late-Neolithic
Period II—Megalithic
Period III—Historical

Each period was clearly sealed by a floor of the subsequent period.

The most significant finds of this excavation were : (a) presence of a well-defined Aceramic Neolithic level, (b) identification of cereal grains and (c) faunal assemblage.

DATA

A. PERIOD IA

The Aceramic Neolithic Period having a deposit of 35 cm to 1.10 m was sealed by a continuous floor of yellow compact clay mixed with *'Chunam'* running in all the trenches. The period is divided into two phases of occupation, marked by the presence of two floor levels, one on the top of the natural soil and the other after a deposit of nearly 30-35 cm.

Settlement

Settlement consisted of large and small dwelling pits cut into the loessic deposits, being circular or oval on plan with narrow mouths and wide bottoms. They varied in diameter from 3.80m to 1.50m at the top (pl. I). Large dwelling pits generally belonged to phase I and were only 20 to 30cm deep unlike dwelling pits were surrounded

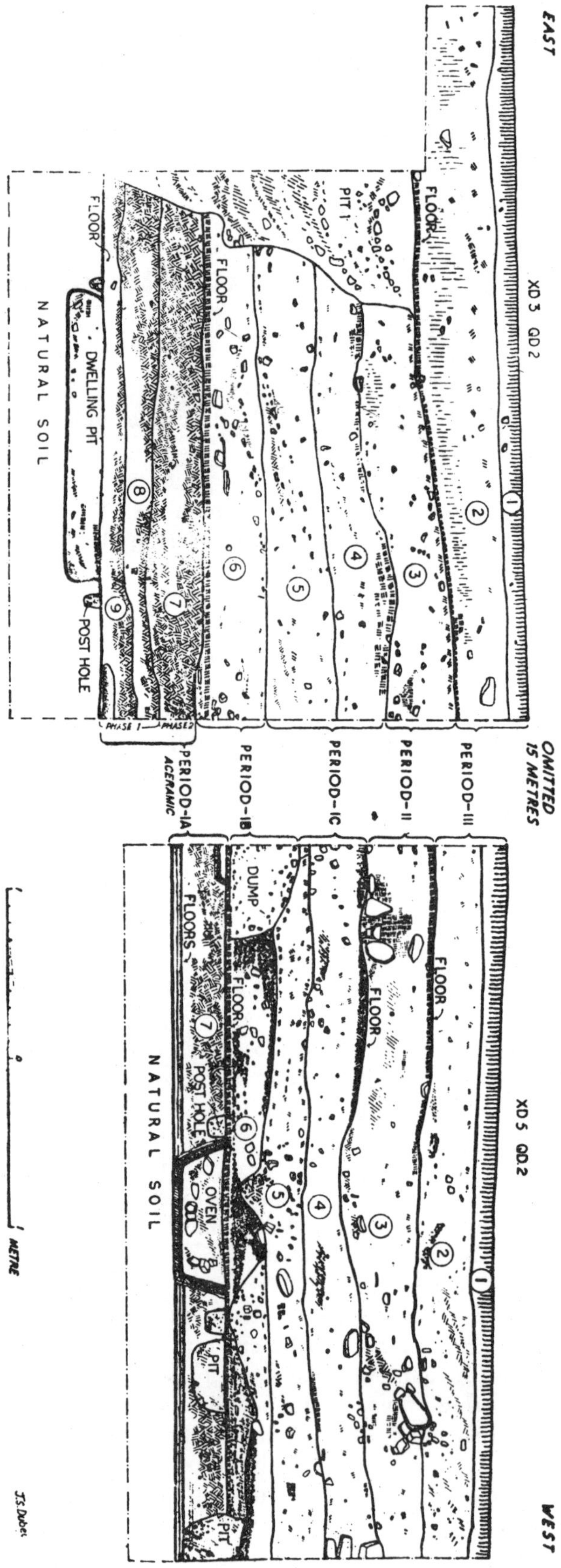
GUFKRAL-1981: DISTT. PULWAMA (J&K)
SECTION LOOKING SOUTH
EAST
WEST
XD 3 QD 2
XD 5 QD 2
OMITTED 15 METRES
PERIOD-III
PERIOD-II
PERIOD-IC
PERIOD-IB
PERIOD-IA ACERAMIC
PHASE 1
PHASE 2
FLOOR
FLOORS
PIT 1
PIT
DUMP
OVEN
POST HOLE
DWELLING PIT
NATURAL SOIL
METRE
J.S. Dubey

Fig. 1

by storage pits and hearths. A number of post-holes, to support structure of grass and reed were noticed around the pits and the hearths. The recovered mud chunks with reed impressions (pl. VII, 11) indicate that most probably the lower portions of the superstructures were plastered with mud to give strength and prevent entry of water and snow from sides. In phase 1, the floors of the dwelling pits and storage pits, all cut into the loessic deposit (top of natural soil) and their working levels in a wide area, were plastered with red-ochre paste. No such treatment was available in the floors belonging to phase 2. Some dwelling pits cut in phase I were subsequently enlarged and used in phase 2 also as indicated by the successive deposits inside these pits. In phase 2, two chambered dwelling pits were also available and were deeper than their counterparts in phase 1. In phase 1 the hearths were rectangular in shape whereas in phase 2 both circular and rectangular hearths made of burnt clay were available. One of the circular hearths had its floor and sides plastered with mud. This circular hearth was 93cm in diameter (outer) and 30cm deep. It had post-holes on its outer periphery. the presence of these post holes and large quantity of ash from inside the hearth alongwith pebbles, indicates that the hunted animals were suspended from these poles and over the fire in the hearths.

The maintenance of floors, covering a wide area around pits, shows that people used to live outdoors during warm seasons and occupy dwelling pits in winter, but roasting of food (both flesh and grains) was done probably outside, for no hearth or fire place have been found inside the dwelling pits so far.

(ii) *Artefacts*

Among the artefacts used by the settlers are polished stone celts (pl. VI, 1, 2, 3), both finished and unfinished, stone points, with one or both the ends sharp, made out of Himalayan Trap. One broken unfinished ring stone (pl. VI, A), pounders and querns. A large quern with a depression on the working surface and showing red ochre paste adhered to it was recovered from the red ochre treated floor near the dwelling pit in one of the trenches.

Twentyseven bone tools, some having the entire body surface polished and others having their working tips alone polished were recovered (pl. III). They were shaped out of long bones, splinters and horns. Most of these were points and arrow-heads. Besides, two awls some piercers and scrapers were also recovered. Of special mention, however, is a polished bone needle with damaged eye. The tips of a large number of tools have been charred to give the required strength to the working ends. Bone tools were mostly made from the green bones, of sheep, goat, cervus and ibex being generally preferred. Arrow-heads were tiny in size like microliths with only their tips charred and polished. Among the ornaments recovered, one cylidrical highly polished spacer bone bead and two steatite beads, one cylindrical and another barrel shaped (pls VII, 128; IV) deserve special mention.

(iii) *Animal Remains*

The animal remains amply demonstrate that in the Aceramic Neolithic Period at Gufkral people were predominantly dependent on wild game. Domestication of a selected variety was just being introduced. The animals represented were wild sheep (*Ovis Orientalis*), wild goat (*Capra aegagrus),* wild cattle *(Bos namadicus),* Red deer *(Cervus elephus)* wolf *(Canis lupus),* Himalayan Ibex (*Capra Ibex)* Himalayan Tahr (*Capra jamlaica),* serow *(Nemorhaedus bubalinus)* and beer *(Ursus).* Sheep *(Ovis aries)* and goat *(Capra hircus)* were the only animals being domesticated (pl. VIII).

With the exception of *Canis lupus,* all the animals hunted were herbivorous. This is possibly due to the fact that these animals were easily available in the surrounding hills and slopes.

Ovis, Capra, Bos and *Cervus* formed the largest percentage of animals hunted, *Ovis* dominating over all (Fig. 2).

(iv) *Grains*

Evidence of grains obtained by floatation technique indicates that in this Period people had already realized the importance of grains for food and were either collecting and/or had started cultivation in a limited area. The second possibility is remote as, so far, no harvesters and good specimen of ring stones have been recovered from this period. However, detailed examination of the grains recovered is underway and may throw

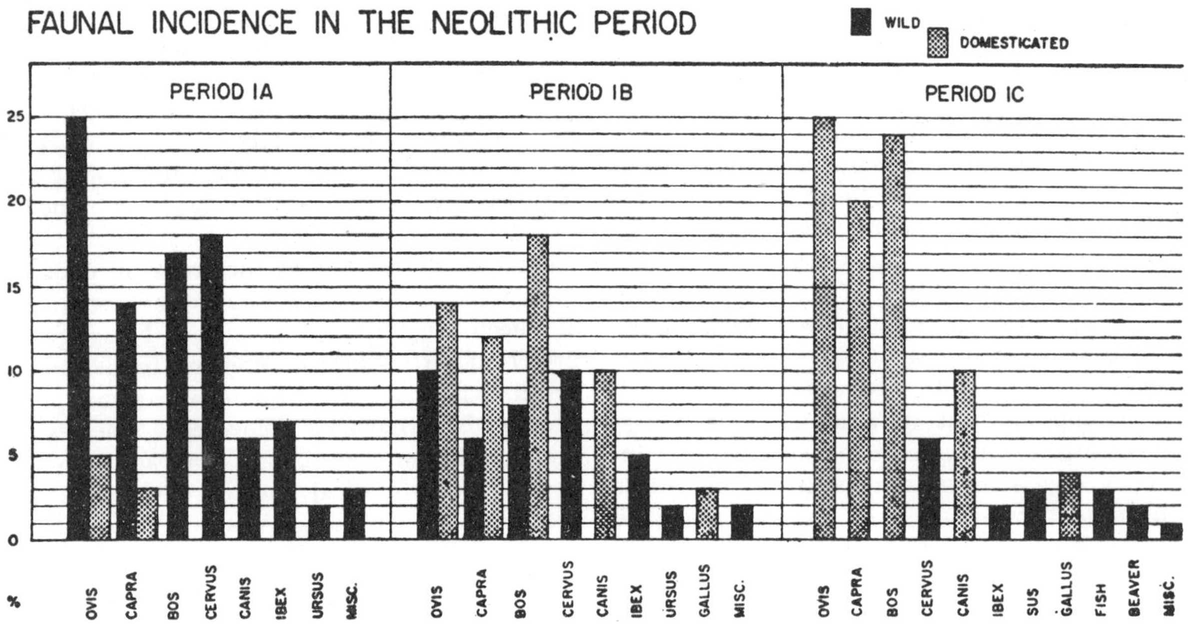

Fig. 2

more light about the species. But one thing is certain that in Kashmir Valley wheat, barley and lentil had much earlier antiquity than rice which is the staple food of Kashmiris in the Valley today and which is grown extensively all over the valley. It will be interesting to investigate as to why and when the earlier grains almost totally disappeared from the Valley and were replaced by rice. What were the circumstances that led to total change in the food habits of the people of the Valley? Was rice introduced with the arrival of a new wave of people? Evidence in this direction is available from the excavation as rice as recovered from Period II, which is marked with the arrival of Megaliths at the site and could be safely dated to *c.* 1000 B.C. pending 14C tests. The following grains were recovered from the Aceramic period :—(i) *Hordeum Vulgare* Linn-Six row barley (ii) *Triticum* sp.—Wheat (iii) *Lens esculenta Moonch*-Lentil, Masur, and (iv) *Lithospermum arvense*—a weedy plant.

B. PERIOD IB

The Period IB is followed without any break and is represented by deposit of 40 cm. Hand made Neolithic pottery made its appearance. Overwhelming percentage was of grey ware with a few sherds of coarse dull red ware. The shapes represented were big jars, bowls, basins and one stem piece of dish-on-stand in coarse dull red ware. The decorations included mat-impressed bases, pinched designs on the neck region and reed impression only on exterior and also both on exterior and interior of the pots. Pottery is mostly incompletely oxidised (pl. II).

Settlement

Settlement pattern of this period is indicated by the presence of a 5 to 7 cm thick floor made of yellow compact clay mixed with *chunam* running throughout in almost all the trenches. At some places this floor was repaired atleast 5 to 6 times. The most important building activity was the construction of mud and rubble walls. A compact mud mixed with '*chunam*' wall-like structure running parallel to each other, 70 cm uniformly wide throughout and having almost same space in between, was also encountered. The nature of this structure will be known after it is fully exposed. There is no dwelling pit in this period. It was characterized by extensive burning activity.

The artefacts included one stone point, one broken ring-stone and nineteen bone tools (mostly well polished points, two piercer cum scrapers shaped out of splinters and one spatula).

(ii) *Animal Remains & Grains*

The Period was marked by sudden spurt in domestication of animals like sheep, goat and cattle. Sheep and goat still dominated the scene with the size of goat getting reduced. Wild sheep, goat and cattle continued to be hunted but in a far lesser percentage. Percentage of dog bones increased with marked reduction in the percentage of bones of wolf. Short horned cattle were present. Presence of bones of red deer, ibex and bear indicates that hunting was still the main source of food. Many of the pieces bore sharp cut marks. In the long bones holes were carefully drilled out to extract bone marrow. Domestic fowl *(Gallus)* was added to the menu. Apart from all the grains of Period IA continuing, common pea (*Pisum arvense* Linn.) was added.

C. PERIOD IC

Period IC belonging to the mature phase of Neolithic Period was represented by a 70-80cm thick habitational deposit and was sealed by a thick whitish floor throughout. It was characterized by the presence of large number of refuse pits and dumps.

Pottery consisted of Grey ware, burnished Grey ware, rough thick dull red were alongwith the introduction of black burnished ware and wheel-turned black burnished ware. A few examples of red gritty ware were also found. All the shapes of Period IB continued and long necked jars were introduced. Dish-on-stand with triangular perforated designs on the stem region on burnished ware was also introduced. Decorations included mat and cord impressed bases; reed impression to create roughened surface of grey and dull red ware; pinched designs on the neck region and incised oblique designs in the neck region in dull red ware; knobbed designs on the neck region of the wheel made black burnished ware (pl.IV). A sherd with graffitti was also recovered (pl. VII 10).

Artefacts

Stone objects were scarce. Only one unfinished stone celt was found. Stone points which had almost disappeared in Period IB make their appearance again in good number (fourteen; pl. VI) Other stone objects included querns, pounders and balls. Double-holed harvesters, one having incised decoration on one side and spindle whorls of both stone and pottery were the important objects which made their appearance in this Period; spindle whorls having large holes indicate the beginning of spinning of thick threads for woollen garments.

One stone engraver used by potters for removing extra clay while finally shaping the pot before drying was also recovered. Other cultural assemblage included terracotta bangles, potsherds with graffitti marks, and terracotta with relief designs. Of special significance is the recovery of a copper hair pin with flattened coiled head from upper levels of this period (pl. VII, 8), similar to one found at Chanhudaro. It may point out to some foreign contacts.

The Period yielded the largest number (forty-one) bone tools, most of which were well polished points. Tips were generally charred and sharp particularly in case of micro tools like arrow-heads. Few awls, one spatula and a harpoon were other tools represented. A bone object with four incised grooves was also recovered.

(ii) Animal Remains & Grains

By this time domestication of animals was complete. The entire herd of sheep *(Ovis aries)*, goat *(Capra hircus)* and cattle *(Bos indicus)* were domesticated. There was considerable reduction in the size of goat and cattle. Sheep and goat continued to dominate the percentage of animals. Two important new species namely pig *(Sus scrofa)* and fish made their appearance. Bones of hare *(Lepus)*, hedge-hog. rodents and beaver were also recovered.

All the grains found in Period IB were also recovered from this period.

Domestication of animals, and advent of harvesters and spindle whorls indicate that by this time the Neolithic people at Gufkral had adopted a well settled life wherein practice of agriculture, cattle breeding and herding and weaving of woollen cloth had become a way of life. Hunting was now restricted to red deer and ibex and that too on a limited scale as the percentage of these animals had considerably reduced in the assemblage. Contacts with the outside world had also started.

D. PERIOD-II

Period II which is associated with the arrival of menhirs on the site has been designated as the Megalithic Period. It is represented by nearly 50-60cm thick habitational deposit. In one of the quadrants near a fallen menhir, a pit cut in layer 3 containing large quantity of packing material comprising of broken pebbles, was exposed. Since not a single menhir is standing and as a huge quantity of broken pebbles are littered all over the site, mostly concentrated near the menhirs, it appears that the menhirs did not have very deep foundation pits. Also indicating that arrival of menhirs was a much later affair. But this needs to be further checked by firmer proofs.

The Period was marked by the presence of nearly 10cm thick floor, running throughout, with few breaks due to pit activities. The Period also witnessed considerable pit activities. A number of refuse pits sinking right upto the natural soil were cut. From these pits large quantity of pottery and animal bones were recovered.

Burnished Grey ware, gritty red ware and thick dull red were continued from the previous period but percentage of thick dull red were and wheel-made pottery increased. Wheel made dull red ware made its appearance, shapes included jars with shapeless rims, long necked jars, bowls, basins, dish-on-stand and medium sized globular jars. Pinched designs, in neck region, incised designs and combed surface obtained by brushing with straw and reeds were available. Vessels with channeled spout were introduced.

Large ring stones, both finished and unfinished were recovered in good number (pls. IV, V, VI & VII). Stone points had almost disappeared. Other artefacts included a copper pin, a wooden bead pls. VII & III), pestles, spindle-whorls with medium sized holes and a miniature pot. The only cowrie shell (pl. VII) found was from this period.

Bone tool industry came to be neglected. Only twenty tools were recovered and that too were not well polished. New innovations were bone handles shaped mostly from tibia of sheep/goat taking advantage of their shape and bone arrow sockets. They were meant to hold smaller tools for easy operation. A fine cobler's awl was also recovered.

All the grains of earlier periods continued. Rice (*Oryza sativa Linn*) and millet *(Eleusive coracana)* were introduced towards the end of this Period.

Animals represented were cattle, sheep, goat, dog, pig, ibex and fowl. It appears that hunting had almost come to a close for amongst bones of wild animals only those of ibex were recovered.

E. PERIOD III

Period III represents the historical occupation of the site. A thick compact floor made of whitish clay was running almost throughout sealing the Megalithic Period. The limited excavations has not yielded any structure except floor levels so far but in the exposed areas in other parts of the mound, thick rubble walls could be noticed.

Hand-made pottery continued but was dominated by wheel-made thin bright red ware. Shapes encountered were jars, bowls, miniature pots, lamps, vases, dishes of Harappan shape, knobbed lids, lid cum bowls, double rimmed pots and cup-on-stand. Few sherds of black painted red ware with stamped designs were also collected. Stone bowls were also found. The artefacts included crude bone tools mostly points, one fine polished bone handle, ring stones, pounders, few stone points and a terracotta huge circular disc (appears to be a halo on the back of the head of an image).

Iron was introduced in this Period. All the grains of the previous period continued with a definite evidence of rice *(Oryza sativa Linn)* from the lower levels of this period.

Animal bones recovered were identified to those of cattle sheep, goat, dog, pig, *felis* (cat), fowl and rodents.

F. RADIOCARBON DATES

The following ^{14}C dates were received from Birbal Sahni Institute of Palaeobotany, Lucknow:

1. BS-356. Neolithic level;
   Period IB, wood charcoal; 3570 ± 110 B.P.
   Sample no. GFK/2/81
2. BS-357, Neolithic level;
   Period IB, wood charcoal; 3470 ± 110 B.P.
   depth 1.70m.
   Sample No. 3 GFK/3/81
3. Bs.358, Aceramic Neoli-3130 ± 100 B.P.
   thic Level; Period IA wood
   charcoal depth 1.80m.
   Sample no. GFK/4/81

4. BS-359, Neolithic level 3980 ± 120 B.P.
   Period IB, wood charcoal
   depth 1.65m.
   Sample no. GFK/7/81
5. BS-360, Neolithic level 3340 ± 100 B.P.
   Period IC, wood charcoal
   depth 1.35m.
   Sample no. GFK/5/81
6. BS-370, Neolithic level 2790 ± 110 B.P.
   Period IC; wood chorcoal
   depth 1.50m.
   Sample no GFK/6/81
7. BS-371, Neolithic level 3570 ± 100 B.P.
   Period IC; wood charcoal
   depth 1.15m.
   Sample No. GFK/1/81

SUMMARY

Excavation at Gufkral has brought to light five periods of occupation right from Aceramic Neolithic to Historical Period. It has for the first time firmly established that in the Kashmir valley there was an Aceramic Neolithic Period before pottery was introduced. It is in this period that process of domestication of selected species of animals was attempted. People had also recognized the food value of various grains like wheat and barley and had started collecting them. Bone and stone tools were manufactured. People lived in open and in pits, i.e. huts with their bottom sunk into the loessic deposits, in order to protect themselves from freezing winds. They kept the floors tidy and beautiful by painting them with red-ochre. Their main occupation was hunting.

In Period IB handmade ceramic was introduced. The Period witnessed the use of jars, bowls, basins, etc. in Grey ware and rough dull red ware. There was a change in the settlement pattern. Pits were discarded and mud and rubble walls were constructed. Well polished bone tools were made. There was a sudden spurt in the domestication of animals.

By Period IC the Neolithic culture had reached the mature stage. In houses, thick whitish floors with *'chunam'* mixed earth were laid. There was now more variety in wares and in their decoration. Large number and variety of well polished bone tools were made. People depended less on large stone objects. With the domestication of animals and agriculture fully achieved, hunting activities declined. People now got spare time to manufacture ornaments and also started weaving of woollen cloth.

Period II at Gufkral was marked by the arrival of menhirs. It is yet to be ascertained whether the same people practised the cult of erecting huge memorial stones or a new wave of people had arrived on the site and started living with the original neolithic settlers. With the menhir phase came to the site, wheel made dull red ware, vessels with channeled spout, copper objects, spindle whorls with medium sized holes, rice and millet, bone tools industry was neglected but bone handles were manufactured.

Period III represents the historical phase with the introduction of iron and wheel made thin bright red ware having jars, bowls, cups-on-stand and lid-cum-bowls. Stamped designs and black on red paintings were introduced.

One season's limited dig at Gufkral has filled some of the gaps in the cultural sequence of Kashmir and has definitely pushed back the antiquity of the Neolithic Culture in the Valley. As the earliest ^{14}C date for Period IB is 3980 ± 120 B.P., the Aceramic Neolihic Period at Gufkral is likely to go back by 400 to 500 years earlier.

Acknowledgements

I am very much thankful to Shri C. Rajagopalan, Assistant Director, Birbal Sahni Institute of Palaeobotany for the ^{14}C dates and to Dr. M.D. Kajale of Deccan College Postgraduate and Research Institute, Pune for identifying tht cereal grains. I am also grateful to Miss Madhu Bala for analysing the pottery. The illustrations in the article are by the courtesy of the Archaeological Survey of India.

Pariar-An Eastern Outpost of the Painted Grey Ware

B. B. LAL, IIAS, Simla
K. N. DIKSHIT, ASI, New Delhi

Situated on the left bank of the Ganga in District Unnao, Uttar Pradesh, Pariar is about 25 km north-west of the district headquarters. It is approachable by a link road which takes off southwards from the Unnao-Hardoi State Highway, near Chakalvansi. The Painted Grey Ware was picked up from here in 1952 by Y.D. Sharma (*IAR* 1953-54 : 38). A few objects of the Copper-Hoard complex had been noticed earlier in a temple at the site. The word Pariar is a distorted form of 'Parihara' which means abandonment; and there is a local tradition that it was here that Sita was abandoned by Lakshmana at the behest of his elder brother, Rama. Bithur, associated with the sage Valmiki, is on the right bank of the Ganga, opposite to Pariar. The tradition also has it that Valmiki gave shelter to Sita in his hermitage.

The ancient mound known as Garhi is largely under occupation by the villagers and it was with great difficulty that suitable spots were found for excavation. Altogether five trenches, named PRR-1 to PRR-5, were laid out at different points of the mound. Of these, only one, viz. PRR-3, laid in the courtyard of the house of one Shri Fakir Ali gave a reasonably clear sequence of the early cultures (Fig. 1), to obtain which was the main aim of our work. However, the collective evidence from all the trenches indicated the following sequence, from bottom upwards:

Period I(?)	Mixed deposit — Ochre Colour, Black-slipped and Black-and-red Wares.
Period II	Black-slipped and Black-and-red Wares.
Period III	Painted Grey Ware.
Period IV	Northern Black Polished Ware.
Period V	Sunga-Kushan levels.

PERIOD I (?)

In the lowest levels of PRR-3, a 60-cm thick deposit of loose brown earth and sand, mixed with occasional hard clods, was encountered. It contained an admixture of the Ochre Colour, black-slipped and black-and-red and burnished grey wares. It is very likely that all these sherds got washed down into this sandy deposit from some nearby areas and thus got mixed up. A few sherds had percolated from this level even to a depth of 1.15m into the natural soil. In the OCW, only a few sherds gave an idea of the shape. The same are illustrated on Fig. 2.

Since the above-mentioned deposit was a mixed one, without any proper stratification, it would not be appropriate to call it a regular occupational period. Thus, the co-occurrence of the above-mentioned four wares may be just a chance and need not necessarily be interpreted as their being contemporaneous. At the same time, the fact that the Ochre Colour Ware does exist in this deposit and does not occur in the subsequent Period, II, shows that some part of the site was under occupation in the pre-Period II stage, though right in trench PRR-3 (as also in the other trenches) we have not encountered any such regular occu-

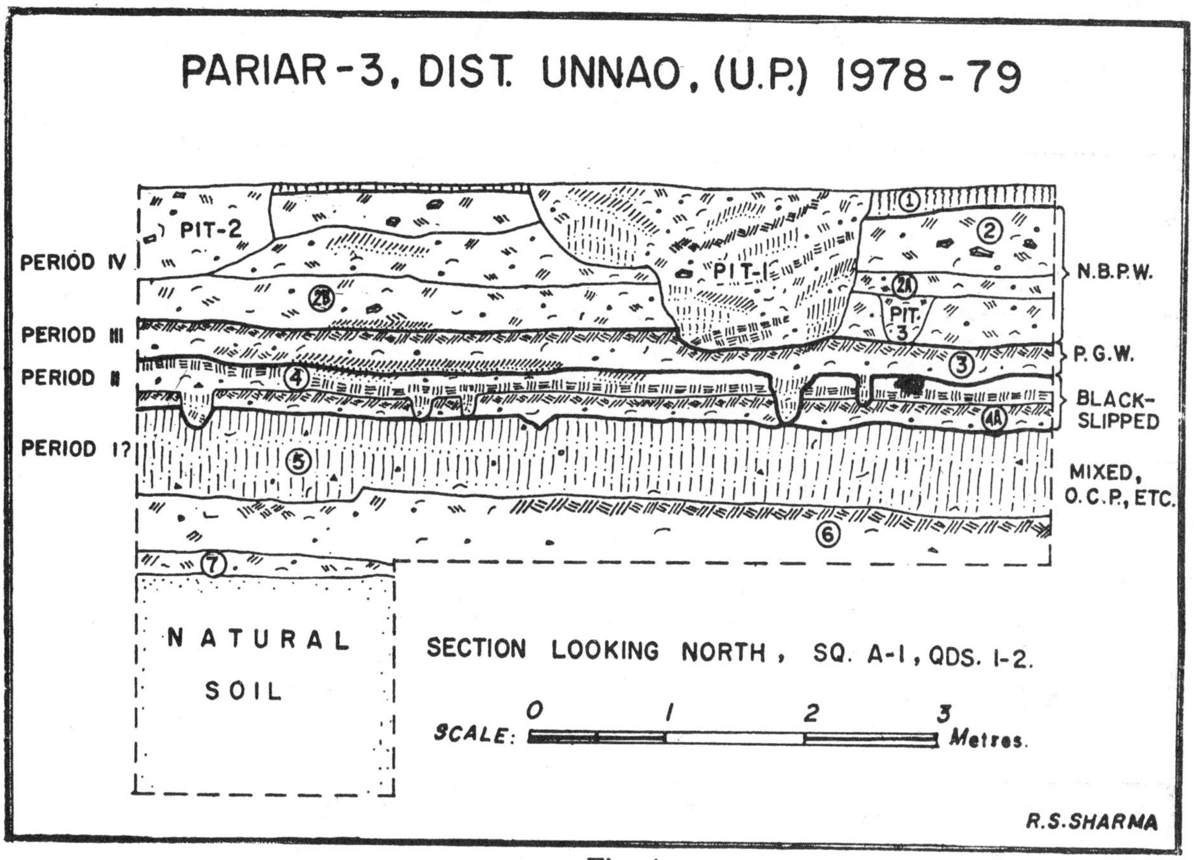

Fig. 1

pation. (Hence the need to have a provisional Period I.)

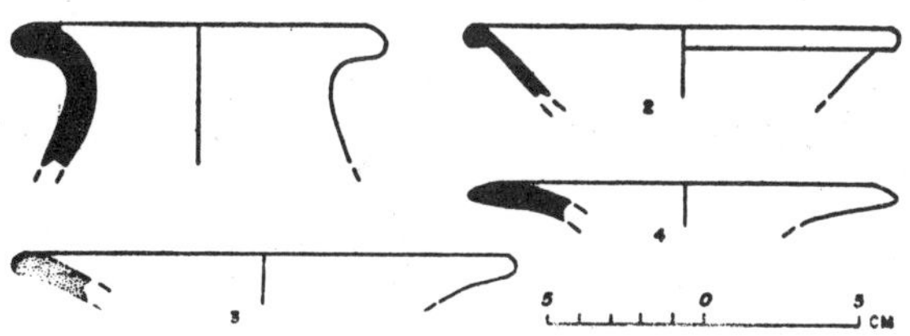

Fig. 2. Pariar: OCW. Period I(?)

PERIOD II

This Period is marked by a regular occupational deposit, about 40 cm in thickness, yielding the black-slipped, black-and-red and associated red wares (Fig. 3). No burnished grey ware was, however, found. Dominant types in the black-slipped ware were the dish and the bowl. Amongst the antiquities, mention may be made of terracotta beads and discs, bone points, copper and stone objects. No structure was found, but a series of post-holes of different sizes and chunks of plaster with reed impressions suggest that the houses were made of wattle-and-daub.

PERIOD III

With a blackish deposit of about 30 cm in thickness, Period III was characterised by the occurrence of the Painted Grey Ware and other associated wares (Figs. 4 and 5). Though not in great abundance, the sherds were nevertheless in sufficient quantity so as to attest to their regular use by the occupants. They were not just odd pieces as, for example, were the ones found at Sringaverapur or even at Sravasti. The shapes represented were the usual dish and bowl. The painted designs, which were quite limited, comprised simple linear and curvilinear motifs (pl. I). In these levels there also occurred the black-slipped and black-and-red wares, though their quantity was less than that in Period II. Lumps of plaster with reed-marks suggested that in this Period also the houses were made of wattle-and-

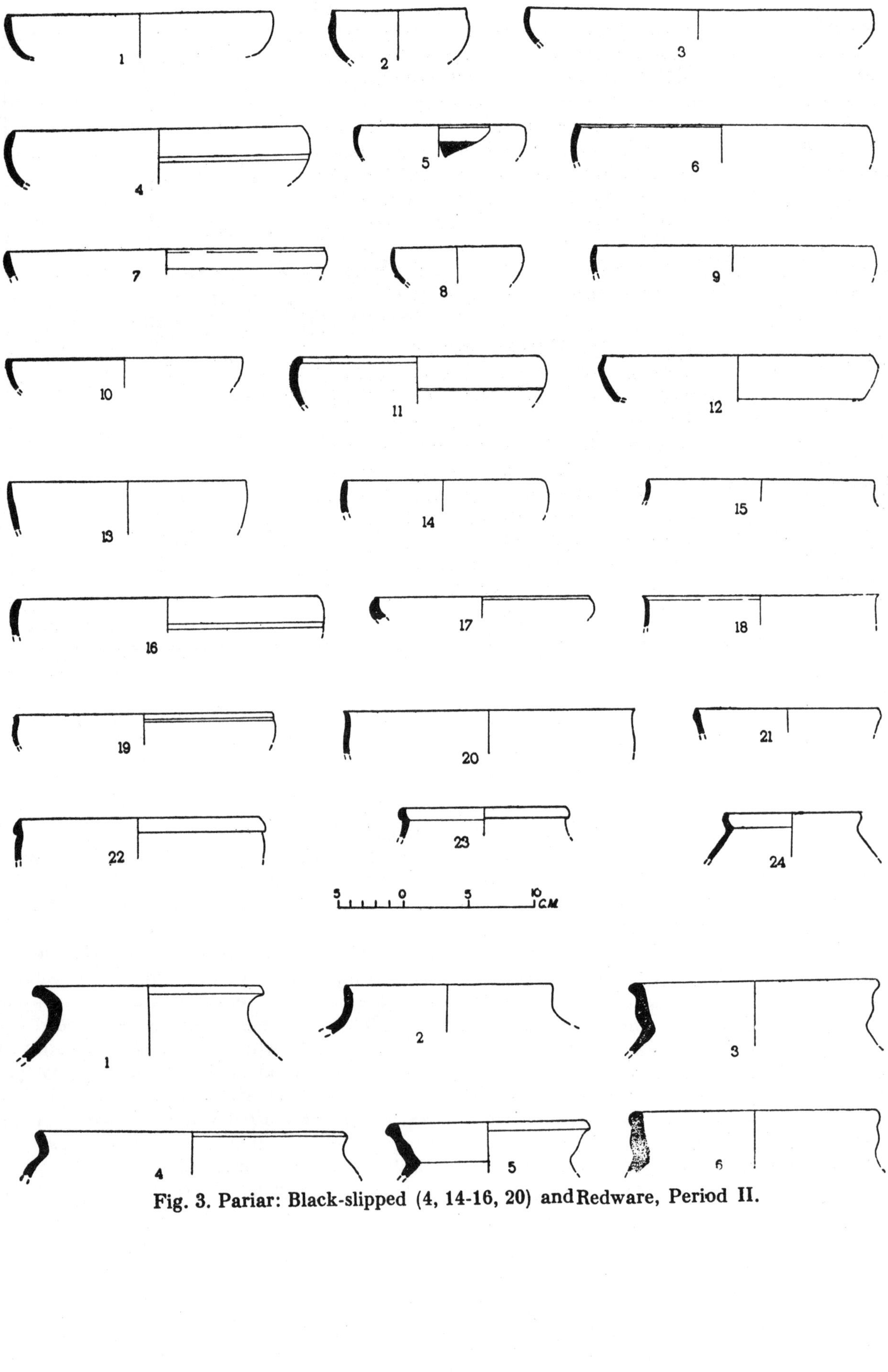

Fig. 3. Pariar: Black-slipped (4, 14-16, 20) and Redware, Period II.

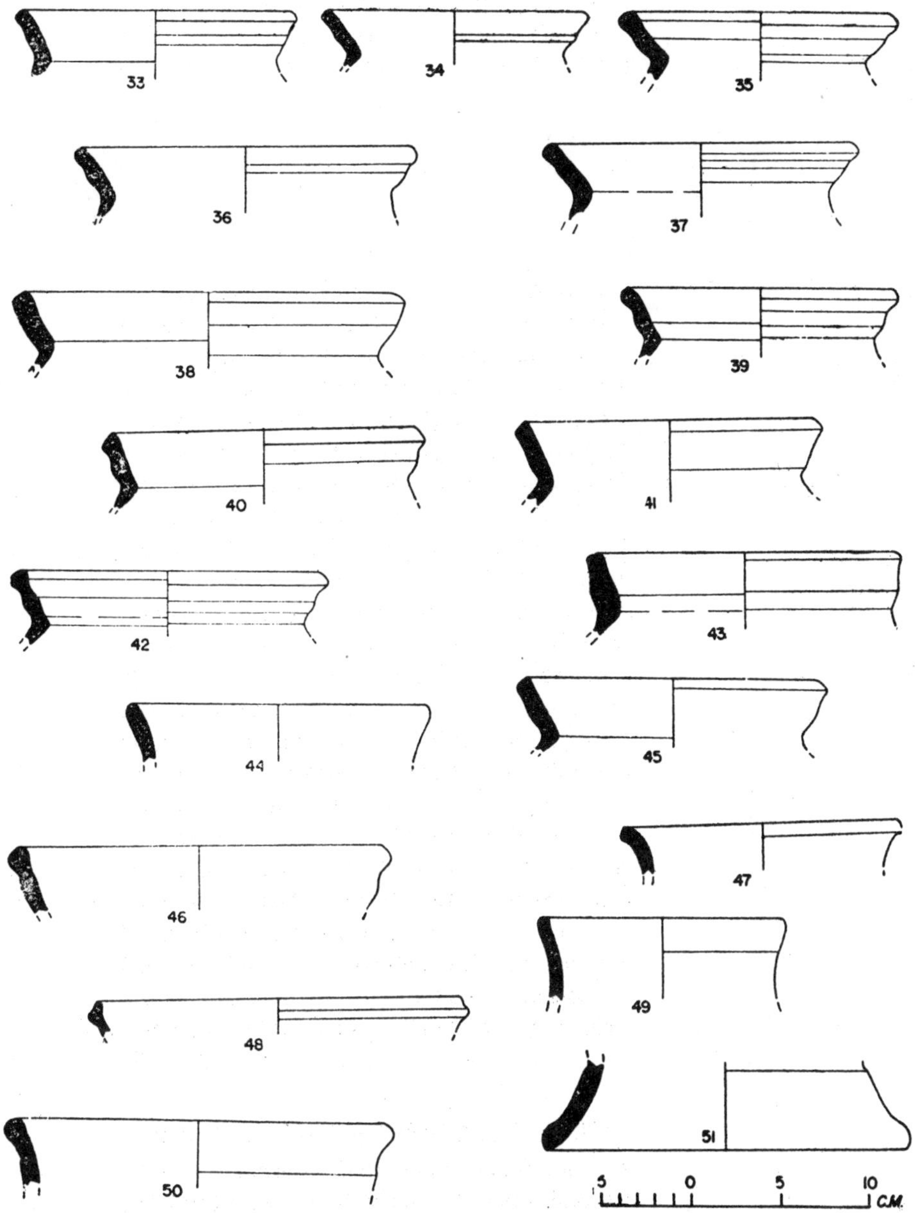

Fig. 4. Pariar: Red ware, Period III

daub. Many-of these lumps showed a sandy deposit on the side that did not bear the reed-impressions. This was obviously the outer side, that was exposed. It is gathered that the addition of sand on the surface may have helped in preventing the action of saltpetre. Amongst the antiquities were *ghata*-shaped beads and discs of terracotta, and bone-points.

PERIOD IV

Continuance of the PGW sherds, though in a limited quantity, was noticed in the early levels of the next higher period which yielded the Northern Black Polished Ware. This occupational deposit had an average thickness of 40 cm. It was further noticed that these early NBPW levels were bereft of the miniature bowl, carinated

Fig. 5. Pariar: Red ware, Period III

handi and the vase known as Ahichchhatra 10A type, which occurred later in the next 60 cm deposit of the same period. Important antiquities of this period as a whole were female figurines, wheels, skin-rubbers, beads, discs, bangles and gamesmen-all of terraccotta; points of bone; antimony rods of copper; and a few objects of iron as well. Amongst the structural remains there was only a terracotta ring-well, with five rings intact, met with in PRR-4.

PERIOD V

A flimsy deposit of the Sunga-Kushan period was noticed as the uppermost three layers of PRR-1 and PRR-2, though the same was not met within PRR-3.

CHRONOLOGY

There are no ^{14}C or TL dates for any of the periods at Pariar. Hence one has to depend on comparative stratigraphy only. Though we did not come across any separate stratum of the OCW, its presence somewhere at the site is indicated, as already mentioned earlier. For comparison, the nearest Ochre Colour Ware sites are Saipai on the west and Sringaverapura on the east. Typologically, the horizontally splayed-out rim of the jar makes Pariar as the extension of the Saipai Complex.

The excavations at Chirand, Sonepur, Prahladpur, Rajghat and Sringaverapura have revealed the various stage of the black-slipped and black-and- red wares. One may notice a sort of general decrease in the thickness of the cultural deposits represented by these wares, from Chirand in the east to Pariar. Atranjikhera, Jakhera, Noh and Jodhpura in the west. At Allahapur there is no separate phase of the black-slipped and black-and-red wares, although these wares dominate the early levels of the PGW and continue with it. The coarse black-and-red and burnished grey wares, of which some examples occur at Sringaverapura in the early levels of Period II but soon peter out, are totally absent from the main black-slipped ware complex at Pariar. All this suggests that the black-slipped and black-and-red ware phase of Pariar has it moorings in the east and that it may be slightly later than the beginning of Period II at Sringaverapur which is assignable to early tenth century B.C. (Lal and Dikshit 1981: 1-7) Thus the beginning of Period II at Pariar may be placed at *c.* 900 B.C. Since there is a very thin (only 40 cm) deposit of Period II at Pariar and there is also a continuity from Period II to III, the appearance of the PGW (which marks the beginning of Period II) at Pariar may be placed in the second half of the ninth century B.C. It may, however, be added that these are only tentative datings and would need to be confirmed.

SOME OBSERVATIONS

1. The generic relationship of the black-and-red ware of these U.P. sites with that of Ahar has been suggested by some scholars but not accepted by most. The types noticed at Pariar, Sringaverapura, Jakhera, Noh and even Jodhpura consist mostly of dishes and bowls which are also devoid of any painting, whereas Ahar has yielded its own characteristic shapes and painted designs. Thus, unless intermediary links, if any, are established, it would be difficult to accept this generic relationship.

2. The limited types and designs in the PGW complex and the thinness (only 40 cm) of its occupational desposit would tend to suggest that at Pariar this culture was in its decadent stage.

3. East of Pariar, the PGW shows a sporadic contact with the contemporary culture like those of the black-slipped and black-and-red wares (e.g. at Sringaverapura) or early NBPW (e.g. at Sringaverapura and Sravasti).

4. In the north-eastern areas of U.P. the northern tributaries of the Ganga, as such Sai, Gomti, etc. were part of the black-slipped and black-and-red ware zone, as noticed in explorations in that region. It may be noted that excavations at Hulas Khera in District Lucknow has not so far yielded any PGW from the black-slipped and black-and-red ware complex.

REFERENCES

Indian Archaeology 1953-54—A Review.

Lal, B. B. and K. N. Dikshit 1981 Sringaverapura: A key-site for the Protohistory and early History of the Central Ganga velley, *Puratattva* 10.

The Pre-Harappans in Punjab

Y. D. SHARMA
Panjab University, Chandigarh

Following the discovery of the pre-Harappan culture at Kalibangan, the older material of Punjab necessitated re-examination and re-evaluation. It was noticed that the lowest levels of Ropar excavated in 1953-55 contain a 60 cm deposit of unmistakable pre-Harappan pottery, although other objects of sophisticated industrial use were obviously borrowed from the Harappans, among which are a typical jar and a large celt of copper. A few Bara ware sherds also occurred in these levels (Sharma 1976). Sarangpur, near Chandigarh, and Bhudan, near Malerkotla, were also broadly pre-Harappan, whatever their date (Suraj Bhan 1967: 1-9; Suraj Bhan *et al* 1978: 67 fn).

Bara culture, named after the type site near Ropar, also needed a re-appraisal. It was noticed that the painted motifs on the Bara ware showed close parallels with those from Baluchistan and Kalibangan. Some pre-Harappan tradition, therefore, appeared to be ancestral to it. The beginnings of Bara site on ^{14}C basis could not be later than *circa* 2000 B.C. and its end obviously later than *circa* 1600 B.C. (Sharma 1973). A date of *circa* 1900 to 1500 B.C. for Bara culture at Sanghol goes very well with it (Sharma *et al* 1982).

Among the sites so far excavated in Punjab mature Harappan culture uninterwoven with the Bara culture existed, if in fact, only at the earlier phase of Kotla Nihang. At other sites mature Harappa and Bara are partners in the cultural make-up of the relevant level. In fact, Bara ware has a dominant share even at such sites as Chandigarh, where Harappan elements are not negligible. The Sutlej-Ghaggar *doab* is so densely dotted with Bara culture sites that the Bara people appear to be the real residents here even if their role was at times subservient in the Harappan socio-economic system.

Bara ware is not reported from the middle Ghaggar in Rajasthan, but it is widely distributed along the Sarasvati and Drishadvati in Ḥaryana. However, its density may not perhaps be as high here as in Punjab. Even in the Ganga-Yamuna *doab* in western Uttar Pradesh it has a widespread distribution.

The pre-Harappans moved north-east from the middle Ghaggar or Sarasvati, not only along the Sarasvati and Drishadvati, but also along other streams now dried up, which originated in the Siwaliks and flowed south-west to swell the waters of the Sarasvati.

RECENT WORK IN PUNJAB

In Punjab, in addition to Sarangpur and Bhudan already mentioned, from Raja Sirkap near Faridkot was collected pre-Harappan pottery in random visits (Sharma 1982). Recent excavations in district Sangrur have now lent relevance to the earlier surface collections and superficial soundings. These excavations cover two sites. The site of Rohira (lat. 30° 35' N, long 75° 50' E), excavated by G.B. Sharma of the Punjab State Archaeology Department, lies about 14 km north-west of Malerkotla, while Mahorana (lat. 30° 28' N, long. 76° E) excavated by the Panjab University under the present author's direction lies 8 km south-west of Maler-kotla on the Nabha-Ludhiana highway.

Till we have more information on Rohira, a brief notice would do. Leaving aside its later three period. Rohira represents apparently the sequenc of Banawali, including the existence of a town wall, but without a bipartite division of the settlement. An enigmatic sealing repeated on four sides of a clay lump recovered here is not of usual. Harappan genre and its relationship is yet to be ascertained (pl I). A standing figure on right perhaps with a bow in hand, a sacred plant in a narrow-waisted tall pot (?) in front and three vertical strokes recalling a Harappan script symbol may be identified in the sealing. From the richness of material the site would appear to have been a town, perhaps both during the pre-Harappan and Harappan occupations.

Mahorana is a large mound with a four-period occupation. The work here was in the nature of a sampling, and accordingly the results obtained should also be viewed as giving only a limited insight into each period. The upper three occupations yielding the Black-Slipped-cum-Painted Grey Ware, Kushan and medieval materials are outside the scope of this paper.

A 2 m thick mantle of yellow sandy clay covering white riverine sand mixed with *kankar* lay here when the first occupants, the pre-Harappans, reached. They occupied the site for a long period, as their average deposit measures three metres in thickness. This long duration, Period I, has been split up into two sub-Periods, IA and IB. The main difference between the two sub-Periods is that while the pre-Harappan pottery occupies a dominant position in the former, the Bara ware does so in the latter, even though this ascendancy has been reached groundly.

Typical pottery, terracotta cakes, bone points, a copper wire and broken razor blade (?), beads of terracotta, steatite and faience, bangles and bracelets of terracotta, shell and faience and a miscellany of other terracotta objects make up the inventory of the pre-Harappan culture in sub-Period IA. There are no beads of semi-precious stones. Terracotta cakes are triangular, round with central depression or oval with constricted waist. Among other terracotta objects may be named querns and pestles, cart frames, hubbed wheels, large balls and gamesmen. Stone has been used for large balls and pounders. Steatite beads are small discular or tiny short tubular, the latter shape being popular also in faience.

Viewed from the classification of pottery at Kalibangan as guide we have at Mahorana Fabrics A,C,E and F, apart from some hard make pots. Vases of different shapes and sizes with concave neck and black-painted upper profile, the body and neck being potted separately and then luted, can hardly be distinguished from Kalibangan pots. Other shapes of this category are short-stemmed small dish-on-stand, medium jar with vertical neck and featureless rim, handled vase shallow bowl with mild carination below rim and miniature jar and dish.

Red ware akin to Fabric C of Kalibangan is both coarse and fine, but mostly the latter. Large dish-on-stand with dish of incurved rim and stand of flaring base, painted jar with beaked or beaded rim, and pedestalled vase are some of the red ware types. Both buff and grey wares are limited in quantity. No basin with internally incised designs representative of Kalibangan Fabric D was found.

Wash and slip of red, or brown hues are fairly common, buff being rare. Among the painted motifs may be recounted bands, loops, single and multiple, the latter resulting in rows of lozenges, arches, series of hatched diamonds making a chequer-board pattern, large spirals with splintered terminals and wavy and zig-zag lines. A potsherd shows part of the figure of a standing stag. The graffiti include some motifs which are close to Harappan script signs. White or cream colour bands are sandwiched between black bands. Slip or paste of these colours is sometimes painted over with characteristic designs in black.

In a representative excavated section the lowest layer above the natural soil is numbered (11). What is unique about Mahorana is the fact that from layer (10) upward the Bara ware is found freely intermingled with the pre-Harappan. It may be present in layer (11) also, but perhaps was not encountered in the limited excavated area. Typical among Bara ware pots are painted globular vases like large *lotas* tnd externally incised vases and jars with Wet Ware rusticated base, some of them bearing soot marks and obviously used as cooking vessels. The curved terracotta stele diagnostic of Bara culture is found in a *tandoor-*

pit cut into layer (9). The base of a footed goblet and some other fragments of Harappan vessels are found in layer (7) and bespeak a restricted contact with the mature Harappans. The numbei of such pots is so small that there appears no likelihood that the Harappans ever had a settlement at the site.

In sub-Period IB mixed pre-Harappan and Bara material continues, but the quantity of the Bara ware which has been on gradual increase from the lowest layer, now crosses the percentage of 50. In layes (10) and (9) taken together perhaps the pre-Harappan and Bara wares are in 60 to 40 ratio. In layer (5), the lowest layer of sub-Period IB, the Bara ware is 60% and the pre-Harappan 40%. In the top layer this proportion changes approximately to 80 to 20 percent.

Otherwise there is little change in the composition of the two Sub-periods. The oval-shaped cake with constricted waist was not recorded from IB levels. Biconical standard beads with large holes (possibly used as spindle whorls) and thick faience bangles occur here in larger numbers. Terracotta bull figurines and a pottery dabber are additional objects. A square steatite bead wtih concentric circles at the corners and another stud-like bead with an intricate rosette motif are unique, particularly the latter, and are a tribute to the bead-

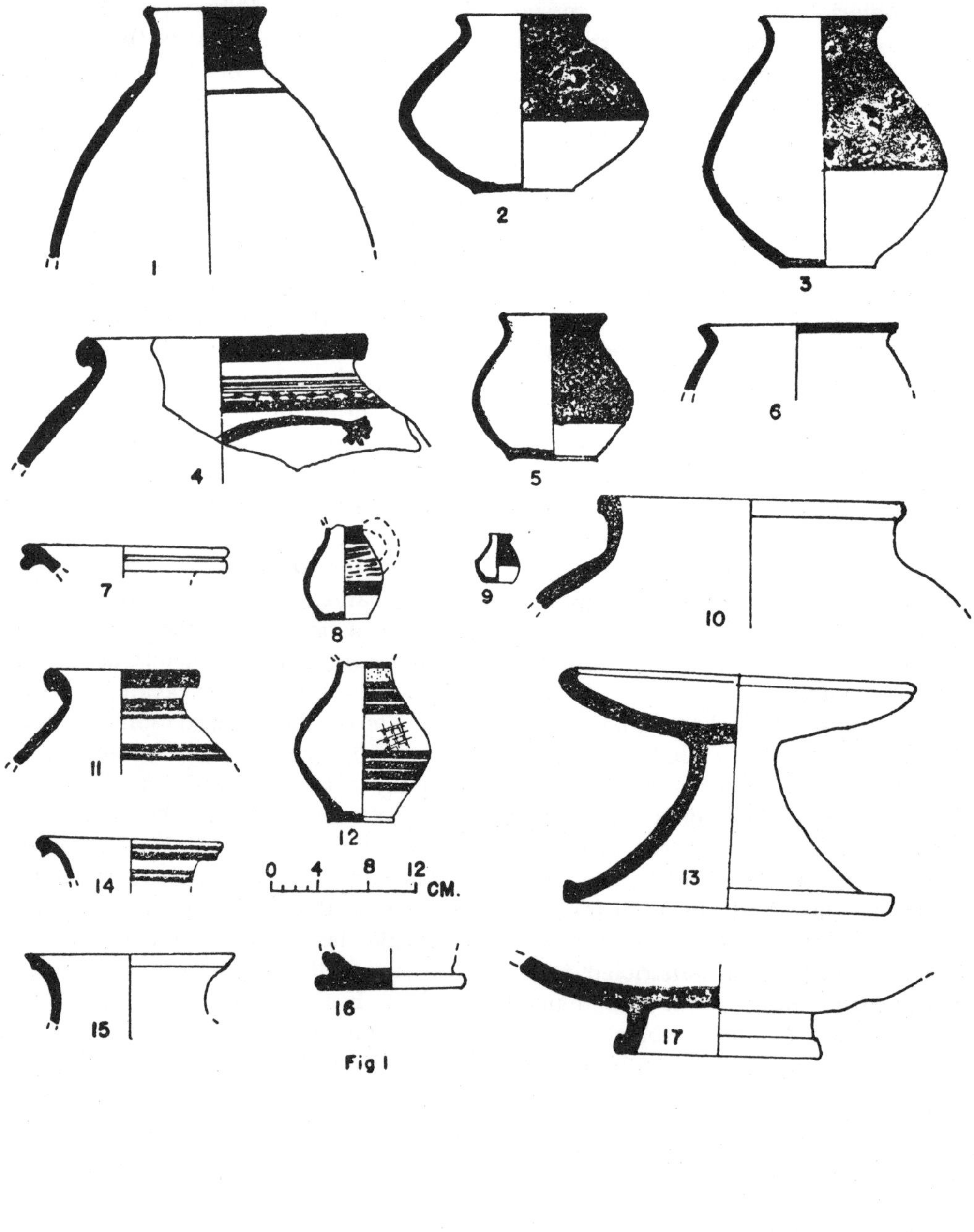

Fig I

maker. A creamish chert blade was a single find of its class. The Bara type terracotta stele occurs frequently. Often it is found in fireplaces and debris of *tandoors,* a fact which had been noticed also at other sites (Sharma *et al* 1982: 72).

On the western slope of the mound nearer the northern corner the extant remains belonged only to Period I. In fact the major part of our information is derived from a 6.50 by 6.50 m area, partly excavated to the natural soil. Mudbrick or

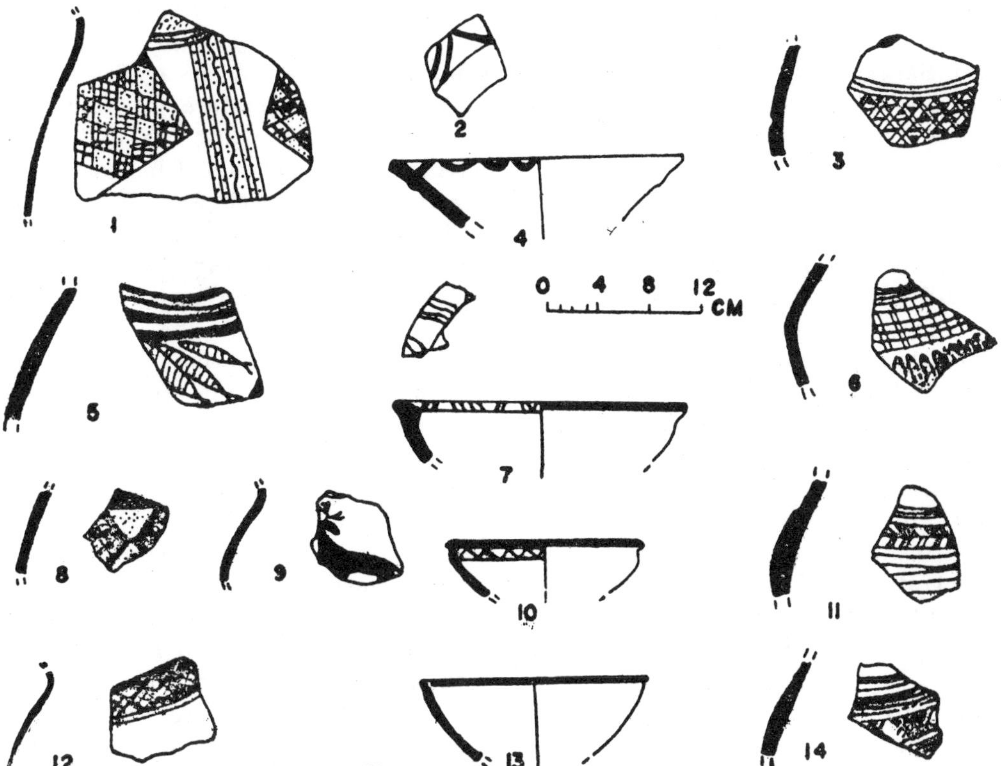

Fig 2

It is noticed that the range of rim-types in vases, jars and large bowls is limited as compared with the pottery at such upstream sites as Ropar, Bara, Chandigarh and Sanghol. The dish with drooping rim is not noticed. Only one pot sherd of internally incised basin, which is typical of Fabric D of Kalibangan and also occurs at Bara, was recovered. The range of painted motifs is also limited, while some of the incised motifs perhaps disappear on the upstream sites. Among the pre-Harappan wares the vase with painted upper profile is rare in sub-Period IB. All this indicates a gradual change and transformation, particularly in the Bara culture, facilitating thus a phasing of the culture. We may perhaps go ever further: what we are witnessing at Mahorana is a gradual transformation of the pre-Harappan to Baran.

mud structures commence from the lowest levels, but they are highly mutilated with short lengths of walls and floors only being now available. The mudbricks were normally of 11 x 22 x 44 cm size.

This area had a series of *tandoors* from the beginning of the occupation. Only two of these *tandoors* were raised overground, others being sunk underground and one of them of sub-Period IB was 1.50 m deep, but the white burnt earth at the base of the *tandoor*-walls was very clearly marked. One of the large underground fireplaces with burnt sides was oval on plan, one end being narrow. Its shape is like small kilns at Bara and other places (Sharma 1976: 12), but it seems to have served here as a *tandoor*. Apparently this area served as a communal bakery from the

In late IB sub-Period the settlement was en-
earliest to the latest days of its occupation.

closed by a 2 m thick platform on the western side. The dimensions and layout of the platform could not be ascertained, but it was fairly wide, perhaps running under the existing fields where dwarf and pale growth of the crop seemed to indicate its existnce. It would appear that its width was not less than 17.50 m, as we were able to locate one end of its width. A section was cut through it and Bara pottery occurred below it and in its make-up. When the site was re-occupied in Period II, the newcomers settled on the platform.

SUMMING UP:—

The origin of the pre-Harappans represented at Amri, Kot Diji and other sites is sought to lie in the Bolan valley and the adjacent area of northern Baluchistan, Afghanistan and Iran, particularly because at Mehrgarh and its neighbourhood (g. Nowsharo) on the Bolan a continuous occupation has been pieced together from the neolithic to the Harappan times. From the lower Indus, according to one view, the pre-Harappans moved east and north-east and having come upon the now extinct stretch of the lower Ghaggar, they continued their march upstream and thus spread into Rajasthan, Haryana and Punjab (Dikshit 1980).

The area of the old Bahawalpur State and its neighbourhood, now in Pakistan, generally known as Cholistan, has been extensively surveyed from 1974 to 1977 by M.R. Mughal (1980), and he records the discovery of 41 Kot Diji-related sites and 32 sites yielding an earlier ceramic, named the Hakra ware by him. No site has be excavated in the area and the nature of relationship between the pre-Harappan and Hakra cultures remains uninvestigated. We may, however, be certain that from Cholistan to the Sutlej there may be more than a hundred pre-Harappan sites. In fact the pre-Harappans had even reached the White Bein across the Sutlej where their existence is clear at Domeli (Sharma *et al* 1982).

The western districts of Punjab have not been systematically surveyed and the sites are being levelled down at a fast pace for cultivation. Even so, judging from the explored area in Mansa Tehsil of Bhatinda district (Joshi 1982) and from the fact that at several sites earlier reported as late Harappan in district Sangrur the pre-Harappan content had been missed, it appears that speaking generally the pre-Harappan settlements in this area lie at a distance of 6-7 km from each other.

The pre-Harappan sites in India are certainly much later than those on the lower Indus. This is clear not only from the available ^{14}C dates but also from the fact that the total nature of Indian pre-Harappan sites bears a distinct impact of the mature Harappa culture in certain features. Apparently after reaching the middle Ghaggar and having spread into the Ghaggar-Sutlej *doab*, the pre-Harappans developed their own way of life and became indigenous in this region. Even though basically and notionally the pre-Harappan culture preceded the mature Harappan, the evolution from the pre-Harappan to the mature-Harappan has not been satisfactorily demonstrated even in Pakistan, much less in India. The Indian pre-Harappans and the mature-Harapppans on the Indus and Ravi are broadly contemporary.

Perhaps the same urge and necessity that drove the pre-Harappans from the lower Indus to the middle Ghaggar also operated in the case of mature-Harappans. Trade and procurement of raw materials would be additional considerations for movement. With their urbanised social and administrative infrastructure and with their advanced and sophisticated equipment they would successfully assault the larger pre-Harappan settlements and would in a way subjugate them. This is what may have happened at sites like Kalibangan, Banawali and possibly Rohira. But the vast majority of smaller settlements would remain untouched. The interaction between the mature-Harappans and the villages of the pre-Harappans would thus be only marginal, mainly confined to the adoption by the latter of some of the sophisticated things of daily life of the former. This is what is perhaps noticeable at sites like Balu in Haryana, Mahorana in Punjab and possibly also in the lowest levels of Ropar. The pre-Harappans continued to live at the same site for several centuries as apparent from reasonably thick deposits at Banawali, Balu and Mahorana. The marginal Harappan impact may perhaps be identified at Mahorana in such articles as a few pieces of pottery, steatite and faience beads, a single chert blade and a fragmentary copper razor blade. The paucity of Harappan material at Mahorana may partly be due to the limited scale of excavation, but one of the main reasons would be that the rural pre-Harappans, conservative by nature, did not need the Harappan articles on a large scale.

The excavations at Mahorana have thrown fresh light also on the Bara culture. Both pre-Harappan and Bara wares and other objects overlapping from the lowest to the top levels at Mahorana make it clear that the Bara culture is not afterall late, even if it survived till very late times. Nor can it be derived from the mature-Harappan culture, even though its origin may not be very clear at the moment, most likely if represents a direct transformation from the pre-Harappan. Some of the incised decoration on the shoulders of its pots is certainly traceable to the Hakra ware (Sharma *et al* 1982 : 73). Other shapes are present at RD-89, a Hakra ware site (Dalal 1981).

Radiocarbon and TL dates are not yet available for Mahorana. This much is, however, certain that the Bara phase of Mahorana and other sites in this region, including perhaps sites in Bhatinda district (Joshi 1982), is much earlier than the phase exposed at Bara and Sanghol. The present author had suggested at least two phases in the Bara culture (Sharma 1982); perhaps a minimum of three phases would be necessary. Compared with the pottery at Bara, shapes and types at Mahorana are limited. The prolification of rim features, painted motifs and incised designs noticed at Bara is absent here. In addition there are perhaps some incised designs at Mahorana, which are no longer current at Bara. The Bara culture may have evolved in Bhatinda-Sangrur belt, but it needs excavation of many more sites before this can be asserted.

The date of Period I of Mahorana is at present a matter of surmise. Considering that the beginnings of the pre-Harappan levels of Kalibangan are placed at *circa* 2400 B.C. on uncorrected ^{14}C basis, we might assume that Mahorana was inhabited for the first time in *circa* 2300 B.C. With a deposit of three metres, and allowing 75 cm for accumulation of a century, the end of Period I may be placed at *circa* 1900 B.C. This wlll go well with the Bara and Sanghol dates, where the more advanced and sophisticated phase of Bara culture has been dated to *circa* 2000 to 1500 B.C. (Sharma *et al* 1982 : 75-76).

Acknowledgements:

Grateful thanks are acknowledged to the Director, Punjab State Department of Archaeology and Museums for permission to publish the photo graph of the clay sealing from Rohira.

REFERENCES

Bisht R.S. 1979 Excavations at Banawali: 19974-77, *Harappan Civilization* (ed) Gregory L. Possehl, New Delhi.

Casal, J.M. 1964 *Fouilles d' Amri,* Paris.

Dalal, Katy 1981 RD 89: A New Hakra ware Site? *Man & Environment* V, Pune.

Dales, G.F. 1979. The Balakot Project: Summary of Four Years of Excavations in Pakistan, *Man & Environment* III, Ahmedabad.

Dikshit, K.N. 1980 A Critical Review of Pre-Harappan Cultures, *Man & Environment* IV, Ahmedabad.

Ghosh, A. 1952 The Rajputana Desert—Its Archaeological Aspect, *Bulletin of the National Institute of Sciences of India* I, New Delhi.

1965 The Indus Civilization: Its Origins. Authors, Extent and Chronology, *Indian Prehistory: 1964* (eds) V.N. Mishra and M.S. Mate, Poona.

Jarrige, Jean Francois. 1982 Excavations at Mehrgarh: Their Significance for Understanding the Background of the Harappan Civilization, *Harappan Civilization* (ed) Gregory L, Possehl, New Delhi.

Joshi, J.P. 1982 Settlement Patterns in Third. Second and First Millennia in India—With Special Reference to Recent Discoveries in Punjab. Paper read at the Seminar, 'The Cultural Heritage of the Indian Village', held on 13th-14th April, 1982. Museum of Mankind, London (cyclostyled copy).

Khan, F.A. 1965 Excavation at Kot Diji, *Pakistan Archaeology* 2, Karachi

Lal, B.B. 1979 Kalibangan and Indus Civilization *Essays in Indian Protohistry,* (eds.) D.P. Agrawal and Dilip K. Chakrabarti, Delhi.

Majumdar, N.G. 1934 Exploration in Sind, *Memoirs of the Archaeological Survey of India* 48, Delhi.

Mughal, Mohammad Rafique, 1971 *The Early Harappan Period in the Greater Indus Valley and Northern Baluchistan (C. 3000-2400 B.C.),* Ph.D. Dissertation, University of Pennsylvania, Philadelphia University Microfilms, Ann Arbor, Michigan, USA (facsimile produced in 1975).

1980 New Archaeological Evidence from Bahawalpur, *Man & Environment* IV, Ahmedabad. Repeated in 1981.

In *Indus Civilization-New Perspectives* (ed) A.H. Dani Islamabad.

Sharma, Y.D. Value of Common Painted Ceramic Designs from Different Sites as Guide to Chronology, with Special Reference to Pottery from Bara (Punjab), *Radiocarbon and Indian Archaeology* (eds) D.P. Agrawal, and A. Ghosh, Bombay.

1976 Transformation of the Harappa Culture in the Punjab, *Archaeological Congress and Seminor: 1972* (ed) Udai Vir Singh, Kurukshetra.

1982 Harappan Complex on the Sutlej (India) *Harappan Civilization* (ed) Gregory L. Possehl, New Delhi.

Sharma, Y.D. and G.B. Sharma, 1982 Bara Culture and its Housing Remains with Special Reference to Sanghol, *Indian Archaeology-New Perspectives* (ed) R.K. Sharma, Delhi.

Sharma, Y.D., G.B. Sharma, and B.S. Nijjar 1982 A New Pre-Harappan Site in Punjab with a likely Neolithic Stratum, *Indian Archaeology-New Perspectives* (ed) R.K. Sharma, Delhi.

Suraj Bhan 1967 New Light on the Ochre Coloured Ware Culture, *Research Bulletin (Arts) Panjab University* 57 (3), Chandigarh.

Suraj Bhan and Jim G. Shaffer, 1978 New Discoveries in Northern Haryana, *Man & Environment II,* Ahmedabad.

Lithic Industries of Bankura

DILIP K. CHARABARTI,
D.K. BHATTACHARYA and
R.K. CHATTOPADHYAY
Delhi University, Delhi

The present paper reports the lithic material collected and studied by the Archaeology and Museum unit of the Department of History, Delhi University, in the course of an exploration in Bankura district, West Bengal, in March 1982. This material involves one newly discovered lower palaeolithic site (in the Silavati valley), 51 microlithic sites in different river-valleys of the district (45 of them are newly discovered) and the microlithic material from 4 protohistoric-historic settlements. Two sites in the last category, Kumardanga in the Tarafeni valley (reported for the first time) and Tulsipur in the Kansavati valley, bear black-and-red ware and do not show any later horizon. The third site, Dihar on the Dwarakeshwar, yields black-and-red ware but its occupation continues up to the mediaeval period. The fourth site, Shulgi on the Silavati, is, on the circumstantial evidence, mediaeval but the eroded river cliff section at the site shows along with mediaeval pottery microliths in some quantity, two small polished celts and a few pieces of iron tools.

A transitional zone between the Chhotanagpur plateau on the west and the Gangetic alluvium on the east the district of Bankura (22° 38' N, 86° 36' —87° 46' E) covers an area of about 6871 sq km. It possesses with some amount of overlap a hilly section in the west, an undulating plain with lateritic gravel beds and rocky outcrops in the middle and an alluvial stretch in the northeast and east. Two major hills, the Biharinath in the northwest and the Susunia further south, attain the heights of 447.8 m and 439.5 m respectively, but the hills of Bankura are usually low, hardly going much beyond 100 m. The Biharinath and its periphery are still forested The Susunia has been largely denuded of its vegetation cover in recent years. Forests still exist in the hills and valleys of the Ranibandh and Raipur Police Stations in the southwest and at least in three major spreads on the lateritic gravels near Sonamukhi, Vishnupur and Joypur in the east-southeast. The forests all belong to the 'Northern Tropical Dry Deciduous —Dry Sal' type of Indian forests. The trees like *asan (Terminalia tomentosa), bahera (Terminalia belerica), piasal (Pterocarpus marsupium), kend (Diospyros melanoxylon), palas (Butea frondosa), mahua (Bassica latifolia),* etc. mingle to some extent with *sal (Shorea robusta).* Wild life (with the possible exceptions of jungle cats and bear) is now marginal. Because of the topography the flow of the rivers is basically from the northwest to the south east. From the north to the south the major rivers are the Damodar, Sali, Gandheswari, Dwarakeshwar, Jaipanda, Silavati, Kansavati, Kumari and Tarafeni. The amount of water in these rivers depends on the rainfall in the western hills. Most of them almost dry up in summer. Rainfall is limited to about 118 cm per annum and this makes Bankura the dryest district in West Bengal. The soil types are sand, silt, clay and different types of loam. Agriculture in the pre-modern days depended on rainfall with marginal help from such irrigation devices as the construction of dams in the slopes and hollows to catch rainwater. The basal geology is dominated by the Archaean metamorphic complex with granitic intrusions. Sedimentary rocks of the lower Gondwona formation (forming the southern part of the Raniganj coalfields) occur primarily in the extreme northwest between Mejia and the Baharinath. Gravels of conglome rates and sandstones of Oligocene-Miocene epochs are scattered throughout the central section of the district. The beds of Pleistocene laterite occur usually in the low levels but occasionally in the higher level as well. Laterite interspersed with associated rocks of sands and gravels is supposed to form the most characteristic geological feature of the district. Iron ore suitable for preindustrial smelting occurs extensively and there is olsa some evidence of copper extraction in the past at Purnapani and Tamakun in the Ranibandh Police Station. Lead ore has been reported in the Ranibandh area and among other things one notices the occurrence of garnet, steatite and different types of stone (Banerji 1968).

THE LOWER PALAEOLITHIC SITES

GUNNIADA HILL, SILAVATI VALLEY (site 43, Khatra P.S.): this hill (more than 100 m high) is a prominent landmark to the south of the Silavati river near a ford called the Amghata crossing. The location of this crossing is near Salanpur. The Guniada hill is isolated, bare, hog-backed and looks reddish in colour. The hill slope is extensive all arround and covered with rock debris, obviously scree material. Chunks of whitish quartz are prominently visible among the debris. At the foot of the hill there are several outcrops (again largely quartz) which have been cut into fragments by erosion. The lower palaeolithic material is limited in quantity but considering the abundance of suitable raw material in the vicinity one would have expected a much larger occurrence of implements. This locality deserves an intensive exploration in future.

There are 6 specimens, all in quartz. (i) Biface —15 by 8 cm — rolled and patinated — flakes detached from the sides—dorsal ridge prominent — anterior pointed end — ventral surface more or less flat—retouchings along the border — well-prepared butt-end. (ii) Biface on shallow flake—10 by 7 cm — a large flake has been detached from the dorsal ridge on the right, forming a sloping surface towards the border. (iii) Side-scraper — 10.5 by 6 cm. iv) Side-scraper — 6.8 by 4.6 cm — convex working edge—abrupt retouchings. (v) Core — small flakes have been detached. (vi) Retouched flake.

MICROLITHIC SITES

A. *THE DAMODAR VALLEY* (sites 1-7): the Damodar drains the northern side of the district and forms its boundary with the adjoining district of Burdwan. It originates in the Chhotanagpur plateau about 96 km west of Ramgarh. It flows for a distance of about 89 km in Bankura district. The river has sandy banks and a low gradient (.64 m per km). The average width is 1484 m. The river receives a large number of seasonal flows bringing in the wet season discharge to its drainage system. The sites are:

(1) *Monor* (MNR): this is about 6 km northwest of Barjora (Barjora P.S.). The location is on the bonks of a local *nullah* called *Monorer jor.* The sections expose red soil mixed with gravel and sand. The implements were picked up from the dry bed and the banks.

(2) *Barjora* (BJA) : the site (Barjora P.S.) is on the western side of the village and close to the Durgapur-Bankura road. The implements were collected form the surface of a lateritic bed or the top of which the local school is located.

(3) *Dejuri* (DJR) : the site (Barjora P.S.) is to the south of the village and near a reserve forest on the Durgapur-Bankura road. The implements were collected from the surface of an undulating, lateritic land and the associated rain gullies.

(4) Ituri, (ITR) : the site (Saltora P.S.) is on the Dishergarh-Bankura road, in the northern end of the village of Ituri. The implements were collected from the local lateritic surface.

(5) *Daiso* (DSO) : the site (Barjora P.S.) is about 1 km west of Dejuri. The implements came from the local lateritic surface.

(6) Kushthalia (KSL) : the site (Gangajalghati P.S.) is about 1 km north of the village of Kushthalia on the Bankura-Gangajalghati road. The actual location is on the right bank of a local watercourse called *Bishindar Jor.* The implements are obtained from the eroded gullies.

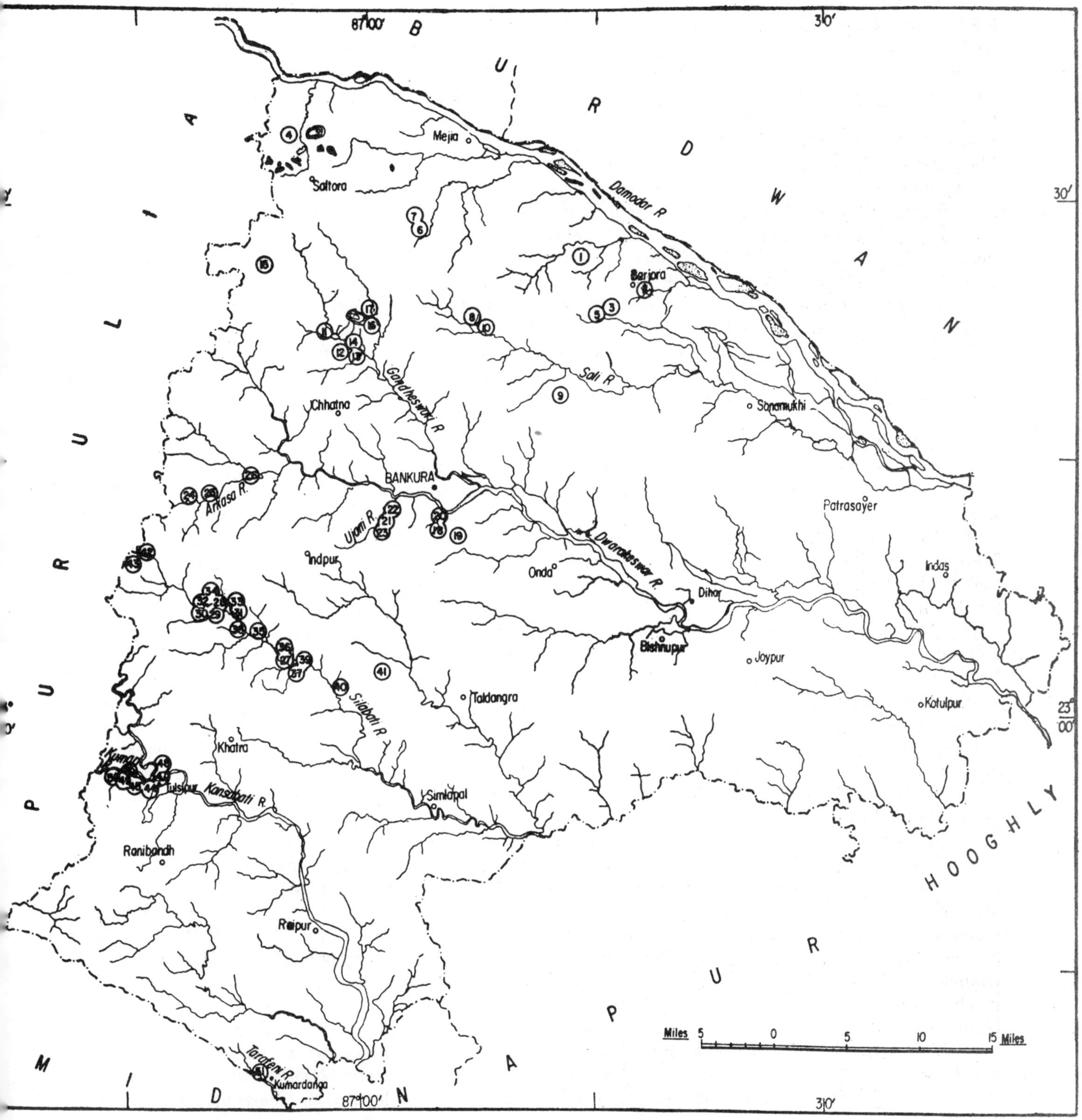

Fig. 1. Map of Bankura showing the sites mentioned in the text.

(7) *Beldanga* (BLD) : the site (Gangajalghati P.S.) is near Kushthalia, on the north bank of the *Bishindar Jor*.

Sites 1 and 3 have been reported earlier (*IAR* 60-61; Lal 1958). The present total collection of microliths from the Damodar system is 79. Table 1 sets forth the sitewise distribution of types. The highest number of finished tools is represented by lunates and obliquely blunted blades. There is no burin in the whole series.. There is a single specimen of scalene triangle. The microliths from these sites are made of various grades of fine-grained rock and are 3.6-1.07 cm in length, 1.2-0.6 cm in breadth and less than 0.5 cm in thickness.

B. *THE SALI VALLEY* (sites 8-10): a tributary of the Damodar this river originates in the western part of Gangajalghati P.S. and traverses a course of about 73 km through Gangajalghati, Barjora, Sonamukhi, Patrasayer and Indus P.S. before it meets the Damodar. This river is locally important because of its irrigation facilities. The sites are :

(8) *Amarkanan* (AMK) : the site (Gangajalghati P.S.) is on the left bank of the Sali. A gravelly and sandy elevated surface near the village school yielded implements.

(9) *Beliatore* (BLT) : a few km south of the Sali the site, an elevated lateritic surface near the local school, yielded implements.

(10) *Kara* (KAR) : the local landmark is the Kara hill (Gangajalghati P.S.) about 122 m high. The Sali flows by its side. The slopes are eroded and yield microliths. It was possible to locate two separate clusters in this area. These clusters are designated KAR(A) and KAR(B).

The Table-2 sets forth the sitewise distribution of types in the Sali valley. It reveals that the Kara area is of special interest. The microliths here are made of yellowish white to grey chert material and the blades measure 4-1 cm in length. Among the tool types one notes burins, lunates, triangles and points which are all finely done. It is also important to note that in KAR(B) some blade fragments go as far as 4 cm in breadth.

C. *THE GANDHESWARI VALLEY* (sites 11-17): a tributary of the Dwarakeshwar this rises near the Susunia hill and flows for about 32 km in a southeasterly direction before joining the Dwarakeshwar near Bankura town. The sites are :

(11) *Pachasimulia* (PSL) : located on the south bank of the Gandheswari the site (Chhatna P.S. yields artifacts from red soil surface of an elevated tract on the river bank.

(12) *Parulia* (PRL) : located on the south bank of the Gandheswari the site (Chhatna P.S.) yielded artifacts from the undulating river bank.

(13) *Paharbeda* (PHB) : located on the south bank of the Gandheswari the site (Chatna P.S. yielded artifacts from the eroded gullies in the river cliff.

(14) *Suyabasa* (SBA) : located on the left bank of the Gandheswari the site (Chhatna P.S.) yielded artifacts from an elevated gravelly surface on the river bank.

(15) *Jamthol* (JMT) : located on the south bank of the Gandheswari the site (Chhatna P.S.) yielded artifacts from the rain gullies near the river cliff.

(16) *Gidhuria* (GDR) : about 1.5 km to the west of the Susunia hill the site (Chhatna P.S.) yielded artifacts from a local eroded surface.

(17) *Dhakorar Jor* : about 1 km to the north of the Susunia hill the site (Chhatna P.S.) yielded artifacts from a local eroded surface.

Site 17 has been reported earlier (*IAR* 1965-66:54). Table-3 sets forth the relevant data. Made of greyish chert and fine-grained quartzite the microliths measure 5-1.5 cm in length. It is important to note that at site 14 (Suyabasa) a tiny neolithic celt (5.5 by 1.9 cm) prepared on dyke material has been found. It is totally ground with a rounded butt and a plano-convex cross-section. There is no reason to doubt the association of microliths and this neolithic celt at the site. Another significant point is that there is not a single geometric type among the present collection of microliths from the Gandheswari valley.

D. *THE DWARAKESWAR VALLEY* (sites 18-20): after the Damodar this is the most important river of the district. This rises in the hills near Hura in the neighbouring Purulia district. In Bankura this flows for about 107 km roughly through the middle of the district before entering Hooghly district and eventually joining the Bhagirathi as the Rupnarayan. The sites are:

(18) *Damodarpur* (DMP): the site (Bankura Sadar P.S.) is located on the southern side of the Dwarakeshwar. The area around the village of Damodarpur is covered by lateritic gravel and the

landscape is undulating and elevated. The surface also contains primary lateritic chunks. The gravelly elevated land covers an area of about 3 sq km. It is important to note that the whole area has been disturbed by quarries for laterite chunks. Two microlithic clusters (designated DMP-A, DMP-B) have been located on the exposed lateritic surface. DMP-A is located in the western part of the elevated land while DMP-B is located in its eastern part. Their mutual distance is tbout 1 km.

(19) *Majuria* (MJR) : the site (Bankura Sadar P.S.) is close to the Damodarpur tract and yields microliths from the gullies on the banks of a local watercourse.

(20) *Dhaldanga* (DHG) : the site (Bankura Sadar P.S.) is about half a kilometre away from the Dwarakeswar bridge near Bankura town towards Damodarpur. The artifacts were collected from surface.

Table-4 sets forth the sitewise distribution of microlithic types in the Dwarakeshwar valley The length of the implements varies between 4.2 cm and 1.5 cm. The material is greyish chert and quartz.

E. *THE UJANI VALLEY* (sites 21-23) : the Ujani is a minor tributary of the Dwarakeswar. The sites are :

(21) *Bhagabandh* (BGB) : the site (Bankura Sadar P.S.) lies in the western side of the village. The artifacts were collected from an elevated surface. Iron ore and slag occurred in the immediate vicinity.

(22) *Krishnanagar* (KSN) : the site (Bankura Sadar P.S.) is about half a kilometre away from the village and near the confluence of the Ujani and the Dwarakeswar. The artifacts occurred on the surface.

(23) *Bhaturi* (BTR) : the site (Bankura Sadar P.S.) is about 1 km away from the village and close to the river bank. The artifacts occurred on the surface.

The Table-5 sets forth the sitewise distribution of microlithic types in the Ujani valley. The artifacts are prepared on a crusty variety of chert and measure almost 6 cm to less than I cm in length.

F. *THE ARKASA VALLEY* (sites 24-26): the Arkasa is a minor tributary of the Dwarakeswar. The sites are :

(24) *Deulbira Temple* (DLRT) : the artifacts occur on the river bank behind the local temple (Chhatna P.S.).

(25) *Deulbira Bridge* (DLRB) : the artifacts occur on the river bank near the bridge on the river.

(26) *Badlar Ghat* (BLG) : the site (Chhatna P.S.) is on the river bank at this spot on the road to Bankura.

The Table-6 sets forth the relevant data. Prepared on greyish chert the artifacts measure 4.5-1.5 cm in length.

G. *THE SILAVATI VALLEY* (sites 27-43) : The largest tributary of the Dwarakeswar the Silavati rises in the Puncha P.S. of Purulia district and flows for 56 km in Bankura district before and flows the Dwarakeswar in Midnapur district. The sites are :

(27) *Patirdanga* (PTD) : the microliths occur on a gravelly surface near the river bank (Indpur P.S.).

(28) *Deulgara* (DLG) : the western side of the local village showed microliths on a surface full of lateritic nodules and some chunks of cherty stone (Indpur P.S.).

(29) *Satir Ghat* (STG) : the context is a pottery-stretch of river bank (Indpur P.S.) The pottery is mediaeval.

(30) *Makrasinitala* (MST) : the context is a high stretch of river bank about 1 km south of the village of Junbediya (Khatra P.S.). Bits of unidentifiable pottery are found at the site.

(31) *Kadamdeuli* (KDL) : the context is a large area of undulating land on the northwestern side of the village (Indpur P.S.).

(32) *Junbediya* (JBD) : the context is a surface full of calcareous nodules in the eastern end of the village (Indpur P.S.).

(33) *Harinbira* (HBR): the context is surface mixed with gravel and sand in the eastern end of the village (Indpur P.S.).

(34) *Bandeuli* (BDL) : the context is a forested tract near the village (Indpur P.S.).

(35) *Giorda* (GRD) : the context is an eroded surface on the river cliff (Indpur P.S.).

(36) *Gobindapur* (GBP) : the context is the topmost portion of the eroded river cliff (Indpur P.S.).

(37) *Benjtabani* (BTB) : the context is an eroded surface on the river bank (Khatra P.S.).

(38) *Silavati Dam* (STD) : the context is an eroded surface near the dam (Indpur P.S.).

(39) *Namokechanda* (NKD) : the context is the eroded river bank near the village of Patirdanga (Indpur P.S.). A large quantity of potsherds, presumably mediaeval, was found in this area.

(40) *Anardihi* (ARD) : the context is an elevated land on the river bank. A fragment of a ringstone was found associated with the microliths (Taldangra P.S.).

(41) *Bibarda* (BBD) : the context is a forested tract near the village (Taldangra P.S.).

(42) *Amghata* (AGT) : the context is the topmost part of the river cliff (Indpur P.S.).

(43) *Guniada hill* (GND) : the context is the surface on the hill slope.

The collection from STG represents a typical collection from this area. The artifacts are made of agate, fine-grained greenish quartzite, chert, dirty chalcedony, etc. The size varies between 4.5 and 1 cm in length, and between 1 and 1.8 cm in breadth. The thickness is less than 1 cm. Even the fluted cores are small and do not exceed 1 cm in thickness. An important feature to notice is the occurrence of pottery, presumably mediaeval, at STG and NKD and of a fragment of a ringstone (diametre 6.5 cm) at ARD.

The Table-7 sets forth the sitewise distribution of microlithic types in the Silavati valley.

H. *THE KUMARI-KANSAVATI VALLEY* (sites 44-50) : with its origin in the Ayodhya hill complex in Purulia the Kumari flows for only 8 km in Bankura before it joins the Kansavati near Ambikanagar. Besides the Damodar and the Dwarakeswar the Kansavati is the third largest river in the disitrict. Rising in the hills around Jhalda in Purulia district this river flows for about 56 km in Bankura district before it enters Midnapur district. A dam has been constructed at the confluence of the Kumari and the Kansavati. A considerable area has been submerged under water because of the construction of this dam. The sites are :

(44) *Ambikanagar* (AKN) : the context is the southern bank of the Kumari near the confluence. Pottery is found in the same place and this pottery is unlikely to be earlier than the mediaeval period (Ranibandh P.S.).

(45) *Mukundapur* (MDP) : the context is the dried-up bank of the Kumari (Ranibandh P.S.).

(46) *Paresnath* (PRN) : the context is the foot of the Paresnath hill (Khatra P.S.).

(47) *Chitgiri* (CTG) : the context is the top section of the cliff at the junction of the Kumari and the Kansavati (Khatra P.S.).

(48) *Gorabari Kansavati colony* (GKC) : the context is close to the modern dam project colony and yields iron ore and slag as well (apart from microliths), (Khatra P.S.).

(49) *Hatikheda* (HKD) : the context is the Kumari bank (Ranibandh P.S.).

(50) *Navachiada* (NCD) : the context is a gravelly surface near the river bank. Sites 44, 46 and 47 have been reported earlier (*IAR* 59-60: 49-50). The artifacts are almost entirely made of a blackish fine-grained rock. The length is 8-3 cm and the width 1-2 cm. The thickness is 0.5-1 cm. The occurrence of pottery at AKN and of iron ore and slag at GKC is noteworthy. Table-8 puts forward the relevant typological data.

I. *THE TARAFENI VALLEY* (site 51) : rising in the hills near Belpahari in Midnapur district this tributary of the Kansavati flows for only 8 km in Bankura district before entering Midnapur district again. Only one site has been located in this valley.

(51) *Durpal* (DPL) : the context is the upper section of the river cliff (Raipur P.S.). The collection does not have any finished specimen.

MICROLITHS FROM PROTOHISTORIC—HISTORIC SETTLEMENTS

A. *Kumardanga* (Raipur P.S.) : the site is very close to the modern village and located on the bank of the Tarafeni river. The Tarafeni has curved out a wide bed in this area, although in March the stream is only a narrow rush of water confined to the middle of this bed. On the river cliff side the site has been partly destroyed but we would suggest that it was a small settlement, hardly 40 m across. Sufficient quantity of good quality black-and-red ware and an unidentified terracotta object of the type reported from the site of Bahiri in Birbhum district (Chakrabarti and Hasan 1981 : pl X, the lower object on the right) could be recovered from the cliff section. Fragments of potsherds, microliths and bone tools were, to some extent, found scattered on the surface which is at present covered by grass. Our field-impression is that Kumardanga is a single occupational site. There was no occupation after the black-and-red ware phase.

We collected 19 microlithic artifacts from the surface. The specimens are made of fine-grained quartz. They are 4.5-1.5 cm in length and 0.8-0.3 cm in breadth. The break-up of artifacts is as follows : fluted core-3, core trimming flake/blade-6, lunate-2, burin-4, point-1, backed knife-1 and retouched blade-2.

B. *Tulsipur* (Ranibandh P.S.) : the site is in the Kansavati valley and was excavated in 1967-68 (*IAR* 1967-68 : 49-50). The report is very brief and incomplete. For instance, it makes no mention of the microliths which must have been found because there was no difficulty for us in collecting 19 microlithic artifacts on the surface itself. A noteworthy feature of this black-and-red ware site is that this has yielded iron throughout.

The microlithic artifacts prepared on a greyish cherty stone and range in length from 5.5 to 2.5 cm. Among the total of 19 specimens the number of debitage is 13. The break-up is : fluted core-4, core trimming blade 6, parallel-sided blade-3. The fluted cores are 3-1.7 cm in length and mainly on tabloid chunks. Blade beds are usually narrow. The core trimming blades are 6-3.5 cm in length, triangular in cross-section and preserve marks of previous blade removal on the dorsal surface. The parallel sided blades are in fragment and 2-1 cm broad. The finished specimens are : burin -1, point -1, retouched flake -2 and retouched blade -2. The burin has been made on the thicker end of a slender blade. One of the facets bears the marks of multiple spalls which intersect with a single scar forming the other facet. The point is prepared on a blade fragment by thick blunting of two equally converging lateral borders. The opposite end indicates a shoulder preparation and the specimen could have been used as an arrowhead. The retouched flakes and blades are unspecific in character.

C. *Dihar* (Vishnupur P.S.) : on the left bank of the Dwarakeswar river this site is well-known for its 10th-11th century temples but recent investigations have brought out black-and-red ware, early historic ware, cast copper coins, beads of semi-precious stone, etc. on the long, flat and reasonably well-preserved mound of Dihar. Interestingly enough, in the present exploration we recovered three glass objects which, on close inspection, give the impression of being microlithic artifacts in glass. The objects have been illustrated in Figure 2. In fact, if the objects were in stone there would have been no hesitation in calling these pieces microlithic artifacts. We do consider them specimens of glass microliths. In any excavation of the site the occurrence of these artifacts on the surface should be kept in mind.

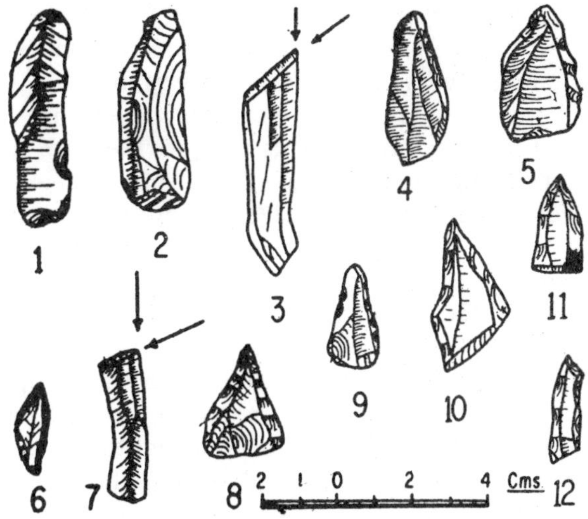

Fig. 2. Lithic artifacts from Tulsipur and Kumardanga. Glass microlithic artifacts from Dihar. Tulsipur 1-6; Kumardanga 7-9; Dihar 10-12 (glass) 1-2: blade; 3: burin; 4: retouched blade; 5: retouched flake; 6: micropoint; 7: burin; 8: point; 9: knife; 10-12 glass artifacts.

D. *Shulgi* (Taldangra P.S.) : the site lies on the left bank of the Silavati. This is a small village which is approachable from a larger village called Brahmandiha (near Harmasra). What is interesting at Shulgi is that there is a mass of potsherds exposed in the upper section of the cliff. This pottery cannot be earlier than the mediaeval period. This inference also gains support from the fact that a mediaeval sculptural piece is known to have been discovered at the spot. The cliff is not straight but sloping and on the slope immediately below the top one notices scattered potsherds which have no doubt fallen from the exposed section above. In this part one finds along with the pottery microlithic debitage (we could not find any finished tool), two neolithic celts and a few pieces of iron implements. The association between the mediaeval pottery and the latter categories of artifacts is hard to deny. There are 11 pieces of microlithic debitage in our collection : 2 fluted cores, 5 core-trimming blades, 2 core trimming flakes and 2 parallel-sided blades. Made of quartz and a greyish cherty stone the artifacts measure 4.8-2.6 cm in length. Of the two neolithic celts one is made on a small flattish pebble by polishing the working edge on two sides. The rest of the specimen is left untouched. The second specimen is a small well-polished trapezoidal celt in a slightly greenish stone. The iron implements are mainly lance-points.

The purpose of the present paper is not to discuss the different issues of Bankura prehistory with reference to all the sites discovered so far but to report the lithic material found in the course of an exploration which only intended to sample the district archaeologically (the historical material will be published in due course). The point which easily emerges out of our work is the frequency of microlithic occurrences in the district. The prehistoric sequence in the area begins with the lower palaeolithic implements (the Dwarakeswar valley, the Gandheswari valley and the Kumari-Kansavati valley which were already known to contain lower palaeoliths, and the Silavati valley where lower palaeoliths have been found by us for the first time) and it is only reasonable to assume that at least some microlithic occurrences in Bankura should be early and fit in the sequence. Only further careful work can establish this. However, once the microlithic tradition was established this apparently continued for a very long period. The microlithic occurrence with black-and-red ware at Kumardanga and Tulsipur is, of course, not surprising but what is of great interest is the association of microlithic artifacts with apparently mediaeval pottery at Namokechanda (site no 39) and Shulgi. Bankura witnessed a great spurt in temple-building and sculpture-making activities in the 10th-11th centuries A.D. We would suggest that there were pockets of microlith-users in Bankura during that period. This is an assumption which may be true of the neighbouring district Purulia as well, although the evidence is not particularly direct there (Chakrabarti *et al* 1982). However, this is still an inference which should be tested by further fieldwork.

TABLE 1

Site	*Tool specimens*	*Debitage*	*Tool types*
MNR	13	7	obliquely blunted blade?4, lunate-4
BJR	13	7	ob. blunt. blade-3, lunate-2, scalene triangle-1.
DJR	27	19	Backed blade-2, ob. blunt. blade-point-1.
ITR	4	4	No tool type
DSO	6	3	ob. blunt. blade-1, lunate-1, micropoint-1.
KSL	10	7	Backed blade-1, lunate-1, notch-1.
BLD	10	7	ob. blunt. blade-1, lunate-1, micro-point-1.

TABLE 2

Site	*Tool specimens*	*Debitage*	*Tool types*
ANK	29	14	Backed blade-1, ob. blunt. blade-5, lunate-6 scalene triangle-2, retouched flake/blade-1
ELT	12	5	ob. blunt. blade-2, lunate-3, ret. flake/ blade-2.
KAR(A)	152	111	ob. blunt. blade-8, lunate-11, Sauveterranean point-1, point-2, denticulate-2, knife-3, burin-3, scalene triangle-6, ret. flake/blade-5.
KAR(B)	64	41	Backed blade-6, ob blunt. blade-3, lunate-4, Sauvet. point-1, point-1, burin-2, flake/ blade-6.

TABLE 3

Site	*Tool specimens*	*Debitage*	*Tool types*
PSL	15	13	lunate-1, ret. flake-1.
PRL	4	4	no tool type
PHB	12	10	ret. flake-1, burin-1.
SBA	24	20	lunate-3, point-1.
JMT	11	10	burin-1.
GDR	9	4	ret, flake-2, Backed blade-2, borer-1.
DKJ	14	9	ret. blade-1, burin-2, side scraper-1, end scraper-1.

TABLE 4

Site	*Tool specimens*	*Debitage*	*Tool types*
DMP(A)	13	10	Backed blade-1, ob. blunt. blade-1, burin-1.
DMP(B)	21	13	Backed blade-1. ob. blunt. blade-2, point-1, crest guiding blade-2.
MJR	6	6	no tool type
DHG	14	13	Ob. blunt. blade-1.

TABLE 5

Site	*Tool specimens*	*Debitage*	*Tool types*
BGB	29	25	Ob. blunt. blade-2, lunate-1, ret. blade-1.
KSN	12	10	ret. blade-1, backed knife-1.
BTR	43	38	Backed blade-2, ob. blunt. blade-2, side scraper-1.

TABLE 6

Site	*Tool specimens*	*Debitage*	*Tool types*
DLRT	5	3	Burin-1, backed knife-1.
DLRB	8	5	Burin-1, ret. flake-2.
BLG	8	8	no tool type

TABLE 7

Site	*Tool specimens*	*Debitage*	*Tool types*
PTD	22	20	lunate-1, end scraper-1.
DLG	32	25	Ob. blunt. blade-1, lunate-3, micro point-1, ret. blade-2.
STG	146	104	Backed blade-1, ob. blunt. blade-5, lunate-10, knife-3. micropoint-2, Sauve. point-4, burin-6, ret. blade-9, denticulate-1, ret. core rejuvenation-1
MST	20	19	backed blade-1.
KDL	8	6	Thumbnail scraper-2.
JBA	8	7	Micropoint-1.
HBR	27	22	Ob. blunt. blade-1, point-1, micropoint-1, end scraper-1, thumbnail scraper-1.
BDL	6	2	Backed blade-2, ob. blunt. blade-1, micropoint-1.
GRD	8	7	Ob. blunt. blade-1.
GVP	36	30	Backed blade-1, lunate-1, burin-1, ret. blade-3.
BTB	16	13	Ob. blunt. blade-2, micropoint-1.
STD	15	12	Lunate-1, point-1, ret. blade-1.
NKD	4	4	no tool type
ARD	6	3	Backed blade-1, lunate-1, micropoint-1.
BBD	10	9	Backed blade-1.
AGT	146	96	Backed blade-3, ob, blunt. blade-2, lunate-6, knife-3, point-10, micropoint-1, end scraper-1, burin-3, ret, blade-11, denticulate-1, ret. core rejuvenation-3, side scraper-1, borer-1, scalene triangle-3, ret. flake-1.
GND	18	11	Lunate-1, point-3, ret. blade-2, borer-1.

TABLE 8

Site	Tool	Debitage	Tool types
AMG	17	10	Obliquely blunted blade-4, lunate-2, side scraper-1.
MDP	25	23	Lunate-1, side scraper-1.
PPN	90	63	Ob. blunt. blade-10, lunate-10, ret. flake-4, truncated blade-3.
CTG	5	5	no tool type
CKC	17	16	Ret. flake-1.
HKD	16	14	Ob. blunt. blade-1, ret. flake-1.
NCD	29	16	Ob. blunt. blade-4, lunate-2, side scraper-1, ret. flake-4, Ob. blunt. blade-4, lunate-2, side scraper-1, ret. flake-4, truncated blade-1, point-10

NOTE: The items in the debitage category in all these tables mean fluted core, core trimming blade/flake and parallel-sided blade.

Acknowledgements

Shri Lilamay Mukhopadhyay of Bankura Christian College and Shri Karunamay Chattopadhyay of Palasdanga village helped us in various ways. Our sincere thanks are due to them.

REFERENCES

Banerji, A.K. 1968 *West Bengal District Gazetteers-Bankura*, Calcutta.

Chakrabarti Dilip K. and S. Jamal Hasan, 1981 The sequence at Bahiri (Chondra Hazrar Danga), District Birbhum, West Bengal, *Man & Environment* 6.

Chakrabarti Dilip K., D.K. Bhattacharya and R.K. Chottopadhyay 1982 Lithic industries of Purulia, *Man & Environment* 7 (forthcoming).

Indian Archaeology—a Review. 1959-60; 1960-61 1965-66; 1967-68.

Lal, B.B. 1958 Birbhanpur, a microlithic site in the Damodar valley, West Bengal, *Ancient India* 14.

Some Aspects of Megalithic Culture of India

H. SARKAR
Archaeological Survey of India, New Delhi

India, as is well known, is extremely rich in megalithic monuments—not merely in number but also in the variety of types (Thapar in Ramachandran 1971: i-x). Further, megalithism continues to be a living practice in certain parts of the country. Another interesting aspect is that the peninsular India occupies an intermediary position between Europe and west Asia on the one hand and east and south-east Asia on the other. Perhaps of all the Asian countries, India has made significant advancement in this sphere of research. This is more because of the long history of the research itself, which began as early as 1823 (Ramachandran 1971: no 17) in this field, than for any concerted effort to unvail the picture of the material culture of the builders, their sources and inspirations, the racial affinity of their authors and several other problems. There cannot be any doubt that for fuller perspective, the study of the megalithic culture of India needs to be viewed not only in terms of researches that have been going on in the countries to its east but also with the discoveries and fresh researches in the Mediterranean countries, in central and western Asia because of the intimate bonds which existed with these regions from a very remote past.

DISTRIBUTION

Let this discussion begin with the question of distribution of megaliths, as the pattern appears to be quite clear. These are essentially funerary monuments and show denser distribution in the peninsular part with greater concentration in the Deccan plateau and belong to a time-bracket varying from *circa* 1000 B.C. to the early Christian era. Several types like urn-burials, dolmens, cists, dolmenoid cist, cairn circle, rock-cut caves, menhirs and alignments, passage grave, hood-stones, umbrella stones, etc.. are found distributed in different parts of the region (Krishnaswami 1949: 35-45; Gururaja Rao 1972: 234-53). In the distribution of different types one may well discern some pattern; and these types, though do not come strictly under the term megaliths, are associated with the same cultural milieu. The two main characteristics of this culture are the use of the Black-and-red pottery, similar to what is called in Egypt as black-topped pottery, and the profuse use of iron. Furthermore, the peninsular India, which falls roughly between 8° N to 20° N latitude, is climatically a hot region with moderate rainfall, the west coast or the Malabar coast being however an area of very high precipitation. Most of the people here are Dravidian speakers, a language not spoken outside the Indian subcontinent.

Megaliths occur sporadically in different parts of northern India and parts of what is now politically known as Pakistan: Baluchistan and the Makran coast (Baluch as well as Persian); Waghodur and Murad Memon near Karachi; Asota near Mardan in the North-Western Frontier Province, all in Pakistan; Leh valley of Ladakh; Burzahom near Srinagar; Deosa near Jaipur; Khera near Fatehpur Sikri, Agra; Deodhoora near Almora; sites in the Districts of

Allahabad and Mirzapur and Varanasi etc., (Wheeler 1948: 300-08).

The third region comprises north-eastern India from the borders of Burma to central India and this tradition is found to be more or less a living tradition of the aborigines. This megalithic tradition, according to many scholars, has affinity with the south-east Asiatic tradition. Broadly speaking, megalithic monuments of some kind or the other are found over different parts of India; while the living tradition is restricted to eastern and central India (Haimendorf 1945: 73-86 and Krishnaswami 1949: 41-42) the ancient tradition along with its various trends and modifications, is confined to the south.

TYPOLOGY

For a discussion on typology it is proposed to exclude the living tradition among the aboriginals who erect menhirs or forked posts, build dolmens or flat sitting stones; these are mostly memorial in nature unlike the south Indian examples which are basically ancient tombs.

Megaliths of older tradition do occur in other parts of India as well; in fact, the megalithic remains of the extra-peninsular region may be subdivided into two broad groups: cairn-circles of Baluchistan in Pakistan and stone-circles of the Ganga basins. The former region has brought to light from the cairn-burials their typical pottery with a band of volutes or spirals, and showing the use of iron and the knowledge of the domestication of horse (Gordon 1954-55; 1972-74). The presence of iron appendage is established in the excavations of the stone circles in the District of Allahabad though the graves in the same region, but falling in the Districts of Mirzapur and Varanasi, despite their family likeness, did not yield iron objects. By and large, typologically there are no basic differences between these groups and the peninsular types. Incidentally Burzahom, in Kashmir, produced good examples of menhirs.

The peninsular India shows bewildering types of megaliths, of which the present discussion may begin with the urn-burials found commonly in the southernmost part of India. At the same time, this has the widest distribution in India and dates back to the protohistoric times. A post-Harappa culture known commonly as Cemetery-H Culture (Wheeler 1947 : 81 and Vats 1940: 203-50), which is decidedly a chalcolithic phase, revealed large painted jars, paintings being on black on red surface, containing post-excarnation burial, a practice followed widely in subsequent times in the megalithic cultures of the east coast, particularly in the southernmost part. However, the cultural appendage of the latter is characteristically of the iron-using megalithic people. That it was just a mode of disposal of the dead is evident from its wide distribution in terms of space and time. Occasionally, in the chalcolithic cultures of the western India, two jars are placed mouth to mouth containing the articulated skeleton; this has, for example, noticed at Nevasa in Maharashtra, a site ascribable to about the fifteen hundred B.C. The anthropometric study shows that the people of Nevasa was a dolichocephalic one (73.9 and 72.4 cranial index) and those of the urn-burial site at Adhichannallur at the extreme south, to cite an instance, has amongst its people a long-headed type as well (Sarkar 1972: 189-205). At the same time, it is not at all desirable to make any specific conclusion regarding the identity of the two peoples. Incidentally, the Cemetery-H people is also a dolichocephalic popula tion. This aspect will be dealt at some length in a subsequent section.

Strictly speaking, the urn-burials, which have a wide distribution in Asia from the protohistoric times, may not be included as megalithic monuments although during the period when megalith builders occupied a prominent place in the history of south India, the people practising urn-burial were influenced by their material culture. Whatever that may be, urn-burials cannot be excluded from the purview of this discussion because these also occur inside the different types of megalithic monuments.

The typological classification of Indian megaliths is, again, fraught with difficulties because of the variation between the surface indications and what is actually revealed in the excavation. Thus a stone-circle on the surface may entomb urn-single, double and multiple-or a sarcophagus, a type found for instance also in Indonesia, a buried cist simulating oblong chamber, and again, this cist may or may not have a port hole, and simple pit. Incidentally, the cist with port-hole is quite common in the Mediterranean region (Childe 1948: 4-13). However, menhirs and alignments do not have any substantial difference between the surface indications and what is buried below them; in fact, there are hardly anything buried below them. In the course of discussion some more examples will be cited to make this point clear.

To list out types of megaliths found in the peninsular India is by no means a simple task, as there are variations in each type. What is attempted here is a broad typological classification and this classification has to be discussed in the context of the distributional patterns that certain types do conform to. Take first the passage chamber-tombs, mostly confined to northern Karnataka around 16° latitude. Some of them appear like the Greek or Latin cross though circular variety is also to be found (Sundara 1975: 137-45). In external appearance they look like dolmens made of rude stones. The passage chambers may be dated, according to the present writer, from *circa* 1000 B.C. to 700 B.C. and are considered as the precursor of other refined types. Some scholars are of the view that several later types evolved out of this early structural form which may have some distant affinity with the passage chamber, polygonal in shape and approached by a passage, of Spain, Portugal, northwestern Portugal, western Wales, Ireland etc., (Sundara 1975 : 148-51). Even in construction these passage chambers, like their European parallels, are usually orthostatic and sometimes even cyclopean. Unlike the European counterparts these contain post-excarnation secondary burial and may be called family onsuary.

The next early group from northern Karnataka, though not as early as the passage chambers, is the port-holed cist or chamber. In fact. there are three types of port-holed chamber tombs: port-holed dolmenoid cists with short passage, port-holed dolmens and oblong dolmenoid cists with port-hole. It is the presence of port-hole in one of the orthostat that gives added significance, for this feature connects this group with the western parallels, particularly to western Asia. These are dated after 800 B.C. (Sundara 1975 : 215).

Like the urn-burials containing post-exposure burials, cairn-circles and dolmenoid cists have a wide distribution. In the area around Madras, in the Chingleput District, there are clusters of dolmenoid cists made of rude stones and interestingly, these are rare on the west coast. Some parallels of this type may be available in several other Asian countries. In such examples of the dolmenoid cist, the stone circle is made of rude granite stones enclosing a chamber built of unhewn, irregular boulders, surmounted by a capstone. The chamber is built of six boulders of different sizes arranged in such a way as to form roughly an oblong (Banerjee and Soundara Rājan 1959: 4-42). It is noteworthy that these dolmenoid cists contain one or more sarcophagus. Taken collectively, the dolmenoid cists conform to several types of which the following are of common occurrence: (a) with multiple orthostats; (b) orthostats with opening simulating port-hole on the east; and (c) orthostats with a U-shaped port-hole in the east (Narasimhaiah 1980: 113-37).

The transepted cist with passage seems to have a specific area of concentration in the Pudukkottai region of Tamil Nadu (Krishnaswami 1949: 38) though it occurs also in the Districts of Coimbatore, Madurai and Thiruchchirappalli. In such cists the chamber is partially or wholly found underground and capped by a huge slab, another slab transcepting the chamber into two. Further, two upright slabs on either side of the port-hole form a passage which is closed in front by a slab; this kind of construction has sometimes been described as antechamber. There are reports of the occurrence of dolmenoid cist with slab-circles in certain Districts of Chittoor in Andhra Pradesh and Kolar and Bangalore in Karnataka (Narasimhaiah 1980: 142-44). It will be too tedious to list out different sub-types of dolmenoid cists which, taken collectively, may constitute a dominant tradition in the south.

The other widespread type is the slab cist in which cists are made of dressed slabs. In such cases slabs are placed vertically either in a pit dug specially for the purpose or even above the ground, in a clockwise fashion. Quite often, these slab cists, generally oblong in shape, are buried deep in the soil, and their surface indication is the occurence of stone circles enclosing a heap of cairns. This type of slab cists may or may not have port-holes; in fact, slab-cists with port-hole is common throughout the peninsula.

Apart from urn-burials (which are basically pit-burials), dolmenoid cists and slab cists, there are two other common types: cairn circles and stone circles. As is evident, cairn circle consists of a heap of stones encircled by boulders; this very surface feature is noticed in case of dolmenoid cists as well. Yet the principal differences are in their contents which lay buried and these conform to three varieties: (i) pits with fragmentary burials; (ii) oblong sarcophagi burials and (iii) burials in pyriform jars or urns. Similarly, the stone circles constitute another ubiquitous element and form the visible evidence of the three kinds of burials enumerated above.

It is evident from the foregoing that typological classification on the basis of the surface indications combined with what are lying beneath the ground may establish overlap or interlocking of cultural assemblages, besides fusion and diffusion of traits and traditions. These variations are, therefore, clearly suggestive of the division of population into various clans and segments, each following certain distinctive rites and traditions. However, there are a few types which by no means be considered as common to all parts of south India. Before coming to these localized types, mention may be made of the occurrence of barrows or earthen mounds indicative of burials underneath (Krishnaswami 1949: 37; Sundara 1975: 145-46); these are without the lithic circle so prominent in the megalithic traditions of the peninsula. They have, however, disclosed urn-burials or sarcophagus interment.

Some of the localized types (Krishnaswami 1949: 38-41), as is evident, are confined to certain geographical areas. For example, Kerala occupying the coast of the Arabian sea has a few distinctive, and perhaps even evolved types, not met with elsewhere. These megalithic monuments are rock-cut caves, hoodstones and hatstones, all cut out of locally-available laterite deposit. The hoodstone is a dome-shaped stone of dressed laterite resting on its flat surface on the ground level, and is known locally as *kudaikallu.* A variant of it is the multiple hoodstone where several hoodstones are surrounded by a circle of clinostatic laterite slabs all converging at the top. Below the hoodstone, in a burial pit, is lodged an urn with usual burial furniture. There are examples in which hatstone or *topikal* occupies the place of hoodstone: a plano-convex laterite slab rests on four quadrantal clinostatic boulders forming below a squarish base and a truncated-top over which rests the hemispherical hatstone.

Like the hatstones and hoodstones, the rock-cut caves are mainly confined to the Malabar coast of Kerala. These caves dug into the lateritic rock are in fact underground excavations having single, double and multiple chambers (Sharma 1956: 93-115). They have generally an oblong entrance shaft and doorway whereas the burial furniture consists of Black-and-red Ware pottery and iron objects, apart from fragmentary human remains. Comparable underground tombs are found in Palestine and Cyprus (Ramachandran 1971: no. 360). It is just a parallelism, for there exists considerable hiatus in terms of chronology. Moreover, the geographical distance has yet to be bridged by intensive exploration. At the same time, it is worthy of note that Kerala remained exposed to maritime activities from very early times.

The northern part of Kerala has yielded a good number of menhirs though they are not so common as the burials caves. Menhirs occur sporadically in the Coimbatore area of Tamil Nadu, northern Karnataka and parts of Andhra Pradesh. Closely allied to menhirs are the alignments consisting of a series of menhirs placed in rows. These are to be seen in parts of Kerala, Karnataka and Andhra Pradesh (Narasimhaiah 1980: 165-66). Some sites in the north-west Andhra Pradesh has yielded as many as forty-three sites, most of the stones here being dressed. Even in Kerala, menhirs of laterite are dressed nicely. The evidence of avenues, in which two or more parallel rows of alignments are found at one place, comes from certain parts of the Deccan. Unfortunately, no cultural material has been found associated with menhirs, alignments or avenues; presumably, these are mostly memorial in nature and may be correlated with the memorial pillars or hero-stones of subsequent times.

DATING

Mention has already been made about the early dates of the passage graves of northern Karnataka. It may be stated here that at Kotia, in District Allahabad, in north India megalithic cultures flourished from the second century B.C. onwards. Thus taking the megalithic cultures of the peninsular India as a whole one may date them from *circa* 1000 B.C. to about the third century A.D. It is necessary here to discuss the evidences in support of these dates.

The megalithic monuments are funerary structures or, in some cases, memorials. These are quite impressive in appearance but very little is known about their habitation. Before coming to the question of dating it is worth-while to have a few words about the settlements of these megalith-builders. Most of the clusters of the megalithic monuments are not associated with any habitation sites close by. There are exceptions and it is these sites which provide clues to compute a chronological scheme. The megalithic habitational deposits have been discovered from: Maski (Thapar 1957: 17), Sanganakallu (Subbarao 1948: 9), Hallur (Nagaraja Rao 1971) and Brahmagiri (Wheeler 1948), in Karnataka; Kunnattur, Sengamedu, Paiyampalli, Tirukkampuliyar etc., from Tamil Nadu (Sundara 1975: 95); Dharanikota, Kesarapalle (Sarkar 1973: 37-74) etc., in Andhra Pradesh. A few ^{14}C dates are also available to supplement the archaeological dating. Here the discussion may begin with Andhra Pradesh where a few sites were excavated in recent times.

Nagarjunakonda (Subrahmanyam *et al* 1975: 165-211) is a site on the river Krishna where extensive excavations were carried out for several seasons and despite the occurrence of two clusters of megaliths no habitational deposit could be traced. This is also the case with Yelleswaram (Sarkar 1969: 16-18) which is situated on the bank of the Krishna opposite Nagarjunakonda. However, this is not the case with Dharanikota, near Amaravati, on the river Krishna, and Kesarapalle in the Krishna-Godavari basin. The first two periods at Dharnikota yielding characteristic Black-and-red Ware have been ascribed to the megalithic culture which was followed by early historical phase. Two charcoal samples from the Early Historical Period I, give dates of 475 ± 100 B.C. and 390 ± 100 B.C. In the circumstances, the megalithic remains may safely be dated to *circa* 300 B.C. This date is further corroborated by the discovery of urn-burials below the Buddhist *stupa*-site at Amaravati. There are reasons to believe that the nucleus of the *stupa* came up during the time of the Maurya emperor Asoka (273-32 B.C.), and on the basis of this evidence the megalithic vestiges may be dated anterior to 300 B.C. In the habitational site, the structural activity of the megalith-builders was represented by hearths with vent-holes, post-holes and drains; one of the important small finds was a goldsmith's mould for ornaments.

At Kesarapalle, the habitational desposit of the megalithic culture, located close to a cluster of oblong cist-burials, was found interlocked with the chalcolithic while the later limit showed an overlap with the historical phase conspicuous by the presence of the Rouletted Ware of Roman association and datable to the first century A.D. The time-span of the megalithic culture calculated on the basis of stratigraphy is, therefore, from the middle of the fifth century B.C. to the first century A.D. (Sarkar 1973: 40-49). The occupational deposit of the megalith-bulders disclosed traces of post-holes, ashy bands, hearths filled in with chunks of burnt earth and ash. Apart from animal bones, iron objects, colour-grinder in stone, pottery discs, stone and terracotta beads, a spacer bead of bone, annular terracotta rings etc., were also unearthed. Thus the evidence from Dharanikota and Kesarapalle shows that the dwellings of the megalith-builders were unpretentious huts built on earth-fast poles, and that the material equipments do not suggest a prosperous economy. The use of iron including evolved types of tools and weapons found in megaliths would certainly indicate a period of developed food-producing economy in which agriculture might have played an important role.

Still earlier date for the megalithic, settlements is available from Hallur (lat. 18° 20′ N., 70° 37′ E.) on the bank of the river Tungabhadra in Karnataka. Here neolithic deposits were found overlapping the megalithic habitational deposits. There are two samples from the overlap phase and these dates are 1105 ± 105 B.C. and 955 ± 100 B.C. Without any hesitation the beginning of the megalithic phase may be dated to *circa* 800 B.C., if not earlier. There are a number of ^{14}C dates which point to the fact that this culture spread in different parts of south India between 500 and 250 B.C. To cite yet another instance, the megalithic deposit at Paiyampalli (lat. 12° 33′ N., long. 78° 27′ E,) in Tamil Nadu has a sample dated to 640 ± 105 B.C. (Ramachandran 1975). By and large, the radiocarbon dates conform to the chronology based on traditional archaeological dating which may range from 1000 B.C. to A.D. 300.

As indicated earlier the urn-burial, the passage grave and the cairn-circle may have an early beginning, and dolmens and slab-cists are likely to be later intrusions. Still later are perhaps the monuments like umbrella stones, hatstones etc., of Kerala and the rock-cut caves of the same region. Considering all aspects of the megalithic monuments, it appears that the slab cists and the dolmenoid cists stand out as one of the three basic features of this distinctive culture, the other two elements being the use of iron and the Black-and-red Ware pottery. Several cultural strains earlier as well as contemporary got mingled up to give rise to a complex megalithic cultural matrix. It was certainly a developed culture in its heyday though the presence of some nomadic people or pastoral population alongside the settled agricultural population can by no means be ruled out.

MODES OF DISPOSAL OF THE DEAD AND STUDY OF HUMAN REMAINS

Generally the post-excarnation burial, either in graves, urns or cists was the dominant mode of disposal of the dead; burial furniture included pottery, iron objects, ornaments and so on. Elaborate rites, including interment of animals, before the burial of the human remains were followed. This type of exposure burial appears to be an intrusive element as in the earlier neolithic or chalcolithic cultures the primary mode of disposal was the extended inhumation burial. Occasionally extended inhumation burial is noticed in the pit-circles of Nagarjunakonda (Subrahmanyam *et al* 1975), Maski (Thapar 1957) and a few other places. Moreover, cinerary urns have been recovered from cairn-circles near Amaravati (Sarkar 1973), while burnt bones are reported from the urn-burials at Raigir, Dornnkal etc. Yet, admittedly, cremation and true burial were rather exotic elements in the megalithic culture.

The anthropometric studies revealed that the megalith-builders were a hybrid population and many sections amongst them believed in the establishment of family ossuary. Yet a distinctive racial strain could be noticed in the skeleton remains found in the oblong cists at Brahmagiri (Sarkar 1972: 124-63c and Yelleswaram (Sarkar 1972: 20-40). Designated as the Scytho-Iranian they were medium-statured, flat-nosed, brachy-mesocephalic people of robust constitution. The same type of people seems to have been present at Piklihal (Allchin 1960) and Maski in Karnataka. This cranial index pople (77-79 cephalic index) appears to be present at Period III of Tepe Hissar. According to some authorities the great migration of these Scytho-Iranians took place between 1000 and 2000 B.C. from the region of Ukraine (Sarkar 1972 : 162). Brahmagiri in Karnataka has also revealed brachycephaly having its affinity with that of Period VI of Sialk (*circa* 1000-800). Some of Skulls from Nagarjunakonda (Gupta, Basu and Dutta 1970: 1-17), and Yelleswaram are brachycranial. On the other hand, cists at Raigir, in Andhra Pradesh, brought to light the remains of a dolicho-mesocephalic people. Furthermore, the autochthonous Australoid element was also present at several sites like Raigir and Yelleswaram.

In a recent study of head-forms from different types of megaliths, it has been shown that the jar-burial people like the one at Adittanular, in the extreme south, appear to possess smaller head-forms, the cranial index being 71.30. It thus falls within the dolichocranial range though verging towards the hyperdolichocephaly. In this study (Sarkar 1972: 202) a comparison is made between the different cranial types occurring in the earth burial, jar burial and cist burial and the result is quite interesting.

	Earth burial	*Jar burial*	*Cist burial*
Hyperdolicho-cranial	33.33%	46.67%	12.50%
Dolichocranial	33.33%	40.00%	20.00%
Mesocranial	14.29%	13.33%	30.00%
Brachycranial	14.29%	-	27.50%
Hyperbrachy cranial	4.76%	-	10.00%

Thus the headform occurs in the highest frequency (46.67%) amongst the people practising jar-burial and it may constitute the earliest stratum; significantly, there is no brachycranial people amongst them. On the contrary, mesocranial and brachycranial people are common in the cist burial - and these cists are mostly slab-cists. In the circumstances, it may well be concluded that real megalithic monuments in the form of dolmenoid cists or slab cists are perhaps connected with a mesobrachycranial people who might have migrated to India from Asia by about 1000 B.C. There must have occurred intermixing and hybridization amongst different groups with the fusion of cultural traits and elements. The conclusion based on anthropometric analysis is no doubt on small samples and might not provide a comprehensive picture. Yet it does furnish certain indications which with the comparison of data from other countries are bound to shed lights on many a darker aspect of megalithic culture in general and dolmen culture in particular.

REFERENCES

Allchin, F.R. 1960 *Piklihal Excavaions,* Hyderabad.

Banerjee, N.R. 1956. The Magalithic Problem of Chingleput in light of recent exploration, *Ancient India* 12, New Delhi.

and K.V. Soundara Rajan 1959 Sanur 1950 and 1952: a megalithic site in District Chingleput, *Ancient India* 15;

Childe, V. Gordon 1958 Megaliths, *Ancient India* 4, New Delhi.

Gordon, D.H. 1954-54 The pottery industries of the Indo-Iranian border: a re-statement and tentative chronology, *Ancient India* 10 and 11, New Delhi.

Gupta, Pabitra, Arabindo Basu and Pratap C. Dutta, 1970, Ancient Human Remains, *Memoirs of the Anthropological Survey of India 20,* Calcutta.

Gururaja Rao, B.K. 1972 *The Megalithic Culture of South India,* Mysore.

Haimendorf, C. Von.F. 1945 The Problem of Megalithic Cultures of Middle India, *Man in India,* XXV, Ranchi.

Krishnaswami, V.D. 1949 Megalithic types in south India, *Ancient India* 5, New Delhi.

Nagarja Rao, M.S. 1971 *Protohistoric Culture of the Tungabhadra Valley - a report on Hallur Excavations,* Dharwar.

Narasimhaih, B. 1980 *Neolithic and Megalithic Cultures in Tamil Nadu,* Delhi.

Ramachandran, K.S. 1971 *A Bibliography on Indian Megaliths,* Madras.

Ramachandran K.S. 1975 *Radiocarbon Dates of Archaeological Sites in India,* Hyderabad.

Sarkar, H. 1969 Megalithic Monuments of Lower Krishna basin *Seminar Papers on the Problem of Megaliths in India* (ed) A.K. Narain, Banaras Hindu University, Varanasi.

1973 Kesarapalle 1962, *Ancient India,* 22.

Sarkar, S.S. 1972 *Ancient Races of the Deccan,* Delhi.

Sharma, Y.D. 1956 Rock-cut Caves in Cochin, *Ancient India* 12.

Subbarao. Bendapudi 1948 *Stone Age Cultures of Bellary,* Poona.

Subrahmanyam, R. *et al* 1975 *Nagarjunakonda 1954-60,* I, Memoirs of the Archaeological Survey of India 75, New Delhi.

Sundara, A. *The Early Chamber Tombs of South India,* Delhi.

Thapar, B.K. Maski 1954: a chalcolithic site of the southern Deccan, *Ancient India* 13.

Vats, M.S. 1940 *Excavations at Harappa,* Calcutta.

Wheeler, R.E.M. 1948 Brahmagiri and Chandravali 1947: megalithic and other cultures in Mysore State, *Ancient India* 4.

A Study of Place Names and Protohistoric Cultures in Andhra-Karnataka

I. K. SARMA
Archaeological Survey of India, Madras

The place and personal names, like warp and woof on a loom' are intimately interwoven with the cultural heritage of an area. I have specially chosen here the study of certain place-names of the sites falling in the culture-fusion zone of Andhra-Karnataka. While for the historical periods, geographical identification and place-name correlations are relatively easy tasks with the help of inscriptions and literary data, no such sources are available for the pre-literate periods.

SOME PLACE-NAMES CONTAINING THE WORDS BUDI, VIBHUTI, etc.

I shall consider here a few important examples only and discuss their cultural significance subsequently. The names are *Budibetta, Budigunta, Budhigunta,* (district Chittaldurg) Budihal (district, Gulbarga), *Budikanama,* (Kudatini village, district Bellary), Budini (district, Raichur) of Karnataka and Budidepadu (district Karnool). *Budikonda, Budidihal, Budili, Bududu, Budanampalli, Budacherla, Budidagaddepalli,* all in district Anantapur of Andhra Pradesh (Narayan Rao 1935-36). These sites with the *Budi* element in their names revealed ash mounds and a few excavated among them yielded Neolithic and Iron age assemblages. If in a village name, the prefix *Budi* is not found, the ancient site within it had preserved its archaic derivation almost captioning the unearthed material culture. This is so with regard to Tordal in district Bijapur. The neolithic burial site is known as *Vibhuti maddi.* The site has, on excavation, yielded black-on-red painted pottery, steatite beads, ground stone axes, short blades, and ash deposits in the habitations of these pastoral folks. Gorkal was another ash mound site with a pre-iron, late Neolithic assemblage and the name is obviously a colloquial form for *Gokal.* At Gudekallu, (district Kurnool) the ash mound site is known as *Narriavulagutta,* the heap or mound of grey cattle and kine. Similarly, at Halakundi village, (district Bellary), the ash mound site goes with the name *'budihal'.* The mound is known a *Vibhutihalli* at *Benakanahalli,* (district Gulbarga). The extensive ash-mound site *Gaudaur* has revealed ancient cattle pens and the name derives from 'go', i.e., cow and cattle. This site is also famous for ancient gold working. At Mallur, district Gulbarga, the ash mound site is called *Budimatti.* The famous Kupigal mound is known as *Kolimidibba*—furnace pit or heap—because of the burnt white scoraceous, ash present at the site along with ancient workings. Atop the mound is a later temple dedicated to Siva. In many other cases, the ash-mound sites are after the cult deity itself. Lingadahalli (district Kurnool), Lingsugur and Sivarpur (district Raichur) belong to this category. The last mentioned site, has revealed, in addition, an impressive cave settlement over the granatold hillock.

Budi is said to be a *Drapidian* word signifying ash in general. When and how this ash came to assume a wider significance in the daily ritual and religious life of India, deserve serious investigation. The Vedic words *Budi,* and *Vibhuti* stood for power and auspice. The *Amarakosa* tells

"*Vibhutir budi raisvaryam animadhika mashtadha; Anima mahima chaiva garima - laghima tatha, Praptih Prakamya misatvam Vasitvam Chashta Siddhayah*" (Rice 1979:8). Thus super human powers consisting of eight faculties were attributed especially to Siva. In the early historical period, the Saivas, specially Pasupatas, *(Patanjalis Siva Bhagavatas* and later on *Lingadharis),* used to smear ash all over the body and wander. The practice of adorning *vibhuti* over the forehead is a custom associated with *Saivas.* The ash mound sites, were pastoral based 'cattle pens' originally associated with Neolithic settlers. (Allchin 1963 : 52-57). Bruce Foote (1916 : 79-96) calls them 'Cinder came sites, while Majumdar and Rajaguru preferred to regard them merely 'Cinder Mounds' for they were not inhabited by man but simply piled cowdung heaps, burnt up later (Majumdar *et al* 1966: 11-13). These cinder mounds were in open and analysis has shown that humified cow-dung was found mixed with clay, quartz and feldspar.

It may be pointed out that these 'ash-site' were not integral with any of the nearby habitations as revealed by the archaeological stratigraphy but separate and distinct in themselves. They were contemporaneous not only with the Neolithic but Megalithic folks of southern Deccan.

Thus these migrant cattle-keepers formed into a distinct living group in protohistoric. India and their mainstay, both of life and ritual, was domestic cattle, *(godhana).* They culturised the early settlers of the Deccan. They not only found here good grounds of habitation for their cattle-pens but the receptive men were ready to absorb the new traits and realised the enormous advantages of the cattle products in their economy. Archaeological evidence vividly illustrates this cultural metamorphosis. In later times the cattle economy was so integrated, became almost inseparable, the pastoral rituals and even the place, house and community names come to be known after the cow-dung heaps and ritualistically burnt ash (Malik 1968: 127). The moving pastoralists *(goshthas)* lead to the emergence of various *gotras (Covah trayante yatra gotrah* (Kosambi 1960: 211-255; Tripathy 1966: 162-68). These *gotras* were headed and protected by the *rishis* and their descendants created the *Pravara pramnparas.* (Sarma 1966: 54-58; Dange 1971). These were perhaps the Aryanisers. Aryanisation, should, therefore be taken as a cultural process, a sort of revolution in living patterns that was brought upon the stone age 'Food collecting - fishing folks' in central eastern and peninsular India. A long period of pastoral activity must have preceded farming in India. The archaeological remains of these *gotra* stages, their huts, and cattle pens, present a poor material culture in the form of a few post-holes, thatched circular or rectangular huts on wooden posts, rammed mud floors, ovens and pits with pottery, cow-dung heaps, etc.

The Vedas vividly delve on their ecology, daily life and rituals (Sarma 1974 : 67; Sankalia 1964: 646). The picture we obtain is a metaphysically rich and highly refined ritual life but meterialistically very poor representing only incipient agricultural economy. It is an utter imbalance, if we may so, but truly Indian. Walter A. Fairservice (Jr.) was certainly not correct and fair when he labelled the Neolithic Culture under "Uncivilised India" (Fairservis, 1971: 320-321.

SITE NAMES SUGGESTIVE OF ANCIENT TRADE LINKS

Pusalapadu is a hamlet in Giddalur taluk of Prakasam district, Andhra Pradesh. Its ancient mound has yielded on surface large number of hand-made black-on-red painted pottery, ground stone axes, microlithic blades, and profuse quantity of steatite beads. The nearby hillock has Megalithic cairns also. A subsequent exploration proved that the place has middle and late stone-age artefacts as well (Sarma 1960: 75-94).

The main point here is the name of the village *Pusalapadu, Pusalu* in Telugu meant beads and *Padu* stands for refuse heap or mound of antiquity. Strangely enough the site is strewn with whitish discular beads all over. The cowherds even now take a stroll on this mound and collect these beads and adorn their necks. These discular beads range from microscopic size to 20 mm. The boys instantly locate the spot once you impress on the form of these discular beads and the field is called *Bandi Pusalachenu* viz., the field of cart wheel shaped beads.

Another village called Ramapuram has yielded material relics of similar type. The specific mound is alike known as *Bandi Pusalachenu.*

Sometime ago, we had occasion to vividly discuss the distributional pattern and cultural importance of these Neolithic painted pottery village settlements of Kurnool and Cuddapah region (Sarma 1967-68: 68-83). Chronologically too they are basically aligned to the early Neolithic farming communities of Andhra-Karnataka. The steatite beads are far and few in the Neolithic-Chalcolithic contexts of Deccan as the well dug sites of Andhra-Karnataka such as Brahmagiri, Piklihal, Maski, Sanganakallu, Tekkalakota, Hallur, etc., revealed. Whereas they are profuse in the chronologically contemporaneous (Harappan and northerly chalcolithic contexts. So the question here is not only abundance or proximity of raw material but also the use, shaping and exploiting of the material for the daily needs. These minute, cylindrical and thin wafer beads of burnt steatite are extraordinarily hard and still bear the marks of the wire-saw used for cutting them. The Neolithic inhabitants of Pusalapadu, so also Ramapuram and Singanapalli could have well been the bead makers at large and supplied these decoratives to the urbanised Indus and advanced chalcolithic settlers of the north. As S.R. Rao, has pointed out even precious metallic objects, Gold and Copper, brought the urban Harappans in closer contact with the Neolithic villages of Andhra-Karnataka and occasionally highly sophisticated finish products both ornaments of gold and weapons and tools of copper, were found in the Neolithic sites (Tekkalakota and Hallur), a circumstance best explanable by the exchange of objects and not merely ideas (Rao 1973: 103-187; Allchin 1962: 195-221). Special distances never barred the commercial and religious contacts between various settlements and groups of men in the protohistoric India. The quantum of such exchanges was, however, governed by the abundance of raw material and other related factors.

From the foregoing, it is clear that a careful analysis of the place-names sheds important side light on the cultural patterns and movements among the protohistoric communities, which have not yielded so far any decipherable inscription to debate on their life and events.

REFERENCES

Allchin, F.R. 1962 Upon the Antiquity and Method of Gold Mining in Ancient India, *Journal of the Economic and Social History of the Orient* V.

1963 Neolithic Cattle Keepers of South India, Cambridge.

Dange, S.A. 1971 *Vedic concept and the Divine Fructification*, Bombay.

Fairservis, W.A. (Jr.) 1971 *The Roots of Ancient India*, London.

Foote, R.B. 1961 *Indian Prehistoric and Protohistoric Antiquities: Notes on their Ages and Distribution.*

Kosambi D.D. 1960 Development of Gotra System, *P.K. Gode Commemoration Volume*, Poona.

Majumdar, G.S. and S.N. Rajaguru, 1966 *Ash Mound Excavations at Kupgal*, Poona.

Malik, S.C. 1963 *Indian civilisation, The Formative Period A Study of Archaeology as Anthropology*. Simla.

Rao, C. Narayana 1934-36 Study of Place Names in Anantapur district, *Jounal of the Madras Geographic Association* X.

Rao, S.R. 1973 Lothal and the Indus Civilization, Bombay.

Rice, Lewis 1927. *Amarakosa* IV.

Sankalia, H.D. 1964 Traditional Indian Chronology, *Journal of Indian History* XLII (1).

Sarma, L.K. 1967 Painted Pottery from Pusalpadu, Andhra Pradesh: And further Explorations in Cuddapah and Karnool districts, *Indica*, Bombay.

1967-68 Patapadu Revisited: A New Painted Pottery culture in South-East India. *Puratattva* 1, Varanasi.

1974 Protohistoric India, Correlation of Vedic, Puranic and Archaeological Sources, *Itihas* 2.

Sharma. R.S. 1966 *Light on Early Indian Society* and *Economy*, New Delhi.

Tripathy, R. 1966 Gotra and Pravara, *Bhavans Journal*, Aug. 14th, Bombay.

Protohistoric Indian Metal Tools for Tillage—A Note

K.V. SOUNDARARAJAN
Archaeological Survey of India, New Delhi

It is well known that the implements of tillage have a bearing upon (a) the stage of progress of the cultivation, whether formative, developed or advanced (b) the knowledge of the botanical growth potential and periodicity of maturing of the seed (c) the softness or hardness of the soil and the subsoil water content and (d) the wear and tear factor of the material of which the implements are made and (e) the technical knowledge of the angle of piercing of the soil consistently to turn the clod effectively.

In this initial stages of cultivation, it is obvious that mostly tools of wood or antler or other such bone material would have been employed, irrespective of factors (a-c) above. The advent of the pre-metallic era of polished stone axes etc. would have introduced the hafting of these as the terminal parts of wooden or other frames or stems and the shape of the stem would have been deliberately adjusted for this purpose. Traction by animals as different from hand driven plough or tillage implement for formative farm usage would have also differed essentially in order that the mechanical advantage gained is optimum. The stone tools of this period, called the 'neolithic' stage, had themselves been variegated to such an extent that we may infer in them the diversification of the farm activity also, such as breaking of the clods (by hafted ring or hammer-stones); hard piercing by sharp tools like the fabricators or piercers; and steady ploughing by tools like the 'shoe-last' celt which last as Gordon Childe who named it so by its typical shape in the Danube Valley in Europe felt—was a type fossil of a finite stage in systematic early cultivation process. When metallic exploration became possible, it was immediately giving rise to a regular *economy* of agriculture, because unlike the wood, bone or stone-made tools, the size of the tool could be forged or cast to an uniform character and could also be multiplied by an easy process of casting moulds. Casting from moulds thus become an advanced stage in cultivation economy which would have had a bearing upon metallic resources, craftsmen of the appropriate expertise and the potential of the society to employ him and thus was clearly a stage further when the distribution of work has been fairly well compartmentalised into technocrats who will be maintained by the community for their expertise. This was the chalcolithic stage of semi-urban and urban phases within it.

Going backwards into time again, the potentiality of the soil may sometimes need tough tools and the formative Neolithic communities who, when they are coeval with chalcolithic communities elsewhere, could afford to borrow some of the hard tools of metal, to accelerate the pace of the cultivation cycle. This is contact-culture and results also in *technology-transfer,* in due course, when the self-sufficiency of the borrower becomes greater.

When copper or bronze was the metal used, as in the earlier part of the metallic age, the pace of growth of both the technique and the peasant occupation would have been gradual, the design element getting more and more variegated and specialised for the particular farm need. When iron metallurgy was understood subsequently, the phenomenal acceleration of the activity of both craft and farming resulted and the economy then variegated itself to such an extent, that modernity in thinking and planning was imparted to it, from the point of view of the activities of cultivation, on a methodical basis, from sowing to reaping, the tools for which could be identified either in types or in designs.

It is in this regard that the graffiti marking on pottery and their antecedent inspiration, if any, have to be evaluated. It has been the general thinking on these graffiti markings of a post-firing nature found on pottery, that they may perhaps be owner's marking on a para-scriptal basis and partly symbolic or of derivative signs (Thapar 1957; Banerjee *et al* 1959; Lal 1960) But if we could consider them as the representations of actual objects or material elements in the vocational life of the people, we seem to be deriving greater insight into the life-style itself, if the presumption that they may represent material equipment of farm life is acceptable (Fig. 1). In this regard, however, we have parallels from

S.NO.	SYMBOL	CULTURAL AFFILIATION	PLACE	REFERENCES
1		HARAPPAN CHALCOLITHIC MEGALITHIC	AMRI	A.I. NO.16, PLATE-I-2
2		HARAPPAN MEGALITHIC	N. ARCOT GMM MEGALITHIC YAZDANI NO. 5	A.I. NO. 16 PLATE-II-3
3		HARAPPAN MEGALITHIC	VIRAMPATNAM	A.I. NO. 16 PLATE-X-C-2
4		MEGALITHIC	MASKI	A.I. NO. 13 FIG. 29-14
5		MEGALITHIC	MASKI	A.I. NO.13 FIG. 29-6
6		UNPAINTED GREY WARE	SONPUR	A.I. NO.16 PLATE-XXXIV-:B-2
7		MEGALITHIC	SANUR	A.I. NO. 15 FIG. NO. 8-24 PAGE-32
8		MEGALITHIC	SANUR	A.I. NO.15 FIG. NO. 8-11 PAGE-32
9		MEGALITHIC	SANUR	A.I. NO. 15 FIG. NO. 8-10 PAGE-32

Fig 1

stone engravings in other countries of the west also of the farm tools which have been so identified with the contemporary tool implements of farming. These relate to the various parts of a tilling implement, such as the shaft, the stilt, the share, the ard, the coulter, the share-mount etc. frantier. This analogy could be applied to the graffiti also.

Our desire in this note is to bring to the notice of scholars, the two types of metallic share that has been recently discovered in protohistoric to early Iron Age contexts in the excavations at Ramapuram by the Archaeological Survey of India where metallic share outfit in iron have been noticed[1]. We shall then compare these with other objects which have been so far not functionally described in their individuality in Iron Age megalithic tool outfit and also to examine if the megalithic graffiti on pottery could be made to yield any comparative date on the equipment or their mounting designs. These also might indicate that animal traction in ploughing as much as manual human application of tillage in standing posture could both have been in use. The standard pattern of equipment for the former is given in Figure 2a while that of the latter could be seen in Figure 2b. These have been discussed in connection with Neolithic sites discovered in north Jutland in Denmark under circumstances which have yielded radio-carbon datings for the wooden remains of the tackle from the 'ard of the plough in most cases, originally made of tough wood, and range from 1490 B.C. to A.D. 120, with intermediate dates of 945 B.C., 710 B.C., 350 B.C. and 330 B.C. (Axel steensberg *et al* 1968:58). It is also seen that the usages have continued through early historic and medieval times upto post-industrial revolution modern Europe when the rock-engravings of these have also been found (Rea 1951: pl. IV. 1). In the Indian context, the matter is particularly relevant since, as an essentially agricultural country, its modes and means of tilling, farming and reaping in India follow a conventional well-ordered course, round the year and the technological increment in tool outfit is not only infrequent, but marginal, design-wise over many centuries.

The two implement remains found in the excavations at Ramapuram are illustrated in Figs. 3 and 4. They both seem to form part of an *ard* end at which the *share* tip is fixed. In view of the fact that they are made of heavy and then costly iron and cast at least in the case of the more elaborate and functionally evolved of the, two specimens, it could be seen that (a) that hard tilling of the soil was envisaged and (b) the permanence of the implement was laid store by and (c) the means of procuring it suitably was available in the community using it. This fragment bears comparision with the Danish tool design seen in Fig. 2a, 28 which are, however, much later and very elaborate, oblong in design and which show the method of mounting of the share. In so far as the stilt design likely to have been used is concerned, as compared with the age of the metal share remains under reference which is datable to *circa* 1000-600 B.C., according to the excavator and found in the strata of Period I relatable to the transition from Protohistoric into Iron Age, we have to compare the megalithic post-firing graffiti marks datable between fifth century B.C.-first century A.D. in

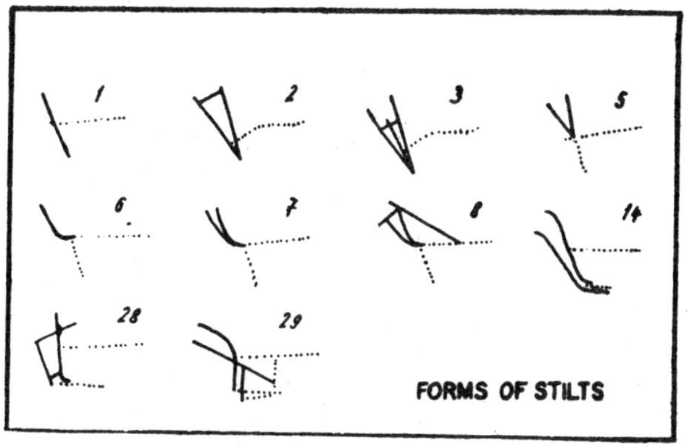

Fig 2a

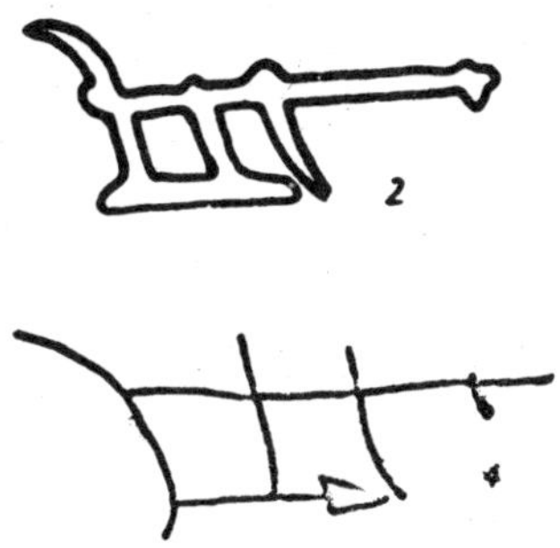

PLOUGHS ON SCOTTISH TOMB STONES

Fig 2b

various excavated remains in upper lower Deccan (Chalcolithic-Neolithic levels) and lower southern India (from the megalithic levels). For supplementary information a conjectural use of the While grave yards are rich in these times and many, corresponding habitation sites are very few, thus showing that for residential purposes, they might have utilised mainly perishable mate-

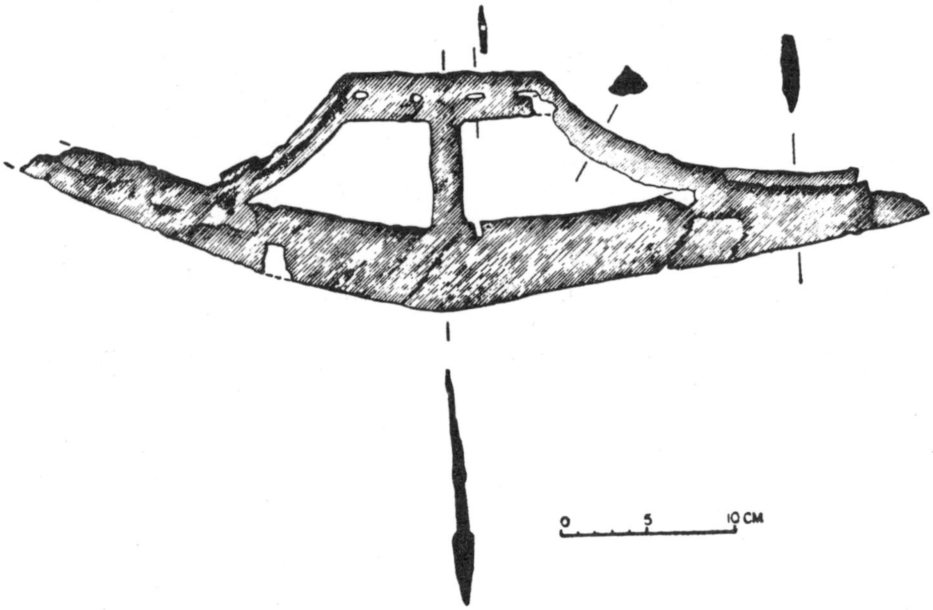

Fig 3

share types found from Ramapuram is given in Fig. 5, suggesting both manual traction and animal traction. Some of these types of the still varieties appear to be sketched in the graffiti. Method of grid share hafting is seen present in the excavated specimens from Ramapuram cited. rials like timber, bamboo and thatch fixed in post holes of circular, or rectangular varieties and these were liable to shift from time to time. They knew coursed stone masonry erection for walls is apparent from the tomb types themselves (as in north Karnataka chamber tombs)

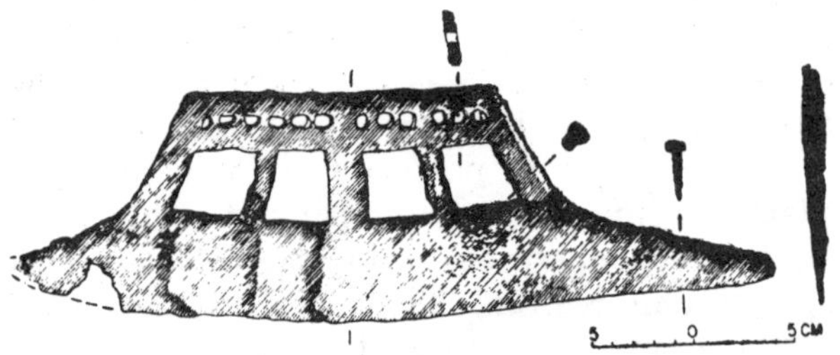

Fig. 4

Thus, we may note that it is in the transition from Chalcolithic to Iron and in the Iron Age itself that tillage and its tools get variegated and should have resulted in great farm prosperity which the megalithic tribes themselves eloquently proclaim in their burials and graffiti marks on pottery as the product of considerable community growth and corporate labour potential.

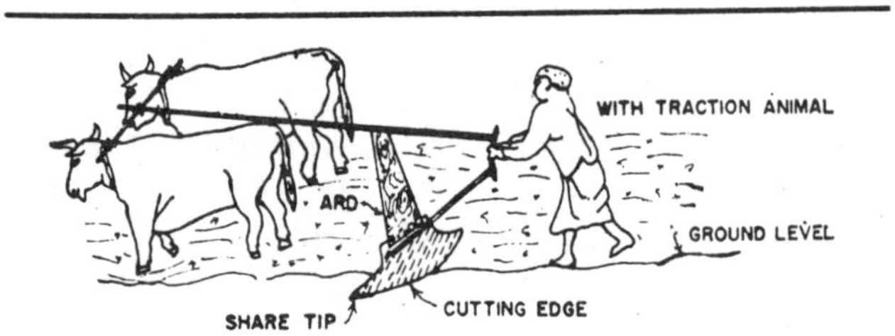

Fig. 5

but they had not thought it necessary to use this for their own residential dwellings.

The second point may be that they were mostly itinerant and land possession has not perhaps been individual or private, but perhaps of the whole community and hence village life as a settled community has not been very much favoured in so far as these communities were concerned. This, however, begins from the early historic times, firmly when further impacts of civic and urban potential enable them to patternise their living style also in residential areas of both farmers and others in a village. The Mauryan and post-Mauryan thrust, the Roman contacts and the reorganisation of communities, on a localised pattern should have resulted in such a sedentary scheme. Thus the chalcolithic matrix does not appear to have influenced the settlement patterns in the early Iron Age-because farm was yet the main focus of activity in Iron Age, and perhaps they lived in scattered units on or around the farm itself but yet isolated the sepulcheres as not only an area to be honoured but also as a consolidated index and show-pieces of their material advancement. If we draw them in a chart it would be like this (Fig. 6).

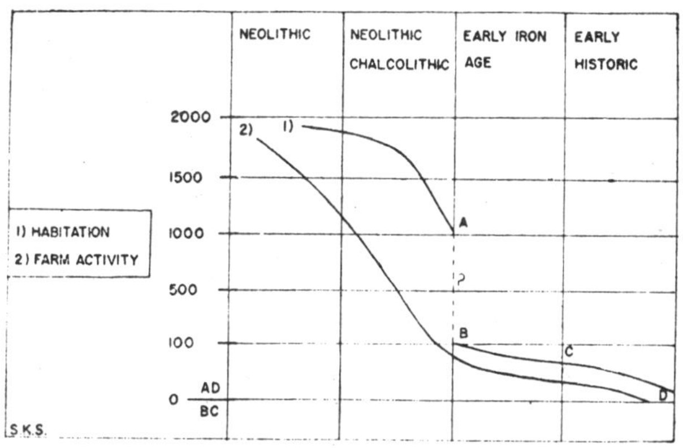

Fig. 6

O.A.D.

Between point A and B of time scale no habitational......is necessarily present. While this occurs from points B-C-D of time scale, because of Iron metallurgical evolution from development however is continuous throughout.

The two lines of the graph shows in each case the progress of farm practices and the gaps and breaks in the occurrence of regular habitations, thereby indicating that regularity in permanent habitations is not necessarily one of the true parameters of farm activities and growth and that their evidence could be at the same time gleaned from the material usage-in contexts other than secular (residential) as in sepulchral (in the - Megalithic graves). This shows also incidentally that a religious or spiritual bias, when it enters the daily life style, shows the material elements in more special preference than in regard to the daily life style itself.

Another tool which is a surface find from Kudavali Sangamesvaram on the Krishna near Alampur, Andhra Pradesh,[2] shows a stone axe (?) of the small/shoe last type which however by its shaft hole, may belong to a late period under Tribal usage, unless it could be claimed as part of the Neolithic economy of the site, which had yielded certainly Neolithic finds also.

This is paralleled, in a similar demographic pattern, in what are *civilizations* (art of living in towns) and what are *cultures* (socio-mental growth). For instance, in the *Indus-Civilization* virtually from 3000 B.C. to 1400 B.C., it had shown a consistent residential bias. But the *Vedic culture* which has seemingly partly or wholly been overlapping with it and continued for a *longer* time at least upto third century B.C. had no such observable and lineal residential bias characteristic to it but should have remained a religious bias, supported by an oral tradition. Thus the period from 1400-250 B.C. becomes a *fallow* period, because sepulchrally also they opted for cremation. For residential patterns, thereafter, due to various local and exotic impacts, the residential and spiritual bias both *mingle* and they become part of the *hybrid civilization* again. Thus it is more appropriate to say that civilization in India was, in early stages, essentially secular and was in dichotomy with farm production which was confined to villages, not giving a preferential treatment for material growth. But when farm development itself had reached a high point in early historic times, and become a potent factor for the socio-economic stability of society, a new civilization is in reborn which we now call the Indian civilization, with secular, agricultural, spiritual and aesthetic dimensions all fused together, and enthusiastically nurtured by the great Imperialista Kingdoms of the past from Mauryans downwards.

NOTES

1. Information kindly furnished by B. Narsimhyya after the objects have been seen by the author at the excavated site.
2. Material in Archaeological Survey of India Collection at Delhi made by Shri Lakshminarayan, photographer, New Delhi.

REFERENCES

Banerjee, N.R. and K.V. Soundara Rajan 1959 Sanur 1950 & 1952: a Megalithic site in District Chingleput, *Ancient India* 15, New Delhi.

Lal, B.B. 1960 From the Megalithic to the Harappan tracing back the graffiti on the pottery, *Ancient India* 16, New Delhi.

Rea, Alexander 1915 *Catalogue of the Prehistoric Antiquities from Adichanallur and Perumbair,* Madras.

Steensberg Axel, Alexander Fenton and Grith. Lerche 1968 *Tools & Tillage* I. 1, GEC., GAD Publishers, Copenhangen.
1970 Tools & *Tillage I.* 3 GEC., GAD Publishers, Copenhagen.

Thapar, B.K. 1957 Maski 1954: A Chalcolithic site of the Southern Deccan, *Ancient India* 13, New Delhi.

Some New Finds in Fatehpur District Uttar Pradesh

D.P. SHARMA
Allahabad

Fatehpur, lies in the lower part of the Ganga-Yamuna *doab.* The ancient trade route from Kausambi to Mathura passed through Fatehpur. Archaeological remains here start right from the neolithic times. Following that, Painted Grey Ware has been reported from Khaga (Tripathi 1976), Galanganath and few other areas in the district. A team from the Archaeological Survey of India had earlier reported N.B.P.W. from several sites (Tripathi 1976). Two Brahmi inscriptions of the fifth and seventh centuries have also been reported from Hathgao and Santo.

POLISHED STONE AXES

In explorations stray polished stone tools were discovered from Brahman Tola, Ukathu, Budvan, Navbasta Begram, Kukara, Ku Kari, Lekiyapur and Bhar-Khanna, lying in Khaga sub-division of this district. The main tool type was a triangular celt of biconvex cross-section (pl I).

THE MOUND OF REH

Reh (lat. 25° 51′ 19″ N, long, 80° 33′ 36″ E) is located on the left bank of the Yamuna, 26 km southwest of Fatehpur town. The mound extends over 2 km along the river Yamuna and is situated just at the confluence of the Yamuna and the Rind. The total height of the river section facing the Yamuna is about 28 km in which there is 6m thick habitational deposit.

The potteries noticed in the section are black slipped, grey, red, and N.B.P. wares. G.R. Sharma reported evidence of conflagration over the N.B.P. deposit at Reh and associated this phenomenon with the invasion of the Indo-Greek king Menander (Sharma 1980). However, the present author, who had discovered Reh and later informed about its discoveries to G.R. Sharma could not notice any such feature at the settlement. Thus the hypothesis of G.R. Sharma is open to serious doubts. But admittedly, only a proper excavation of the site will provide the final answer.

Other archaeological finds at Reh are soakage jars, ring-wells, terracotta figurine of a drummer of Saka-Parthian style and stone sculptures of Surya, Vishnu and Sheshsai Vishnu of the early mediaeval period. Stone image of Surya is, however, interesting since in it seven wives of Surya are depicted (pl II).

REH INSCRIPTION: THE TRUTH

The author brought to light in early 1979 a Brahmi inscription from Reh which was subsequently published by G.R. Sharma, my teacher. It occurs on the lower part of a broken victory-pillar which has been converted into a siva-linga and placed in a rectangular *argha,* erected in the early mediaeval period. (pl III). There are only four lines in it, the top three are complete, and the fourth is largely missing. The language of the inscription is Prakrit (pl IV).

The inscription reads as follows:

1. *Maharajas rajrajas*
2. *Mahamatas trataras dhami*
3. *Kas jaya tas cha a pra*
4. *Jijasa.................ras*

On the palaeographic grounds this may be dated anywhere between 150 B.C. to A.D. 100. G.R.

Sharma (1980) places it around 150 B.C. and reads the name of Menander in the fourth line. He then concludes that this inscription announces the victory of Menander. Some leading historians and palaeographists are, however, of the opinion that the Reh inscription does not belong to Menander. This may be ascribed to some Saka-Pahlava (Mukherji 1980: 245) or Kushan (Verma 1981: 38) ruler. The reading of Menander in the inscription has not been supported even by D.C. Sircar. Prof. G.C. Pande too does not find the letters spelling the name of Menander. Inspite of personal efforts of S.K. Muttu, the then Additional District Magistrate of Fatehpur, the Reh inscription, soon after its discovery, was buried under a cemented platform in a modern-temple by the local people on the 7th March, 1979.

INSCRIBED EKA-MUKHA SHIVA-LINGA FROM MAGILGAO

Magilgao is 8 km east of Khaga on Allahabad-Kanpur road. The inscription is in two lines on the lower part of the *lingam* which is under worship at the local temple. It is partly blurred. It belongs to King Virasena of Bharasiva Naga dynasty. On palaeographic and iconographic grounds the image and the inscription can be assigned to a period extending from the last quarter of the second century A.D. to the first few years of the third. The inscription reads "*Om Virsena Naga pho.....sya.... Siri maharaja ..ten .....s'ivam Kari tena naga*". The *lingam* measures 68x21 cm and its material is Mathura red sandstone. A trident, the Ujjain symbol and a palm leaf are depicted on the *lingam,* which are characteristic of the Naga kings, as are normally found on their coins (Fig.1).

Another Brahmi inscription of King Virasena has been reported from the village Janakhat in Farukhabad District of U.P. Palaeographically, the inscription of Janakhat is similar to that of Magilgao. This discovery tends to confirm the observations of K.P. Jaiswal who once observed that the Kushan power had been thrown from *Madhyadesa* by the Nagas.

DECORATED BRICK TEMPLES

The brick temples of the Gupta period in Fatehpur district were first reported by V.S. Agrawal.

The author explored some new brick temples

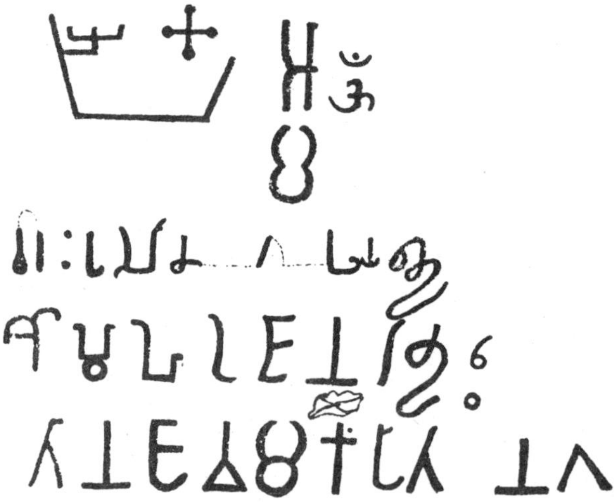

Fig. 1

of the early mediaeval period. On the basis of architectural features, art styles, sizes of bricks used, and potteries they can be ascribed to the period from the end of the Guptas to Harsha. Architectural style of the brick temple of seventh-eighth century, in Fatehpur follows the Gupta style. These temples were noticed at Korari, Thithora, Tinduli, Santo and Sarcan villages. The basement of some ruined brick-temples, of late Gupta period, having only the foundation of the *garbhagriha* with double corner at the grund-plan, are similar to the Bhitargaon brick-temple. These are located at Gambhiri, Santo, Assothar, Chitapur and Reh.

Korari (45° 41′ N, 80° 40′ E): It is 20 km south-west of Fatehpur city. Here four brick-temples were recorded in which two are completely ruined and the other two are somewhat preserved. Temple No. 1 is double storeyed, its height is about 8 m and the upper storey is covered by double Hindu dome. The porch of *garbhagriha* has circular roof while the *garbhagriha* itself has pointed dome. The most important architectural feature of this temple is its *sikhara,* which looks like the frutsum of cone, it has arch similar to that of Bhitargaon group of temples in Kanpur district. Moulded burnt-bricks, used in this temple, have floral and scroll designs. Similar bricks with anthropomorphic figures have also been reported from Lodgao, 5 km from this temple (Shukla 1981: 34). The bricks used in the temple measure 22x22x6 cm and 32x21x5.5 cm and are similar in design and size with the bricks used in Gupta monuments at Sarnath in Varanasi and

Bhitari in Ghazipur district (Misra 1979). On the basis of art style of a fragment of sculpture found a little away from the temple, its architectural devices and associated archaeological material, including the pottery, these temples can be assigned to the period from the last phase of the Gupta Period to the beginning of the seventh century A.D. The author also discovered three stone idols of Ganga, Yamuna and Seshsai Vishnu (pl IV).

Bahua (25° 50′ N, 80° 40′ E): It is 22km from Fatehpur, on Fatehpur-Banda Road. Here one brick-temple with carved door-jamb is still intact. The temple is about 4 m high and is single storeyed with a flat roof. The temple has double recessed type corners at the ground plan, similar to the temple of Bhitargaon. The size of bricks used in this temple is 25x18.5 cm. The roof of the temple is made in lantern pattern. Stone lintels and stone slabs are used in roof to support the temple. One full lotus flower is carved on one of the slabs used in roof. Female figures of early mediaeval period are depicted on the temple door. On the basis of the art style and the pottery of Gupta Period found near the mound, this temple can be dated to the sixth-seventh centuries A.D.

Tipinduli (26° 30′ N, 80° 35′ E): It is 26 km north-west of Fatehpur. Here, a decorated double storeyed brick-temple was noticed. The architectural style is similar to that of temple of Korari of the eighth century.

Thithora (25° 54′ N, 80° 39′ E): It is 19 km south-west of Fatehpur. Here one burnt-brick *panchayatana* temple was recorded. Bricks used on the outer face are chiselled as well as engraved into geometric patterns and it appears that the recessed portions of the temple were filled with plaster which must have produced very striking effect. It belongs to eighth century.

Saton (25° 46′ N, 80° 59′ E): It is 23 km north-east of Fatehpur. Here one brick-temple of the time of the Vardhan dynasty (seventh century) was noticed. This temple has double dome and its outer surface is profusely decorated with carved brick-work divided into equal faces of vertical grooves. A late Brahmi inscription of Vardhana dynasty has already been reported from the lintel of the temple. This inscription reads '*Om jayadittyaputra Durgedittya Kirttih*'. Some scholars are of the opinion that Jayaditya mentioned in this inscription is Harshavardhan.

REFERENCES

Jaiswal K.P. *Andhakarugeen Bharata* (Hindi), Varanasi.

Misra, Tej Narain 1979. *Pracheen Bhartiya Inton Ka Aanyayan* (Hindi), Ph.D. Thesis, Unpublished.

Mukherji, B.N. 1980 *Mathura and Society,* Calcutta.

Sharma, G.R. 1980 *Reh Inscription of Menander and Indo-Greek Invasion of Ganga Valley,* Allahabad.

Shukla, Vimal Chandra 1981 Ladgawan ki Puratanik Sampada, *Allahabad University Hindi Magazine,* Allahabad.

Tripathi, Vibha 1976 *Painted Grey Ware and Iron Age Culture in India,* New Delhi.

Verma, T.P. 1981 Uttar Pradesh Ke Abhilekh, *Uttar Pradesh* (Hindi), Puratattva Anka (May), Lucknow.

Writing Indian Art History: A Search for Valid Approach

S. P. GUPTA
National Museum, New Delhi

Some two decades ago, Dr. Grace Morley, the then Director National Museum, New Delhi, candidly remarked, "Everything said and done, Indian scholars have as yet not produced a single book which could rightfully be claimed as a book of history of Indian art; we have several outstanding works but they all concern either iconography or philosophical background of Indian art." Has this position changed since then? One has only to consider the themes of our so-called 'art history' seminars held during the last two decades to appreciate the observations of Dr. Morley. The themes include 'The Gupta Art' (Varanasi); 'Indian Plastic Art' (Nagpur), 'Mediaeval Court Art' (Hyderabad); 'Aspects of Technique in Indian Art' (Ahmedabad), 'Transmission of tradition in Indian Art' (Chandigarh), etc. All of them are important and meaningful but none tries to break new grounds. None tries new models, new approaches, new frames of reference. Even our respected art journals, such as the *Lalit Kala* and *Marg,* are not coming forward to devote even a single column for exchange of views on 'art history' as such.

The writing of a comprehensive and multifacteted history of Indian art has for me a few basic propositions which should be constantly refined and reformulated with increasing insight.

To begin with, periodization evolved for social and cultural history, which includes history of art, when tied with the rise and fall of ruling dynasties limits itself to worst absurdities, too obvious to be enumerated here in details. Only one instance may do. The so-called 'Mauryan polish', it has now been conclusively proved, continued through the Sunga, Kanva and early Kushana times (Gupta 1980: 313) and, therefore, neither the 'Mauryan polish' now remains a sure guide for declaring a piece of art as 'Mauryan' in date nor it is any more true that the 'Mauryan art' with all its contents and character ended with the Mauryan rule. Let us, therefore, now drop the old theories and old terms which somehow kept our vision on chronology and periodization in Indian art history within the four walls of the life-spans of kings and their geneological tables. Instead, let us find out some meaningful alternatives currently used in Social sciences which emphasize the role of dynamic and evolving cultural processes. In order to do that, let us clearly understand that all objects we deal with in art and archaeology are the products of culture and not culture itself. Thus, instead of perpetuating terms like 'Mauryan Art' and 'Sungan Art', let us use terms like 'Formative Period—Phase I' and Formative Period-Phase II, respectively. Similarly, in place of 'Kushana Art', we may use terms like 'Early Urban Period-Dynastic Art' and 'Early Urban Period-Popular Art'. For the Gupta Art, we may use 'Mature Urban Period-Classical Art'. For the rest also we may evolve new terms which are equally in consonance with the social-cultural history of India which is seen within the frame-work of an evolving phenomenon. These are only a few suggestions. I am only hinting at the possible *directional changes* in the field of Indian art history and nothing more.

The second point which possibly also needs immediate attention concerns *rigid stands* of our art scholars on congnate terms, such as it is 'Religious art', 'Secular art', 'Indigenous art', 'Vedic art', 'Dravidian art', 'Aboriginal art', and many other. Our trouble is that we do not see 'art' as a part of life, as just one item of the Indian culture as a whole. Thus, Indian art, when seen in its totality in the wider context of Indian history, turns out at every stage of its development 'multi-linear'. Crudely putting, it is 'mixed', i.e., partly religious and partly secular; partly indigenous and partly foreign; partly classical and partly folk. 'Mauryan art', for example, was neither completely Persian, nor Hellenistic, nor Vedic, nor Folk yet it was each one of them when seen in terms of individual roots. But, it is common knowledge, when a culture or cultural item is seen in terms of totality, the 'whole is simply not the total of all the available 'singles'. In other words, the roots of the Formation period of Indian art (i.e. Mauryan-Sungan) have been varied, its development multi-linear, and its manifestations pure and simple Indian.

The corollary of the above conclusion is that the art of every country is a unique creation of its own history—political, economic, physical, environmental, social and cultural. Valid Indian art history can, therefore, be written only with reference to Indian. 'historical situations', a term which takes into consideration all the above mentioned and many other factors which governed the life of man in India through the millennia. Every student of history knows that all historical situations are complex. They stand on the shoulders of a variety of interactions, challenged and responses. Geography, economy, cultural heritage, ruler's will, people's mobility, oral traditions, and the basic 'psychy' of a people, etc., go a long way to determine the complexity of historical situations; hence of art. Can we at all appreciate the so-called Mauryan art and Kushan art without having complete understanding of all these factors in the third century B.C. and first century A.D., respectively? Could we still tie up Indian art in the tail of 'West Asian' art of 3rd century B.C. as Coomarasawamy did in 1921?. Had Coomaraswamy, and recently even John Irwin (1976) considered the factor of historical situation he would have reached an entirely different conclusion, I have clearly shown elsewhere (Gupta 1980: 273-283) that the three thousand years of pre-Mauryan history of West Asia (including Egypt and Greece) clearly shows that while the political drama that was played there kept India completely outside its arena, amongst the countries of this region there were intensive and extensive warfares. One may ask how does it matter in art history? It matters a lot. The Egyption art's influence on Asia Minor's art, Asia Minor's art's influence on Mesopotamian art, Greek art's influence on Egyption and Persian and Parthian art, all followed the part of bloody wars won and lost in cyclic order in that part of the world. The art of West Asia, therefore, assumed a particular character with contents called 'Court Art', a term which stand for what is often called the 'art of propoganda, since it is aimed at boosting the personal image of the king as a great warrior. On the other hand, the Indian art when goes to Central Asia or China or Sri Lanka or various countries of South-East Asia, it follows the routes traversed by traders, monks and philosophers. This is precisely the reason why Indian art right from the Mauryan times had the character and content which was entirely different from that is observable in the art of West Asian countries (Gupta 1980: 300-302). Should we still then keep on calling the Mauryan art as 'Court Art' as Niharranjan did in 1950, and again in 1975? Similarly, how long we will be debating whether the secular art and architecture of an already burnt and dead Persepolis (in 330 B.C.) gave birth to Asokan pillars and their art, (250 B.C.) or the religious heritage of the Vedic period can offer valid explanations for all kinds of Mauryan art, from the pillars to the nude mother-goddess? The *history* of the so-called Mauryan period—natural, cultural, social and political—will have to be used as weights and measures before we can determine the quantum and character of contribution of each of the factors which created the particular form, called Mauryan Art, with its particular 'meaning'. How can there be straight-jacket answers? Taking rigid positions on the basis of single factors will be the negation of historical approach to Indian art.

This brings us to yet another problem—the problem of value—judgement in art, using repeatedly superlatives does not make an art better than what it is intrinsically. But then how to measure the quality in a work of art? Is art appreciation an unbridled horse? In other words, how 'quality' can be rescued from the clutches of Victorian language and be turned, at least in a few area, into 'quantity' and made measurable objectively? I shall leave the well-known 'six criteria of good art' propounded by ancient Indian scholars *(roopa, lavandya, sadrisya,* etc.) since they are not quantifiable. Instead, I shall press into service the science of Physical Anthropology since it can be used with great profit in specific situations of time and space in which people of several nationalities and physical types actually met, interacted and the art that they produced reflects this 'mixture' so to say.

The need is repeatedly felt when one works in the field of Chinese Central Asian art or Bactrian art or Sogdhian art because in them we find the representations of people of various nationalities, who used to traverse the famous Silk Routes, which can possibly be identified by this method than by personal impressions. Even the problem of cross-breeds can be established by quantitive analysis. Usages like Chinese face, Tibetan face, Iranian face, Indian facial features, Mongoloid elements and 'partially Iranian and partially Chinese' and 'partially Chinese and partially Indian' are at present arbitrarily used, a situation which can possibly be identified by this method. The method is that of indices (singular, index). By measuring different parts of head and face of human beings and grouping them according to certain formulae we understand the physical types they belong to. In each case two measurements are taken—length and breadth (say of nose or of head)—they are then divided, the latter by the former, and the resultant factor is multiplied by 100. It gives us numerical values, called indices, which are used as ratios. A group of indices when found recurring gives us an insight into the population structure.

$$\text{Head Index} = \frac{\text{Maximum Head Breadth}}{\text{Maximum Head Length}} \times 100$$

By using this formula we group our painted or sculpturutl heads of the donors, devatas and others' which do not always fall into the category of ideal forms' in Central Asian art. The same formula is used to get facial index, nasal index, etc. Any introductory book on physical anthropology will be able to guide the art historian; it is so very basic and simple. We in the Department of Central Asian Antiquities of the National Museum, New Delhi, are trying to involve a method with the help of which the data can be fed to computers and definitive results obtained.

Anthropology is, however, not the only science on which Indian art history can draw; 'archaeology from the earth' also lends helping hands to solve many of its riddles. Pottery for example can be used to date the earliest Gandharan sculptures which largely remain undated for the simple reason that we do not know exactly which era the Kushanas used in their inscriptions (Van Lohuizen-de-Leeuw 1949: 1-10)— the year 1 of Kanishka is placed in first century B.C. (50 B.C.), in first century (78 A.D.), in second century (144 A.D.) and also in third century (278 A.D.). Excavations conducted at Shaikhan-Dheri, Swat Valley by A.H. Dani (1966) has shown that the levels which have yielded the earliest evidence of Gandhara sculptures have also yielded the coins of Kanishka and a large number of the red ware types which are securely placed in the first century A.D. at various sites, including Taxila, Charsada and Thareli, i.e., from Potwar to Gandhara. Thus, on the basis of pottery, it can safely be said that the birth of Gandhara School of Indian Art has to be placed in the first century A.D., neiher in first century B.C. nor in second or third centuries A.D.

Those who are interested in writing a book of Indian art history will also have to study the subject of ethno-archaeology and use that knowledge in solving many problems. The reason is very simple. Indian art is not exclusively the product of great Indian religions-Vedic, Buddhist and Jain. A lot of what is often dubbed as 'folk' and 'aboriginal' has gone into its make-up. Every region has to tell the same story. Every period of Indian art has openly or stealthly incorporated them. Malti Nagar of the Deccan College, Pune, has done pioneering work in this field keeping in view both enthnological art and art as seen in archaeological finds of the same region to offer historical perspective to it. She often wonders how the Vedic mother-goddesses like Aditi and Prithvi are seen by us, the art historians, in the prehistoric and protohistoric terracotta, bone and stone female figurines from sites which are not at all likely to have been influenced by the alleged Vedic concepts at that period of time. She has particularly in mind the figurines from early second millennium Nevasa, Inamgaon, etc., in the deep Deccan (Sankalia 1978). Why do we really not call them non-Vedic elements of the Hindu pantheon? It is absolutely frustrating to see some of our respected Sanskritists waging wars to prove that all forms of Indian art can be traced to the holy Vedas.

There is still another situation, but of a similar kind. We have now a fairly complete history of changing patterns of cultures in northern India from the hills of Baluchistan, through the plains of Indo-Gangetic divide, the rolling sand-dunes of northern Rajasthan and the riverine tracts of the Ganga in Bihar and Bengal from about 7000 B.C. to the contemporary period. All kinds of studies have been made—the reports of Archaeological Survey of India, the journals and monographs published by non-Governmental professional bodies like the Ethnographic and Folk Culture Society, and books like *Ancient Indian Folk Cults* (1970) by V.S. Agrawal, present mines of information on the non-Vedic practices in vogue, often as undercurrents but constantly interesting with higher religions. As a case-study, I will draw the attention to the ring-stones of the 'Mauryan-Sungan' times found at sites starting from Taxila in the north-west and reaching Pataliputra in the east. They depict nude 'mother-goddesses '—but which mother goddesses, Vedic or non-Vedic? Neither Moti Chandra explained it nor V.S. Agrawal (Gupta 1980: 53-77). In which Veda the Mother Goddess, complete in nudity, is offered fowls—a Patna Museum specimen clearly shows this ritual (Gupta 1980: pl. 31c)? Do we draw enough from our oral traditions and Folk cultures to understand our past as-it-was?. In this context we would deal with yet another aspect of social dimension of art. In Tibet, and also in Chinese Central Asia, there have been two kinds of *tankhas* or banners one which were meant for 'worship' and the other, meant to fulfil various social-personal ends, such as 'saving the child from illnesses', 'praying for the rebirth of the dead in heaven', and 'safe journey to a distant land'. A few examples, there is a banner (National Museum, New Delhi, collection) which shows Padmasambhava in a heavenly scene of Amitabha with a stupa drawn at its back. It is clearly an example of the latter category. The presence of stupa at the back indicates that it was commanded by a man who could not build a stupa for his dead relative, hence this *tankha*. It also indicates that he wanted for the dead the rebirth in the Sukhavati heaven of Amitabha but whose own deity was Padmasambhava. There is yet another *tankha* which shows seven Bhaishajyagurus. Obviously, it was meant to call the gods of medicine to help the ailing man recover from his illness. There is a fragmentary *Mandala* with us from Dun Huang caves which depicts along the margins various ferocious figures intertwined with a number of snakes, in the centre there was possibly a figure of Hariti (now missing). According to Lokesh Chandra it was meant to save children from different diseases (each figure represents one disease). In other words, these banners were connected with the everyday life of men, women, and children and unless we add this dimension to our studies of these banners, is it possible for us to write the proper history of art?

Let us go to natural sciences, such as geology. For the Pala sculptures I have often come across the term 'black-stone'. Even the two famous torsoes from Harappa are called red stone torso' 'black stone torso'. The same ignorance about stones is shown when sculptures from the Deccan are dealt with, when they are in fact made on basalt. Eastern Coast stones—from khandolite in Konarka to granite in Mahabalipuram—are very often just casually treated at if the quarry, the stone, its properties, the particular kinds of techniques and the tools it demands for its handling are not the valid concerns of our art historian. If someone takes these studies, like K.R. Srinivasan (1964), fine; if not, does not matter. Can we ever hope to write a proper history of Indian art without the basic knowledge of petrology and solid geology? Those who feel they can, to say the least, they do not understand what 'art history' is.

Geomorphology and Climatology are also as much the concern of art historians as of natural scientists. Why are temple roofs in the lesser Himalayan zones from Assam to Kashmir highly sloping and why the gods and goddesses of the hinterland India are shown clad summarily in a piece of light cloth can be understood properly, to a large extent, in terms of natural history. Some scholars have hinted at it but not dealt with it adequately.

There are many other areas in the world of sciences which can be used by us for the proper and comprehensive understanding of the history of Indian art. We have only to organize inter-disciplinary meets at various levels for intensive dialogues to locate them. The only apprehension which some scholars of Indian art have expressed to me in low tone is that if we start doing it, science will evertake art, as it has already done in the field of archaeology world over. The fear, I guess, is not completely unfounded, but the reward will be tremendous in terms of exactitude. Is it not a fact that what is not exact is also not truthful? To my mind, there is enormous amount of credibility gap between a art historian and the common visitor to a museum gallery. Just go to the Modern art galleries and ask a few questions to the visitors and it will become apparent. Let me emphasize, it is equally true of the history museums at varying degrees of comprehensibilty, of course.

All this brings us back to the second part of the observation made years ago by Dr. Morley—that in India in the name of history of art only iconography and cognate subjects remained the valid subjects of scholarly concern. It is not difficult to know the underlying reasons for it since they are simply historical. Antiquarinism in modern times has been a product of European Renaissance of its late phase. In India, it naturally started with the coming of the Europeans. From William Jones (late 18th century) onwards, we in India received a number of civil servants who got passionately involved in exploring our antiquarian remains. In the late 19th century, however, a large number of Indians became close associates of these scholars. During the period we see three kinds of British and Indian scholars emerging on the horizon—one who had no other interest except scholarly, second who were motivated to serve the cause of Christianity by exposing the dark side of Hinduism, and the third, as a reaction to the second, who worked under nationalist motivation—all of them were undoubtedly seroius scholars whose contributions can never be minimized, such as those of Max Muller, but the fact remains that all of them worked under the stresses and strains of one kind of motivation or the other, and this made all the difference.

However, one thing was common to all of them—serious studies of classical languages, Sanskrit in particular. In Sanskrit literature Kalidas attracted them very much. Then the Vedas and Vedanta. Then the epics and the Puranas, along with texts on the manifestations of gods and goddesses. Thus, whatever the underlying motivation of a scholar, one who chose to deal with the Indian art was also a Sanskritist, wholly or marginally. Obviously, even in the 20th century the hang-over of the 19th century continued.

In the first half of 20th century the scholar who wrote the most, who earned enormous amount of name and fame, and who exposed the 'greatness' of Indian art to the Western world was Ananda K. Coomaraswami, a first rate Sanskritist and an avowed 'nationalist', who was denied the Curator's post in a reputed Museum of India. Obviously, his approach and methodology became the model for all his contemporaries and late contemporaries like Stella Kramrish, a distinguished teacher and art critic in the University of Calcutta; V.S. Agrawal, as usual punished for his learning by his bosses, but greatest among Indian scholars of art, who worked in Mathura, Delhi and Varanasi; C. Sivaramamurti, the outstanding Sanskritist and Museum man who worked in Madras, Calcutta and Delhi; Krishna Deva, a noted field-archaeologist turned art-historian, Kapila-Vatayayan, a great authority on classical Indain dances turned to art history, and many others, dead and living. Niharranjan Ray, of course, tried to inject the element of 'social background' into art studies but it only remained a fad with him, he never showed in his own writings any deep concern for it. Pupul Jayakar, on the other hand, shows great insight into Indian folk art but her main concern has been contemporary India. B.N. Goswami has broken some new grounds but only as far as locating source-material of a group of miniature paintings in the bahis, or hand-written records, of Pandas, or priests in holy places, who traditionally maintain a kind of *vansavalis,* or geneological tables. Karl Khandalavala, extremely knowledgeable in bronzes, paintings and manuscripts, also follows the trodden paths. John Irwin is obssessed by cosmogony and Mulk Raj Ananda tries to locate the 'third eye' into the inner perceptions of a viewer. There are many other very competent contemporary scholars of Indian art, like R.C. Agrawal, P. Pal, Pramod Chandra, M.A. Dhaky, U.P., Shah and R. Nagaswami, but they all show concern for the same—style, school, iconography, literature, philosophy, and other cognate topics. In other words, there are definite historical reasons for the kind of 'art history' we have been practising in India for the last hundred years or more. No one can question the questions which our art scholars have been raising and answering—all of them have been absolutely valid, but what Dr. Morely had hinted at, and I am trying to expand that in my own way (she never spelt out anything to me beyond the observation quoted above), concerns something else and at a different level of understanding and writing—who can deny the fact that we have no single book dealing with Indian art in such a comprehensive manner which may really be called 'history' of Indian art. The emphasis is clearly on comprehensive, i.e., one which covers all aspects. So far we have been dealing with only a few selected aspects, to the exclusion of many others, mainly because our art students do not get even elementary instructions in those fields of study which can sharpen their eyes to appreciate the Indian art from all possible angles and not from the angle of iconography and literature only. This can be achieved only by making the subject of art multi-disciplinary and allowing its development in many directions not easily conceivable at present. Let it grow like anthropology, archaeology and sociology. Let us add new dimensions to our studies and see what fruits it bears. If we now fail to do it, it will remain stagnate, and the scholarship bred in an stagnant pool own't smell fresh.

At the end, I would like to point out that no one need entertain the fears that in the process of making the inter-disciplinary model for the history of Indian art, asthetics will loose its place in art appreciation and the vocabulary of the art critics will suffer since at their own levels they stand by the side of literature, poetics also, which concern the problem of translating the abstract feelings and emotions into words which help the listeners and readers conjure up the same emotions and feelings which actually lie hidden in the works of art. Art appreciation is, therefore, a craft with all its implications, e.g., tools of proper words, long period of practice, highest kind of imagination, etc. And the excellence in craftsmanship cannot be universalized by any method of science. Similarly, iconography and iconometry will also not suffer since without them the one important limb of Indian art will be completely missing, the eyes, I mean, through which we penetrate the meaning of Indian art. Cosmology, cosmogony and literature will also retain their own places of importance since they represent the vehicles riding which we enter the very soul of Indian art. But what I want to plead is that there are still many other aspects of Indian art history which are beyond these, and in them both the social sciences and natural sciences can help us to such a great extent which I fear we do not bother to comprehend. Finally, let me reiterate what I have been striving to communicate so far: a comprehensive history of Indian art has yet to be written and it cannot be written so far as we do not make it inter-disciplinary and give proper training to our coming generation.

REFERENCES

Agrawala, V.S. 1970 *Ancient Indian Folk Cults,* Prithvi Prakashan, Varanasi.

Comaraswami, A.K. 1921 *History of Indian and Indonesian Art.* Dover Edition 1927.

Dani, A.N. 1966 Shaikhan Dheri Excavations, *Ancient Pakistan* II.

Gupta, S.P. 1980 *The Roots of Indian Art,* B.R. Pub-Corp., New Delhi.

Irwin, John 1976 "Asokan Pillars", a Reassessment of the evidence, *Burlington Magazine* CXVIII.

Ray, Niharranjan 1975. *The Mauryan and post-Mauryan Art.* Revised Edition, I.C.H.R., New Delhi.

Sankalia, H.D. 1978 *The Pre-Historic Art.* Vikas, New Delhi.

Srinivasan, K.R. 1964 *Cave Temples of the Pallavas* Archaeological Survey of India, New Delhi.

Van Lohuizen do Leeuw, J.E. 1949 *The "Scythian" Period* E.J. Brill, Leiden.

A Unique Patravahaka Yaksha Image from Ahichchhatra

SHASHI ASTHANA
National Museum, New Delhi.

The National Museum, New Delhi, acquired in 1978 a Yaksha figure in round from the Archaeological Survey of India. It is carved in mottled red sandstone of Mathura-Agra region. The image was discovered at Ahichchhatra. It is a monolithic image of late third century A. D. although S. B. Singh (1979 : Pl. 2A) has, to our utter surprise, dated it to the 9th-10th century A. D. It is shown seated in *bhadrasana* on a sufficiently high pedestal. The body is bare except for a *dhoti* covering the lower portion. One end of the *dhoti* has been used as *udarabandha,* going round both the upright leg and the bulging belly (pls. IA—B). The hands are completely missing but the verticality of the armpits clearly shows that they were raised in the fashion of the Pitalkhora and Aghapur yaksha images (pl. II). In its present condition it is comparable with another image from Ahichchhatra in the National Museum, New Delhi, collection. The top of the head is flat, except for two boat-shaped grooves which clearly shows that anciently some village-folks used it as a hone for sharpening their iron axe-heads. It compares very well with the similar grooves on another yaksha figure from the same site. In this connection it may also be mentioned that even the back of this image shows depressions which were caused by similar actions of the village-folk.

The yaksha appears to have carried over its head a bowl. This is absolutely clear from a comparative study of this image with similar other images. We may, therefore, clearly see that it formed a special category of the yaksha images. We may call it *patravahaka* or bowl-carrying category.

The figure is of a very charming and youthful yaksha, probably the youngest in age when compared with other yaksha images of bowl-carrying category. His lovable round face given a boyish look, with most innocent but enchanting smile which is nearer to the early Gupta feel (pl. III).

THE MYSTERY OF TRIPUNDRA

The image is however marked by a feature which never came to our notice earlier, there is a *tripundra* on the forehead. It contains a group of three parallel straight lines; when seen from above they are slightly concave or concentric with closed ends. It is placed exactly in the centre and slightly above the line of the eye-brows It is identified with the *tripundra* of sandal paste or ash generally applied by a Saiva on his forehead these days.

In this connection, probably it is essential to make it clear that *tripundra* should not be confused with wrinkles on the forehead generally seen on the image of the same category with slightly grim face. As may be observed, the wrinkles are of different shapes and sizes, and they neither form a homogenous group nor they are concentric. Similarly, their placement on the forehead is erratic—sometimes they are in between the two eye-brows and sometimes here and there above them in the naturalistic fashion.

Further, our close observations showed us that the *tripundra* marks were engraved anciently. We have made detailed observations of this feature on three counts : colour, patination, and weathering. Our findings are that in colour the marks match with the colour of the rest of the body if they had been freshly scratched, the colour would have been whiter, brighter and fresher than what they are. In face, inside the grooves they are slightly darker than the rest because of two factors : there occurred some weathering of the stone because of its long time exposure to the sun and rain, and, therefore, now there appears thin film of patination, a usual product of the chemical weathering of stones. There is also some accretion of silica particles, clay and other foreign elements, although of late they have been cleaned by our laboratory.

In the absence of any other known test to detect the difference between old and new scratches, we are convinced that the *tripundra* marks are old. But how much old they are, by one thousand years or seventeen hundred years, there is absolutely no way to establish. The only remark that we would like to make is that on the present showing the yaksha images of the *patravahaka* category were generally not made in the post-Kushan period. Obviously, these images did not serve any purpose to the worshippers either in the Gupta period or during the mediaeval period. The image in question, therefore, might have fallen in disgrace within a century of its birth. Why should, therefore, anyone other than the sculptor or one of his contemporaries be made responsible for these marks?

The *tripundra* is now the well-known mark of the Saivaites. It, therefore, raises some significant iconographic issues since *tripundra* does not appear in religious texts before the early medieval times, i.e., not before the 9th-10th century. It may be recalled that *tripundra,* as our knowledge goes so far, appeared almost along with the *urdhva-pundra* of the Vaishnavites and *Urdhva-pundra* has also not been reported in the context of ancient Vaishnavas until at least the 11th century A.D. It has, therefore, to be explained whether *tripundra* appeared independently in the later part of the 3rd century A.D. Further, on the present showing, it is more or less clear that *tripundra* is first applied to Siva-lingas and then on the human body, and, therefore, when Siva-bhaktas apply it on their forehead they do so primarily as a reflection of the *tripundra* on the linga, and secondarily to establish their sectarian mark. Therefore, as a minimum requirement to establish the lines on the forehead of this image as Saiva *tripundra* we must also be able to show one example of Siva-linga of the contemporary period with the *tripundra* mark. Not only that, in a sense, we have also to establish the prevalence of Siva temples during the 3rd century A.D. at Ahichchhatra.

We confess we have no answer to all these questions, but we will like to present some circumstantial evidence to show that there was a perfect historical situation in the words of Prof. Niharranjan Ray for the existence of not only a Saiva yaksha but also Siva images and Siva temples in the Kushan times.

Belonging to the early centuries of the Christian era we have several depictions of Siva in the anthromorphic form on the coins of Kujala Kadphises, Vima Kadphises, Kanishka and Huvishka. We have also a beautiful head with a third eye on the forehead from Mathura and now housed in the National Museum, New Delhi. Belonging to the same period, we have a number of *lingas,* which were in regular worship. At Nagarjunakonda (District Guntur, Andhra Pradesh) Archaeological Survey of India has excavated the remains of a number of Saiva temples including those dedicated to Karttikeya. An inscription from the same site and belonging to the 3rd century A.D. records the erection of a Pushpabhadra-swami temple. Patanjali in his Mahabha-*shya* clearly mentions the prevalence of worship not only of Siva but also yaksha and other Saiva gods. At Ahichchhatra itself we have a monumental Saiva temple of the Gupta period whose plans and proportions may imply the existence of an earlier stage of temple building activities devoted to the Saiva temples since the Ahichchhatra temples as they have come down to us show several periods of construction. At Mathura and Sonkh we have now the remains of a large number of temples devoted to several Buddhist and non-Buddhist gods and goddesses, including the Nagas. In areas between Mathura and Bharatapur passing through Agra there are several sites where the evidence of ancient Saiva shrines with *lingas* worship still exist. We, therefore, feel that it is not impossible that yaksha of Saiva group existed in these shrines, particularly when we have got ample evidence of the yakshas having being incorporated in the Saiva pantheon as Kubera and ganas.

As far as the actual place at Ahichchhatra, from where the present image is said to have come, is concerned, it may be pointed out that it is a high mound outside that fortified area but near the southern gateway of the town. It has not yet been excavated, what lies below the surface is anybody's guess. May be, there is a temple below it, or else, there is just a platform on which the image once stood.

But the question does not end here. We have also to see whether there was any other image with these marks which belonged to the same period and also to the period immediately succeeding the Kushans. There is some evidence. R. R. Tripathi, the Director, Allahabad Museum, informed S. P. Gupta that one Mr. Tandon of Allahabad brought a fairly big Kushan terracotta male head with exactly similar marks but its whereabouts are not known. However, there is another yaksha image of the *Patravahaka* category, found at Mathura. It also shows traces of a *tripundra* on the forehead. At present it is housed in the Mathura Museum. Belonging to the Gupta period is an image in the Mathura Museum which bears five horizontal marks on the forehead. In any case it is *panchangulaka* rather than *tripundraka*. That is all that we could gather from different sources we could tap during our enquiry. We shall feel happy if someone enlightens us more on the subject.

But closely connected with the problem of *tripundra* is the problem of the bowl on the head of these yaksha images. What does a bowl signify when shown in this particular manner? According to Coomaraswamy (1971 : 65) it was an *achamana kumbhi* for storing water used by the devotees of a Buddhist shrine, for washing hands and feet before entering the temple. He did not agree with the suggestion given earlier by Vogel that it represents the begging bowl (*bhiksha-patra* of the Buddha), since according to him some Buddhist texts, like the *Chullavagga,* make it clear that a begging bowl should not be decorated (most of the bowls bear geometrical and floral designs). R. C. Agrawal (1970:63-65) does not go into the functional aspect of these bowls, because of the attitude of the hands, he calls these figures as Bharavahaka or Atlantees. We, however, beg to differ from all these scholars. To begin with, we feel that the bowl was more symbolic than functional. The bowl of the Pitalkhora yaksha is more or less solid since the intended depression was never carried to its logical conclusion although the rest of the image was finished to the last details. Obviously, neither water could be kept in it nor offerings be placed on it in any significant amount. The examples in which the bowls are hollow and which could contain some liquid, their holding capacity will not allow more than a handful of water, which we feel, is never sufficient even for a couple of visitors if they start using it for washing hands and feet. They could also not contain more than two to four handful of dry offerings. In order to understand its symbolic nature we may have to go to other sculptures. Belonging to the Ikshavaku period (3rd century) we have a sculptured slab from Nagarjunakonda in the National Museum, New Delhi, with two standing dwarf figures which may be identified as yakshas, each with a basket on his head. Obviously, they are carrying flowers. In the Mathura Museum there is one Kushan panel which clearly depicts a *devata* or a Royal person with a handful of flowers, possibly taken out of the basket being carried by a *yaksha-gana.* The two *patravahaka yakshas,* one in the Lucknow Museum and the other in Mathura Museum which bear-dedicatory inscriptions to Buddhist establishments may be analogous with the Nagarjunakonda examples, but the same cannot be said of the remaining ones. If some of these yakshas were Saiva as we have tried to suggest have, then it is possible that the bowl was symbolic of something else. Within the *Gangavatarana* panel of Mahabalipuram we have a *yaksha-gana* by the side of Siva who is shown carrying bounty, obviously for distribution among the devotees. There are a number of stone and bronze *Bhikshatanamurtis* of Siva of the Chola period which show separate images of dwarfs or ganas or yakshas carrying bowls on their heads. It is, therefore, possible to imagine that yaksha with *tripundra* symbolically carried in the bowl on the head, the bounties which Siva distributed to the devotees.

There is, however, one snag—the *yakshaganas* carrying baskets on heads are generally in standing posture while our example is in sitting posture on self-same pedestal, like other examples from Ahichchhatra, which are likely to have been independent gods worshipped in their own right. In that case it will be a Saiva yaksha and not yaksha-gana or Kubera. In any case, it is a riddle whose solution is till largely unsettled.

Acknowledgements

I am extremely thankful to Dr. S.P. Gupta who located this sculpture near a well in Ahichchhatra village in 1975, informed Shri M.N. Deshpande, the then Director General, Archaeological Survey of India, and got this priceless object collected from the site for the museum with the help of Sri W.H. Siddiqui, Superintending Archaeologist, Agra Circle of the Survey, under his personal supervision. Much of the discussion that goes in this article is the product of many rounds of my talks with him.

REFERENCES

Agrawal, R.C. 1970 Atlantee yaksha statues in the National Museum, New Delhi, *Journal of the U.P. Historical Society,* XVIII, (N. S.), I-II Lucknow.

Coomaraswamy, A.K. 1971 *Yaksha,* II, New Delhi.

Singh, S.B. 1979 *Archaeology of Panchala Region,* Delhi.

Some Literary References to Chinese Pottery in India

K. K. MOHAMMED
Aligarh Muslim University, Aligarh.

Chinese pottery is made out of kaolin (Aluminium silicate) and feldspathic rock (Silicate Potassium and Aluminium). Feldspathic rock is ground to powder, mixed with kaolin and the mixture is exposed to an intense heat of the order of 1450° C. It is painted only in metallic oxides, because the oxides had to be heated considerably to attain the state for permanent fixing on the pot.[1] A number of motifs were also freely used by the Chinese to make the pottery attractive.[2] The first reference about porcelain is made in a Chinese book of Han dynasty (206 B.C.-A.D. 220). Since then production continued throughout its long history and its high watermark was registered by the exquisite wares of the Ming dynasty (A.D. 1368-1644).

India's commercial and cultural relations with China is attested by various references: mention of Chinese silk in *Arthasastra* mention of Kanchipuram (Huang-tche) in the accounts of Pan-Kou (Ist contury A.D.) (Shastri 1938:382) and the Chinese coin of the first century B.C. found at Chandravally., Ibn Batuta found Quilon (Kerela) as a thriving mart of Chinese merchandise (Gibb 1929). Chinese travellers of fourteenth and fifteenth centuries like Wang Ta Yuan (A.D. 1330-1349), Fei-Hsin (A.D. 1436) and Mahuan (A.D. 1451) speak about Chinese Porcelain trade with south India (Shastri 1938). The trade in Chinese pottery was so profitable that the Quilon people not only mastered the technique of its manufacture but began marketing their imitation products as the originals. Yaqut, Qazvini, Muhalhil and Friar odoric have spoken very high of this pottery and its sale as Chinese porcelain in West Asian countries (Nainar 1942 : 206:208; Moti Chandra 1977:203).

In medieval north India the first to mention China's trade with India are: All-Biruni and Islami (Elliot and Dowson 1968:69) Husain 1976:237). During the Sultanate time this ware was imported mainly to south India. Perhaps this was the reason why contemporary writers are silent about its import to Sultanate Kingdom. Porcelain must have occupied a prominent place in palaces and noble houses of the Sultanate period. But the volume of trade between India and China in porcelain might have been only marginal. Though the ware has been reported from a number of excavated sites from medieval levels, we are not sure if they belonged to the Sultanate or Mughal period.[3] With the advent of the Mughals however trade in porcelain became very brisk. All the emperors and nobles had a number of Chinese porcelain in their personal possession. It was valued so much that often it found a prominent place in the list of articles offered to emperors to please them. The emperor carried it wherever he went, because of the belief that the pot split into two, or changed its colour, the moment it came in contact with poisonous food. At a time when there were wars and murders, treacherous and otherwise for kingship and empere, it was the most trusted triend and one of the highly needed one. Humayun had given special instruction to Jouhar, his cupbearer, to give him drinking water only in China-cup (Stewart 1904:163). In fact it possessed none of the poison testing capacity. But the popular belief that it did possess such quality, prevented khansamas and bearers from making an attempt on the life of the king. This was also used as decorative pieces in the niches of Mughal noble houses (Bernier 1968:247-48). In almost all the paintings of the Mughals, the niches are shown invariably adorned with porcelain pieces.[4]

All the Mughal emperors had porcelain wares in their personal possession. Babar is said to have taken Chinese cups along with him even when he went on an excursion to a nearest place on 18th August 1519. The birth of Akbar was celebrated by distributing musk placed in a China cup (Stewart 1904:65-66) Akbar always had his dinner in porcelain dishes imported from China. (Smith 1958:298). However, according to Abul Fazal, Akbar used to have his meals in gold, silver, copper and Chinese plates. When Akbar died in 1605 he left in his treasury at Agra a beautiful porcelain worth twenty five lakh rupees. (Lurrd 1977:291). Besides celadon, other kinds of Chinese potteries, were also imported in Akbar's empire. During the region of Jahangir, nobles, merchants, and foreign dignitaries invariably presented Chinese porcelain to the emperor alongwith other valuables to mark, an occasion or to get a social favour from the king. The gift or Asaf Khan to Jahangir on Thursday the 22nd included Faghfuri and Khatai (Northern Chinese) porcelain (Rogers *et al* 1909:132). Valuables sent by Khan Duran on 7th New Year's day also contained Khatai porcelain. In the tenth regnal year Lashkar Khan sent twenty cups and plates of Khatai porcelain along with many other items. Nine pieces of Chinese pottery were sent by Murtaza Khan to Jahangir. On 5th Urdibhistor 11th regnal the envoy of the king Bisampur had brought to Jahangir's court many valuables along with China ware. In the month of January 1618 some Dutch merchants went to the Mughal court with gifts of Chinese ware, sandalwood, parrots and cloves. The importance of the ware can be understood from the fact that once Jahangir had imprisoned an officer for breaking a China cup and made him an advance of five thousand rupees to meet the expense of a man going to China to procure a similar one[5]. On 12th October 1617, Thomas Roe visited prince Shahjahan in his private room, where he offered the prince a small gold Chain in a China cup as presents. Puritan Aurangzeb also liked this beautiful ware. The list of items presented to Aurangzeb by the Ambassdor of Holland Monsieur Adrican included Chinese ware. The East India Company had no porcelain trade in India worth speaking, but the Dutch made prosperous trade in it. We are told that their entire estate at Masulipatam was in China ware.

Excavations in different parts of the country have yielded a wide variety of Chinese porcelain. Of them the most important sites in south India are Arikamedu, Kaveripattinam (Chola country) Kayalpattinam, (Pandya Nadu) Kanchipuram, Kodungallor, (Kerla) Hampi, Golkunda, Malwan (Surat) and Vadapadra (Vadodara). The fact that at Kaveripattinum celadon ware was found in the excavations along with the coins of Raja Raja (A.D. 985-1014) throws light about its age. This is further proved by the occurrence of two Chola coins of the time of Raja Raja, I in the Mathilakam excavation along with celadon ware, found at Arikamedu has all the characteristics of the Sung and Yun Lung chung wares, meant for export trade. Arikamedu specimens have been ascribed to *circa* tenth-eleventh centuries. However a piece of pottery with *Yueh* foot ring and sand adhering to it, according to some scholars, belong to an earlier dare.

Chinese ware has been reported from a number of north Indian sites. Excavations at Purana Qila in New Delhi, Adilabad, Vijayamandal, Khilokri, Ambari in Gauhati, Champaner and Atranjikhera have yielded Chinese procelain in profusion. The Purana Qila porcelain ware bore painted inscriptions made under the great Ming dynasty in the Cheng Hua Era. Another epigraph recorded a fair tale in verse. This was perhaps a treasured possession, for quite a few fragments bear evidence of their being joined by means of iron rivets. Some Chinese fragments from Champaner bore inscription in Devanagiri characters. The exploration at Fatehpur Sikri has yielded a number of Chinese potsherds with inscriptions.

Chinese pottery was a luxury item. The ware was used only by the upper class, as the common men could not purchase it because of its exorbitane price. The growing case of life in Agra, Fatehpur Sikri, Delhi and other urban centres of the Mughal empire stimulated the demand for luxury goods like porcelain, and raised up a class of entrepreneurs who organized the required long distance caravans, and created a mechanism of distribution. It is true that it was available in China at a cheap price. Ibn Batuta says that the price of this pottery in China was equal to that of an ordinary pottery in our country. According to Marco Polo for a Venetian goat one could purchase porcelain cups. On reaching India its price shot up because of its high demand. Hawkins says that the price of a piece in Jahangir's possession was Rupees ninety. In the later part of fifteenth century price of Chinese porcelain shot up because the supply of cobalt from the cobalt mines of Baluchistan failed, this price continued upto the middle of the sixteenth century. Later it increased further. Smith is of the opinion that Chinese porcelain was used only by Muslims and caste prejudices prevented Hindus from using it. He is also of the view that Hindus always preferred fragile pottery because of caste restrictions. This argument ignores the fact that deluxe wares such as the Painted Grey Ware and Northern Black Polished Ware, were used in large parts of India by Hindus at a much earlier date. Excavations at Ropar, Bairat, Sonpur and Kumrahar have yielded potteries repaired and rivetted by copper wire or pins. It is true that the Hindu masses preferred fragile pottery but this was hardly the case with the Hindu upper class where life style was more or less the same as that of the Muslim aristorcrats. The Chinese porcelain piece found at Champaner, bearing Devanagri inscription proves point beyond doubt.

NOTES

1. Important oxides used for colouring are cobalt, copper, iron, manganese, tin and colloidal gold mixed with chloride of tin.
2. Frequently used motives are bat, pomegranate, *swastika*, eight triagrams stork, tortoise, deer, flaming wheel, conchshell, wind instruments, state umbrella canopy lotus, vase, pair of fish, endless knot, waves, clouds, dragons, hare, tiger, fox, rat; pig, cock, monkey, goat, horse, musical instruments meanders, diaper pattens, thunder fret, pines, bamboo and Buddhist and Chinese mythology.
3. Some porcelain pieces excavated at Purana Qila, bore painted inscription made under the great Ming dynasty in the Cheng Hra Era (A.D. 1465-87) which of course is an indicator of China's porcelain trade with the Sultanate Kingdom.
4. Akbar Nama *(circa* 1600-1605) Chester Beatty Library, Dublin Vol. 2 ff 176, 176, 201 (reproduced in Arnold & Wilkinson) Babar Nama *(circa* 1680-5) British Museum, or 3714 ff 252 reproduced in Suleiman, Miniatures of Babur Nama, Tashkent, (1961) pls. 23, 32, 33, 37, 95. Album of Jahangir, Chester Beatty Library. Dublin (reproduced in Arnold and Wilkinson) Joc. cit pls. 58-59; Album of separate miniatures, No. 24 pl. 88. For their shapes, see S.P. Verma, Art and Material culture in the paintings of Akbars Court, Delhi, 1978, pls. XXXVIII to XLIII.)
5. A China dish belonging to Jahangir was broken by an officer when the emperor was not in the camp. Knowing fully well, the importance of the ware the officer sent a man to China to procure a similar one. When the emperor came to know about it, he severly flogged him and imprisoned him. On the interference of a prince, a quarter of his Jagir was restored and five thousand Rupees were also given to procure a similar one. Jourdain who tells the story with some variation says rupees fifty thousand was given to the man to get a similar dish (Early Travels in India, P. 168). Terry has also given a brief anecdote of the incident.

REFERENCES

ARMAD 1910 *Annual Report of Mysore Archaeological Department.*

Bernier 1968 *Travels in the Mughal Empire,* Delhi

Elliot and Dowson 1968 *History of India as told by its own Historians*

Gibb H.A.R. 1929 *Travels of Ibn Batuta* (tr). London.

Hussain A.M. 1976 *Futub's-Salatin* (tr), Bombay.

Moti Chandra 1977 *Trade and Trade Routes in Ancient India.* New Delhi.

Nainar 1942 *Arab Geographers Knowledge of South India,* Madras.

Rogers and Beveridge 1909 *Tuzuk-e-Jhangiri I,* London.

Sastri K.N. 1938 *Indian Historical Quarterly* XIV.

Smith V.A. 1958 *Akbar the Great Mughal,* Delhi.

Stwart C. 1904 *Tazkirat-al-wagiat* (tr).

Composite Images of Lakshmi and Vishnu: Some Observations

M.C. JOSHI
Archaeological Survey of India, New Delhi.

Recently, the National Museum (New Delhi) has added to its collection an interesting eight-armed Vaishnava bronze (height 26 cm) of Nepali origin which can be dated to *circa* fifteenth century A.D. on stylistic grounds. The image is of a composite character showing the Lakshmy-arddha (half-Lakshmi and half-Vishnu) form of Vishnu (pl. I) which is termed in Nepal as the combined representation of Vasudeva and Kamalaja.

The figure of the composite deity (Lakshmy-arddha-Vishnu) stands on a double-petalled lotus pedestal and is vertically marked on its proper right and left by iconographic traits of Vishnu (Vasudeva) and Lakshmi (Kamalaja), including her single prominent breast, respectively. Of the eight hands of the deity, those on the right (proper) hold *chakra, sankha, gada,* and *padma,* the usual attributes of Vishnu whereas those on the left have *kalasa, darpana* (mirror), *utpala (kamala)* and *pustaka* as emblems of Lakshmi. The treatment of ornaments and lower garments with fine decorative patterns (pl. II) also differ on either part of this sculpture of which a conspicuous feature is the top knot like longish protuberance on Vishnu's side of the crown (pl. III). The sculpture is neatly executed and bears an impress of pleasing conventionalism of contemporary images of Nepal.

The icon under reference, however, has a few parallels from India. An early specimen of this class depicting the composite form of Vishnu and Lakshmi riding a *garuda,* originally from Kashmir, is now in the Pan-Asian Collections (U.S.A.) according to Pratapaditya Pal (1975:76). It is a bronze image executed somewhat clumsily but with considerable details and it has been dated by Pal to twelfth century A.D. The figure has all the eight attributes of the unified form of Vishnu and Lakshmi of which those associated with later are e.g. (top downwards) *pustaka, darpana, kalasa* and *padma.* The eight handed garuda carries also the *amrit-kumbha.*

Another example of the composite icon of Vasudeva and Kamalaja has been located from an ancient temple at Baijnath (Kangra) in Himachal Pradesh (pl. IV). It is in stone and could be dated on the stylistic basis to about the beginning of the thirteenth century A.D. In this finely executed relief with elaborate details, the order of holding the attributes differs from already discussed Kashmir type, yet it also represents the composite divinity seated on a *garuda* with eight arms, who is flanked by a male and a female attendant on either side. The Lakshmy-arddha Vishnu holds in four of its right hands (from top downwards) *chakra, sankha, padma* and *gada.* Similarly, on the left side, attributes carried by the diety comprise an oblong *darpana, kalasa, pustaka* and *kamala.* A partly carved *kirita-mukuta* serves as the head-dress of masculine side (Vishnu portion). Other ornaments include a beaded-*vanamala* and *haras* besides usual items of jewellery which vary mostly on male and female parts of the deity's body, like the ear-drops and bangles. The feminine part is further decked with striped *sati* covering almost the entire leg and an ornate shoe (pl. IV).

Certain verses of *Silparatna,* a sixteenth century text, cited by Kalpana S. Desai (1966: 396) offer explanation for composite Lakshmi-Narayana images called as 'ekibhuta-vapu' (united body) of Vishnu and Lakshmi. D.C. Sircar (1970: 132), in this connection, draws our attention to an older evidence preserved in an expression *Kamalardhangina-Vishnu* used in the Sitala temple inscription (from Gaya) which contains a clear reference to combined form of Lakshmi *(Kamala)* and Vishnu. The inscription which dates in the latter half of the eleventh century records the construction of certain shrines including that of Lakshmyarddha-Vishnu.

Commonly, the concept of Ardhanarisvara is related to Sivism and the association of similar iconographic theme with Vishnu or Vishnuism poses certain problems for a student of Indian art and religion. Pal (1970: 141) has tried to trace the genesis of the concept of dualism (*Prakriti* and *Purusha)* of the Sankhya philosophy and in the Buddhistic idea of *upaya* and *prajna.* According to him, this idea was already there in the Panchratra texts: "In describing the higher or 'pure' creation the *Ahirbudhnyasamhita* states that in the eighth part of the cosmic night *(paurusi—ratri),* the *Sakti* of Vishnu, awakened by His command, 'opens her eyes' *(unmesa).* The *Samhita* further explains this phenomenon: Sakti, which was so far indistinguishable from the 'windless atmosphere', or 'motionless ocean' of the Absolute, existing only as it were in a form of 'darkness' or 'emptiness", suddenly, "by some independent resolve *(kasmaccit svatantrayat),* flashes up, with an infinitely small part of herself, in her dual aspect of *kriya* (acting and *bhuti* (becoming), that is Force and Matter."

Whatever may have been the philosophical factors for the origin of Arddhanari-Vishnu, it has to be kept in mind that the idea did not seem to have found favour with the Vaishnavas as can also be understood from the absence of such images in Vishnu shrines. Perhaps for a Vaishnava the very thought to worship the half male and half female Vishnu, the sole grantor of ultimate refuge, with intense devotion and *saranagata-bhava* may hardly be meaningful to arouse any appeal. It has also to be remembered in this context that Vishnuism does not give equal position to Vishnu and his spouse. Lakshmi is, no doubt, regarded by Vaishnavas as the bestower of the glory and prosperity having her abode in Vishnu's heart or chest for being his beloved *(Vishnu-vallabha),* but she was always considered to be inferior to the Supreme lord of the universe *(sarvalokekanatha).* It is, therefore, unlikely that later Tantras had earlier Vaishnava influence on them to introduce the Arddhanari concept of Vishnu.

In our view, it is only under the liberal Sakta-Saiva influence that the composite images of Vishnu and Lakshmi were conceived and carved, for only the medieval Sakta Tantras could transform Vaishnava beliefs and forms into Sakta-Saiva concepts and themes and could properly interpret them in their own terminology.

Lakshmana Desikendra's *Saradatilaka,* a Tantrika work composed in the eleventh century A.D. (Bhattacharyya 1982: 73), is perhaps the earliest text mentioning the Lakshmyarddha form of Vishnu, within a proper context, as representative of Vaikuntha (Vishnu) and Kamalaja. The *dhyana* is an under:

vidyuchchandranibham vapuh Kamalaja Vaikunthayorekatam
Praptam snehavasena ratnavilasadbhusabhiralankritam
vidyapankajadarapanam manimayam kumbham sarojam gadam
sankham chakrammuni vibhradamitam disyachchiyam vah sada
51 xiii patala, Saradatilaka

The *Sardatilaka* (*vi, patala*) gives Arddhanarisvara Siva and Arddha-Lakshmi Hari *(arddha-Lakshmi Harih sakshaddvatatra samirita*) equal importance as divine manifestations in connexion with the *sadhana* of the goddess Sarada. Further, the following verses of the same text demonstrate actual significance of the Arddhanarisvara concept in the Sakta terminology treating even the half body of Siva as a creation of his own consort, viz., the Supreme-Energy in female form without the beginning or the end, who the creates of the speech and words.

Anadyanta sambhor-vapushi kalirddhena vapusha

Jagadrupam Sasvasrijati mahaniyamapigiram
Sadartha sabdartha stabhatanata Sankara-vadhu
Bhavad-bhuyad ...... bhavajanita duhkhaugha-samani
64-65, *xxi patala, Saradatilaka*

Most probably, as can also be inferred from its name, the *Saradatilaka*, appears to have been compiled in Kashmir as a text connected with the *Srishti Krama* of the Kaulas, wherein Vishnu becomes almost as much important as Siva, for, he is the spouse of Kamala, one of the principal Mahavidyas (connected with Shodasi) whose male counterpart could be no other than Siva himself under the name of Vishnu. The following verse quoted in *Sakta Pramoda* (V.S. 1957: 61) would support our contention:

Vande-Lakshmim-Parasivamayim suddhajam-bunadabham
Tejorupankanaka-vasana sarrvabhushojvalangim
bijampuramkanaka-kalasa hemapadmam, da-dhanam
Adyasakti sakalajanani Vishnu-Vamanka-Sanstham

It may be observed in the above verse that there is a special reference to Lakshmi as *Para Sivamayi* (embodiment of *Para-Siva)* and Vishnu. *Vamanaka sanstham* (occupying the left side or lap of Vishnu) whose attributes include gold vase, golden lotus and *bijapura* or citron. The last named object is a purely Saiva-Sakta symbol indicative of knowledge/learning of Agamas and Nigamas which in the sculpture under reference is replaced by a manuscript.

Saradatilaka also includes in it the *sadhana* of Vishnu, Narasimha and Purushottama but within the frame of Sakta thought and *acharas*. An interesting feature associated with the Tantrika worship of Vishnu is the *anaganyasa* wherein the *devata* associated with heart is mentioned as Arddha-Lakshmi Hari (cf. *Hridi Arddha Lakshmi-Hari-devatayai namah; Sakta Pramoda,* V.S. 1950: 552.)

It would thus be clear from what has been discussed above that the composite form of Vishnu and Lakshmi is a product of Saiva-Sakta thought and not of the Vishnuite ideology.

Acknowledgements

I am grateful to Shri B.S. Nayal, Archaeological Survey of India for drawing my attention to the Lakshmyarddha Vishnu sculpture from Baijnath, Kangra, H.P. The photographs are by the courtesy of the National Museum and Archaeological Survey of India, New Delhi.

REFERENCES

Bhattacharyya, N.N. 1982 *History of the Tantra Religion,* New Delhi.

Desai, Kalpana S. 1966 Some Lakshmi-Narayana Images from Western India, *Journal of the Oriental Institute XIV,* Baroda.

Pal, Pratapaditya 1970 *Vaisnava Iconology in Nepal,* Calcutta.
1975 *Bronzes of Kashmir,* Munshi Ram Manoharlal Publishers Pvt. Ltd., New Delhi.

Sircar, D.C. 1970 Ardhanari Narayana. *Foreigners in Ancient India and Lakshmi and Sarasvati in Art and Literature* (ed) D.C. Sircar, Calcutta.

Door-Jamb at Kayavarohana: A Reappraisal

P.K. TRIVEDI
Archaeological Survey of India, New Delhi.

Kayavarohana, known in history as the original seat of ancient Lakulisa cult, is normally identified with Karvan (22° 5′ N, 73° 15, E), a small village situated in Dabhoi taluka of district Vadodara in Gujarat. It is well connected by road as well as rail. It is a railway station on Miyagoam-Dabhoi narrow gauge section of Western Railway, about 8 km to the east and 11 km to the west respectively from Miyagoam and Dabhoi. Archaeological potential of this place is testified by ancient mounds, numerous temples and sculptures.

The door-jamb under study forms a part of Ekadasalingeshvara Mahadeva temple, a lately raised edifice, approachable by a descending flight of steps near the tank Kasi-Kund in the *Suthar-Ovari* locality. It is locally known as *'Torana'* and is at present fixed in a brickwork provided with a wooden lintel, which is further covered by brick masonry (pl. I). Whether it was brought and re-fixed here with the support of masonry work or it is where it originally was, could not be ascertained, although local tradition ascribes Kasi-kund or Vaidyanatha Mahadeva as the original seat of these stelae. It was first noticed by D.R. Bhandarkar (1908:42) and the sketchy description made by him is as under:

> "Near Pancheswar, into the entrance to *Ovari* or flight of steps near kasi-kund have been stuck up the jambs of an old door frame. Each has three mouldings, and those of the ends are each divided into four panels surmounted by a *kirtimukha*, with, in case of one (proper left jamb) a fluted portion of the shaft. In the panels of the jamb on the proper right are from the top (1) a goddess seated on a throne supported by two lions at the ends, and with four hands, two holding a sword, and a shield, and the remaining a rosary and a lotus, (2) a standing Surya (3) a domestic scene of a male seated on a throne and a female on a foot-stool, and (4) a standing Siva (Photo No. 2913). On the outermost moulding of the other jamb are from the top: (1) a figure seated on apparently a Garuda, but with two hands, one empty and other bearing a bird on the palm, (2) a standing Vishnu, (3) another home scene similar to just referred to, and (4) a standing Siva (Photo No. 2914). On the innermost moulding are at the bottom Yamuna and Ganga, on the proper right and left respectively".

The door-jamb is of *subhaga,* i.e. *trishakha* variety. The innermost band, *ratna-shakha,* middle, *gandharva-shakha* and the outermost *rupa-shakha,* put together is surmounted by *hiragrahanaka.*

The proper right shaft exhibits motifs and figures as below:

(a) RATNA-SHAKHA : The innermost *ratna-shakha* is filled up with diamond and pearl designs and on its lower end is depicted the goddess Yamuna.

1. *Yamuna:* The river goddess is shown standing on her mount tortoise and carries a pot in her hands. She is adorned with beaded *kundalas, hara, ratna-keyuras, valayas,* a hanging scarf and an undergarment secured by means of a girdle bedecked with *uruh-jalak.*

(b) *GANDHARAVA-SHAKHA:* It is embellished with flying *vidyadharas,* musicians, *maladharis* and warriors holding shields and swords.

Below is portrayed a male Naga figure.

2. *Naga:* To the left of Yamuna is a standing Naga under the shadow of a fine hooded snake. He wears two tiered *jata-juta* terminating into a bun on the top and decorated by a bejewelled fillet on forehead. His left hand carires an indistinct whereas the right hand rests on thigh. He has been shown wearing a necklace *(hara)* with a square pendant plain *valayas, ratna-keyuras* and *patra-kundalas.* On his waist is seen a girdle and a scarf entwined around his right arm. Near the feet is carved a *upasaka.*

(c) *RUPA-SHAKHA:* This exterior branch portrays following figurines from bottom upwards.

3. *Siva as dvar-pala:* The lowermost niche of *rupa-shakha* consists of a pair of pilasters surmounted by *makara-mukhas,* sprouting pearls which terminate into a trifoiled bunch and contains a figure of four armed Siva in the form of *dvarpala* in *tribhanga.* He carries akimbo, a trident and *sarpa* and wears *karanda-mukuta,* large ear-rings, necklaces, a sacred thread, armlets, bracelets, and a fine stringed *mekhala,* is decorated with *jalak* securing the lower garment. On his lower left side was perhaps portrayed a devotee (damaged) in *anjali-mudra* and on the right Skanda, seated on a peacock.

4. *Mithuna:* Inside a square, bordered with circular beads, is shown a couple. Potbellied man's hair is combed and arranged into a bun. He wears ornaments and sits on a two tiered pedestal. His right hand is raised in an attitude of discussion while left hand holds a cup. The lady looking towards him is shown sitting on a legged stool in easy posture. Her raised left hand carries an indistinct while the other one is placed on the thigh of man. Her breasts, and faces of the couple have been defaced due to weathering.

5. *Surya:* Two armed standing Surya is seen in *samabhanga* holding lotuses in both the hands. He wears a flattened *kirita-mukuta, padma-kundalas, niska-hara, vanamala* and other ornaments. Below are depicted his two consorts Usha and Pratusha in *tribhanga* pose. The figure is carved inside a niche consisting of a pair of pilasters surmounted by *makara-torana.*

6. *Durga:* Inside a square niche bordered wtih beads, is carved a figure of four armed Durga seated in *lalitasana* on a lion throne. She carries *varada-cum-akshamala,* a sword, shield and *vajra.* She is adorned with necklace, armlets, bracelets and head-dress of *dhammila* variety. Behind her head is a plain halo flanked by a *maladhari* on either side. The upper most niche is surmounted by a *kirtimukha* with two small lion figures each looking in opposite directions.

Proper left shaft of the jamb reveals the following in opposite directions.

(a) *RATNA-SHAKHA:* Like the right one, this branch too is exquistely carved with diamond and pearl motifs. Below is shown a figure of Ganga.

7. *Ganga:* Corresponding to Yamuna has been portrayed Ganga, with her vehicle *makara* or crocodile. She carries *kalasa* in both hands. She, too like her counterpart Yamuna, wears choicest hair-do, ear-rings, *valayas* and *nupuras.* Her lower garment is fastened by a *mekhala* decorated with *uruh-jalaka.*

(b) *GANDHARVA-SHAKHA:* This branch depicts warriors with swords, shields and *vidyadharas* in various dancing poses. Like corresponding *shakha* one male naga figure has also been portrayed.

8. *Naga:* He carries a defaced object in right hand whereas the left hand is in akimbo. Unlike his counterpart depicted in right stele, he does not put on sacred thread and is accompanied by a pair of male dwarfs. In addition to conspicuous knot on the waist band arrangement of five hoods, a scarf and rendering of hair style shows the master-manner of the ancient Karwan stone workers.

(c) *RUPA-SHAKHA:* From bottom upwards exhibits figures in the order given below:

9. *Siva as dvarpala:* Four armed male deity is shown carrying *nilotpala, sarpa, trisula,* and in akimbo. He wears *karanda-mukuta,* neck ornaments, *keyuras, valayas* a multi-stringed *mekhala,* a long garland and *nupuras.* Below is depicted a female and a standing male devotee, wearing a *kaupina* presumably in *anjali-mudra* respectively on left and right sides.

10. *Upasaka:* A couple in worship is depicted inside a rectangle with beaded border. The male

is in an attitude of *namaskar-mudra* and the lady carrying a garland is also worth taking note of.

11. *Harihara:* The earliest representation of Harihara in Gujarat is found on the door-jamb of Roda Temple No. III in district Sabarkanatha and dates back to *circa* eighth century. This four armed syncretistic male deity has been portrayed standing in *samabhanga* and chronologically may be put immediately after that of Roda Temple No. III. Siva half of right side is shown carrying *nilotpala* and trident (pl. II). A male attendant in *katihasta* with Nandi-head above is also shown. The left hands hold a *cakra* and conch, and below have been modelled a Garuda figure in *virasana* with folded hands. The deity wears a long *dhoti* fastened by a waist-band and a scarf hangs on his elbows, and is ornamented with a *kiritamukuta,* ear-rings, a *niska-hara* and *yajnopavita.*

12. *Karttikeya:* Seated Karttikeya is represented alongwith his mount peacock. He carries *varada* and a peacock in the right and left hands and puts on a bejewelled crown, ear-rings, a torque and is flanked by a pair of *maladharis* on top.

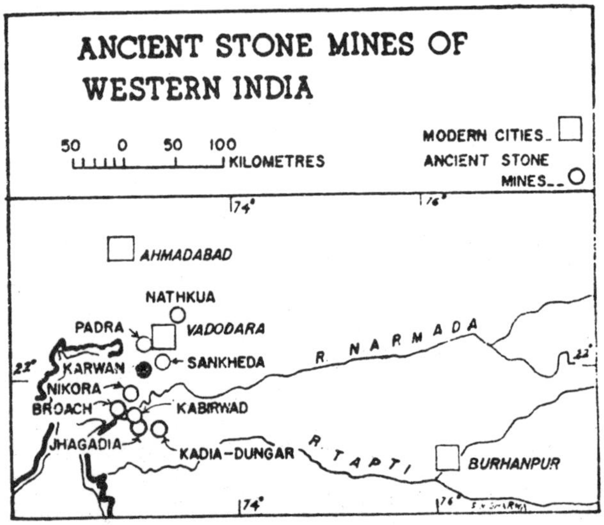

Fig 1

The stone in which the art piece has been worked is marine cretaccous sandstone which was most probably brought from the ancient mines of Nathkua or Sankheda in the district Vadodara or from the stone quarries of Kadiadungar in Jagadia taluka of Broach district. R.N. Mehta (1971-72:4) while commenting over the ancient routes, has observed, 'At least one route followed by this trade seems to run from Kadiadungar to Jagadia and after crossing the river Narmada near Kabirwad and Nikora moved through Kanama and reach Karvan, the famous *Lakulisha* site (Fig. 1). Kanama is the area roughly including the parts of Padra, Baroda, Miyagam, Dabhoi and Broach talukas.

While discussing the sequence of Solanki temples Dhaky (1961: 10) has observed that though the craftsmanship of this doorjamb is a little inferior *its ratna-shakha* preserves the reminiscence of Roda temple no. III. As far as the *gandharvashakha* is concerned he is of the view that its more evolved from could be seen in some Solanki temples of later date. Shah and Mehta had once remarked (1951: 164), 'Deterioration of medieval period has not yet darkened the vision of the artist as can be seen from the innermost panels of *purana-ghata* and foliage motifs in association with floral arabasques and lozenges or from the panels of the male and female kinnaras.' Loose sculptures lying at Karvan date right from *circa* fourth to eleventh century and of them, some have not only been carved out in the identical material but also exhibit resemblance with the modeling of the figurines on the door-jamb under discussion. On the basis of artistic peculiarities it may be dated to early half of ninth century. Vadodara had already come under Rashtrakuta rule in the beginning of the ninth century as gleaned from a copper-plate grant of the Rashtrakuta king Karka Suvarnavarsha, dated to A.D. 812. So far as Rashtrakuta art traits are concerned it would be rather too early to judge from the meagre evidence. 'The arches in the sections or the motif on the top of left side stele show unmistakable Pratihara influence on this beautiful specimen of art'.

Acknowledgments

The author is grateful to Sarvashri R. Gupta and Laxminarain for the photographs and Shri S.K. Sharma for the preparation of the map, incorporated in this paper.

REFERENCES

Bhandarkar, D.R. 1908 *Progress Report of Archaeological Survey of India, Western Circle, for the year ending 31st March 1908.*

Dhaky, M.A. 1961 Chronology of Solanki Temples of Gujarat, *Journal of Madhya Pradesh Itihas Parishad 3.*

Mehta, R.N. 1971-72 Rhyolite Mines of Kadia-Dungar, *Journal of M.S. University of Baroda* XX-XXI 1, Baroda.

Shah, U.P. and R.N. Mehta 1951. A Few Early Sculptures from *Gujarat, Journal of Oriental Institute* I(2), Baroda.

Are The Defences of Kausambi Really as old as 1025 B.C. ?

B.B. LAL
Indian Institute of Advanced Studies, Simla

A stir was created in 1960 when G.R. Sharma published his report, *The Excavations at Kausambi—1957-59*, in which he spoke of the defences at the site as having been built in the eleventh century B.C., and also referred to a brick-complex contiguous to one of the revetments of the defences as being a *syena-chiti* (eagle-shaped altar) for a *purusha-medha* (human sacrifice). While the latter will constitute the subject-matter of another paper by the present writer, in this paper it is proposed to discuss only the defences and their dating.

Not that the present writer is the first one to offer his comments on this topic, K.K. Sinha (1973: 231-38) and A. Ghosh (1973: 80-81) already took up the matter and expressed their doubts about such a high antiquity for the Kausambi defences. The provocation to write this paper comes from what transpired at the Indo-Soviet Joint Seminar on Copper-Bronze Age Cultures of India and Central Asia, held at Allahabad from 16-19 February 1982. At this seminar a paper by G.R. Sharma and his colleagues, B.B. Misra and J.N. Pal, was presented in which, amongst other things, the high antiquity of the Kausambi defences was reiterated. In the course of the debate that followed, R.S. Sharma took up the issue and expressed his grave doubts about such a high antiquity. He called upon G.R. Sharma to substantiate his case, whereupon the latter very cryptly replied that R.S. Sharma was free to hold his views and he (i.e. G.R. Sharma), his own. The debate appeared to take rather an acrimonious turn.

All this set the present writer thinking and he paid two visits to Kausambi, one along with K.N. Dikshit in March 1982, and another with K.V. Soundara Rajan in April 1982, to examine the issue with an open mind. This exercise was, of course, preceded, accompanied and followed by an in depth study of the Kausambi report referred to above.

A close look at the sections across the defences (Sharma 1960: Figs. 3 and 4; relevant parts of these are reproduced here as Figs. 1 and 2) raised the first serious doubt about Rampart 1 having been a rampart at all. The doubt arose because of two observations: (i) the ***absolute horizontality*** of the deposits constituting the rampart, and (ii) the presence of *'ancient humus'* capping these deposits. It is the experience of all excavators that the layers/deposits constituting mud-ramparts have a tendency to slope down from the apex. Indeed, this is what would normally happen when some soil is brought from elsewhere and dumped to form a bund or a rampart. Rarely, if at all, would the constituent deposits betray such absolute horizontality as do the ones shown in the published section. Secondly, unless the surface had been abandoned for a very long time, chances of the formation/deposition of "ancient" humus are very meagre. With these initial doubts, the writer probed into the textual part of the report and found to his great surprise the following observations made by Sharma himself:

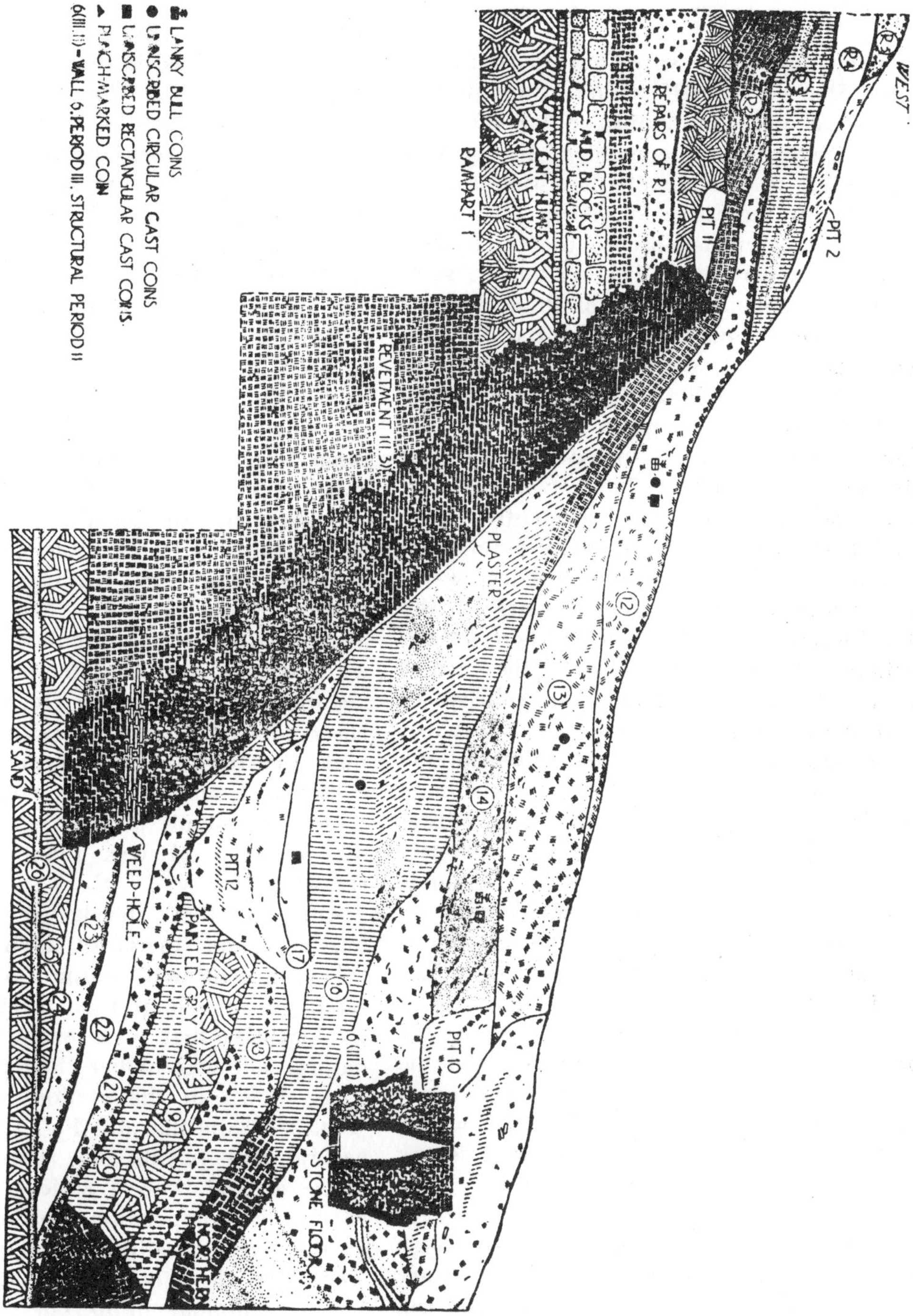
WEST
PIT 2
PIT 11
REPAIRS OF R.I.
MUD BLOCKS
RAMPART I
REVETMENT III(3)
PLASTER
PIT 10
PIT 12
WEEP-HOLE
PAINTED GREY WARE
STONE FLOOR
SAND
NATURAL SOIL
LANKY BULL COINS
UNINSCRIBED CIRCULAR CAST COINS
UNINSCRIBED RECTANGULAR CAST COINS
PUNCH-MARKED COIN

Fig 1

> 'The core of Rampart 1 was built of hard, compact and thoroughly rammed clay, evidently excavated from the natural soil. *It is significant that the first rampart is completely devoid of pottery and other material indicating human association.*' (page 27)

Thus, altogether there were four facts, all recorded by Sharma himself either through the aforementioned section-drawing or textual description, which agitated the mind of the present writer. To recall, these were: (i) the absolute horizontality of the successive deposits constituting Rampart 1; (ii) complete absence therein of pottery or any other material indicating human association; (iii) the superimposition of these deposits by 'ancient humus'; and finally (iv) the observation that these deposits were 'hard, compact and thoroughly rammed'. While all these observations/statements of Sharma were perfectly in order, the only place where he appears to have gone wrong was his remark that the 'hard, compact and thoroughly rammed clay' had 'evidently' been 'excavated from the natural soil'. The points that arose in the mind of the present writer were: Had the earth been brought from a quarry in the natural soil elsewhere and redeposited here for the construction of the rampart, *normally* the various deposits would not have remained so exclusive of one another as are seen in the section-drawing. In the process of dumping, some intermixing would have taken place. Secondly, even assuming that the earth had been quarried from the natural soil, some pottery and other material previously existing at the site or even that used by the builders themselves would have normally found its way in the dump. Thirdly, the absolute horizontality of the dumped material is a remote possibility, and finally if a rampart is built and subsequently repaired, there is not much chance of *'ancient humus'* getting deposited in between the two stages. Under the circumstances, the question that came to the mind of the present writer was: could these deposits be the various layers constituting the natural soil itself, *in situ*?

This led him to examine the various parts of the site where rain-gullies had provided rough and ready sections for observation. A preliminary look at these sections showed that the natural soil was very high and consised of a series of horizontal deposits of the kind shown in the section-drawing referred to above. The next step, therefore, was to check up the level of the top of Rampart 1 *vis-a-vis* that of the available natural soil in the various rain-gullies. For this purpose, the top of Rampart 1, as shown in the section-drawing (Fig. 2 of Sharma and Fig. 1 here) was assumed to represent a height of 100mm. With this as the starting point, Lal Singh Mamani Surveyor of Excavation Branch-II, Archaeological Survey of India, measured with a Dumpy level the heights of the natural soil in the various rain-gullies located from the eastern to the western end of the site. A very rough sketch plan, drawn on the spot during the course of the day, showing the approximate location of the these gullies is given here with (Fig. 3). From this plan, it would be seen that the exposed top of the natural soil in locality marked A, which lies between the excavated area of the defences and the Ghoshitarama Monastery is 101.800 m. In the same rain-gulley, further to the south-west it is 103.630 m (Locality B). In Localities C and D, which fall in a rain-gulley to the south-west of the excavated defence area, the readings were respectively 101.920 m and 101.870 m. In Locality E, marked on the edge of a rain-gulley to the east of the white-washed modern temple-complex dominating the landscape of the site, the natural soil was observed as high as 102.950 m. Lal Singh then took the trouble of carrying his levels further to the west, and in *nullah* which lay to the north of the stone-built palace(?)-complex, the level of the natural soil was found to be 102.670 m (Locality F).

Although these levels were taken somewhat hurriedly and, therefore, their absolute accuracy to every centimetre cannot obviously be vouchsafed, this much at least is clear that in all the six localities that were examined the top of the natural soil was higher than the top of Rampart 1 as shown in the section across the defences (Fig. 2 of Sharma and Fig. 1 here). Further, the natural soil in all the rain-gullies referred to above also showed a series of successive layers varying in composition, hardness, colour, etc. as do the layers constituting the so-called Rampart 1. *Therefore, there is little doubt that Rampart 1 is not a man-made affair but natural soil itself in situ.*

At this point one may draw attention to another observation by Sharma himself, made in

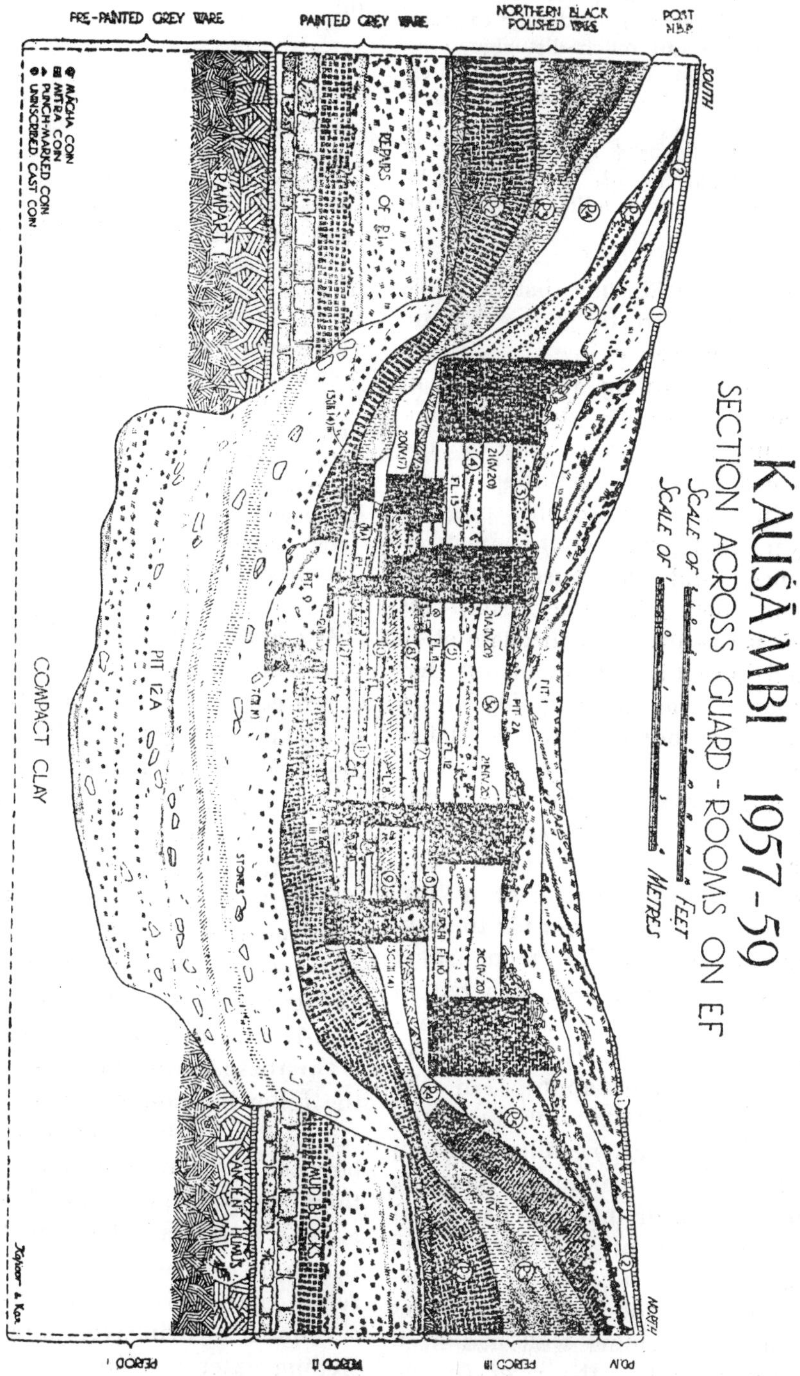
KAUŚĀMBI 1957-59
SECTION ACROSS GUARD-ROOMS ON EF
SCALE OF FEET
SCALE OF METRES
PRE-PAINTED GREY WARE
PAINTED GREY WARE
NORTHERN BLACK POLISHED WARE
POST NBP
SOUTH
NORTH
RAMPART
REPAIRS OF B1
MUD BLOCKS
PIT 12A
COMPACT CLAY
MĀGHA COIN
MITRA COIN
PUNCH-MARKED COIN
UNINSCRIBED CAST COIN
PERIOD I
PERIOD II
PERIOD III
PD.IV

Fig 2

connection with the "ancient humus":

> "At the top of Revetment 1, accumulated a deposit of an average thickness of 4 ins. (maximum 7 and minimum 3 ins.). This level was evidently exposed for a very long period without much disturbance so that the decayed vegetation led to the formation under favourable climatic conditions, of this thin deposit of black colour. *It is to be noted that this ancient humus has been exposed in the course of excavation in other areas of the site and also can be seen in the sections made by rain-gullies even outside the ramparts.*"

It must go to the credit of Sharma that he made most of his observations correctly, but evidently failed to grasp their significance.

The normal way of excavating a defence wall is to carry the section well into the habitation area so that not only is the *inner face* of the defence wall obtained but the habitation layers are also exposed. Thus alone it becomes possible to identify the layers that preceded the construction of the defences and the ones that got accumulated during their life-time. Had his trench gone further westwards into the habitation area, Sharma would have himself found out that his so-called Rampart 1 was an *unending affair,* for the natural soil, as shown above, stretches right across the site.

A question might perhaps now be put to the present writer himself, viz. if Rampart 1 is not a rampart and is only the natural soil *in situ,* where was the need to build the revetment of kiln-fired bricks? The answer to this is not far to seek. Since at and near this part of the mound some important structures were built, need was felt to *protect the edge from further erosion.* Plate I accompanying this paper shows an almost identical situation at Sringaverapura. In the photograph is seen a revetment of kiln-fired bricks, partly intact and partly fallen. From behind it peep the various horizontal deposits constituting the natural soil of the river bank. At the top may be seen parts of a structure and brass-bells associated with a close-by temple-complex (not seen in the photograph) to protect which from erosion the retaining wall had been built. In the left foreground is the river Ganga, with its banks receding in the far distance.

Now to the dating of the defences.

On page 22 of his report Sharma states: "The beginning of the fortification may be dated to c. 1025 B.C.". Some of the factors that appear to have led him to assign such an early date were as follows:

> "The early defences at Kausambi closely recall the Harappan citadel. The mud-packed rampart revetted externally with baked bricks in the so-called English bond in alternate courses of headers and stretchers, battered back to angles of 20° to 40°, bastions at intervals, rectangular towers and underground passage built on corbelled arch, are significant features of architecture at Kausambi with prototypes for each one of them in Harappan architecture."
>
> "It is equally significant that P.G. Ware occurs at Kausambi two structural periods after the original construction of the defences." (Sharma 1960: 6).
>
> "Pottery associated with the earliest defences offer numerous links with Navdatoli and Rangpur and other sites in Kathiawar....Pottery types at Rangpur and other western Indian sites, similar to those at Kausambi occur in late Harappan or immediately post-Harappan context and their Harappan origin in these sites is undoubted." (Sharma *ibid:* 6-7).

Altogether there are four points in Sharma's above statements, viz. that (i) the revetment of kiln-fired bricks (Revetment 1) of the defences at Kausambi is similar in its constructional style to the revetment of the defences at Harappa; (ii) the corbelled arch of the 'underground passage' (or a drain?) is similar to that of the drain emanating from the Great Bath at Mohenjo-daro; (iii) Rampart 1 was 'two periods' earlier than the occurrence of the PG Ware; and (iv) the pottery associated with the earliest defences at Kausambi has its parallels in the Harappan and immediately post-Harappan pottery at Navdatoli, Rangpur, etc.

On these points the present writer has to offer the following comments, seriatim.

(i) The only similarity that is discernible between the Kausambi and Harappa revetments is their stepped (i.e. sloping) exterior. This is such a general feature that one finds it in most cases where an effective revetment is to be provided to retain the deposits at the back. Even the recent revetment of Sringaverapura shown on pl. I has a sloping exterior. So have the retaining walls of the first century A.D. tank unearthed at this very site. Thus, no dating-importance can be attached to this feature.

In this context, a very noteworthy point is the size of the bricks used in the revetment at Kausambi, viz. 51.5x33.5x7.5 cm (Sharma *ibid:* p1, 4). The Harappan bricks have a very set ratio of thickness, breadth and length, which is 1:2:4, the actual size being either 7½x15x30 cm or 10x20x40 cm. The Kausambi bricks have neither this ratio nor the size. In fact, the size of the Kausambi bricks falls in line with that obtainable in the case of bricks at other early historical sites in the Ganga valley itself.

(ii) As regards the corbelled arch, it may be mentioned that this was the prevalent method of constructing an arch prior to the introduction of what is known as the 'true arch'. This again, therefore, has no dating value.

(iii) The relative stratigraphical position of the P.G. Ware *vis-a-vis* Rampart 1 has been shown by Sharma in his Fig. 4 (here reproduced as Fig. 2). In this figure what has been marked as "Repairs to Rampart 1" is shown as being associated with the P.G. Ware. Derivately, therefore, Rampart 1 has been marked as pre-P.G. Ware. Since Rampart 1, as shown earlier, is nothing but the natural soil, there is no rampart of the pre-P.G. Ware times. Further, one does not know about the exact nature of what has been termed as "Repairs to Rampart 1". However, if one turns one's attention once again to Sharma's Fig. 3 (here Fig. 2) one notices that even this deposit is retained by Revetment 1 and, therefore, had existed prior to the latter. If that be so, as it seems to be, Revetment 1 would be posterior to the deposit containing the PGW. As regards the find of a few PGW sherds in layers 19 and 20 which lie against Revetment 1 and are, therefore, later than it, it may be stated that these layers are not regular occupational strata but constitute fallen material from the habitational levels at the back. Such layers can contain anything from A to Z that existed at the sites prior to the fall. At Sringaverapura, K. N. Dikshit and the present writer got plenty of NBPW sherds from layers that lay against the medieval walls. That does not mean that the medieval walls are pre-NBPW.

(iv) That the so-called Harappan pottery from Kausambi has no similarity whatsoever with the Harappan pottery has already been dealt with by the present write in a paper which he presented at the Srinagar Seminar (Lal, 1982:335-38). Hence the same is not repeated here. (In fact, in this very issue of *Puratattva* K. N. Dikshit has dealt with this topic in fuller detail.)

From the foregoing it would be amply clear that there is nothing Harappan about the Kausambi defence nor are they even pre-PGW.

In that case, what is the likely date of these defences and what is the basis of such a dating?

It has already been shown above that Rampart 1 is nothing but the natural soil *in situ.* Thus, if Rampart 1 is not a rampart at all, the deposits which have been termed as "Repairs to Rampart 1" also cease to have any meaning in terms of a rampart. The first real rampart, therefore, would be what has been called as Rampart 2 by Sharma (of his Fig. 4; Fig. 2 of this paper). As would be seen from this drawing, it is not the first thing to have been built in the NBPW period: there is some NBPW deposit *prior* to the construction of this rampart. The rampart is, therefore not assignable even to the Early NBPW Period.

Now, if one has a further look at the drawing, one finds that associated with this rampart (i.e. Rampart . of Sharma) are punch-marked and uninscribed cast coins. This would mean that the rampart was built after these coins had also come into being.

On the basis of the evidence from Sravasti, Rajghat, Kausambi itself (Sharma 1960:23) and even Sringaverapura (Agrawal, Bhandari, Lal and Singhvi 1981:171), the emergence of the NBP Ware is unlikely to have been much earlier than the beginning of the seventh century B.C. From most of these sites it is also known that the punch-marked and uninscribed cast coins did not come into being right at the beginning of the NBPW period. These may go back at the most to *circa* sixth century B.C.

Thus, Rampart 2 of Sharma, which is really the first rempart, is unlikely to be earlier than *circa* sixth century B.C. It may very well be even somewhat later.

The answer then to our initial enquiry is that *the defences at Kausambi do not go back to 1025 B.C., as held by Sharma. These may have come into being about half a millennium or so later.*

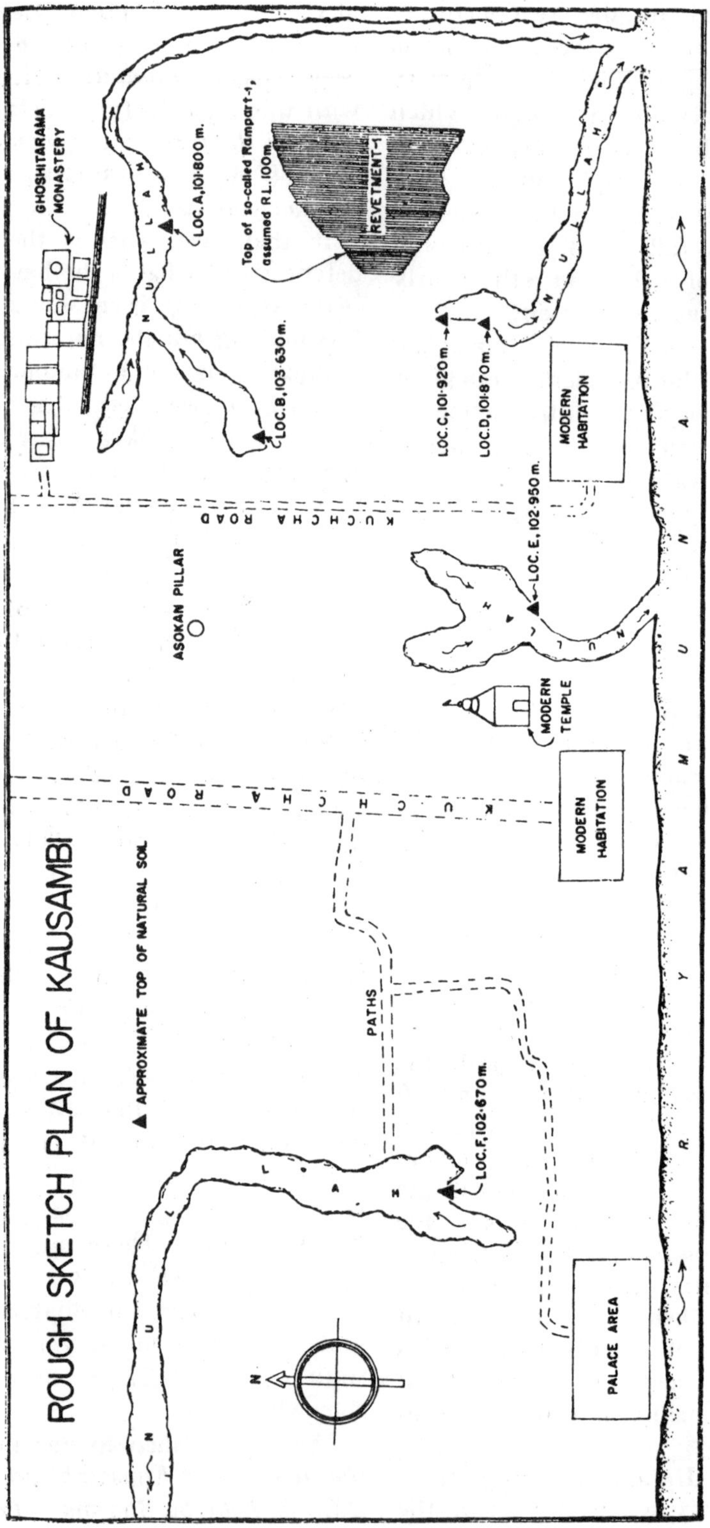
ROUGH SKETCH PLAN OF KAUSAMBI
▲ APPROXIMATE TOP OF NATURAL SOIL
GHOSHITARAMA MONASTERY
LOC.A,101·800 m.
Top of so-called Rampart-1, assumed R.L.100m.
REVETMENT-1
LOC.B,103·630 m.
LOC.C,101·920 m.
LOC.D,101·870 m.
MODERN HABITATION
KUCHCHA ROAD
ASOKAN PILLAR
LOC.E,102·950 m.
MODERN TEMPLE
MODERN HABITATION
KUCHCHA ROAD
PATHS
LOC.F,102·670 m.
PALACE AREA
N
NULLAH
NULLAH
NULLAH
NULLAH
R. YAMUNA

Fig 3

REFERENCES

Sharma, G.R. 1960 *The Excavations at Kausambi 1957-59*, Allahabad, Department of Ancient History, Culture and Archaeology, University of Allahabad.

Ghosh, A. 1973 *The City in Early Historical India* Simla, Indian Institute of Advanced Study.

Sinha, K.K. 1973 Stratigraphy and Chronology of Early Kausambi—A Reappraisal, *Radiocarbon* and *Indian Archaeology*, (ed) D.P. Agarwal and A. Ghosh, Bombay, Tata Institute of Fundamental Research.

Lal, B.B. 1982 West was West and East was East, but When and How did the Twain Meet? The Role of Bhagwanpura as a Bridge between Certain States of the Indus and Ganges Civilizations, *Harappan Civilization—A Contemporary Perspective* (ed) Gregory L. Possehl New Delhi, Bombay, Calcutta.

Agarwal, D.P., N. Bhandari, B.B. Lal, and A.K. Singhvi 1981 Thermoluminescence Dating of pottery from Sringaverapura—a Ramayan Site. *Proc. Indian Acad. Sci (Earth Planet Sci.)* 90(2).

The Use of Arch in the Kushan Palace At Kausambi

K.V. Soundara Rajan
Archaeological Survey of India, New Delhi

The Kushan palace excavated at Kausambi has been reported in detail (Sharma 1968:1-41). The important reference made is to the existence of the arch principle in the 1st-2nd Century A.D. and technical basis for the development of the same has been elaborately discussed in the above. This is a matter of universal interest and in the Indian context of crucial importance.

On *prima facie* grounds, the problem is mainly twofold: (a) whether the fringe area on the river front where these arched usages are seen could be considered as an integral part of the rest of the Kushan excavated here in the quadrangular layout (b) whether the arched principles show any features which could be considered as sufficiently early or only mediaeval. It is to be noted that the palace complex is itself laid in two or more structural phases according to the excavator and using flat slabs and semi dressed stones. The chambers, as excavated, are all available only at plinth level. They do not show any subterranean feature, which is seen only in the river front area, alleged to be a part of the palace complex with its 4th phase. It is therefore essential that this river front area should be examined carefully to confirm whether they had any well integrated character with the rest of the palace where in structural materials that are used, it shows consonance and whether its layout carries any functional unity or continuity with the rest of the structure.

On a thorough examination of the land around it and the type of pottery it yields, it is seen that this pottery as collected from the surface, variously on the debris used in the structures at or around the arched passages and also generally in the immediate vicinity for model study shows three broad groupings (a) those which are typically of the late NBP and post NBP stage (b) of the early historic stage (*c.* Ist century A.D.-4th century A.D.); and those (c) which are truly mediaeval. These are documented in the appendix. While the first is of the antecedent matrix, and the second contemporary with the Kushans and after, the third is totally unrelated to the structure of the palace and may be seemingly coeval with certain mediaeval accretions made to the earlier structure (which must have been lying in ruins then), but with a visible outline and thus induct a mediaeval phase here.

According to the excavator:

(1) This 'Kushan' structure belongs to the IVth stage (1st-2nd century A.D.) and the walls of this period are built over the foundation of phase III.

(2) Composition of the mortar and plaster and their constituent elements do not show variation of any fundamental nature. The total impression given, however, is one of having been done in *haste, which is evident, by intermixing of brick and stone of irregular sizes in thick mortar joints and heavy coatings of plaster compensate this (italics present author's).* Nowhere else however is this hybrid use of brick and stone attested to at Kausambi.

(3) morphologically and functionally, the four centred pointed arch, segmental arch, semi-

elliptical vault, and the dome with foliated profile (both circular and elliptical) are seen. Function and position of keystone at the corner was thus fully familiar to its builders.

(4) Examples examined in coeval times are from 1st-3rd century A.D.-Toprah Kala and Janbas Kala (USSR) and Balkh 1st century A.D. (Afghanistan). No drawing however is available of the arches there.

(5) The rooms and halls of the central and eastern blocks and galleries were filled with large heavy fragments and materials provided were domical and can aptly be called *sikharas*. These are of brick and thick lime mortar and heavy plaster; horizontal and vertical laying is noticed. Corbelling technique is indicated in the offsetting of intrados and extrados. Radial technique of brick setting is entirely absent here. The most significant construction emerging from the restoration is the *sikhara*-like shape. This is closely associated with the majority of Hindu temples, and had already evolved in its typical north Indian characteristic in 1st-2nd century A.D. and was a popular roofing done on secular structures like palaces of kings.

Kharavela's record, Sikhara etc. Milnda Panha-Gopura torana, Anga Vijya (Kushan age) text of the Buddhists mentions Kottaha, Kadikatorana, Gopura, etc. *Amarakosa* refers to kuta, sikhara and sringa.

Ramayana mentions royal buildings of Ayodhya-'Kuta' is used.

The conclusions of the excavator are:

1. Kushan architecture was hybrid—Bhitargaon and Mripurkhas, under their influence rose to the occasion and evolved the true *sikhara*.

Answering and examining these, we may note :

1. If Kausambi's early structural tradition is not followed in the Kushana phase and is hybird, the impact it had on the succeeding ages at least do not bear out any such continuance of this hybrid technique or function or tradition elsewhere.
2. If it is a hurried construction, it is certainly not bad construction at that rate, since even in a hurried creation, such typical arch features are clearly envinced which should imply a long antecedent tradition in better material.
3. Thick mortar is never used in Hindu temple which, till the 12th century A.D. virtually, is of dry-bound without mortar and requires specific explaining (from early Gupta times onwards). Even in brick structure, heavy mortar is never used and lime mortar often not used.
4. The true arch-vault types are absent at Dhamekh Stupa Sarnath, Bhitargaon, Mirpurkhas and upto Vikram Sila stage (8th-11th century A.D.) and do not show any evidence of any link with true arch techniques and all astylar corbelling In fact, in Vikramsila there are clear instances of stone construction of the underground vault chamber for the monastic cells wherein the true keystone arched vault has never been employed, but the indigenous vault where the stone slabs had been laid in radial lines but mainly on the principle of corbelling, and had thus suffered gravitational thrust and had got dilapidated. Nonetheless, these vaults which are dated by the excavator to the first half of the 9th century A.D. at Vikramsila do not show the true-arch principle. Even early Sultanate architecture upto A.D. 1231 is of astylar corbelling. In Dhamekh and Adhaidin Ka Jhonpra, Ajmer, the curved vertically foliated dome/arch profile is already shown but it is astylar entirely. The function and position of keystone at the crown gets familiar only from 1250-80 A.D.

The comparision between Afghan and USSR types and Indian is neither close nor technically relatable. The function of this subterranean cell at Kausambi is different from the load-bearing arch devices, for which keystone is necessary. No upper structures have been shown extant here having true arch principles and, where discussed, are of corbelling type and no radial techniques of brick-setting are seen here according to the excavator himself. To agree that the same craftsman showed keystone arches for non-functional subterranean vaults and only corbelled ones for superstructural domes is, to say the least anomalous. Literary references quoted do not clinch any point other than terminological or linguistic. The mere theoretical projections of drawings showing the different arch pattern do not by themselves prove that these are the oldest in India. It is possible to show even in the Islamic construction, the functions where these changes of centres of the arch-curve are based on differing character of structures. The archaeological evidence, even stratigraphically, from the bonding, if any, of these structures with the main palace walls here, do not show them as integral to the earlier structural phases.

The fact that all the samples of lime mortar have similar proportions does not prove anything except that all these structures where mortar is involved are of similar tradition. These mortar types are not seen in this manner of application, in the earlier phases at Kausambi nor in succeeding periods, except after the 12th century A.D. The Chemist's notes also indicated only a probability that *surkhi* is not used, except in one instance. The actual fact is that *surkhi* is not an invariable component in early mediaeval mortar but is utilised mostly where the stone work is more and in the case of brick work, this may differ. Thus, its presence or absence besides the nature of the lime mortar which will always be local and not imported, and thus could be of available quality cannot prove or disprove anything.

We shall now examine what is the type of bonding, if any, the arched tunnel passages have with the main structure. These can be examined in two parts: the features that are found laid against the 'palace structure' platform in the centre on the river front and those features of the arched passages themselves. The first shows only a hotch-potch reconstruction which are running partly resting over the original palace plinth offsets and which are applied to the back wall of the hidden inner corners of the plinth. The sketch (Sharma Fig 1) shows the structural features of this accretion, as could be seen from the river side, and tells its own tale on the mode of its erection which, to say the least, is an improvised re-use of old materials in mixture of brick and stone, and totally uncoursed, with underpinning of brick here and there, amidst stone work.

As regards the arched tunnel passages, it is seen that they show:

(a) the arch principles (to be detailed below)
(b) they involve a heavy laying of mortar of the kankar lime and sand mix amidst underssed grey schistose sandstone,
(c) All their parts longitudinally are well integrated but transerverely are mere cross-wall arches abutting on the outer pre-existing face of the earlier plinth and are thus clear accretionary constructions.
(d) Their size and height clearly show that they were subterranean for unseen movement along the edge of the structure from one end to the other. There are some fragments of domes which are lying upon the top of the palace wall terrace which are themselves parts of the mediaeval reconstruction of this structural level after the end of phase IV and perhaps are coeval with the arched structural remains. These show concave facial design elements which appear to be part of a lotus or fluted interior ceiling faces and intrados of drum and domes here—a feature which became very popular everywhere in upper India in the Tughlaq and post Tuglaq Pre-Mughal stages, some stone carvings of lintels and jambs have also been reused as sill-stones and could themselves be of the same stage as the mediaeval stage (12 century A.D. onwards) referred to above. If they are of vertical double curved profile in domes, rich arched principle in astylar corbelling is also seen as stated already only in the early Sultanate period as in Adhaidin Ka Jhonpra mosque arches at Ajmer (*c.* 1230) and do not have a corresponding usage elsewhere in Hindu-Buddhist India.

Now coming to the 'arched' features themselves, they show invariably a well-coursed jamb feature on either side of thin, dressed slabs of more than a dozen courses interspersed with bricks also, and with mortar packing at the top of the springing of the arch and the first voussoir stone. The laying of these voussoir stones are suggestive of a full and well mastered understanding of the arch-vault principle which is particularly having the characteristic 'V' shape key stone point found, which instead of one single key stone is in pieces of two angular slabs with mortar packing of stone jelly in betwen. This can be extensively seen in Tughlaq structures in Delhi, such as at Tughlaqabad and depict an already achieved total mastery of the arch principle, while still using only rubble stones and slabs. Even admist these voussoirs, bricks have been interspersed showing that they were using available old fragments.

Now the issue whether such a constructional, feature of a 'true' arch could be envisaged at the early period of 1st century-2nd Century A.D. is to be discussed. On the one hand, consistent with the subterranean character of the vaulted arch passages, the curve of the arch is a shallow segment and not semicircular although in one larger instance a four centred arch is also shown. The same, if they are standing above the base level, as chambers, would have been of semi-circular arches or even with high vertical drummed domes or vaults. That apart, the very character of these, utilizing coarse building materials evince that the technique of a 'true' arch has been fully mastered and were subesequent to their manifestation in regular dressed stones first, and translated in subsequent stages on rubble stone and brick. We know that in the consideration of constructional devices, style and technique are two distinctive features, the latter depicting the inherent knowledge of the working principle, and the former a veneered patterning of it on an aesthetic plane. Thus, styling always becomes subsequent to the initial introduction of the technique and the first introduction of a technique is in ideal building materials like wood, or cut stone or well cut bricks and subsequently when such ideal building materials are not readily available, the mastery of the technique already achieved enabled the mason to improvise with any material and, in such a case, the use of mortar is more profuse to give a solid strength to the structure. This is what happened at the close of the Delhi Sultanate stage from A.D. 1190-1280 whereafter the Khalji stage introduced the true arch in ideal circumstanced, as in Alai Darwza. Therefore, the succeeding Tughlaq masons who had mastered the technique could adopt it using any rough or coarse raw material .and create structures of excellent finish and superstructural details which hide the coarse stone work below.

Taking all these into consideration, a conclusion would appear reasonable that the accretionary vaulted and arched features found on the river side end of the palace remains at Kausambi are more likely to be mediaeval and perhaps may go well with the mediaeval Islamic village close by, with other grave remains which occur there, and are not liable to be considered certainly as of the Kushan times. The pre-existing use of vaults and arches in Indian context before and after the period of the Kushans, as at Sarnath (Dhamekh Stupa), Bhitargaon, and Vikramsila (sub-terranean vaults-early 9th century A.D.) all shows principles which are not relatable to the true arch or the true vault. If the Kushans could show it at Kausambi in such a facile manner even in rough workmanship, there was no reason why they have not left any bequeathal behind, this also becomes somewhat anomalous in the mechanics of technical traditions and their growth. The constructional materials and devices adopted here, have been, even according to the excavator, no where else seen at Kausambi. Why such a sudden and short lived digression in constructional techniques, without any functional continuation thereafter anywhere else, should occur has not been satisfactorily answered yet. The technical geometric analysis of the architypes shown do not necessarly imply that they have to be only Kushan. The pottery in the area has already ben shown to be including mediaeval sherd types also. It would thus require much more than what has been so far adduced by the excavator to make them pre-mediaeval, to say the least not to mention, Kushan.

REFERENCES

Sharma, G.R. 1968 *Kusana Studies*, The University of Allahabad, Allahabad.

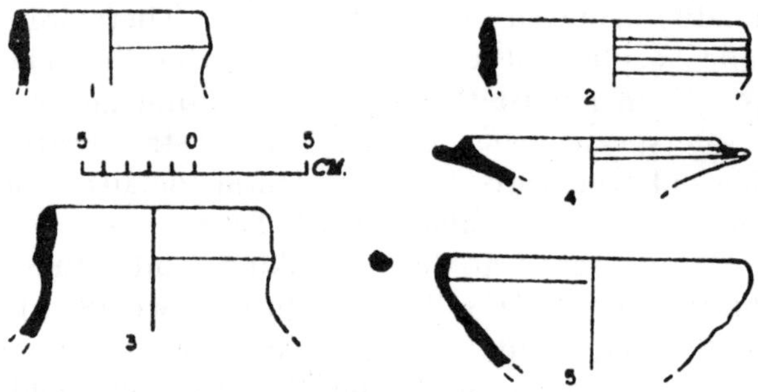

Fig 1

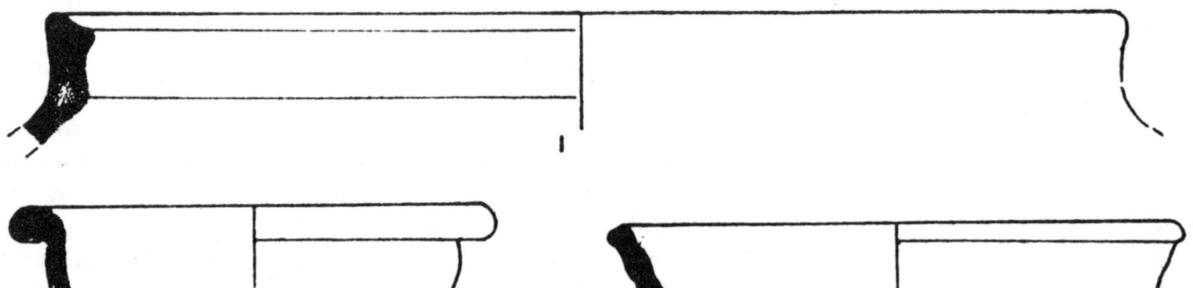

Fig 2

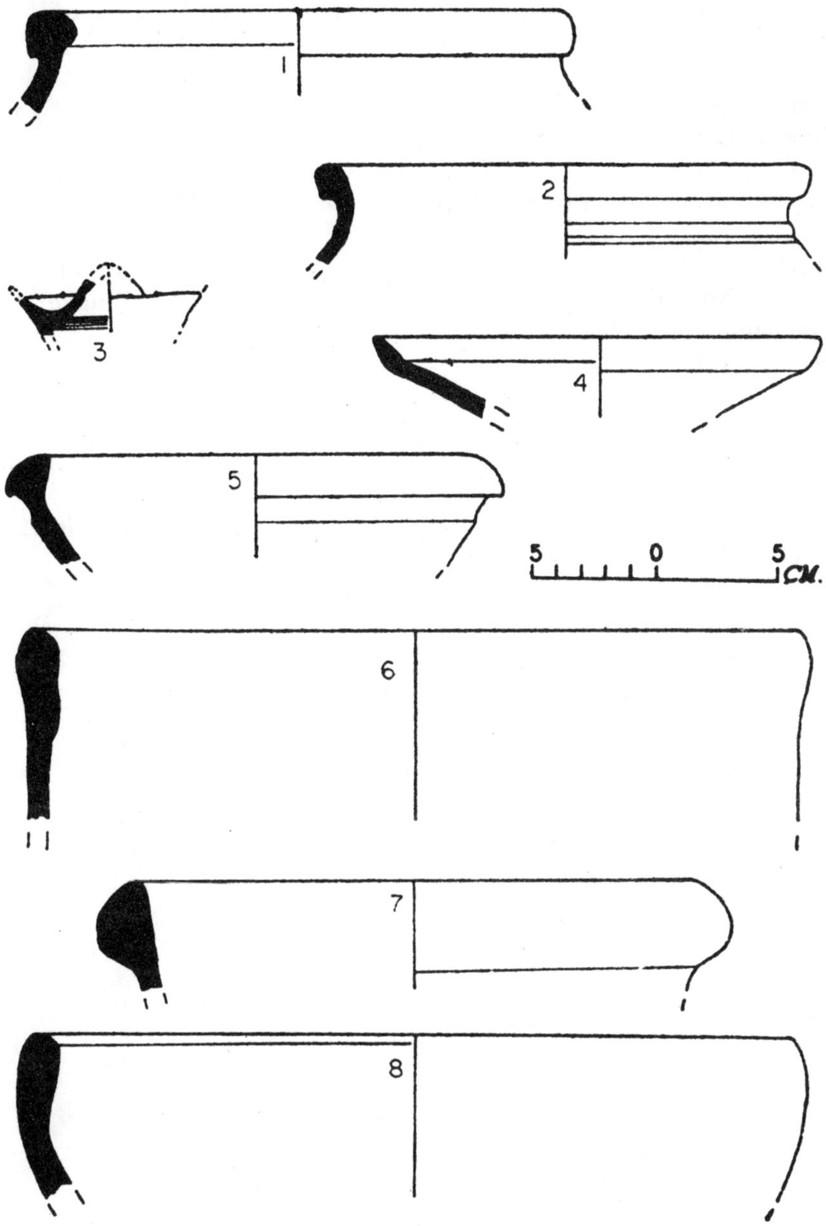

Fig 3

APPENDIX

Fig. No.	No.	Parallels where available	Appropriate Period
Fig. 1	1.	Hastinapura Fig. 18-variant of XXXI-g	
	2.	Variant of Ahich chhatra 10A	
	3.	Hastinapura Fig. 18 Variant of XXXI-e	Pre-christian
	4.	Rajghat Fig. 16, No. 21.	
	5.	Hastinapura Fig. 20 Variant of 1	
Fig. 2	3.	Hastinapura Fig. 26, No. XVA	Early Historical
	4.	Fig. 20, Variant of IC	
	5.	Fig. 16, No. XXIII A	
	8.	Rajghat Fig. 13, Variant of No. 33 (Handmade)	
Fig. 3	1.	Rajghat Fig. 24, Variant of No. 12	Medieval
	2.	Fig 21, Variant of No. 7.	
	3.	Fig. 24, No. 15.	

Is The Early Pottery from Kausambi Harappan ?

K. N. DIKSHIT
Archaeological Survey of India, New Delhi

While excavating at Kausambi, District Allahabad, G. R. Sharma claimed: 'Apart from the defences which were built on the Harappan model, many types of pottery from Kausambi are analogus to pottery types of Harappan origin in western India (Sharma 1960: 7). Recently Sharma (1980:68-70, 79) has compared this pottery as well as some more pottery from the monastery (Ghositarama) area, some pottery from sites like Onaur, Unchdih and Kakoria with Bhagwanpura, a site on the Saraswati in Haryana. The types according to him are button-based goblets, dishes-on-stand, lid-cum-bowls, beakers, high necked jars and dishes of dishes-on-stand.

While engaged in the excavations at Sringaverapura, a site located in the same district, the author had chances to examine this pottery thoroughly alongwith B.B. Lal and B.K. Thapar. In order to understand the stratigraphical position of this pottery, the Kausambi was also visited with B.B. Lal, K.V. Soundara Rajan, H. Sarkar and H.K. Narain. We have to offer the following comments.

KAUSAMBI TYPES COMPARED WITH TYPES FOUND AT BHAGWANPURA IA

Sharma 1980:69	Our Comments
1 Beaker with a featureless rim and round base.	Survival of the Neolithic and Chalcolithic type noticed at Chirand.
2, 3 Bowls in coarse fabric	No such bowls were reported from late Harappan sites
5 Bowl with ring base	Hulas II (PGW)
4, 6, 7, 8, Dish-on-stand in coarse fabric	Similar stems were found at Mathura-I (PGW), HST-II and Hulas-III (NBP)
9 Raised horizontal bands	These are different from Harappans. It is analogus to the ribbed ware associated with the NBPW period.
10 Jar	General type

ONAUR AND UNCHDIH POTTERY COMPARED WITH BHAGWANPURA IA POTTERY

Sharma 1980:70	Our Comments
1-5 Miniature pots	No 1 is a lid, whereas others are the part of miniature pots

6, 7, 8 Basins	**Present at Sringaverapura in the upper NBPW Complex (Period III)**
10, 11, 12 Bases	**Wrongly published in inverted position. They are the upper parts of the pots. In *IAR* 1969-70, these pots are correctly published. No. 10 was found at Ayodhya in NBP levels.**

Most of these bowl or basin types are presentin Sringaverapura (Period III)

KAKORIA POTTERY TYPES COMPARED WITH TYPES FOUND AT BHAGWANPURA IA

Sharma 1980-79	Our Comments
1-2 Button based goblet	It is a part of lid, complete example comes from **Kausambi.**
3 Miniature pots	General types
7, 8, 9, 10 Bowls & jars	Present at HST II & in the early levels of SVP III (NBPW)
4, 6, 11 Bowls and jars	General types
12, 13 Raised horizontal bands	It is a ribbed ware associated with NBPW.

Sharma compared a fragment of a basin with an out-turned rounded rim of Kausambi with Alamgirpur and Lothal IIB (Sharma 1960: Fig 10-47). But there is no such type available at Alamgirpur.

B. B. Lal who also examined these early potteries from Kausambi, observed that button-based goblets are the knobs of the lids, beakers are the lower parts of the elongated vessels, sometimes cylindrical and sometimes conical and dishes-on-stand are not exclusively confined to the Harappan culture. In fact "it was observed that there was nothing in the pottery from Kausambi, Kakoria, etc. which could really lay claims to being Harappan in the true sense" (Lal 1982). K. K. Sinha is also of the view that "The Kausambi pottery types for which a similarity with Navadatoli types has been claimed are mostly of an indistinctive type which could have been evolved independently any where at any time (Sinha 1979:234). According the typological parallelism lose much of their significance".

For comparision, it should be brone in mind that the Indus pottery is sturdy, well fired and well levigated. The regular striation marks suggest the possible use of fast spinning wheel. It has sand or lime or both as degraissants. The majority of pots are utilitarian in character with flat as well as round bases. The pottery was dressed by way of applying slip which varies from a thin wash to thick coating coloured either red or cream. It is generally the upper parts of the pots which are covered with slip, whereas the lower portion is left roughned and sometimes found decorated with a cord. A few of the sherds also have graffiti marks which also occur on the seals. The fabric is well known for typical painted designs arranged in horizontal registers on a carefully prepared ground. The complete painted pots are rare. It appears that in the later stage of Indus civilization different types of wares such as pre-Harappan survivals, Harappan and also some non-Harappan wares like Cemetry-H and Jhukar coalesced and continued. The painted pottery is replaced by less intricate designs and plain unpainted ware with new pot-forms. The incised decorations are confined on the exterior but the famous metallic ring of the pottery is there. At Ambkheri and Bahadarabad representing a degenerate stage of Harappa culture, the types-goblets, beakers and perforated jars are absent. The typical incised designs noticed at Atranjikhera, an Ochre-coloured ware site, have not found place further east.

The early pottery from Kausambi is ill fired and coarse in texture. The surface treatment is poor and the slip is thin. The pottery of this group including other sites show a general decadence in fabric, potting and treatment of surface, whereas the late Indus pottery is different in character and cannot be compared with it. This pottery is, in fact, the associated red ware found in eastern India with black-and-red and black slipped wares phase at Chirand, Sonepur, Prahladpur, Ayodhya and Rajghat and with the PGW sites in the western U.P. at Hastinapura, Hulas and Mathura (Fig. 1). At Sringaverapura a few of these types were found in the early NBPW levels.

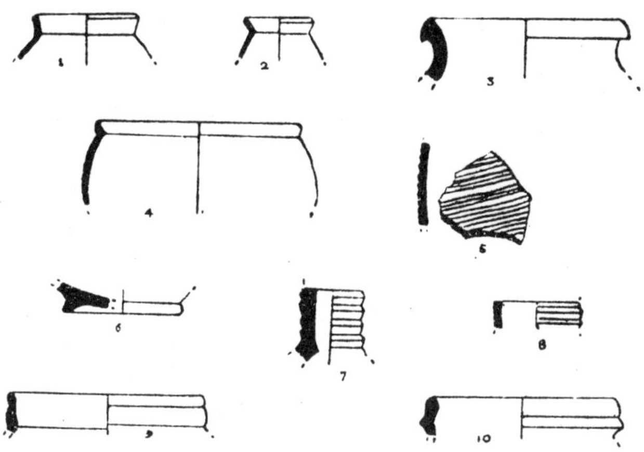

Fig 1

REFERENCES

Sharma, G.R. 1960 *The Excavations at Kausambi 1957-59.* Allahabad. Department of Ancient His. Culture and Archaeology, University of Allahabad.

1980 *History to Pre-History*—Archaeology of the Ganga valley and the Vindhyas.

Lal, B.B. 1982 West was West and East was East, but When and How did the Twin Meet? The Role of Bhagwanpura as a bridge between certain stages of the Indus and Ganga Civilization, *Harappan Civilization—A Contemporary Perspectives.*

Sinha,, K.K. 1973 Stratigraphy and chronology of early Kausambi—A reappraisal, *Radiocarbon* and *Indian Archaeology, Bombay.*

NOTES AND NEWS

Ayodhya: Mythical and Real

In one of the previous numbers of this journal (Joshi 1978: 98-102), I raised many issues relating to the interpretation of Vedic and epic traditions in archaeological terms.

Important points discussed therein included, besides the nature of early references to Ayodhya, theory of Aryan invasion of Harappa and archaeology of Hastinapura and Mahabharatan traditions.

I am grateful to Prof. Lal (Lal 1981: 45-49) for questioning my observations on Ayodhya as mentioned in *Taittariya Aranyaka* (1.27). His main objections read as under:

> 'One really wonders as to how Joshi envisages his Ayodhya of the mortals, on the one hand, ceased to exist long before the composition of the *Taittariya Aranyaka* and, on the other, to have come into being well after the same *Aranyaka.* Further, Joshi has to answer: 'Who was this Rama and why and when he did come to be associated with modern Ayodhya?'

Lal, after citing a number of textual references, concludes that the word 'Ayodhya' in the Vedic context has not been used as a proper noun but only in the sense of 'invincible'. At the same time, he feels that eight-chakras and nine-dvaras are respectively indicative of eight plexuses beginning with *muladhara* and nine gates (outlets) of human body like the eyes, nostrils, ears, etc. The major difficulty in accepting the interpretation of Lal is that that the number of the *chakras* (plexuses) is believed to be only six without *sahasrara.* With latter's inclusion their total number would be only seven (Hinze 1979: 25ff.) and not eight as inferred by him. Besides it is doubtful whether by the time the *Atharvaveda* was compiled, the concepts associated with *kundalini* or *shatchakras,* etc. had developed?

On the basis of the relevant passage of *Taittariya Aranyaka,* whatever was inferred to by us about Ayodhya earlier (i.e. it was either a mythical city or if at all it existed ever, it was wholly forgotten by the time the text under reference was compiled), was on account of the occurrence therein of adjectives like *ashtachakra, navadvara devanampura, hiranmayakosa,* and *amritenavritampuram* qualifying it. The adjectives seem to be allegorical in character indicating the personal beliefs or impression of the composer of the hymn about the phenomenon involved. The references thus betray a meaningful symbolism.

Coming to the historical period, the earliest reference relating to Ayodhya as a settlement is available in the *Samyukta Nikaya* (Feer 1890: XXII. 95.I) locating it not on the Sarayu but on the Ganga (cf. *ekam samayam Bhagava Ayogjhayam viharati Gangaya nadiya tire).*

Ayodhya mentioned by Valmiki in his *Ramayana* as the capital of Kosala is often identified with a small town of the same name in district Faizabad, Uttar Pradesh, on the right bank of the Sarayu or the Ghagra. But a critical examination of the geographical data available in Valmiki's narratives does not justify the commonly accepted identification of ancient city with the modern one. The major points of disagreement are as under:

According to Valmiki's description, Ayodhya was situated at a considerable distance from the river Sarayu flowing at that time in a westward Direction and joining Ganga at some distance:

> *Adhyardha-Yojanamgatva nadi paschyan-mukhasritam*
> *Sarayu punyasalila dadarsa Raghunandanah*
> 119, CX. *Uttarakanda*
> *Adhyardhayojanamgatva Sarayva dakshinetate*
> 11. XXII *Balakanda*

Tau prayantau mahaviryau divyam Tripathagam nadim
Daddrisate tatastratra Sarayvah sangame subhe
5. XXIII. *Balakanda*

The location of modern Ayodhya however does not tally with the details given in the above cited verses; for instance, the present city stands in the close proximity of the river and not one-and-a-half *yojana* away from town site. According to D.C. Sircar (1966:386) one *yojana* is equal to nine miles (14.4 km) and therefore one-and-a-half *yojana* would be thirteen-and-a-half miles. Even if this distance is taken to be somewhat less than what has been stated by Sircar, it would hardly justify the present location of Ayodhya in terms of the epic.

Further, the Sarayu today flows eastward and not westward *(paschanmukhasritam)* and joins Rapti (ancient Achiravati) and not Ganga which is contrary to the Ramayanic references (5. XXIII. *Balakanda)* (Fig. 1).

13. XIV. *Raghu.*
Anvitah pativatsalyad grihavar jam-Ayodhyaya
97. XV. *Raghu.*

Kalidasa, thus used the two terms, Ayodhya and Saketa, as synonyms. The same tradition is recorded in *Adhyatma-Ramayana* a post-classical text (cf. *Sakete Lokanatha prathitagunagana gano*..........." 57. VII *Balakanda;* and *Ayodhyabhimukham gatva kinchidduram tato yayah*...... ...." 57. V. *Ayodhyakanda)*.

It would be interesting to note that Saketa is mentioned as a separate town from Ayodhya in the early Pali literature situated at a distance of six or seven leagues (*yojanas*) from Sravasti. Located on the trade route linking Sravasti with Kausambi and other towns to further south (Joshi 1974), ancient Saketa was in fact an important town during the Maurya-Sunga period. According to classical and post-classical Brahmanical literature, it appears to be identical with modern Ayodhya.

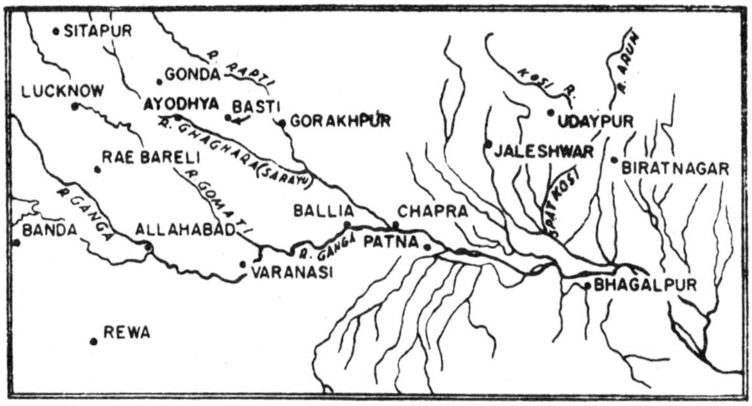

IMPORTANT RIVERS IN EAST UTTAR PRADESH & BIHAR

Fig 1

The problem of identification of ancient Ayodhya does not end here for the *Raghuvamsa* of Kalidasa presents a slightly different picture. In this text the capital of Raghuvamsis has been referred to as Ayodhya as well as Saketa as can be observed below:

Prasada-vatayana lakshya bandhaih
Saketanaryonjalibhih Pranemu

Hieun Tsang (Watters 1961) however, locates A-Yu-te i.e., Ayudha or Ayodhya 600 *li* (120 miles) to the east-southeast of Kanyakubja (Kanauj) and about a mile south of Ganga. Scholars have identified Hieun Tsang's A-Yu-te with modern Ayodhya in district Faizabad taking Ganga to be a mistake for Sarayu; but this does not seem to be convincing, for present Ayodhya is definitely more than 120 miles from Kanauj. It is also unlikely that

Hieun Tsang who himself travelled within this area would commit such a blunder. Perhaps, the Chinese traveller followed the Buddhist Tradition as available in *Samyukta Nikaya.*

On the basis of what has been discussed above, it may be inferred that Ayodhya of present day stands over the remains of Saketa of early Buddhist literature of which Asvaghosa, the author of *Buddha Charita,* was probably a native. The Brahmanical tradition confirming the present location of Ayodhya could thus be traced back to the Gupta period. It may now be desirable to search for the site of earlier Ayodhya somewhere else also, so that diverse facets of literary tradition could be verified.

Archaeological Survey of India,
New Delhi.

M.C. JOSHI

REFERENCES

Adhyatma Ramayana (Hindi Tr), Munilal, 15th edition, Gorakhpur, V.S. 2027.

Dwivedi, Rewa Prasad 1973 *Raghuvamsa Darpana* I, Patna.

Feer, M. Leon 1890 *Samyukta Nikaya* III, Pali Text Society, London.

Hinze, Oscar Marcel 1979 *Tantra Vidya* (English Tr.) V.M. Bedekar, Delhi, Patna, Varanasi.

Joshi, M.C. 1974 Early Historical Urban Growth in India: Some Observations, *Puratattva* 7, 1974-75.

1978 Archaeology and Indian Tradition: Some Observations, *Puratattva* 8, 1975-76.

Lal, B.B. 1981 Was Ayodhya A Mythical City?, *Puratattva* 10.

Sircar, D.C. 1966 *Indian Epigraphical Glossary,* Delhi, Varanasi, Patna.

Srimad-Valmikiya Ramayana I and II, V.S. 2017, Gorakhpur.

Walter, Thomas 1961 *On Yuan Chwang's Travels in India* (Indian Edition), Delhi.

Prehistoric Investigation in the Gambheeram Valley: Visakhapatnam Coast

Explorations in the Gambheeram Valley and its environs (18° 40′—18° 55′ N, 83° 10,—83° 30′ E) of Visakhapatnam district, Andhra Pradesh, have revealed in the discovery of eighteen prehistoric sites, such as Bhimendrapalem, Pappalavanipalem, Madhyakadamam, Dibbadapalem, Sontyam, Mamidilova, Gudilova, Dukkavanipalem, Gambheeram, Madhurawada, Marikavalasa, Rushikonda, Vadapalem, Bhimunipatnam, Lankalipalem, Mangalipalem, Gangavaram and Venkatarajapuram. These are located on either banks of the river, foot-hills and on the coast. The prehistoric material was found on the eroded surface of the gravels and soils. The material was also noticed in the sections of nallas. Sections were scraped at Madhyakadamam and Sontyam and trial trenches were dug at Madhyakadamam, Mamidilova, Gudilova, Madhurawada and Rushikonda to confirm the stratigraphic horizons of different cultural phases. The cultural material ranges from Lower Palaeolithic to Neolithic (Fig. 1).

A varied picture of stratified layers is observed in the valley. However, a comprehensive stratigraphy for the valley is reconstructed on the basis of the strata represented at a few sites. Four gravels alternated by four soil layers were observed in the valley.

Blocks of stone, nodules and chunks form the basal gravel (Gravel—I) which rests on weathered bedrock. At a few places this is cemented. The brownish soil is the binding matrix. The thickness of this gravel varies between 50-150 cm. Lithologically this gravel is composed of Khondalite. This is devoid of any archaeological material. Sealing the Gravel-I is brown soil, which ranges in thickness between 10-90 cm. This is also sterile. The next layer that follows is ferruginous gravel (Gravel-II) and consists of large, angular ferruginous pellets. It ranges in thickness from 60 to 100 cm. Late acheulean artefacts are recovered from the top of this gravel. Yellowish soil covers Gravel-II. Its thickness ranges from

40 to 60 cm. Calcretes are seen within the layer but always more profuse towards the top. This layer is sterile. Next in the sequence of layers is pebbly gravel (Gravel-III) composed of round to sub-round pebbles. This gravel ranges in thickness between 50 to 150 cm. This is the horizon for Middle Palaeolithic culture. Overlying this gravel is the yellow soil. This is very compact and clayey. This is a thin layer ranging between 20 and 40 cm. On the top of this layer, there is small pellety ferruginuous gravel. Its thickness varies between 15 and 20 cm. This is the horizon for Upper Palaeolithic cultural material. Finally, red soil forms the top surface. This ranges in thickness between 50 and 200 cm. Mesolithic and Neolithic cultural material occur within this soil layer (Fig. 2).

The cultural material collected from the Gambheeram Valley and its environs consists of stone artefacts characterising Lower, Middle and Upper Palaeolithic, Mesolithic and Neolithic. The material is recovered mostly from the eroded surface. The finished forms include handaxes (47.14%), cleavers (10.00%), discoids (2.86%), Choppers (18.57%), picks (2.14%) and scrapers (15.71%), while cores (34), flakes (45), stone hammers (5), and split blocks of stone (15) constitute the biproducts. Most of the tools are made on flakes. They have wide platforms near the butt. Flake scars are small and shallow, while deep flake scars are occasionally noticed. Handaxes of different shapes are bifacially worked. They have a flat surface (facet like) at one of the lateral sides towards the butt. Some of the tools have a groove across the breadth on the dorsal surface. Choppers are massive and elongated. Cleavers are made on thin flakes. Elongated, pointed and massive tools are identified as picks. On the basis of technique of manufacture these tools are assigned to Late Acheulean phase. Gravel-II is the horizon for this cultural phase. Quartzite, medium to coarse grained and vein quartz are the raw materials. Occasional use of quartz and sandstone are also seen. (Fig. 3).

GAMBHEERAM RIVER VALLEY AND ITS ENVIRONS

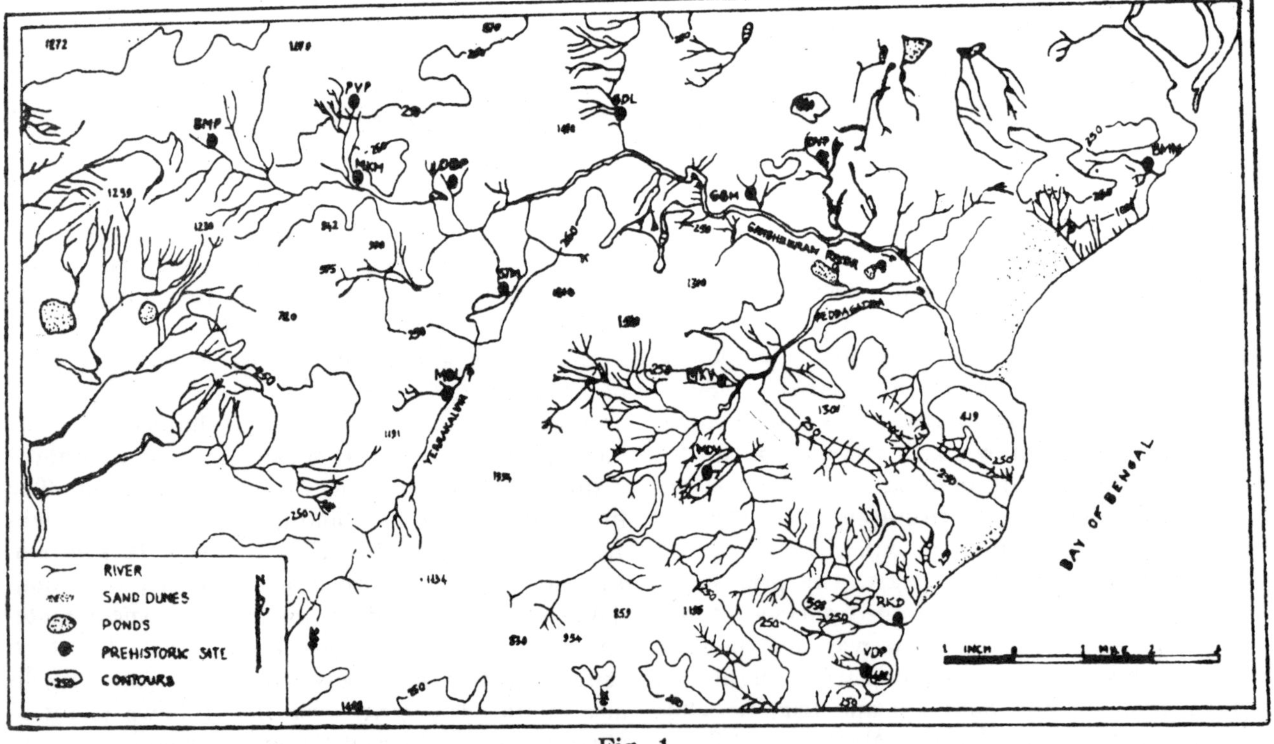

Fig 1

The Lower Palaeolithic cultural material comprises both finished forms (142) and waste (99).

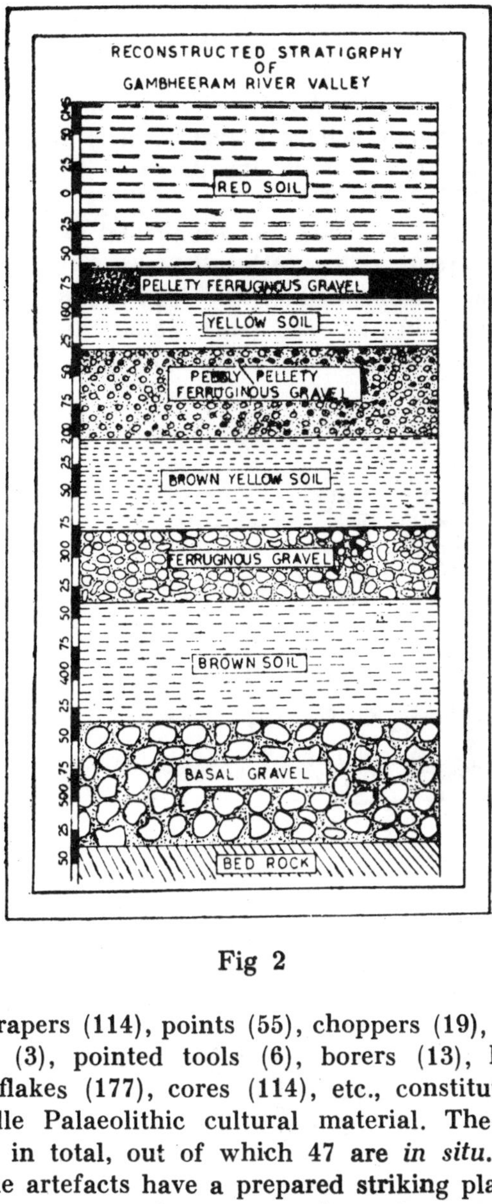

Fig 2

Scrapers (114), points (55), choppers (19), hand-axes (3), pointed tools (6), borers (13), burins (3), flakes (177), cores (114), etc., constitute the Middle Palaeolithic cultural material. The artefacts in total, out of which 47 are *in situ*. Most of the artefacts have a prepared striking platform with one or two facets. A small notch on the dorsal surface at the distal end of the points is conspicuous. This appears to have facilitated hafting. Though the flake element of the acheulean continues in this phase, the size of the flake diminishes, as the method of detaching these flakes is prepared core type. Points fall under leaf (34) and triangle (21) shape. They include simple (39) and tanged (16) specimens. Scrapers (114) are distinguished on the basis of retouched edge into single side (37), double side (11), convex (24), notched (22), side-cum-end (8), end (4), and round (8) scrapers. Medium to fine grained quartzite (46.43%), vein quartz (23.41%), quartz (21.03%), and chert (9.13%) are the raw materials used. Gravel-III is the horizon for this culture.

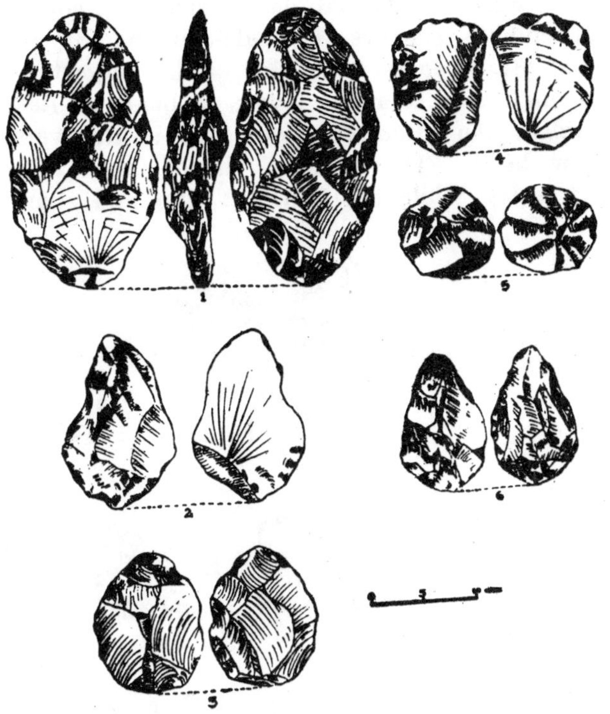

Fig 3

The Upper Palaeolithic of Gambheeram valley is characterised by blade-burin industry. It includes blade tools such as backed blades (124), points (167), burins (73), borers (52), scrapers (164), transverse arrow heads (28) and simple blades (230). However, a few of these tools are made on flakes. The flake elements accounts for 20.41% of the total artefacts. The biproducts are cores, core flakes, flakes and chips. The total artefacts are 1819 in number. Majority of the blades are asymmetrical, while those on quartz are parallel sided. The backed blades include backed points (36) and backed knives (88). Points on blades (102) and flakes (65) constitute 19.93% of the tool kit. They include tanged (72) and simple (95) points. The simple points have a notch on the dorsal surface at the distal end. Burins constitute 8.71% of the finished forms. The burins fall under central (33), bevelled (29), transverse (3), convex (7) and concave (1) categories depending on the position of spalls. Scraper is another predominant tool type and constitute 19..57% of the total tool kit. These are made on blades (110) and flakes (54). The scrapers are further categorised depending on nature of working edge. They are single side (55), double side (52), convex (17), end (8), concave (17), side-cum-end (8), and round (8), scrapers. One side of the majority of the single side scrapers, either on blade or flake is thick. An interesting tool type is transverse arrow head. They are 'U' shaped, with three thick sides, while the fourth is thin and sharp. The thick sides are not blunted. They look like chisels. Chert (41.23%), glassy quartz (5.66%), milky quartz (33.04%), cherty quartz (19.35%) and quartzite (0.71%) are the raw materials exploited. Small pellety gravel (Gravel-IV) underlying the red soil is the horizon for Upper Palaeolithic (Fig. 4).

Mesolithic evidence is found all along the Gambheeram valley. With little exception microliths are associated with 'bad lands'. They are found in the red soil about 70-80 cms. below the surface. Microliths are also recovered

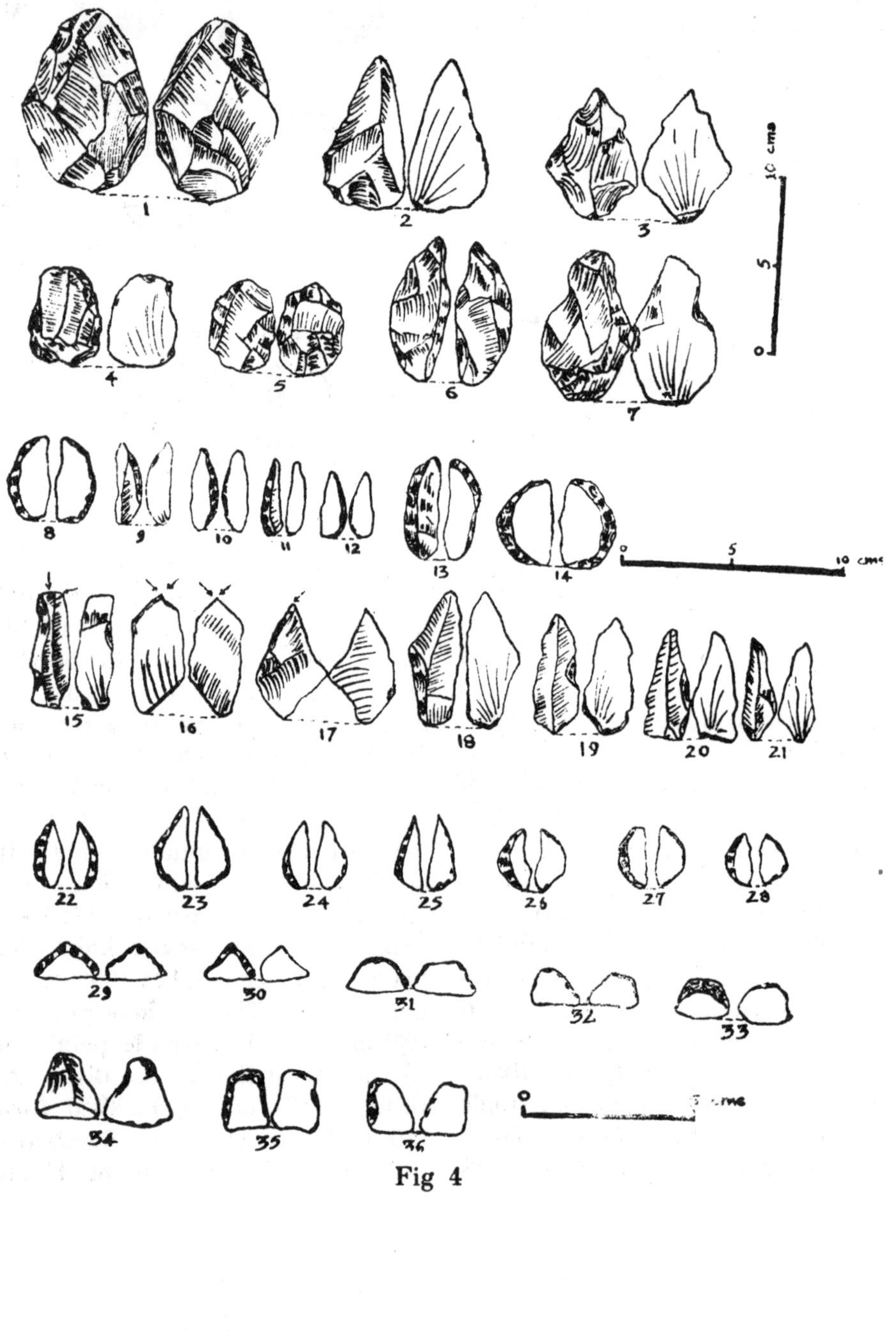

Fig 4

from the ancient beach sands. The collection amounts to 4543. Of these 2498 are finished forms while the rest are biproducts. Backed blades (20.50%), points (12.33%), scrapers (28.18%), chisel edged tools (1.12%), borers (4.88%), burins (3.64%) and simple blades (29.34%) constitute the finished forms. The backed blades include lunates (172), points (170), knives (126), triangles (25) and trapezoids (19). It is surprising to find perfect backed specimens measuring 10 x 5 x 3 mm. The artefacts show improvement in the technique of manufacture from those of Upper Palaeolithic. This is evident in the case of blunted back pieces. Though, there is considerable reduction in the size of these tools, perfection in blunting to get geometric forms is clear. Other than the backed pieces, scrapers and points are the dominant tool types. Retouch on both the surfaces is found on several scrapers. One lateral side is invariably thick among the single side scrapers. Points are distinguished into those with tang (46.75%) and without tang (53.24%). Of these, points on blade account 77.60%. Quartz (74.75%) is the chief raw material, while cherty quartz (10.0%) and chert (15.25%) are occasionally used. The Mesolithic industry of Gambheeram is of geometric and aceramic.

Neolithic evidence has been recorded all along the Gambheeram valley. Trial trenches have revealed the Neolithic horizon at a depth between 50 and 60 cm. below the surface. The cultural material includes ground and polished tools, thin and slender blade tools, mace heads, saddle querns, rubber stones, stone tablets, carnelian beads and pottery.

P. VIJAYA PRAKASH

Deptt. of Anthropology
Andhra University
Waltair

Lalapur: An Acheulian Site in District Banda (UP)

For the reconstruction of the ways of life of Stone Age man, the study of camp or living sites has been emphasized by almost all the prehistorians. Some of the primary sites like Adamgarh, Bhimbetka, Sihawal, Nakjhar-Khurd, Patapara and Bhaghor, Sidhi district, (Sharma and Clark 1980) in Madhya Pradesh, Chirki-Nevasa in Maharashtra, Hunsgi (Paddaya 1977; 1978) and some cave sites in district Karnool of Andhra Pradesh and Lalitpur in Uttar Pradesh were systematically excavated. Attention has also been drawn to the study of open-air sites in understanding geographical setting and environmental evolution of a site. The work of Jacobson (1975:280-297; 1978) in district Raisen and V. D. Misra at Maihar in Satna district of Madhya Pradesh are two examples of this kind.

The stray investigations carried out in a sporadic manner, right from the later half of the nineteenth century, have indicated the archaeological potentiality of district Banda. Against this background, the author carried out explorations in district Banda, which lies between latitudes 24°53′ and 25°55′ N, and longitudes 79°59′ and 81°34′ E. As a result of extensive explorations carried out a number of sites ranging from the Lower Palaeolithic to the Neolithic have been discovered.

In this note, an attempt is made to put the preliminary results of the finds of Lalapur (25°13′ N and 31°9′ E), an Acheulian surface site. The site is situated on the Ohan river in Karwi tahsil of Banda district on Allahabad-Banda road, about 100 km. from Allahabad. The site lies on the northern edge of the extension of the Vindhyan Hills, where the Central Indian Uplands fall away into the low-lying alluvium of the Ganga-Yamuna Doab. The solid geology of the site is marked by the Archaean (Bundelkhand gneiss), the Upper Vindhyan, the Pleistocene and Recent (Holocene) formations. The 'Bundelkhand gneissic rocks' are the earliest formations. The next in succession are the Upper Vindhyan formations composed of fine grained sandstones, shales and lime-stones. Sandstones are by far the most common rocks.

The site experiences typical monsoon climate with the characteristic four months of rainy seasons (July to October), followed by eight months of dry period of winter and summer. The mean annual precipitation varies from 75 to 100 cm. of which 80% falls between July to September. We are well aware that it is misleading to discuss a region only in terms of present day conditions. There is no gravel formations at Lalapur, but silty cliff-sections are to be found at a number of points at the site. Thus it can, reasonably be inferred that at Lalapur, the Ohan Valley has been subjected to climatic fluctuations during the Pleistocene.

The hills in and around the sites are generally covered with stunted jungles. Among the chief trees tendu *(Diosypron melanoxylon)*, sej *(Lagerstreemia parvifolia)*, Saj *(Terminalia Tomentosa)*, achar (*Buchanania latifolia*), dhawa (*Anogeissus latifolia)*, bamboo (*Dendroolamus strictus*) deserve special mention. Bushes of Khair (*Acacia katechu)* and ber *(Zizyphus jijuba)* are also very common. Among the sporadic trees, mention may be made of mango (*Mangifera indica*), banyan *(Ficus bengelenis)*, Jamun *(Eugenia jambolana)*, neem *(Azadirachta indica)* and Chhul or dhak *(Butea frandosa)*.

Like the flora, the fauna is also quite rich and diverse. Antelopes, gazella, wild bears, jackals, foxes, rabbits and porcupine, etc., are common wild beasts, Carnivores are present but are of rather low density.

MODE OF OCCURRENCE: The lower Palaeolithic artifacts have, mostly been collected from the eroded bed of Jariha nullah which joins the Ohan near Lalapur. Jariha *nullah* is a recent ravine situated behind the Maharshi Valmiki Sanskrit Pathashala and in the northern side of the Asawara Devi hlils. The Ohan, a perennial tributary of the Paisuni, the latter a tributary of the Yamuna, at Lalapur flows today, through a narrow and restricted channel but indeed, beneath the hills towards the north, the dry course of what must have been once a large stream, can still be discerned. Only a few Lower Palaeolithic tools have been collected from the southern side of the hills.

INDUSTRY : In all 115 artefacts, for distribution see table, have been collected from the site.

The tools have been collected mainly from surface in slightly disturbed archaeological context. Some of the tools appear to have been worn out or weathered surface due to association with the reddish clay. Otherwise, the tools are not rolled or abraded. The artifacts exhibiting stone or hand hammer characteristics are rare in the collection; the majority of the tools indicate an overall preponderance of cylinder hammer-technique. The tools exhibit small, and tiny, shallow flake-scars with symmetrical outlines, thin sections and even surface. The fined-grained grey/brown quartzite has been employed as chief raw-material. The tools are fashioned either on cores or flakes but a substantial number of cleavers are fashioned on chunk pieces.

Sl. No.	Units	Numbers	Percentage
1	Cleavers	42	36.53
2	Handaxes	14	12.17
3	Scrapers	12	10.44
4	Flakes	10	8.69
5	Cores	14	12.17
6	Waste	23	20.00
	Total	115	100.00%

MATERIAL ANALYSIS

Systematic classification of artifacts is essential for proper study. Following the works of D.A. Roe (1964: 245-269; 1968: 1-82) some metrical analysis of cleavers, handaxes and scrapers is attempted. These measurements and indices will help us to gather certain information concerning an artifact group.

CLEAVERS

There are 42 cleavers. Flakes seem to have been taken from the unprepared cores. However, in some examples the front shows a series of scar-beds along the margin directed towards the central area, which indicate the striking of the flake from the prepared cores.

These are basically parallel-sided, convergent, divergent. These may be further classified as follows, taking into consideration the trend of butt and the position of the edges in relation to the long axis:

a) 1— Round butt and oblique edge,
   2— Round butt and convex/splayed edge,
   3— Round butt and straight edge.

b) 1— Pointed butt and oblique/guillotine edge,
   2— Pointed butt and concave edge,
   3— Pointed butt and straight edge.

c) 1— Truncated convergent butt and oblique edge,
   2— Truncated convergent butt and straight edge.

Some specimens are subjected to trimmings on both the longitudinal margins to regularize the shape of the tools.

The working edge in some specimens makes an angle of 76°-80° range with the major axis. Some specimens belong to the 81°-85° range and the rest to 86°-90° range.

Length:

The length of the cleavers has a range of variation from 11 cm to 21 cm. These values are divided into class interval of 10 mm.

Length of Cleavers: Lalapur-Banda (U.P.)

Length in cm	Number	Percentage
10.1-11	6	14.30
11.1-12	5	11.90
12.1-13	3	07.14
13.1-14	8	19.05
14.1-15	4	09.52
15.1-16	3	07.14
16.1-17	'4	11.90
17.1-18	3	07.14
18.1-19	x	—
19.1-20	3	07.14
20.1-21	2	04.77
Total	42	100.00%

Breadth: The breadth of the cleavers ranges from 6 cm to 17 cm. The table given below shows the frequency distribution of each class interval.

Breadth in cm	Number	Percentage
6.1-7	6	14.30
7.1-8	7	16.67
8.1-9	4	09.52
9.1-10	3	07.14
10.1-11	5	11.90
11.1-12	12	28.57
12.1-13	2	04.77
13.1-14	2	04.77
14.1-15	x	—
15.1-16	x	—
16.1-17	1	02.36
Total	42	100.00%

In contrast to length values, the breadth values have rather a limited range of variation. The highest proportion of breadth values falls in the class 11.1-12 cm and nearly 60% are confined to three class intervals, namely, 6.1-7 cm, 7.1-8 cm and 11.1-12 cm.

Thickness: The thickness has a range varying from 2 cm to 8 cm.

Thickness in cm	Number	Percentage
2.1-3	2	4.77
3.1-4	11	26.19
4.1-5	15	35.71
5.1-6	7	16.67
6.1-7	6	4.30
7.1-8	1	2.36
Total	42	100.00%

The most frequent thickness has a value between 4.1-5 cm and the next frequent thickness is represented by the class interval of 3.1-4 cm and thus nearly 60% of the thickness values are confined to these two successive class intervals.

HANDAXES:

The handaxes number only fourteen. These include specimens made on cores and flakes. (a) Ovates—4, (b) cordates—3, (c) subtriangular forms—7.

Heavy and thick specimens are conspicuous by their absence. Handaxes are generally thin and their cross-sections are oval or biconvex or lenticular. The tip-end is either pointed, rounded or spatulate.

SCRAPERS (ON CORES AND FLAKES):

These are twelve in number, side scrapers (6), round scrapers (4) and end-scrapers (2).

FLAKES:

There are only ten flakes; irregular, divergent and parallel-sided, mostly with plain, unfaceted platforms. Some specimens show signs of scarring and bruising along the edges.

CORES:

These are fourteen, pyramidal, discoidal globular and formless.

In India, unlike Africa, we are still lacking precise and reliable stratigraphic evidence for distinguishing the sub-cultural phases of Acheulian. Some scholars thus (Joshi & Marathe, 1976: 1-12) have made an attempt to resolve this problem by resorting to statistical methods. While analysing the significance of Cleavers in Indian Acheulian industries, Joshi (1940:39-40) observes that Cleavers generally predominate in the late Phase of Acheulian. It is interesting that even in Africa (Clark 1969) the cleavers predominate over handaxes in the Acheulian transition. Cleavers predominate over handaxes (3:1) at Lalapur also. The Lower Palaeolithic industries from the adjoining regions of Lalitpur and Maihar (Mishra 1977:1-21) are also cleaver dominated Acheulian in character. Considering the quantitative characters and techno-typological features, the Acheulian assemblage from Lalapur may, tentatively be assigned to the Upper Acheulian tradition in India.

University of Allahabad
Allahabad

J. N. PANDEY

REFERENCES

Clark, J.D. 1969 *The Kalambo Falls Prehistoric Site*, Cambridge University Press.

Jacobson, J. 1975 Early Stone Age Habitation sites in Malwa, *Proceedings of the American Philosophical Society* 119.

1978 Acheulian surface sites in Central India, Paper read at the *Seminar on Recent Advances in Indo-Pacific Pre-history* held at Poona from 19th — 22nd December, 1978.

Joshi, R.V. 1970 Significance of Cleavers in Indian Acheulian Industries *Archaeocivilization* (Antiquities Nationalet, Internationales, Nouveile Series) 7-8.

Joshi, R.V. and A.R. Marathe 1976 Metrical Analysis of Hand axes from Chikri on Pravara (western Maharashtra, India) *Puratattva* 8.

Mishra, V.D. 1977 Lithic Industries of Maihar, Satna (M.P.) A Preliminary Study, *Some Aspects of Indian Archaeology*, Allahabad.

Roe, D.A. 1964 The British Lower and Middle Palaeolithic — Some Problems, Methods of study and Results, PPS 30, 1968. British Lower and Middle Palaeolithic Handaxe groups, *PPS* 34.

The Alleged Upper Palaeolithic Bone Mother Goddess from Belan

The sole purpose of this note is to reopen the question of identification of a bone object found 'associated with the Upper Palaeolithic assemblage in the Belan Valley' of Uttar Pradesh. It was discovered by Prof. G. R. Sharma and his associates Pers. communication R. K. Varma; pl. I.

Although even at that stage strong doubts were expressed by practically every one who had some experience of handling such objects from European sites, yet the worse happened when the Indian and foreign delegates to the International Pacific Conference held at Pune in 1978 disagreed with Prof. Sharma on this issue. Since all these opinions remained unprinted a myth has been perpetuated and I feel it my duty to put the things straight.

The object in question is pure and simple harpoon so commonly found at Upper Palaeolithic sites on the continent. The two largely preserved projections in the centre are barbs and not hands of the goddess. That there was another set of these barbs also at the base of the extant top is more than clear in the sharp cut-marks and the remaining incipient projections. The drooping nature of the barbs should not make us close our eyes to the obvious. The shouldered tenon hardly needs any comments for experts. My own experience in handling such objects in the museums of France now makes me come out with my opinion, which incidentally most of the prehistorians in the world share.

National Museum
New Delhi

S. P. GUPTA

Indus Sealing From Hulas

The sealing, excavated under the direction of K. N. Dikshit of the Archaeological Survey of India from the Harappan site of Hulas, district Saharanpur, Uttar Pradesh, is an impression from a rectangular stamp-seal. The text comprises 3 signs and is complete. The line is to be read from right to left as usual. The script is in the mature Harappan style. (pl 1).

The 3 signs are (from the right) No. 249, 169 and 342 in the sign list. The text is already known from No. 2600 (Mackay 1937 : No. 600), No. 5404 (Vats 1940 : No. 1241) and No. 6128 (Mackay 1943 : pl. LI-28) respectively from Mohenjo-daro, Harappa and Chanhu-daro. The text also occurs on the reverse side of a copper tablet from Mohenjo-daro (No. 2912).

If the middle sign (No. 169) is taken as a variant of sign (No. 162) the text can also be compared with No. 4650 (Vats 1940 : 650) from Harappa.

There are also a large number of texts (about 80) in which the present inscription occurs as part of longer lines (Mahadevan 1977 : pl. 624-627).

Indian Express
Madras

IRAVATHAM MAHADEVAN

REFERENCES

Mackay, E. J. H. 1938 *Further Excavations at Mohenjo-.daro,* Delhi.
1943 *Chanhu-daro Excavations* 1935-36, American Oriental Society, New Haven.

Mahadevan, Iravatham 1977 *Indus Script, Texts Concordance and Tables,* New Delhi.

Vats, Madho Sarup 1940 *Excavations at Harappa,* Calcutta.

Dangwada (Ujjain)-A Chalcolithic Site

The ancient site of Dangwada is situated on the northern bank of the river Chambal, about one km west of the village Dangwada on the Ingoria-Indore road and 26 km from Ujjain via Ingonia in Tehsil Badnagar. To ascertain the extent of the Kayatha and Malwa chalcolithic cultures, this extensive site was subjected to excavations jointly by the Directorate of Archaeology and Museums, Government of Madhya Pradesh and Vikram University, Ujjain, the author and V. S. Wakankar being its co-directors. The surface finds from this site included sturdy Kayatha ware, microliths, painted black-on-red pottery, punch marked coins, and other early historical antiquities. Further, the presence of a Siva temple, called Boreshvar Temple, originally built during the Paramara period, but repaired subsequently, indicated that the site might yield a long sequence of cultures. The work of two seasons (1978-79 and 1979-80) here has proved beyond doubt that Dangwada was a very important centre of activities during the Chalcolithic period.

The 'L' shaped mound, major part of which appears to have been washed away by the river, is 15 m high, 150 m wide and 340 m long. Eight trenches were laid, two of which were on the two slopes of the mound.

The following is the sequence of the cultures as worked out on the basis of the excavations.

PERIOD I

The average thickness of the habitational deposit in the heart of the mound is about 5.45 m. It is divisible into two sub-phases, viz. I A and 1 B, representing Ahar and Malwa Chalcolithic Cultures, with a thickness of 1.10 m and 4.35 m, respectively. Period—IA (Ahar Chalcolithic)

Since the excavations were confined to an area measuring 2 x 2 m in DGW VII and 3 x 2.5 m in DGW I, the number of finds was limited. It is distinguished by the presence of twelve microliths, mostly parallel-sided blades and a few cores, meagre copper, three stone pestles, a ball and some potsherds of painted black-on-red, incised grey wares and lustrous red ware. The white painted designs on black-and-red ware comprise of simple bands, straight and wavy lines, strokes and dots (Fig. 1). Painted black and red has a pre dominance over the plain black and red ware. The types represented in black and red ware are deep bowls and dishes. The designs on the painted black and red are also restricted, viz. simple bands around the body, small vertical strokes on the exterior of the rims and occasionally on the interior and hatched diamonds. The plain red ware has in most cases corrugated shouldered vases.

Terracotta naturalistic bulls and archaic bull forms auguments the finds. From a deposit of 40 cm in DGW I in Layer (32) as many as 12 but figurines of various types have been picked up. From DGW VII a large number of animal bones, a pair of burnt animal teeth and a jaw were recovered. The two pot-burials in DGW III layer (12) yielded two urns of burnished red ware with corrugated shoulders and applique decorations. These pots contained a few burnt bones, possibly human. The burial rested on the virgin black soil. A few microliths were also picked up from the vicinity of the burial.

No structural remains except a floor consisting of small pebbles and measuring 1.00 x 0.70 m was exposed in DGW I layer (29). Period IB (Malwa Chalcolithic)

The maximum deposit of this sub-period in DGW I is 4.30 m. The remaining two trenches, i.e., DGW IV and VII being on the two slopes of the mound, have an average thickness of about 3.00 m only. Since the DGW VI was not excavated upto the natural soil, its total deposit is not known. The excavated area of DGW IV, VII covered 2 x 7 m and 14 x 11 m respectively. It is from these two trenches that the maximum number of finds and structural remains of outstanding merit have been brought to light. This sub-period has been divided into four sub-phases.

I B—(i) : It yielded only typical Malwa chalcolithic pottery along with a limited quantity of the Ahar pottery and microliths, and stone objects, like querns, pestles, balls, hammer stones. No structural remains were noticed.

I B—(ii) : The maximum number of finds and structural remains came from this phase. The most notable is a shrine measuring 1.20m in length and 0.70 m in width, and made of burnt bricks duly plastered with mud. Although no objects were found in the shrine itself, the presence of a few terracotta objects, symbolic of mother goddess and a few mini-lamps were found lying in close proximity of the shrine near the north-eastern corner of DGW VII. At a distance of 1.15 m towards the south of this shrine, was 1.15 m towards the south of this shrine, was exposed a sacrificial pit, rectangular in shape and measuring 1.95x1.50 m. The pit was full of charcoal. Thick burnt logs of wood were seen placed on all the four sides, which must have been originally plastered with mud. Another spectacular discovery at DGW VII was a structural complex possibly of religious significance. Here a small chamber contained square and hollow pot stands, jars and other pottery types. Another room adjacent to the above had an opening made of mud pillars surmounted by a round arch. As still larger and rectangular room of which a number a post-holes were exposed in DGW IV yielded painted and plain pottery, charcoal and charred grains, terracotta bulls of various types, steatite bead, etc. The ceramic industries of this sub-phase are almost the same as in sub-phase (i) except that the Ahar types are very few in number and the painted designs are more elaborate and the animal designs make their appearance.

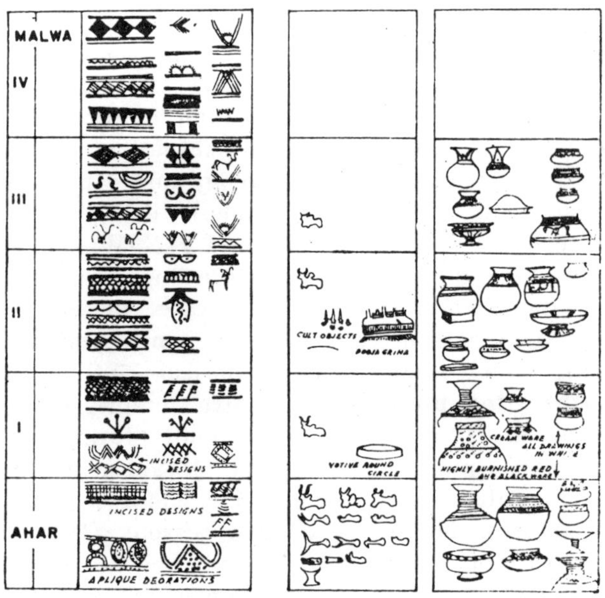

Fig 1

I B (iii) : This sub-phase is noted for an elliptical structure standing on wooden pots (Fig. 2) and a kitchen complex containing besides a few posts, one terracotta ladle with a perforated handle and painted on its exterior from DGW VII and a copper chisel, a terracotta mould for copper axes and another, kitchen complex from DGW IV. Four storage jars containing charred grains were also recovered from here. The important finds of this deposits are bone tools, including a chisel, terracotta ear-lobe, and stone and terracotta ball (marbles). There is a higher percentage and variety of painted designs on pottery.

I B (iii): This sub-phase is noted for an elliptical deposit, going to a depth 3.72 m the exact nature and extent of which could not be ascertained. Towards the south of this deposit was a dump. Whether it could be a part of some rampart or a bastion is a matter of conjecture only. A rectangular house measuring 5 x 6 m standing on wooden posts in DGW IV also belongs to this sub-phase. The painted bull designs on pottery are conspicuous by their absence. Similarly, the fabric of the pottery in general is poorer than that at the earlier sub-phase. The painted designs are confined to simple bands, wavy lines and occasional hill symbol. The site has suffered from large scale conflagrations.

The discovery of a terracotta mould for casting bronze axes, abundant use of terracotta bulls and bull forms, besides the figurines of terracotta mother goddess, a triple shrine (Fig. 3), *yajna-kundas* and a large number of houses, including an apsidal structure (Fig. 2) are some of the outstanding features of this site. It is proved beyond doubt that the chalcolithic people of Dangwada performed *yajnas,* as testified by the sacrificial pits, which were quite elaborate. It may be worth recalling that Navdatoli also yielded such an evidence (Sankalia *et al* 1971: pl. IVB).

Unlike Navdatoli, wher circular plans of houses were very common, Dangwada people preferred rectangular plans. But sometimes apsidal ended houses were also built. Mud wall became a regular feature with an average thickness of 20 cm. The roof stood on wooden posts, which were usually of square section, their foundation being very deep like eastern Malwa, whereas at Besnagar (Range mound) lumps of clay were used to strengthen the posts.

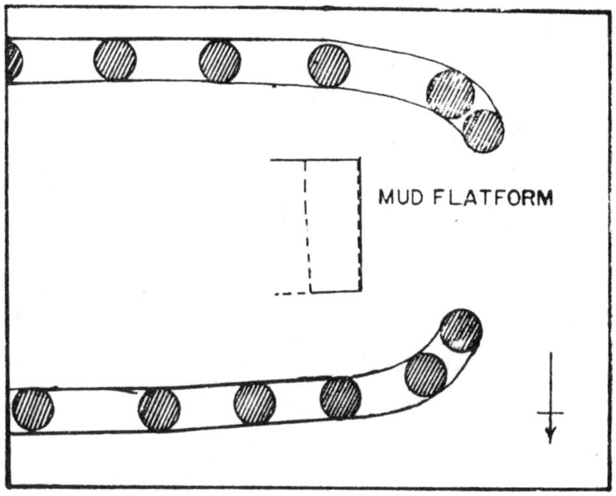

Fig 2

Recent excavations at Runija (Ujjain), conducted during 1980-81, also a joint work of the author and V. S. Wakankar, indicated still more vigorous architectural activities in the upper levels of Malwa chalcolithic deposits, as evident from a huge mud wall, with very thick wooden beams and still thicker mud roof. Here too, the chalcolithic phase came to end with a large scale conflagration.

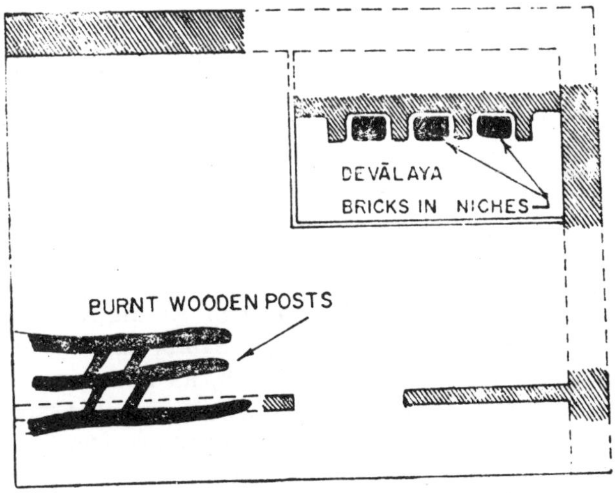

Fig 3

It is, however, surprising that Kayatha culture which is available in many sites of this region, is conspicuous by its absence and that chalcolithic deposits here have only Ahar and Malwa wares.

However, two post-cremation burials from period. IA (DG WIII) are noteworthy, so also a potsherd carrying a painting of *Pashupati* (?) in black-on-red and a pot-stand with incised animal figures on the exterior.

Thus, Dangwada excavations have not only yielded information on the architectural activities of the chalcolithic people of Malwa, particularly the apsidal plan, but also given an indication that their religious activities were much nearer to those of Vedic Aryans.

Archaeological Survey of India,
New Delhi.

M. D. KHARE

REFERENCES

Sankalia, H. D., S. B. Deo and Z. D. Ansari 1971 *Chalcolithic Navdatoli, The Excavations at Navdatoli 1957-59*, Poona-Baroda.

The Ganeshwar Culture-An Appraisal

The village Ganeshwar (District Sikar, Rajasthan) is about 10 km south-east of Neem-ka-Thana. The site which is situated to the north-east of the village, is quite denuded and is rising about 3 to 4 m from the surrounding plains. The pottery is strewn all over the surface in an area of about 200 x 200 m. The mound slopes towards a low lying area which accumulates the rain water. Locally, this tank is called Kulhade-ka-Johad. In 1978 an extensive survey was carried out along the banks of river Kantli from Neem-ka-Thana to Pilani lying in districts Sikar and Jhunjhunu (*IAR* 1977-78: 46-49). During our survey the site of Ganeshwar which was explored in 1977 by the Department of Archaeology and Museums, Government of Rajasthan, was also visited.

The topography of Ganeshwar region is dotted with the hillocks of Aravalli ranges and sand dunes which form the part of Thar desert. These hillocks provide drainage to rivulets originating in this region to north through Kantli river, to the north-east through Sota, Sahibi and Dohan and also to south-west direction. As the source of these non-perrenial rivulets is in a limited area, the deflection of their minor currents from one divide to another cannot be ruled out. This tri-junction is important in other ways also as to its north lies the settlements of the pre-Harappans and Harappans, to its north-east the settlements of the Ochre-Coloured Ware and to its south-west of the Ahar Culture.

The published data on Ganeshwar is inadequate, as nowhere, the excavator has mentioned about the occupational thickness of the deposit and the area tapped for the excavations. Other details such as structures etc. are also not known (Agrawal 1978 : 123; 1981 : 59-62; 1982 : 125-134). In 1979 the excavations at Ganeshwar revealed a red ware industry having exterior decorations. The pottery is treated with drab red slip which in certain cases has peeled off due to the exposure to climatic conditions. In the absence of any published data we are using here the types picked up in our exploration (Fig. 1).

Agrawal (1981 : 59-63) has reported a variety of Copper objects such as arrow-heads, rings, bangles, spear-heads, chisels, fish-hooks, rods, nails, spiral headed pins, blades and flat celts (from the writings of the excavator, it is not clear what has been reported from excavations and what has been collected from the godown of Sub-Treasury, Neem-ka-Thana). Most of these objects contain 97% of pure copper and are totally devoid of tin content. However, tin is present, 1% and more, as deliberate alloying material both in Harappan and Central Indian Chalcolithic cultures. But in copper-hoard objects there is no tin (Nautiyal *et al* 1981 : 48-51). A microlithic industry was also noticed at Ganeshwar, but the details of the types have not been reported. A round terracotta cake was also noticed (Agrawal 1982). However, it is not clear from the details whether there is a thumb impression in the centre, a characteristic of Harappan terracotta cakes.

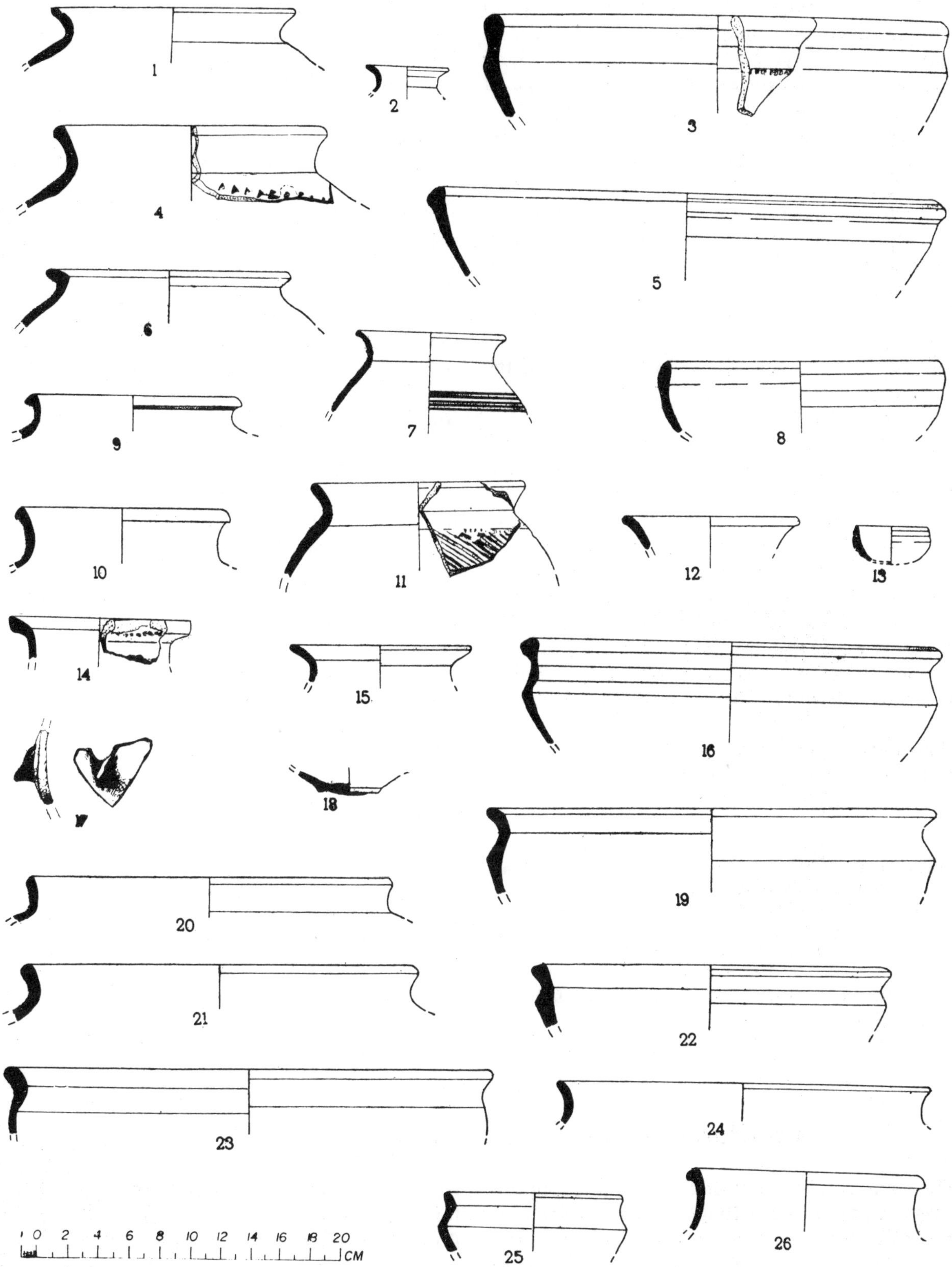
1
2
3
4
5
6
7
8
9
10
11
12
13
14
15
16
17
18
19
20
21
22
23
24
25
26
1 0 2 4 6 8 10 12 14 16 18 20
CM

Fig 1

The pre-Harappan and Harappan fabric were found quite different when compared with Ganeshwar. The potforms and incised designs of Ganeshwar have no parallels in Indus region. The Ganeshwar culture has nothing to do even with the so-called Ochre Coloured Ware of Upper Ganga-Yamuna *doab*. The main types in Ganga Valley (from Upper *doab :* type site Ambakheri) such as jar with horizontally splayed out rim, dish-on-stand with drooping rim, bowl like lid with central knob and everted rim, basin with undercut rim and ring-stand are absent at Ganeshwar. In central *doab,* Atranjikhera, no doubt, has some typological affinities but here the pottery has not been found alongwith copper objects and microliths.

Ahar, (Sankalia *et al* 1969) Bagor (Misra 1973 : 295-305), and Kayatha (Ansari and Dhavalikar 1975) are the type sites representing different stages of cultural development in their respective regions. At Ahar from Period IA to Period IC, a red ware industry having incised decorations on outer side is present. Typologically and from incised motifs point of view this pottery is similar to Ganeshwar. It has also revealed a large number of copper objects especially flat celts and a limited number of microliths. Bagor has also yielded a similar complex but there the pottery is handmade. The arrow-heads too draw parallels from Ganeshwar. The site at Kayatha is also important as the pottery, copper objects and microliths have similarity with Ganeshwar complex.

It may be mentioned that the type bowl with an externally carinated shoulder is confined only at the sites of Kayatha, Ahar, Malwa and Jorwe cultures. This type never found place in Haryana and western Uttar Pradesh or in northern Rajasthan representing the contemporary distribution zone of Indus Civilization. The incised motifs are present at Atranjikhera, but the nearest source for the contact appears to be Bara culture which is well known for its incised design. The Ganeshwar people while moving towards Ahar came in contact with the users of painted black and red ware, already noticed with the Harappans in Gujarat. This comparative study also brought forth a point that the Ganeshwar culture did not survive in isolation but flourished alongwith Aharians and other indeginous people in the riverine valleys of Banas and Chambal. As it has not been studied stratigraphically in relation to other cultures, it may be placed somewhere in the middle of the third millennium B.C. till the ^{14}C and TL dates are not forthcoming.

Archaeological Survey of India
New Delhi

K. N. DIKSHIT
A. K. SINHA

REFERENCES

Agrawal, R. C. 1981 Recent Explorations in Rajasthan, *Man & Environment* V.

Agrawal, R. C. and Vijay Kumar 1982 Ganeshwar Jodhpura Culture: New Traits in Indian Archaeology, *Harappan Civilization—A Contemporary Perspective* (ed) Gregory L. Possehl, New Delhi, Bombay, Calcutta, Oxford.

Ansari, Z. D. and M. K. Dhavalikar 1975 *Excavations at Kayatha,* Poona.

Indian Archaeology—A Review 1977-78.

Misra, V. N. 1973 A New Prehistoric Ceramic from Rajasthan,*East and West* (New Series) 23 (3-4), Rome.

Nautiyal *et al* 1981 Some New Analyses on the Protohistoric Copper Artifacts, *Man & Environment* V.

Sankalia, H. D. *et al* 1969 *Excavation at Ahar* (Tambavati), Poona.

Pre-Harappan Pottery From Distt. Saharanpur, U.P.

The eastern most limit of the Harappan culture extends at present upto Hulas in District Saharanpur, which covers the northern-most part of the plains of the Ganga-Yamuna *doab* in Uttar Pradesh. The area of this district is shaped like a triangle with its base on the south. This triangular formation is again divided by river Hindon, which flows from the north to the south, into almost two equal triangles. A number of small channels and streams, old and new, cut the land and flow through the region. Situated between two mighty rivers, the Ganga and the Yamuna, the fertile land of this district attracted settlers from very early times. More than seventy habitational sites have been located during the course of explorations carried out by the author and his colleagues during the sixties. These are mainly located in the central and the western parts of the districts. The cultural milieu suggests that these sites ranged from the Harappan to the late-Harappan phase.

In the present state of our knowledge, the pre-Harappan or Kalibangan I Culture is available in the east upto Dhansa, near Nazafgarh in the Union territory of Delhi. So far as District Saharanpur is concerned, it has been *terra incognita* in respect of the existence of 'pre-Harappan' culture. However, recently the author got an opportunity to re-examine the entire material collected by him during explorations in that area. During this process he found some 'pre-Harappan' pot-sherds along with Harappan and Late Harappan material from Naya-Bans in Nakur Tehsil, and a few at other sites in the district.

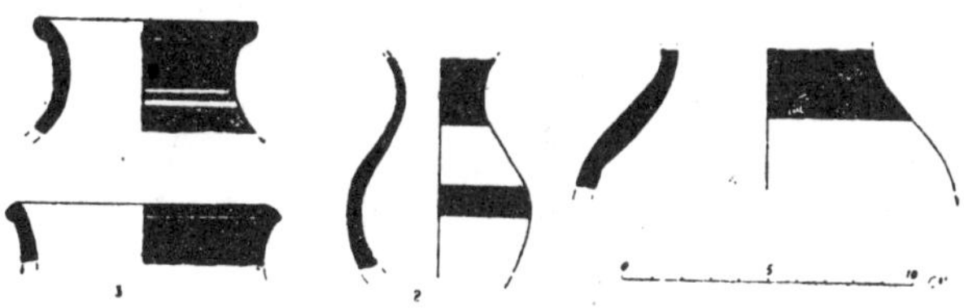

Fig 2

Naya-Bans is situated about 4 km south of Nakur, which is about 28 km south-west of Saharanpur. The site is overlooking in the west, the low lying flat lands of Yamuna Khadar, which has been cut into two by the road coming from Nakur. A good quantity of Harappan pottery was picked up from here. However, a few of the pot-sherds did not fit well into Harappan ceramic assemblage and the identity of these remained elusive till the recent examination.

The evidence provided by Naya-Bans regarding the occupation of land between the Ganga and Yamuna, by the people who may be called 'pre-Harappans' is no doubt meagre at this stage, but it calls for thorough investigation.

DESCRIPTION OF POTTERY FROM NAYA-BANS

1. Fragment of a miniature vase in dull red ware with out-turned rim, painted in black. A broad horizontal band on concave neck; completely oxidized core, of fine fabric. Surface collection.
2. Miniature vase of dull red ware, with concave neck and globular body, painted in black showing horizontal bands on neck and shoulder. Incompletely oxidized core, of medium fabric, showing a creamish slip. Surface collection.
3. Fragmentary vase of bright red ware with slightly out-turned rim, painted in black showing a thick horizontal band on the neck; completely oxidized core, of fine fabric. Surface collection.
4. Fragmentary jar of bright red ware painted in black with thick band on neck and bulbous body; completely oxidized core, of fine fabric showing bright red slip. Surface collection.

Archaeological Survey of India
New Delhi

SHANKAR NATH

Khatoli-A Protohistoric Site in Haryana

Khatoli (Lat. 28° 5' N., Long. 76° 15' E), in district Mahindragarh is located on Delhi-Jaipur road, at a distance of 85 m from Delhi. The mound touches the eastern bank of the river Sahibi.

This single culture site measures 35 m x 35 m and is nearly 2 m higher than the surrounding ground level. A trial trench, measuring 2 m x 2 m, was laid in the centre of the mound. It revealed 1.60 m deposit running through six layers. Layer (1) that forms the top loose humus, is characterised by light brown sand with patches of greyish clay. The pottery is mainly a coarse red ware; the main types being vases, *handis* with and without perforation, and basins. Layer (2), also light brown in colour, is composed of sand, clay, charred bone pieces and charcoal bits. Layer (3) is dark brown in colour and is composed of clayey earth, compact in texture. The main finds include pottery charcoal bits, terracotta pieces, charred

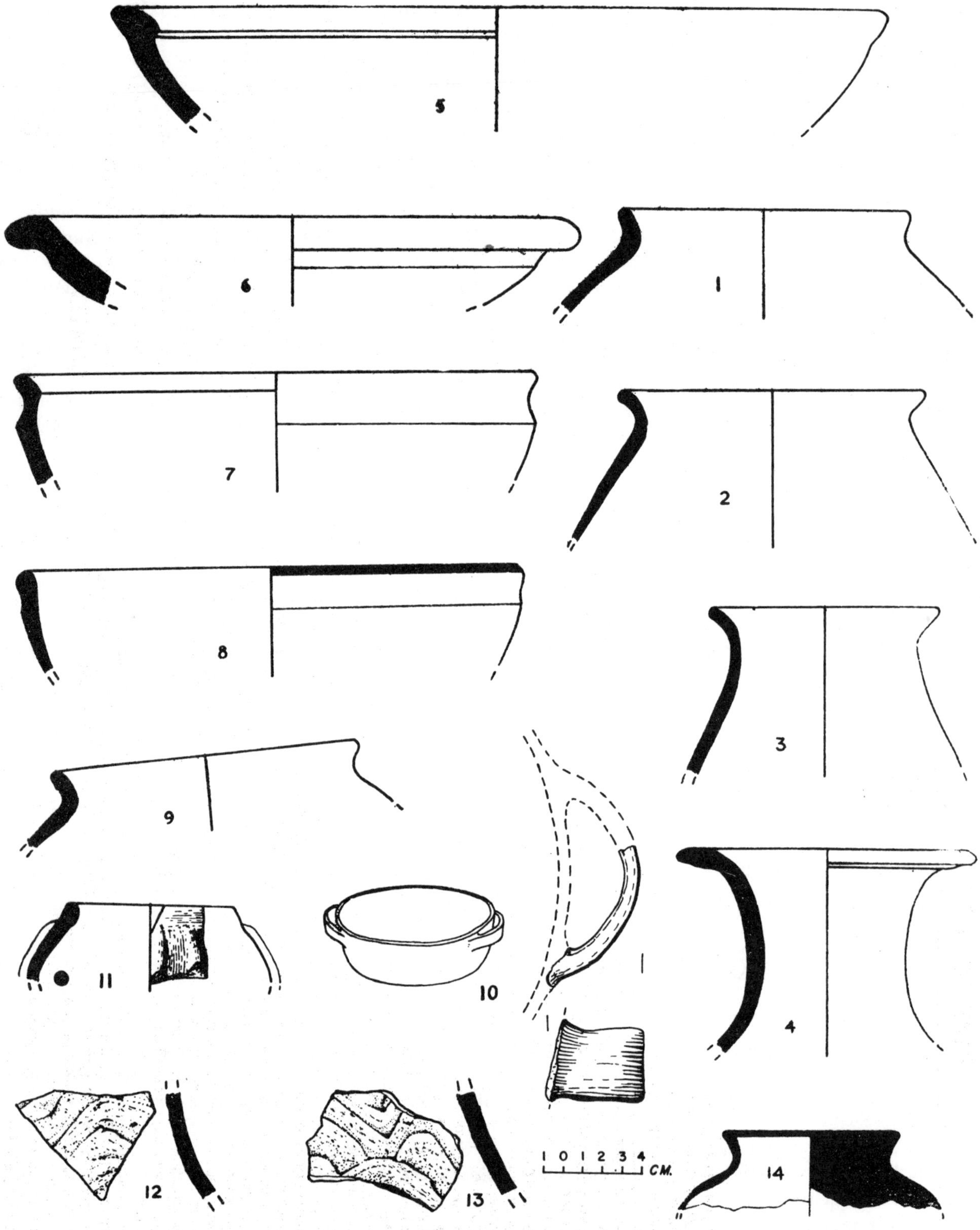

Fig 1

bones, stone pieces and beads. The plain tarracotta cakes and stone pieces could have been used in preparing the floors of the houses. The antiquities include a bronze ring and a hook, tubular faience beads, beads of jasper, and pieces of terracotta cakes, a few of which bear finger impressions in the centre. The pottery includes red ware and grey ware. The red ware includes vases with out-turned rim having a black painted band on the top of the rim. The paintings also include loop pattern and simple bands. The main types are *handis* and bowls. The lower part of some of the vases are ribbed, and also have triangular incised-pattern on the ribs, probably executed with nail. A few thick grey ware sherds have also come from this layer. Pieces of *handis,* small vases and bowls on black-and-red ware were also noticed in this layer. Layer (4) is darker and more compact than that of layer (3). The finds include stone pieces, terracotta cakes, some bearing finger impressions, chunks of burnt clay with reed impression. A few bronze objects, e.g., hooks were also found in the layer. This layer yielded examples of red ware and coarse red ware. The red ware bears brown slip and is well fired. The paintings comprise of black horizontal bands and leaf patterns. The type are vases with splayed rims, platters, miniature *handis,* handles, etc. The coarse red ware types are bowls, basins and *handis.* The incision comprise of oblique nail impressions on the ribbed bands on the belly of the pot, leaf pattern, checked designs, and simple incised lines. The white painted black-and-red ware showing fork pattern has also been found, though in this layer in much less quantity. Bowls of thick grey ware variety have also been noticed. Layer (5) and (6) comprise of pinkish, sandy and yellowish loose sand, respectively. Layer (6) has some river deposit. The pottery in these two layers is rolled and as such it is a re-deposited material. The pottery of layer (5) includes plain coarse red ware, burnished red ware, black-and-red ware. The plain coarse red ware types include vases with out-turned rim and vases with splayed rim. The decoration on the pot comprise of horizontal incised lines topped by roughly painted horizontal bands. The two horizontal bands were crossed by oblique bands at regular intervals. This also include rim of perforated vase, having black painted oblique lines. Basins and *handis* were also noticed. The burnished red ware types are vases, bowls, basins, and *handis.* The black-and-red ware has also been recovered in equal quantity, the main types being platters, basins and bowls having paintings, executed in grey pigment against a black surface. The lower part of the coarse red ware have rusticated and ribbed lower surfaces, the ribs being decorated with nail impressions. A few pots have also incised designs which comprise of opposed triangles. Below this is the natural soil.

It is clear from the foregoing account that the layers (3) and (4) represent the occupational deposit of the protohistoric men. Some types, mainly vases with splayed rims, perforated *handis,* pieces of tarracotta cakes bearing finger impressions, faience and jasper beads may show that they belong to the Late Harappan phase. The wares like white painted black-and-red ware, Cream slipped ware and others show that culture influences penetrated into this region from south Rajasthan, across the Aravallis. The early dwellers lived in huts plastered with clay, as is indicated by clay chunks bearing reed impression. The work executed was limited in nature and is still in progress. The evidence has to be corroborated by trial digs at other sites also.

Archaeolgical Survey of India
New Delhi

R. P. SHARMA

Harappan Furnaces

The purpose of this note is to examine the use and the construction of Harappan furnaces found at Mohenjodaro, Harappa, Chanhudaro, Lothal, Tarkhan-wala-Dera, Sarangpur, Kotla-Nihang Khan and Hulas. There are several kinds of furnaces and ovens which can be divided into two broad types :

1. Intermittent

2. Continuous

They occur in different forms, such as oval, oblong, circular and pear-shaped. Some are raised with mud bricks and some are cut into the natural soil. A fine paste of clay is applied for smoothness along the walls of the pit. Generally, these types of furnace will be jutting out nearly 7 to 9 cm above the ground level. Oval shaped furnaces are more common.

From Mohenjodaro Mackay (Mackay 1976) found a quantity of copper ore in small pieces together with a little piece of lead and it is quite possible that a metal-smith worked here with a furnace in close vicinity.

From Harappa, sixteen furnaces, all situated in trench IV, mound F, were discovered (Vats 1940). They are of three kinds :

(a) Part of round pottery jar.
(b) Cylindrical pits dug in the ground with or without brick lining.
(c) Pear-shaped pits dug in the ground with or without brick lining.

There was only one jar furnace and it consists of three-fourths of a round pottery jar with its lower parts embedded in earth. It contained ashes. This kind of furnace, with charcoal as fuel, is still used by goldsmiths in India.

There are two examples of cylindrical shaped furnaces. The walls of this furnace are mud plastered and along with ashes a lot of high vitrified slag was found in it. This indicates evidence of intense firing. The remaining thirteen furnaces are all pear-shaped on plan.

At Tarkhan-wala-Dera mud bricks having four courses were used for construction. An oval-shaped structure, possibly furnace, which was partly jutting out and partly underground yielded Harappan pottery. The top of the wall was covered with mud. One complete dish was obtained from this structure.

At Kotla-Nihang Khan in the eastern Sector, several such kilns were noticed in a row, partly underground and partly jutting out of the surface. From one of these kilns were recovered fragments of three terracotta bangles. A similar kiln was also noticed at Bara and it yielded a small painted vase. (Sharma 1976 : 12).

At Sanghol furnaces or small kilns were found at several places in structural phases 2, 3 and 4. Near some of these kilns were found pieces of faience bangles. Although not many objects were found from inside or in the vicinity of these firing enclosures, it is evident that Bara people were engaged in considerable industrial activities. It may be assumed that beads, bangles and other small objects were being fired in these kilns. In this connection the discovery of 92 micro-gold-beads and agate beads, some of which unfinished, a chert weight and a few copper chisels, which were found inside near the large corner enclosure of room 2 of phase 4 is significant (Sharma *et al* 1982 : 72-82). A series of furnaces were noticed from Moharana (see Y. D. Sharma in this issue).

From Daulatpur (Singh 1977) the existence of walled constructions, round to oval in shape and burnt inside, most probably designed as ovens or *bhattis* were noticed. Along with ash and pottery, animal bones were also found in these enclosures, which may have been used as refuse-pits, once they fell into disuse as kilns.

J. P. Joshi (1978) has also reported oval structures of burnt earth from Bhagwanpura, Dadheri, Nagar and Katpalon.

Similar small kilns or furnaces were also found at Hulas in western Uttar Pradesh (Dikshit 1981). Two small furnaces one circular and other oval shaped were unearthed from the Harappan levels. These were plastered with fine clay paste. No evidence of burnt or mud brick was noticed in their construction. The oval furnace (*IAR* 78-79 : pl. XXXIVA) yielded a complete dish-on-stand along with Harappan potsherds and two more broken dishes. Perhaps this was used for baking the pottery under careful supervision of the potter. In the vicinity of the circular furnace, a good percentage of cylindical faience beads were found. At Hulas bricks, either burnt or of mud were never used for construction of furnaces like Tarkhan-wala-Dera. Further, these kilns were cut into the ground level and plastered with fine clay occasionally. Minor objects of specific nature were baked in these furnaces under high temperature.

Two kilns were noticed at Lothal (Rao 1980). One of them was circular on plan and has two chambers one above the other. The brick wall and floors of both the chambers were plastered with mud. These were possibly used for baking pebbles and beads of semi-precious stones. Beads in different stages of manufacture, partly baked pebbles, fragments of earthen bowl used as containers for baking the pebble and finished beads were found from this furnace. Due to intense heat, the mud-plaster on the wall turned red and the bricks were virtified.

Copper-smith's furnace from phase III is more or less a circle on plan with a rectangular projection for the supply of fuel. Pots containing the metal, were introduced through the enclosure wall. A bowl with copper traces and a rod were found here. Near the second furnace also one copper pin was encountered which go to prove that structure was used by copper-smith. In both the cases crucibles were placed directly on burning coal as it is done even today.

This survey revealed that the small furnaces were used for the firing of specialised items including pottery. These can be also termed as ancient industrial kilns. In late Harappan stage small furnaces are less in number in comparision to its availability on matured sites. The large furnaces (Oval-shaped) noticed at Bhagwanpura and Daulatpur were possibly used for some other purpose for firing of certain objects on large scale such as pottery etc. This inference is drawn from the massiveness of Daulatpur structure. The absence of small furnaces at Daulatpur and Bhagwanpura indicate that at this stage of Indus Civilization the specialised craftsmanship was more or less on decline.

Archaeological Survey of India,
New Delhi

D. V. SHARMA

REFERENCES

Dikshit, K. N. 1981 The excavations at Hulas and further exploration of the upper Ganga-Yamuna doab. *Man & Environment* V, Pune. *Indian Archaeology—A Review* 1978-79.

Joshi, J. P. 1978 Interlocking of late Harappan culture and Painted Grey Ware Culture in the light of Recent Excavation; *Man & Environment,* II, Ahmedabad.

Mackay, E. J. H. 1976 *Further Excavations at Mohenjo-Daro,* New Delhi (reprint).

Rao, S. R. 1980 *Lothal—A Harappan Port Town,* New Delhi.

Sharma, Y. D. 1982 Harappan Complex on Sutlej (India) *Harappan Civilization—A Contemporary Perspective* (ed) Gregory L. Possehl, New Delhi.

Sharma Y. D. and G. B. Sharma 1982 Bara Culture and its Housing remains with special reference to Sanghol, *Indian Archaeology—New Perspectives,* Delhi.

Singh Udaivir 1977 Late Harappan culture as revealed by the excavation at Mirzapur and Daulatpur District Kurukshetra (Haryana) paper read at the Seminar on *Indus Civilization—Problems and Issues,* Indian Institute of Advance Study, Simla.

Vats, Madho Sarup 1940 *Excavations at Harappa,* Calcutta.

A New Tool-Type of the 'Copper Hoards'

This note is presented primarily to get more information from scholars on a particular tool type. To us, this tool-type adds a new dimension to our understanding of the way of life the users of the 'hoards' may have practised in the prehistoric period. Apparently, it is a moderately long simple copper blade with broad cutting edge. The opposite end has a small shouldered tenon meant to be hafted in a wooden handle, a device commonly adopted by villagers in many parts of northern India, even to this day. The portion near the tenon of the blade is slightly bulging. Some of the examples from northern India, around Delhi particularly, also show similar features. The tool is locally called *khurpi* and is used primarily in removing unwanted grass from agricultural fields. It is a specialized tool whose function is not variable. In other words, it is an agricultural implement.

There are three to four examples of this type in the State Museum, Lucknow, although only one is complete (pl. I); the rest are fragmentary, with tenon broken off since the junction of the blade and the tenon is the weakest point in this implement. At least two examples of this tool-type came also from Bithur, near Kanpur, whose photographs I have obtained from the Archaeological Survey of India, New Delhi, whose courtesy I acknowledge here. Thus, so far, this type of tool comes from the alluvial lands of the Ganga in Uttar Pradesh. But I suspect, it should occur even in the plains of Haryana. The reason is not far to seek. Whatever may have been the mode of life of the 'Hoard' people in southern Bihar, Orissa and Madhya Pradesh, where there are large tracts of rocky soil, in the Indo-Gangetic divide, where alluvium is predominant, they are likely to have engaged themselves, at least partially, in agricultural pursuits. In case, the surmise of B. B. Lal is correct, that the 'Hoard' people used Ochre Coloured Pottery in the Ganga-Yamuna *doab*, as has of late been demonstrated at Saipai, district Etawah, where the tools and pottery have been found together, then the 'Hoard' people will now turn out to be agriculturists and not remain mere nomadic hunters or itinerant coppersmiths.

National Museum
New Delhi

S. P. GUPTA

A Unique Terracotta Figurine from the Jorwe Levels of Daimabad

In the excavation of the Chalcolithic site at Daimabad, situated on the left bank of the river Pravara, a tributary of the Godavari, in Ahmednagar district of Maharashtra, one terracotta figure was recovered from the surface of the fifth floor of House No 38 belonging to the Jorwe Culture (1400 B.C.—1000 B.C.) which represents Phase V in the sequence of cultures revealed at the site (*IAR* 78-79:46-52). Being the only one of its kind so far discovered in the chalcolithic context of the country, it is described here.

The terracotta, made of fine clay and pink in colour, has a rectangular or oval-shaped base or platform, 5 cm long and 3.5 cm broad, and convex under surface. On the upper surface of this platform, almost in the middle of one of its longer sides, has been moulded in high relief, a head with neck of a male figure with a combed long beard and obliquely combed long hair over the head (pl. I). The head is tilted to its left. The face is elongated and has a slit mouth and eyes. The elevation in the centre of the face forms nose. The clay pillet in applique on the left represents ear on that side. A similar clay pillet represented ear on the right side too but is now missing, leaving a depression on that side. The beard is very prominent or in high relief and lies more on the left side of the chin. The portion below the beard merges with the upper surface of the platform. The obliquely combed long hair on the head look like *jata*. The neck is massive and merges with the longer side of the base. When viewed from the back-side, the prominence on the under surface of the platform below, the neck closely resembles the back of the male figure. The longer side of the platform below the neck seems to represent broad shoulders of the male figure whereas the curved arms seem to have been depicted along the breadth of the platform in such a way as to suggest that the male figure is holding in his arms three female figures which are represented by heads moulded in high relief in a row along the other longer side of the platform. One of the female heads is damaged and the other two are in a fairly well-preserved condition. The one at the extreme left has eyes, slit mouth and short nose. The forehead of the central figure is slightly broken. Otherwise it possesses all the features of that on the extreme left. The ears of all the three females are represented by pillets in applique. The faces are in a straight position and they face upwards, as if lying in state. The hair on the head have not been depicted as in the case of the male figure. A close examination of the two well-preserved heads, however, shows that there is an elevated flat portion over the head depicted in such a way as to give an impression that the heads are covered with cloth up to the upper line of forehead. The neck of each figure is finely moulded and the shoulders below the neck, being joined with each other form the longer side of the base. The back of each of the figures is represented by separate slight prominance below the neck on the under surface of the base. The portion below the throat on the front-side broadens below and merges with the upper surface of the platform. Patches of red ochre occur over the entire surface of the terracotta.

The terracotta depicts a male, perhaps a deified sage, holding in his arms, three females, his consorts, unified with him. They seem to be posthumus representations in the memory of the sage and his consorts. From the presence of extant patches of red ochre over the entire surface of the find it is apparent that the object was in religious use and represents a cult object. It was found lying over the floor which was covered with the debris of the collapsed mud-walls of the house.

This circumstantial evidence may also suggest that, while in use, the object was placed in a niche provided in one of the walls of the house.

Archaeological Survey of India
New Delhi

S. A. SALI

Maltese Cross on Protohistoric Pottery

"The Maltese Cross or Cross of eight points is one of the best known crosses still in common use. As a general rule the adjective accompanying the word Cross indicates the shape and course of the arms as they move out from a centre." (Encyclopaedia Americana 8, p. 246).

It appears to be the earliest symbol adopted by man and considerable importance has been attached to it much before Christ who was crucified on the Cross. The angles of crosses may have had astronomical meaning to the ancient people. Besides the Hindus and Buddhists in India and China, the Persians, Assyrians and Babylonians were also using it.

During the course of search for symbols and designs on Indian protohistoric pottery, eight sherds have come to light which have Maltese Cross: two from the Pre-Harappan millieu from Kalibangan, District Sriganganagar, Rajasthan; two from Banawali, District Hissar, Haryana one from Raja Sirkap, District Faridkot, Punjab; one from Lakshmirwala, District Bhatinda, two from late Harappan levels from Banawali and Mitathal, Haryana and one from the overlap phase of Late Harappan (Figs. 1 and 2) and Painted Grey Ware at Bhagwanpura, District Kurukshetra (Joshi and Madhu Bala 1982: pl. 16.9). It may be seen in the accompanying figures 1 to 4 and 11 that while these are examples of perfect Maltese Cross, others show stylistic variations. It may perhaps be pertinent to mention here that Thapar while discusing the pre-Harappan pottery from Kalibangan (*IAR* 1962-63: 20-24) has reported squares with triangles at the corners very feebly resembling Maltese Cross' (*IAR* 1961-62: Fig. 14, 43).

Surprisingly enough, the Maltese Cross is not available in its *characteristic form* from typical Harappan design-repertoire. For comparative study, fig. 1-5, 6, 7, 8, 9 and 10 are Harappan specimens, already described by Starr (1941: 56-58, Fig. 97-98), who has observed, "strangely enough the Maltese Cross, so popular in Iran and Mesopotamia, does not appear on Harappan ware. There can be little doubt that the Maltese Cross sprang from the balanced geometrical grouping of four stags around a central hub, as we see it in *Samarra*, abb, 23, nr. 23, which in turn may have come from the less stylized arrangement of Samarra, abb, 20, nor. 20. At Tal-i-regi (Khusu) in Fars, as illustrated in Persis, pl. xxv, 53, the stag has almost ceased to be recognizable, prominence being given largely to the cross-like bodies. At Musyan (*Del. en Perse*, VIII, fig. 177) we have further examples showing the progress of simplification where only the conventionalized antlers remain to show its origin. The Maltese cross in various parts of Iran (Macown 1942) and Elam, early in late, often retained serrated or pronged outer edges as faint reminders of their naturalistic origin (*Persepolis*, pl. xxii; *Inn. Asia*, iii, pl. cxiii, Md. (R.R.) II.03; *Reconn.*, pl. xiii, Khur. B. ii. 200; *Persian Art*, iv, pl. 3, C)."[1]

The discovery of these pot-sherds throw interesting light on the provenance of Maltese Cross on the pre-Harappan pottery. What does it signify? Is it a simple expression of an art motif or a depiction of religious or mystic symbols or have some astronomical significance? It can be anybody's guess. *Ne plus ultra.*

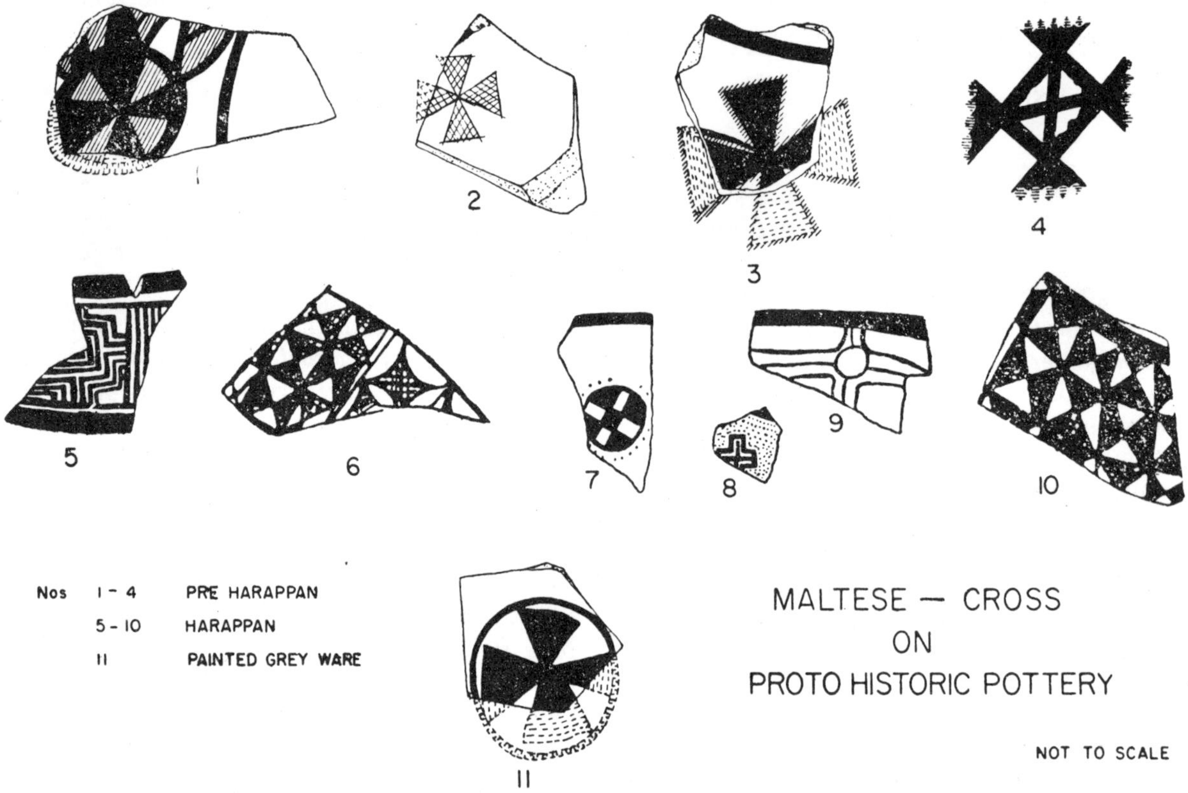

Fig. 1

1. Fragmentary pot-sherds of red ware painted on a rusticated surface in black and white on shoulder, making a design of Maltese Cross in fabric B^2, fully oxidized, having fine core. From Kalibangan Pre-Harappan levels; 2. Fragment of a big jar in Pre-Harappan thick grey ware, fabric F, having incised design on shoulder making a design of Maltese Cross with triangles filled with lozenzes, of medium fabric from Raja Sirkap: Surface collection; 3. Shoulder part of a thick jar in dull red ware showing Maltese Cross under a horizontal band, painted in black, bordered by white, having incompletely oxidized core of medium fabric, fabric A. From Lakhmirwala. Surface collection; 11. Fragment of a dish in fine grey ware painted in black, making a design of Maltese Cross, fully oxidized, having fine core from Period IB, Bhagwanpura. Figurs 4, 5-10 already described elsewhere.

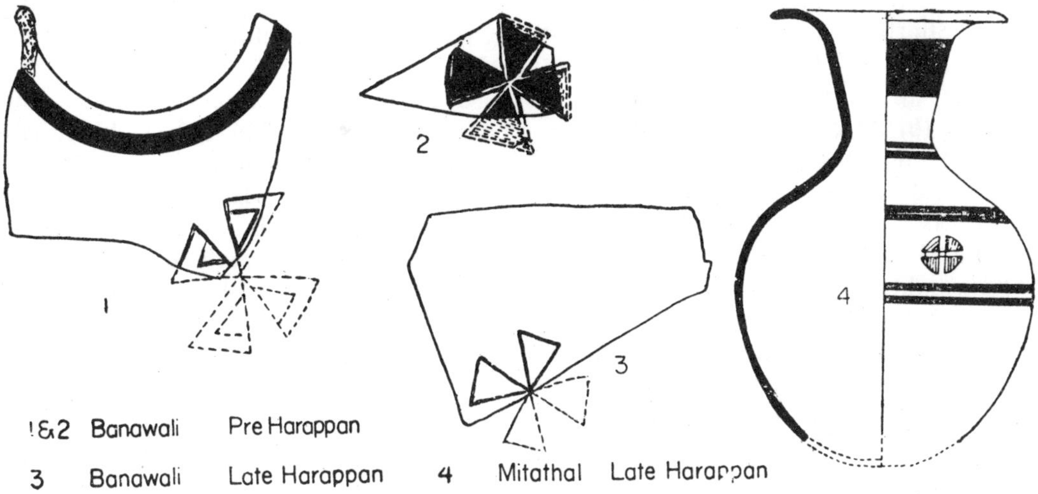

Fig. 2

NOTES

1. Fig. 9 page 20 nos. 21, 22, 27, fig. 10, p. 32 nos. 7, 9, 25, 53, 62, 77, 118, 120, 126, 127; 133; fig. 11. p. 34 - nos 47, 48, 99, fig. 12 p. 38 - nos 6, 63, 71 75, 86, 116, p. 41, no. 52 (Macown 1942)

2. Fabric A - Carelessly potted red to pinkish in colour painted in black and sometime with white over a dull surface; Fabric B - with a red slip and having rusticated surface; Fabric F-Thick Grey coloured pottery (*IAR* 1962-63: 20-40).

MADHU BALA

Archaeological Survey of India,
New Delhi.

REFERENCES

Indian Archaeology — A Review 1961-62; 1962-63

Joshi, J.P. and Madhu Bala 1982 Manda a Harappan site in Jammu and Kashmir, *Harappan Civilization — A contemporary Perspective* (ed) Gregory L. Possehl

Macown, D.E. 1942 *Comparative stratigraphy of early Iran*, Chicago.

Star, R.F.S. 1941 *Indus Valley Painted Pottery.*

The Distribution and Types of Beads in the Gangetic Valley

The material has been chosen only from those sites which have been published in full (Lal 1954-55; Dikshit 1952; Sinha 1967; Sharma 1969; Narain & Roy 1968; Narain & Singh 1977; Mitra 1972; Deva & Misra 1961; Altekar & Misra 1959; Sinha & Narain 1970; Sinha and Verma 1977 and Chakrabarti and Jamal Hassan 1982).

DATA

AGATE—1. Spherical—(a) Ahichchhatra: stratum I-IX (pre 300 B.C.—A.D. 1100); (b) Sravasti: Pd. III (4th-5th cent. A.D.); (c) Kausambi: sub-Pd. III (125-50 B.C.); (d) Rajghat: Pd. III (beginning of Christ. era-end of third cent. A.D.); (e) Kumrahar: Pd. II (A.D. 150-500). 2. Standard truncated bicone circular—(a) Sravasti: upper level of Pd. II (125-50 B.C.). (b) Tilaurakot: rampart filling (third—second cent. B.C.). 3. Standard cylindrical circular—(a) Rajghat: Pd. I-III (800 B.C.—A.D. 300); Pd, V (A.D. 700-1200). 4. Standard cylinder hexagonal—(a) Tilaurakot: rampart filling (third-second cent. B.C.). 5. Standard barrel circular—(a) Rajghat: Pd. IV (A.D. 300-700); (b) Tilaurakot; rampart filling (third-second cent. B.C.). 6. Standard twisted pentagon—(a) Rajghat: Pd. III (beginning of Christ. era-end of third cent. A.D.). 7. Standard barrel lug-collared tabular—(a) Rajghat: Pd. III (beginning of Christ.

era-end of third cent. A.D.); (b) Achichchhatra: unstratified. 8. Shortbarrel circular—(a) Ahichchhatra: stratum IV C (A.D. 100-350). 9. Short cylinder circular—(a) Ahichchhatra: stratum III b (350-750 A.D.); (b) Rajghat: Pd. I-II (800 B.C.—early cent. A.D.); (c) Tilaurakot: rampart filling (third-second cent. B.C.). 10. Square tablet (a) Kumrahar: Pd. IV (A.D. 300-450). 11. Spacer—(a) Rajghat: Pd. I (800-300 B.C.). 12. Barrel circular—(a) Kausambi: Pre-struct V—sub-Pd. VIII (400 B.C.—A.D. 325) (b) Vaisali: Pd. Ib (300-150 B.C.). 13. Long barrel circular—(a) Hastinapur: Pd. II (1110-800 B.C.); (b) Ahichchhatra: stratum V (beginning of Christ. era—1st cent. A.D.); stratum III (350—A.D. 750); stratum I (A.D. 850-1100); (c) Sravasti: early level of Pd. I (600-500 B.C.); (d) Prahladpur: mid phase-late phase (500-21 B.C.); (e) Tilaurakot: pit I (third-second cent. B.C.); Phase B of Pd. I (second cent. B.C.); (f) Sonpur: Pd. II (650-200 B.C.); (g) Rajghat: Pd I—VI (800 B.C.—British time). 14. Long cylindrical circular—(a) Hastinapur: early level of Pd. III (600-500 B.C.); (b) Kausambi: pre-struct. V (400-350 B.C.); (c) Rajghat: Pd. I (800-300 B.C.); Pd. III (beginning of Christ. era-end of third cent. A.D.); (d) Sonpur Pd. III (200 B.C.—A.D. 200). 15. Long barrel elliptical—(a) Hastinapur: early level of Pd. V (A.D. 1100-1200). (b) Sravasti: early level of Pd. II (275-200 B.C.). 16. Long bicone cylinder hexagonal (a) Rajghat: Pd. III (beginning of Christ. era-end of third cent. A.D.). 17. Long cylinder square (a) Rajghat: Pd. I (800-300 B.C.). 18. Circular (a) Pataliputra Pd. II (A.D. 1500-500). 19. Conical with flattened circular base—(a) Kumrahar: Pd. II-IV (650-200 B.C.). 20. Convex cylindrical (a) Kumrahar: Pd. II-IV (150 B.C.—A.D. 450). 21. Drum-shaped (a) Kumrahar: Pd. IV (A.D. 300-450). 22. Disc—(a) Rajghat: Pd. II (third cent. B.C. beginning of Christ. era) 23. Discoid spacer (a) Vaisali: Pd. Ib (300-150 B.C.). 24. Globular (a) Rajghat: Pd. I (800-300 B.C.); Pd. V-VI (A.D. 700—British time). 25. Tinny barrel circular (a) Kausambi pre-struct V (400-350 B.C.). 26. Truncated barrel—(a) Sonpur: Pd. II (200 B.C.—A.D. 200). 27. Tapering lenticular—(a) Rajghat: Pd. III (800-300 B.C.); (b) Ahichchhatra: stratum VI (Ist cent. B.C.—beginning of Christ. era.) 28. Toggle shaped—(a) Rajghat Pd. III (beginning of Christ. era-end of third cent. A.D.). 29. Tablet shaped, hexagonal in section—(a) Kumrahar: Pd. IV (450-600 B.C.). 30. Rectangular cornerless—(a) Ahichchhatra: Stratum I-II (A.D. 750-100).

EYE-BEAD. 31. Spherical—(a) Ahichchhatra: stratum VII (300-200 B.C.); (b) Rajghat: Pd. II (third cent. B.C.—beginning of Christ. era), Pd. V (A.D. 700-1200). 32. Short oblate—(a) Sravasti: early level of Pd. I (6th-5th cent. B.C.). 33. Convex bicone—(a) Sravasti: mid level of Pd. II (200-125 B.C.). 34. Cylinder circular—(a) Kausambi: (no-date). 35. Flattened hexagonal—(a) Kausambi: (no date). 36. Convex circular—(a) Ahichchhatra: stratum I (A.D. 850-1100). 37. Barrel shaped—(a) Kausambi: sub-Pd. V (A.D. 25-100) sub-Pd. VI (A.D. 100-175).

ETCHED BEADS: 38. Long barrel with connected pentagons in two rows and marginal bands:—(a) Kausambi: sub-Pd. III (125-50 B.C.); (b) Hastinapur: late level of Pd. III (400-300 B.C.); (c) Sravasti: early level of Pd. II (275-200 B.C.); (d) Rajghat: unstratified;(e) Sonpur: Pd. III (200-B.C. —A.D. 200). 39. Long barrel circular with diamond shaped designs and zonal bands—(a) Rajghat: Pd. III (beginning of Christ. era-end of third cent. A.D.). 40. Long barrel circular with four zonal bands—(a) Sravasti: early level of Pd. II (275-200 B.C.). 41. Spherical with eight-dotted concentric circle—(a) Tilaurakot: rampart filling (third-second cent. B.C.). 42. Spherical with connected pentagons—(a) Ahichchhatra: stratum IV b (A.D. 100-350). 43. Spherical with connected pentagons in two rows—(a) Rajghat: Pd. V (A.D. 700-1200); (b) Tilaurakot: rampart filling (third-second cent. B.C.). 44. Spherical with a dotted spiral—(a) Tilaurakot: pit 1 (third-second cent. B.C.). 45. Spherical with a wavy band—(a) Tilaurakot: pit 1 (third-second cent. B.C.). 46. Cylindrical with white chalcedony bands—(a) Kumrahar: Pd. III (A.D. 100-300). 47. Four sided with a white band—(a) Kumrahar: Pd. IV (A.D. 100-350).

LEECH SHAPED: 48. Oval—(a) Ahichchhatra: pit 1. 49. Oval with lug collared—(a) Sonpur: Pd. III (200 B.C.—200 A.D.). 50. Flattened—(a) Sravasti: early level of Pd. I (600-500 B.C.). 51. Long elliptical—(a) Tilaurakot: pit 1 (third-second cent. B.C.).

AMETHYST: 1. Long barrel flattened hexagonal—(a) Tilaurakot: Phase B of Pd. I (second cent. B.C.); (b) Sonpur: Pd. II (650-200 B.C.); (c) Rajghat: Pd. III-IV (beginning of Christ. era-

A.D. 700). 2. Long barrel elliptical—(a) Ahichchhatra: stratum VIII (300-200 B.C.). 3. Long convex hexagonal—(a) Ahichchhatra: stratum VIII 300-200 B.C.). 3. Long convex hexagonal—(a) Sonpur: Pd. II (600-500 B.C.). 4. Long cylindrical hexagonal—(a) Sonpur Pd. III (200 B.C.—A.D. 200). 5. Long leaf-shaped plano-convex—(a) Tilaurakot: phase B of Pd. I (second cent. B.C.). 6. Short truncated convex hexagonal (a) Hastinapur: mid level of Pd. III (500-400 B.C.). 7. Short flattened barrel hexagonal—(a) Sravasti: Upper level of Pd. II (125-25 B.C.). 8. Short twisted truncated bicone triangular—(a) Tilaurakot: rampart filling (third-second cent. B.C.). 9. Standard bicone hexagonal—(a) Rajghat Pd. IB (600-400 B.C.). 10. Elliptical hexagonal—(a) Sravasti: lower level of Pd. I (600-500 B.C.); (b) Ahichchhatra: stratum III a (350-A.D. 750). 11. Elliptical plano-convex—(a) Ahichchhatra: stratum III a (A.D. (350-750). 12. Triangular faceted—(a) Sonpur: Pd. II (650-200 B.C.). 13. Tiny hexagonal—(a) Sonpur: Pd. III (200 B.C.—A.D. 200); (b) Kumrahar: Pd. II (150 B.C.—A.D. 100). 14. Drop pendant—(a) Sonpur: Pd. III (200 B.C.—A.D. 200).

BERY: 1. Tiny short—biconical hexagonal tablet—(a) Kausambi: sub pd—II (200-125 B.C.). 2. Flattened hexagonal cylinder—(a) Kausambi: sub-pd III (125-50 B.C.).

BONE: 1. Spherical—(a) Sravasti: mid level of Pd II (200-125 B.C.); (b) Kausambi: sub-pd IA—IB (350-200 B.C.); sub-pd III—V (125 B.C.—A.D. 100) sub pd VIII (250—A.D. 325); (c) Sonpur: Pd.

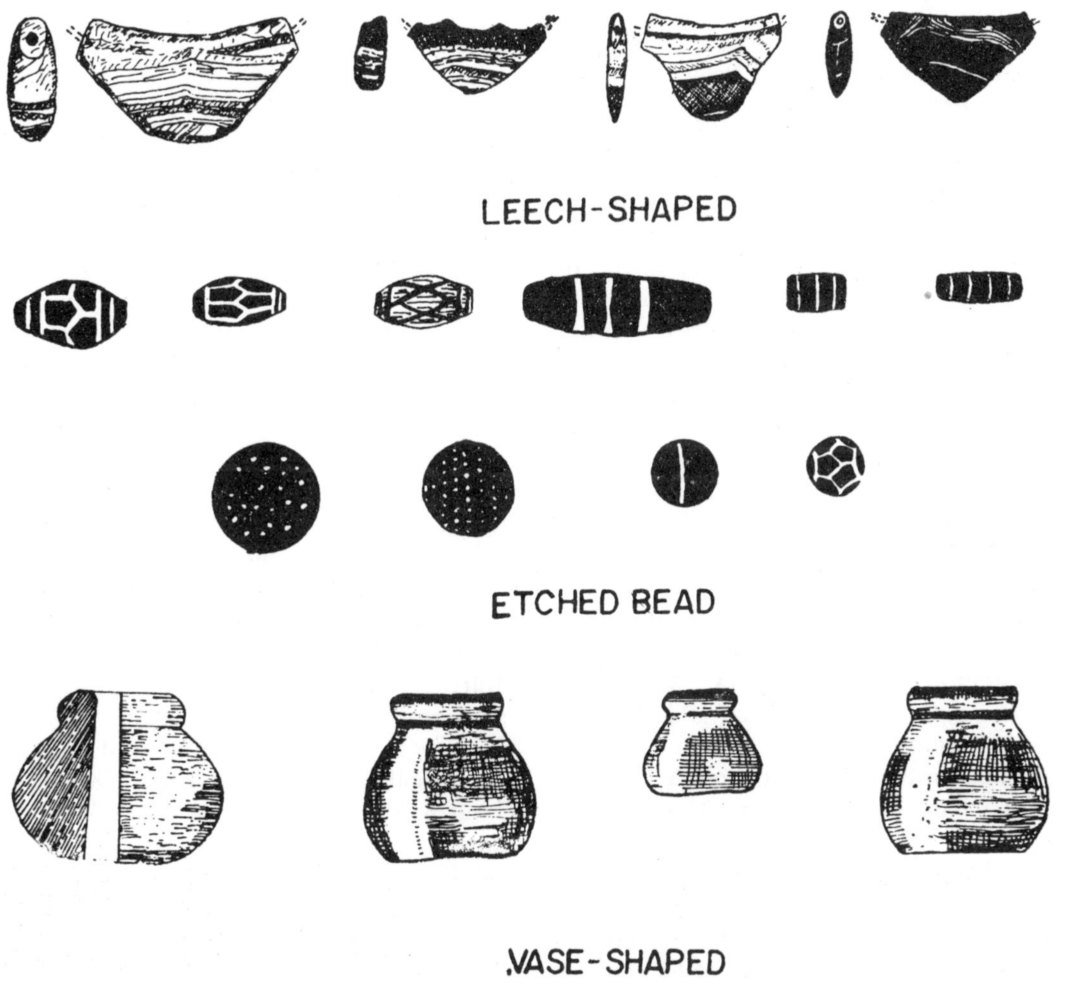

Fig 1

II-III (650 B.C.—A.D. 200); (d) Rajghat: Pd I-IV (800 B.C.—A.D. 700). 2. Spheriod—(a) Hastinapur: mid level of Pd II (1000-900 B.C.). 3. Standard cylindrical circular—(a) Rajghat: Pd. I (800-300 B.C.). Pd III (beginning of Christ. era—A.D. 300); Pd V (A.D. 700-1200). 4. Standard bicone circular with lug collared (a) Sravasti: mid level of Pd. II (200-125 B.C.). 5. Standard barrel gadrooned—(a) Hastinapur: mid level of Pd. II (1000-900 B.C.). 6. Short cylindrical circular—(a) Tilaurakot rampart filling (third-second cent. B.C.). 7. Long barrel—(a) Sonpur: Pd. II (650-200 B.C.). 8. Long barrel oval—(a) Prahladpur: mid phase (500-163 B.C.). 9. Long cylindrical circular (a) Ahichchhatra: Stratum I (A.D. 850-1100). 10. Long inconspicuously barrel circular—(a) Tilaurakot: Pit I (third-second cent. B.C.). 11. Cylindrical—(a) Sonpur: Pd. II (650-200 B.C.). 12. Disc—(a) Rajghat: Pd. IV (A.D. 300-700). 13. Rectangular—(a) Pataliputra: Pd. II (150 B.C.—A.D. 500). 14. Apple—(a) Pataliputra: Pd. I (600-150 B.C.).

CARNELIAN: 1. Spherical—(a) Hastinapur: early level of Pd. IV (second cent. B.C.—beginning of Christ. era); (b) Ahichchhatra: Stratum IV (A.D. 100-350); Stratum I (A.D. 850-1100); (c) Sravasti: early level of Pd. II (275-200 B.C.); (d) Kausambi: sub-Pd. IA—VI (350 B.C.—A.D. 175); (e) Rajghat: Pd. I-VI (800 B.C.—British time); (f) Kumrahar: Pd. II (150 B.C.—A.D. 600); (g) Sonpur: Pd. II (650-200 B.C.). 2. Standard barrel circular—(a) Sravasti: mid level of Pd. I (500-400 B.C.). 3. Standard bicone haxagonal—(a) Rajghat: Pd. III (beginning of Christ. era—third cent. A.D.). 4. Standard spherical: (a) Prahladpur: mid phase (500-163 B.C.). 5. Short bicone hexagonal—(a) Rajghat: Pd. I (800-300 B.C.). 6. Short barrel circular—(a) Ahichchhatra: stratum VIII (300-200 B.C.); (b) Rajghat: Pd. I (800-300 B.C.); Pd. III-V (beginning of Christ. era—A.D. 1200). 7. Short bicone square—(a) Rajghat: Pd. I-II (8th cent. B.C.—beginning of Christ. era). 8. Square barrel—(a) Kausambi: Pre-structure V (400-350 B.C.); 9. Long barrel circular—(a) Ahichchhatra: stratum I-II (A.D. 750-1100); (b) Rajghat: Pd. I-II (800 B.C.—beginning of chist. era; Pd. IV (A.D. 300-700); (c) Sonpur: Pd. II-III (650 B.C.—A.D. 200). 10. Long barrel hexagonal—(a) Ahichchhatra: stratum I (A.D. 850-1100); (b) Sravasti: lowtr level of Pd. I (600-500 B.C.); (c) Kausambi: sub-Pd V (A.D. 25-100); (d) Rajghat: Pd. IV (A.D. 300-700). 11. Long barrel-triangular—(a) Kausambi: sub-Pd III (250-325 B.C.). 12. Long barrel square—(a) Ahichchhatra; stratum I (A.D. 850-1160). 13. Long cylindrical circular—(a)Kausambi: sub Pd. III (125 B.C.—50 B.C.); (b) Sonpur: Pd. II (650-200 B.C.). 14. Long bicone cylinder hexagonal—(a) Prahladpur: Late phase (163-21 B.C.). 15. Long truncated bicone hexagonal—(a) Rajghat: Pd III (beginning of Christ. era—end of third cent. A.D.); (b) Ahichchhatra: stratum I (A.D. 850-1100). 16. Long cylinder square—(a) Rajghat: Pd. IV (A.D. 300-700); (b) Sravasti: lower level of Pd. I (600-500 B.C.). 17. Circular tabular—(a) Rajghat: Pd. I (800-300 B.C.); Pd. III (beginning of Christ. era—end of third cent. A.D.). 18. Circular plano-convex—(a) Rajghat: Pd. VI (A.D. 1200—British time). 19. Barrel circular—(a) Vaisali: Pd. Ib (300-150 B.C.); (b) Pataliputra: Pd. II (150 B.C.—A.D. 500); (c) Sonpur Pd. III (200 B.C.—A.D. 200); (d) Kausambi: sub-Pd. V-VI (A.D. 25-175). 20. Tiny barrel circular—(a) Prahladpur: early phase (673-500 B.C.). 21. Disc—(a) Tilaurakot: Pit 1 (third second cent. B.C.). 22. Dagger pendant—(a) Ahichchhatra: unstratified deposit; (b) Sravasti: early level of Pd. II (275-200 B.C.); (c) Vaisali: Pd. Ib (300-150 B.C.). 23. Faceted bicone twisted pentagonal shaped—(a) Ahichchhatra: stratum I (850-1100 A.D.). 24. Pyramid shaped—(a) Rajghat: Pd. I (800-300 B.C.); Pd. IV (A.D. 300-700).

ETCHED BEAD: 25. Spherical with white dots—(a) Rajghat: Pd. III (beginning of Christ. era—end of third cent. A.D.). 26. Spherical with eight dotted concentric circle—(a) Rajghat: Pd. III (beginning of Christ. era—end of third cent. A.D.). 27. Spherical with spotted—(a) Kausambi: pre-struct III-IV (500-400 B.C.). 28. Spherical with four sets of double convex-lines—(a) Tilaurakot: pit 1 (third-second cent. B.C.). 29. Standard cylinder circular with two zonal bands—(a) Tilaurakot: rampart filling (third-second cent. B.C.). 30. Short cylindrical circular with zonal bands—(a) Ahichchhatra: stratum I (A.D. 850-1100). 31. Small standard cylinder—(a) Kausambi: pre-struct-V (400-350 B.C.). 32. Long barrel with connected pentagons in two rows and marginal bands—(a) Ahichchhatra: unstratified deposit. 33. Long barrel circular with diamond shaped designs and zonal bands—(a) Ahichchhatra: unstratified—deposit; (b) Rajghat: Pd. III (beginning of Christ. era-end of third cent. A.D.). 34. Long cylindrical circular with three zonal bands—(a) Tilaurakot: pit 1 (third-second cent. B.C.). 35. Long convex ellipsoidal with three zonal bands, the middle band crossed by a series of small horizontal lines—(a) Tilaurakot: phase B of Pd. I (second cent. B.C.). 36. Flat trapezoidal with strips—(a) Vaisali: Pd. Ib (300-150 B.C.). 37. Multifaceted with broad lines on each facets—(a) Kausambi: sub Pd. III (125-25 B.C.).

LEECH SHAPED: 38. Oval—(a) Vaisali: Pd. Ib (300-150 B.C.). 39. Lenticular long—(a) Ahichchhatra: surface.

CHALCEDONY: 1. Spherical—(a) Ahichchhatra: stratum VIII (300-200 B.C.); (b) Kausambi: Pre struct-IV (450-400 B.C.); sub Pd V (A.D. 25-100); sub Pd. VIII (A.D. 250-325); (c) Rajghat: Pd. I (800-300 B.C.); Pd. III-VI (beginning of Christ. era-end of third cent. A.D.); (d) Kumrahar: Pd. II-III (150 B.C.—A.D. 300); (e) Sonpur: Pd. II (650-200 B.C.). 2. Spherical but flat at two end and having two rows of pentagonal facets (a) Kumrahar: Pd. III (A.D. 100-300). 3. Standard truncated bicone pentagonal with ground flats—(a) Ahichchhatra: stratum VI (100 B.C.—beginning of Christ. era). 4. Standard cylinder circular—(a) Rajghat: Pd. I (800-300 B.C.). 5. Standard diamond shaped tabular—(a) Tilaurakot: pit 1 (third -second cent. B.C.). 6. Square barrel—(a) Kausambi: Pre-struct-IV (450-400 B.C. 7. Short truncated bicone pentagonal—(a) Tilaurakot: phase B of Pd. I (second cent. B.C.). (b) Ahichchhatra: stratum III b (A.D. 350-700). 8. Long barrel circular—(a) Ahichchhatra: stratum III (A.D. 350-750); (b) Rajghat: Pd. III-IV (beginning of Christ. era—700 A.D.); (c) Sonpur: Pd II (200 B.C.—A.D. 200). 9. Long barrel hexagonal—(a) Ahichchhatra: stratum I (850—A.D. 1100); (b) Kausambi: Pre-struct V (400-350 B.C.); (c) Pataliputra: Pd. I (600-150 B.C.); Pd. III (A.D. 1700 and after). 10. Long truncated bicone circular—(a) Tilaurakot: rampart filling (third-second cent. B.C.). 11. Tablet shaped—(a) Kausambi: sub Pd. III (125-50 B.C.). 12. Truncated bicone hexagonal—(a) Ahichchhatra: stratum I (850-1100 A.D.).

ETCHED BEADS: 13. Long cylinder circular with unconspicuous zonal grooves round the body without any trace of colour (a) Tilaurakot: pit 1 (third-second cent. B.C.). 14. Long inconspicuously convex circular with six zonal bands—(a) Tilaurakot: pit 1 (third second cent. B.C.).

CHERT:—1. Spherical—(a) Rajghat: Pd. I-V (800 B.C.—A.D. 200). 2. Long barrel circular—(a) Rajghat: Pd. I-IV (800 B.C.—A.D. 700); Pd. VI (A.D. 1200—British time.). 3. Long cylinder tabular—(a) Rajghat: Pd. III (beginning of Christ. era-end of third cent. A.D.). 4. Disc shaped—(a) Rajghat Pd. IV (A.D. 300-700).

CHINA CLAY:— Circular, decorated with dots—(a) Vaisali: Pd. III (A.D. 1700—and after).

CLAW:—1. Dagger—pendant—(a) Sravasti: early level of Pd. I (600-500 B.C.).

COPPER:—1. Spherical—(a) Kausambi: sub-Pd. IA (350-275 B.C.); sub-Pd. VI (A.D. 100-175); sub-Pd. VIII (A.D. 250-325). 2. Spherical but with 12 facets, flat at both ends—(a) Kumrahar: Pd. II (150—B.C.—A.D. 100). 3. Standard barrel circular—(a) Sravasti: early level of Pd. I (600-500 B.C.); (b) Rajghat: Pd. I (800-300 B.C.). 4. Short barrel circular—(a) Sonpur: Pd. II-III (650 B.C.—A.D. 200). 5. Short cylinder circular—(a) Sonpur: Pd. IB (1000-650 B.C.). 6. Long barrel circular—(a) Sonpur: Pd. II (650-200 B.C.). 7. Long barrel square—(a) Sravasti: mid level of Pd. II (200-125 B.C.). 8. Long cylindrical circular—(a) Sravasti: early level of Pd. I (600-500 B.C.); (b) Rajghat: Pd. I (800-300 B.C.); (c) Ahichchhatra: stratum VIII (300-200 B.C.). 9. Barrel shaped like a conch shell—(a) Ahichchhatra: stratum I (A.D. 850-1100). 10. Cylinder and conex—(a) Kumrahar: Pd. III (A.D. 100-300). 11. Oblate disc elliptical—(a) Tilaurakot: rampart filling (third-second cent. B.C.). 12. Toggle-bead, cylindrical with conical ends—(a) Ahichchhatra: stratum V (beginning of Christ. era—A.D. 100).

CORAL: 1. Spheroid—(a) Rajghat: Pd. I-III (800 B.C.—A.D. 300): Pd. V (A.D. 700-1200). 2. Standard cylinder circular—(a) Rajghat: Pd. I (800-300 B.C.). 3. Disc-shaped—(a) Rajghat Pd. I-V (800 B.C.—A.D. 1200). 4. Long cylindrical circular—(a) Rajghat: Pd. III (beginning of christ. era—end of third cent. A.D.); Pd. IV (A.D. 300-700).

CITRINE:— 1. Long cylinder hexagonal—(a) Tilaurakot: Pit I (third-second cent. B.C.).

CRYSTAL:— 1. Spherical—(a) Ahichchhtra: Stratum I (A.D. 850-1100); (b) Sravasti: early level of Pd. II (275-200 B.C.); (c) Rajghat: Pd. I (800-300 B.C.); Pd. IV (A.D. 300-700); 2. Spherical, lug collared—(a) Rajghat: Pd. IV (A.D. 300-700). 3. Short truncated bicone hexagonal—(a) Rajghat: Pd. I (800-300 B.C.); Pd. IV (A.D. 300-700). 4. Short truncated convex hexagonal (a) Tilaurakot: rampart filling (third-second cent. B.C.). 5. Short cylinder hexagonal—(a) Ahichchhatra: stratum III c (A.D. 350-750). 6. Standard bicone twisted pentagon—(a) Rajghat: Pd. IV (A.D. 300-700). 7. Standard circular lenticular—(a) Tilaurakot: layer (2) (second cent. B.C.—beginning of Christ. era.). 8. Long barrel circular—(a) Hastinapur: mid level of Pd. III (500-400 B.C.); (b) Ahichchhatra: stratum I (A.D. 850-1100). (c) Rajghat: Pd. II-IV (beginning of Christ. era—A.D. 700); Pd. VI (A.D. 1200—British time); (d) Tilaurakot: rampart filling (third-second cent. B.C.); (e) Sonpur Pd. II (650-200 B.C.). 9. Long barrel triangular—(a) Ahichchhatra: stratum VI (100 B.C.—beginning of Christ. era). 10. Long hexagonal—(a) Hastinapur: late level of Pd III (400-300 B.C.); (b) Kausambi: pre-struct. V (400-350 B.C.); (c) Rajghat: Pd. III (beginning of Christ. era—end of third cent. B.C.). 11. Long barrel oval (a) Hastinapur: late level of Pd III (400-300 B.C.). 12. Long barrel elliptical—(a) Tilaurakot: rampart filling (third second cent. B.C.). 13. Long cylindrical circular—(a) Sonpur: Pd. III (200 B.C.—A.D. 200). 14. Long cylindrical Hexagonal—(a) Ahichchhatra: stratum IV c (A.D. 100-350); (b) Kausambi: sub-Pd. VI-VII (A.D. 100-250). 15. Long bicone cylinder hexagonal—(a) Ahichchhatra: stratum IV c (A.D. 100-350). 16. Long ellipsoid lenticular—(a) Tilaurakot: pit I (third-second cent. B.C.). 17. Long cylinder square—(a) Rajghat: Pd. I (800-300 B.C.). 18. Long cylinder rectangular—(a) Rajghat: Pd. II (beginning of Christ. era—end of third cent. A.D.); (b) Vaisali Pd. III (A.D. 100-300). 19. Lenticular hexagonal—(a) Ahichchhatra: stratum IV c (A.D. 100-350). 20. Barrel circular—(a) Kausambi: sub Pd. VI (A.D. 100-175). 21. Cornerless cube—(a) Tilaurakot: phase A of Pd. I (third cent. B.C.). 22. Bicone hexagonal—(a) Ahichchhatra: stratum I (A.D. 850-1100). 23. Bicone hexagonal with irregular facets—(a) Ahichchhatra: stratum III b (A.D. 350-750). 24. Toggle bead (a) Rajghat: Pd. IV (A.D. 300-700). 25. Twisted hexagonal with facets and convex circular—(a) Kausambi: sub Pd. VII. (A.D. 175-250). 26. Truncated convex (one side short, the other disc) hexagonal wedge—(a) Tilaurakot: Phase B of Pd. I (second cent. B.C.). 27. Drop pendant—(a) Tilaurakot: pit 1 (third-second cent. B.C.). 28. Sword-shaped pendant—(a) Tilaurakot: pit 1 (third-second cent. B.C.).

FAIENCE:— 1. Spherical—(a) Ahichchhatra: stratum III (A.D. 350-750). 2. Short barrel circular—(a) Kausambi: sub-Pd. V (A.D. 25-100). 3. Long barrel circular—(a) Ahichchhatra: stratum III (A.D. 350-750); (b) Kausambi: sub-Pd. IV (500 B.C.—A.D. 25); (c) Rajghat: Pd. I-V 800 B.C.—A.D. 1200). 4. Long cylinder hexagonal—(a) Kausambi: sub-Pd. VI (A.D. 100-175). 5. Cornerless cube—(a) Ahichchhatra: stratum III (A.D. 350-750); (b) Kausambi: sub Pd. VII (A.D. 175-250). 6. Amalake shaped (a) Ahichchhatra: stratum III (A.D. 350-750); (b) Rajghat: Pd. II (third Cent. B.C.—beginning of Christ. era). Pd. VI A.D. 1200—British Time).

GARNET:— 1. Spherical—(a) Kausambi: sub-Pd. III (125-50 B.C.). 2. Long cylinder hexagonal—(a) Tilaurakot: pit 1 (third-second cent. B.C.). 3. barrel rectangular—(a) Tilaurakot: rampart filling (third-second cent. B.C.). 4. Biconical hexagonal—(a) Kausambi: sub-Pd. IV (50 B.C.—A.D. 25). 5. Biconical circular—(a) Kausambi: sub-Pd. IB (275-200 B.C.). 6. Cornerless cube lug collared—(a) Tilaurakot: Phase B of Pd. I (second cent. B.C.). 7. Ellipsoid—(a) Tilaurakot: rampart filling (third-second cent. B.C.).

GLASS:— 1. Spherical—(a) Hastinapur: early level of Pd. II (600-500 B.C.); (b) Ahichchhatra: stratum IX (before 300 B.C.); stratum I (A.D. 850-1100); (c) Sravasti: mid level of Pd. II (200-125 B.C.); (d) Kausambi: sub-Pd. II (200-125 B.C.) sub-Pd. IV (A.D. 25-100); sub-Pd. VIII (A.D. 250-325); (a) Rajghat: Pd. I (800-300 B.C.); Pd. III-VI (beginning of Christ. era—British Time); (f) Kausambi: sub-Pd. III (A.D. 100-300); (g) Pataliputra: Pd. III (A.D. 1700 and after); (h) Sonpur: Pd. III (200-B.C.—A.D. 200). 2. Standard barrel circular—(a) Sravasti: early level of Pd. II (275-200 B.C.); early level of Pd. III (5th cent. A.D.); (b) Kausambi: sub-Pd. IA (350-275 B.C.); (c) Rajghat: Pd. II-V (300 B.C.—A.D. 1200). 3. Standard cylinder circular—(a) Tilaurakot; rampart filling (third second cent. B.C.); (b) Rajghat: Pd. II-V (300 B.C.—A.D. 1200). 4. Standard cylindrical circular—(a) Ahichchhatra: stratum III (A.D. 350-750); (b) Rajghat: Pd. I-IV (800 B.C.—A.D. 700). 5. Standard spherical—(a) Prahladpur: mid Phase

(500-163 B.C.). 6. Standard barrel hexagonal—(a) Ahichchhatra: stratum I (A.D. 850-1100). 7. Short cylinder circular—(a) Tilaurakot: rampart filling (third-second cent. B.C.); (b) Vaisali: Pd. III (100-300 A.D.). 8. Square barrel—(a) Kausambi: sub-Pd. V-VII (A.D. 25-250). 9. Short cylinder square—(a) Kausambi: sub-Pd. V-VIII (A.D. 25-325). 10. Short truncated bicone—(a) Tilaurakpt: rampart filling (third-second cent. B.C.). 11. Spherical (a) Tilaurakot: rampart filling and Pit 1 (third-second cent. B.C.). 11. Spherical (a) Tilaurakot: rampart filling and Pit 1 (third-second cent. B.C.). 12. Spacer—(a) Rajghat: Pd. III (beginning of Christ. era—end of third cent. A.D.). 13. Long barrel circular (a) Kausambi: sub-Pd. V (A.D. 25-100); (b) Rajghat: Pd. I-IV (800 B.C.—A.D. 700); (c) Prahladpur: late Phase (163-B.C.—21 B.C.); (d) Vaisali: Pd. Ib (300-150 B.C.); (e) Sonpur: Pd. II (650-200 B.C.). 14. Long cylindrical circular—(a) Rajghat: Pd. III-IV (beginning of Christ. era—British time); (b) Vaisali: Pd. IB (300-150 B.C.). 15. Long cylindrical hexagonal—(a) Ahichchhatra: stratum I (A.D. 850-1100); (b) Kausambi: sub-Pd. II (200-125 B.C.); 16. Long cylinder square—(a) Tilaurakot: surface. 17. Long barrel square—(a) Ahichchhatra: stratum III a (A.D. 350-750). (b) Rajghat Pd. III (beginning of Christ. era—end of third cent. A.D.). 18. Barrel circular—(a) Vaisali: Pd. Ib (300-150 B.C.). 19. Barrel tabular—(a) Rajghat: Pd. IV (A.D. 300-700). 20. Barrel with lug-collars, lenticular—(a) Ahichchhatra: stratum IV a (A.D. 100-350); (b) Rajghat: Pd. II-IV (300 B.C.—A.D. 700). 21. Bicone pentagonal—(a) Ahichchhatra: stratum I (A.D. 850-1100). 22. Cylindrical square with double chamfered edge—(a) Ahichchhatra: stratum I (A.D. 850-1100). 23. Cornerless cube—(a) Ahchchhatra: stratum I (A.D. 850-1100). 24. Cylinder but convex in the centre collared—(a) Kumrahar: Pd. III (A.D. 100-300). 25. Cyilndrical with facets—(a) Kumrahar: Pd. III (A.D. 100-200). 26. Cylinder and convex collared—(a) Kumrahar: Pd. III (A.D. 100-300). 27. Circular tablet—(a) Kumrahar: Pd. III (A.D. 100-300). 28. Curved pendant—(a) Tilaurakot: Pit 1 (third-second cent. B.C.). 29. Disc shaped—(a) Kausambi: sub-Pd. V (25—100 A.D.); sub Pd. VIII (A.D. 250-325). 30. Disc oblate—(a) Rajghat: Pd. I (800-300 B.C.); Pd. III (beginning of Christ. era—end of third cent. A.D.); Pd. V-VI (A.D. 700—British time). 31. Drum shaped—(a) Kumrahar: Pd. III-IV (A.D. 100-450). 32. Globular—(a) Rajghat: Pd. III (beginning of Christ. era—end of third cent. A.D.); Pd. (A.D. 700-1200); (b) Vaisali: Pd. II (150 B.C.—25 A.D.). 33. Tablet; (a) Rajghat: Pd. III (beginning of Christ. era—end of third cent. A.D.). 34. Elliptical circular—(a) Ahichchhatra: stratum VIII (300-200 B.C.); (b) Kumrahar: Pd. V (A.D. 450-600). 35. Elliptical tabular—(a) Ahichchhatra: stratum V (beginning of Christ. era—first cent. A.D.). 36. Elliptical and collared—(a) Kumrahar: Pd. III (A.D. 100-300). 37. Elliptical circular—(a) Tilaurakot: Pit 1 (third-second cent. B.C.). 38. Irregular shape—(a) Kumrahar: Pd. III (A.D. 100-300); (b) Rajghat: Pd. III-V (beginning of Christ. era—A.D. 1200).

GNEISS:— 1. Long truncated bicone elliptical (a) Tilaurakot: layer 2. (first cent. B.C.—beginning of Christ. era).

GOLD:— 1. Completely deformed—(a) Kausambi: sub-Pd. IA (350-275 B.C.).

GRANITE:— 1. Spherical—(a) Vaisali: Pd. IV (A.D. 300-500). 2. Peculiar Shape—(a) Kumrahar: Pd. III (A.D. 100-300).

IVORY:— Spherical—(a) Rajghat: Pd. III (beginning of Christ. era—end of third cent. A.D.). 2. Standard truncated bicone—(a) Rajghat: Pd. IC (400-300 B.C.). 3. Collared tablet shaped—(a) Rajghat: Pd. III (beginning of Christ. era—end of third cent. A.D.); Pd. V (A.D. 700-1200). 4. Disc—(a) Rajghat: Pd. II (300 B.C.—beginning of Christ. era). 5. Dagger pendant—(a) Sonpur: Pd. II (650-200 B.C.); (b) Rajghat: Pd. IV (A.D. 300-700). 6. Long cylinder elliptical—(a) Rajghat: Pd. V (A.D. 700-1200). 7. Tablet shaped—(a) Rajghat: Pd. III (beginning of Christ. era—end of third cent. A.D.).

JASPER:— 1. Spherical—(a) Kausambi: sub-Pd. IA (350-275 B.C.); sub-Pd. VIII (A.D. 250-325). 2. Barrel circular—(a) Sonpur: Pd. II (650-200 B.C.). 3. Cornerless cube—(a) Ahichchhatra: unstratified deposit. (b) Kausambi: sub-Pd. V (A.D. 25-100). 4. Disc—(a) Kausambi: sub-Pd. II (200-125 B.C.). 5. Double hexagonal—(a) Rajghat: Pd. II (300 B.C.—beginning of Christ. era.). 6. Faceted twisted pentagonal—(a) Rajghat: Pd. IV (A.D. 700-1200); (b) Ahichchhatra: unstratified deposit. 7. Hexagonal and bi-pyramidical—(a) Kumrahar: Pd. III (A.D. 100-300). 8. Long barrel circular—(a) Rajghat: Pd. I (800-300 B.C.); Pd. III (beginning of Christ. era—end of third cent. A.D.); (b) Prahladpur: mid phase (500-163 B.C.); (c) Sonpur: Pd. II (650-200 B.C.). 9. Long barrel flattened hexagonal—(a) Rajghat: Pd. I (800-300 B.C.); Pd. III (beginning of Christ. era—third cent. A.D.). 10. Truncated biconical hexagonal—(a) Kausambi: sub-Pd. V (A.D. 25-100). 11. Twisted pentagonal bicone—(a) Kausambi: sub-Pd. III (125-50 B.C.).

LAPIS-LAZULI:— 1. Disc—(a) Kausambi: sub-Pd. VIII (A.D. 250-325). 2. Globular—(a) Rajghat: Pd. III-V (beginning of Christ. era—A.D. 1200) 3. Long cylindrical circular—(a) Rajghat: Pd. I (800-300 B.C.); Pd. V-VI (A.D. 1200—British time); (b) Prahladpur: mid phase (500-163 B.C.). 4. Long cylinder hexagonal—(a) Rajghat: Pd. IV (A.D. 300-700). 5. Long cylinder pentagonal—(a) Sravasti: early level of Pd. I (600-500 B.C.). 6. Oblate —(a) Kausambi: sub-Pd. VIII (A.D. 250-325). 7. Standard cylinder circular—(a) Kausambi: sub-Pd. V (A.D. 25-100). 8. Standard barrel circular—(a) Kausambi: sub-Pd. V (A.D. 25-100). 9. Short cylinder circular—(a) Rajghat: Pd. II-VI (A.D. 300—British time).

LIME STONE:— 1. Standard barrel circular—(a) Sravasti: late level of Pd. II (125-50 B.C.).

MARBLE STONE:— 1. Spherical—(a) Vaisali: Pd. IB (300-150 B.C.).

ONYX:— 1. Long cylinder circular—(a) Hastinapur: mid level of Pd. III (5th-4th cent. B.C.). 2. Oblate. (a) Tilaurakot: layer 2 (first cent. B.C.—beginning of Christ. era).

OPAL:— 1. Spherical—(a) Kumrahar: Pd. II (150 B.C.—A.D. 100).

PASTE:— 1. Spherical—(a) Rajghat: Pd. IV-V (A.D. 300-1200). 2. Short cylinder circular—(a) Rajghat: Pd. V (A.D. 700-1200); (b) Tilaurakot Pit 1 (third-second cent. B.C.). 3. Long tapering cylinder circular—(a) Rajghat: Pd. I (800-300 B.C.); Pd. VI (A.D. 1200—British time). 4. Disc—(a) Rajghat: Pd. I (800-300 B.C.).

QARTZ:— 1. Spherical—(a) Rajghat: Pd. II (third cent. B.C.—beginning of Christ. era). Pd. IV-V (A.D. 300-1200). 2. Cylindrical and convex—(a) Kumrahar: Pd. III-IV (A.D. 100-450). 3. Collared pendant—(a) Kumrahar: Pd. III (A.D. 100-300). 4. Collared barrel elliptical—(a) Kausambi: sub-Pd. VI (A.D. 100-175). 5. Collared tablet shaped—(a) Rajghat Pd. II-III (300 B.C.—A.D. 300). 6. Hexagonal—(a) Kumrahar Pd. IV (A.D. 300-450). 7. Hezagonal and cylindrical—(a) Kumrahar: Pd. III (A.D. 100-300). 8. Hexagonal and convex—(a) Kumrahar: Pd. III (A.D. 100-300). 9. Long cylinder rectangular (a) Rajghat: Pd. II (300 B.C. —beginning of Christ. era). 10. Long barrel circular—(a) Sravasti: early level of Pd. II (275-200 B.C.). 11. Long cylinder square (a) Rajghat: Pd. III (beginning of Christ. era—end of third cent. A.D.). 12. Long barrel hexagonal—(a) Ahichchhatra stratum VIII (300-200 B.C.); (b) Rajghat: Pd. I-V (800 B.C.—A.D. 1200). 13. Tablet shaped—(a) Rajghat: Pd. V (A.D. 700-1200). 14. Pendant—(a) Kausambi: sub-Pd. VIII (A.D. 250-325).

SHELL:— 1. Spherical—(a) Vaisali: Pd. Ib (300-150 B.C.). 2. Standard cylinder circular—(a) Rajghat: Pd. IV (A.D. 300-700). 3. Barrel shaped—(a) Vaisali: Pd. Ib (300-150 B.C.). 4. Barrel gadrooned—(a) Kausambi: sub-Pd. VI (A.D. 100-175). 5. Cornerless—cube-(a) Kausambi-Sub-Pd. IV (50 B.C.—A.D. 25). 6. Circular with flatened sides—(a) Pataliputra: Pd. II (750 B.C.—A.D. 500). 7. Circular tablet—(a) Kausambi: sub-Pd. IV (50 B.C.—A.D. 25). 8. Circular tabular—(a) Ahichchhatra: un-stratified deposit. 9. Cylinder tabular—(a) Kausambi: sub-Pd. VIII (A.D. 250-325). 10. Circular disc (a) Rajghat: Pd. II-IV (300 B.C.—A.D. 700. 11. Dagger pendant—(a) Sravasti: late level of Pd. I (400-300 B.C.). 12. Disc cylinder square—(a) Sravasti: early level of Pd. II (275-200 B.C.). 13. Disc with optical lines—(a) Kausambi: sub-Pd. VII (A.D. 175-250). 14. Flat lenticular disc—(a) Kausambi: sub-Pd. II (200-125 B.C.). sub-Pd. VIII (A.D. 250-325). 15. Flat circular lug collared—(a) Kausambi sub-Pd. VIII (A.D. 250-325). 16. Long bicone barrel circular—(a) Prahladpur: mid phase (500-163 B.C.). 17. Long barrel hexagonal (a) Sravasti: late level of Pd. I (400-300 B.C.). 18. Mother of pearl beads flat circular disc—(a) Kausambi: sub-Pd. V (A.D. 25-100). 19. Rectangular lenticular—(a) Kausambi: sub-Pd. IV (50 B.C.—A.D. 25). 20. Rectangular discs—(a) Rajghat: Pd. III (beginning of Christ. era—end of third cent. A.D.). 21. Short cylindrical circular—(a) Kausambi: sub-Pd. II-V (200 B.C.—A.D. 100).

SILVER:— 1. Spherical ribbed with horizontal growing—(a) Tilaurakot: Pit 1 (third-second cent. B.C.).

SUNDARY STONE:— 1. Short cylinder—(a) Kausambi: sub-Pd. V (A.D. 25-100). 2. Rectangular pannel bead—(a) Kausambi: sub-Pd. III (125-50 B.C.).

SOAP STONE:— 1. Circular tablet—(a) Kumrahar: Pd. III (A.D. 100-300). 2. Faceted hexagonal (a) Sonpur: Pd. III (200 B.C.—A.D. 200). 3. Long barrel oval—(a) Sonpur: Pd. II (650-200 B.C.). 4. Long cylindrical—(a) Sonpur Pd. III (200 B.C. A.D. 200). 5. Lion faced sacorpean body—(a) Sonpur: Pd. III (200 B.C.—A.D. 200).

STONE:— 1. Irregular shape—(a) Kumrahar Pd. IV (A.D. 300-450). 2. Round and tablet shaped —(a) Kumrahar Pd. III (A.D. 100-300).

WHITE STONE:— 1. Spherical—(a) Vaisali Pd. I (600-150 B.C.).

TERRACOTTA BEADS:— 1. Vase-shaped—(a) Hastinapur: early level of Pd. III (600-500 B.C.); (b) Ahichchhatra (unstratified); (c) Kausambi Pre-struct-II (550-450 B.C.); sub-Pd. VIII (A.D. 250-325); (d) Sravasti: late level of Pd. I—mid level of Pd. II (500-125 B.C.); (e) Rajghat Pd. I-VI (800 B.C.—British time); (f) Prahladpur: sub-Pd. I A-IB (673 B.C.—21 B.C.); (g) Tilaurakot; Pd. IA-II (third cent. B.C.—beginning of Christ. era (h) Vaisali: Pd. I (500 B.C.—A.D. 100); (i) Pataliputra: Pd. I (600-150 B.C.); (j) Sonpur: Pd. II (650-200 B.C.); (k) Bahiri: Pd. II (500-200 B.C.). 2. Pear shaped—(a) Hastinapur: late level of Pd. IV (second-third cent. A.D.); (b) Sravasti: early level of Pd. III (4th cent. A.D.); (c) Pataliputra: Pd. I (600-150 B.C.); (d) Sonpur: Pd. III (200 B.C.—A.D. 200). 3. Standard truncated bicone circular—(a) Hastinapur: late level of Pd. V (14th-15th cent. A.D.); (b) Rajghat: Pd. III (beginning of Christ. era—end of third cent. A.D.). 4. Standard bicone twisted pentagon—(a) Rajghat: Pd. VI (A.D. 1200—British time). 5. Standard chamfered cylinder circular—(a) Tilaurakot: Pit 1 (third-second cent. B.C.). 6. Standard bicone circular—(a) Hastinapur: mid level of Pd. III (500-400 B.C.). 7. Spherical—(a) Hastinapur: mid level of Pd. IV (Ist cent. B.C.—Ist cent. A.D.); late level of Pd. IV (second-third cent. A.D.); (b) Ahichchhatra stratum V-III (beginning of Christ. era—A.D. 750); (c) Kausambi: sub Pd. II (200-125 B.C.); sub-Pd. VIII (A.D. 260-325); (d) Rajghat: Pd. I-II (800 B.C.—beginning of Christ. era). (e) Tilaurakot: Pit 1 (third-second cent. B.C.); (f) Vaisali: Pd. IV (A.D. 300-600); (g) Pataliputra: Pd. II (150 B.C.—A.D. 500). 8. Short blunt-edge lenticular circular—(a) Hastinapur: late level of Pd. III (fourth-third cent. B.C.). 9. Short blunt edged bicone circular—(a) Hastinapur; late level of Pd. II (8th cent. B.C.). 10. Short-truncated bicone circular (a) Tilaurakot: Phase B of Pd. I (second cent. B.C.). 11. Square amulet—(a) Sonpur: Pd. III (200 B.C.—A.D. 200). 12. Sphercial: (a) Prahladpur: unstratified deposit. 13. Spacer fluted—(a) Sonpur: Pd. II (650-200 B.C.). 14. Long ill shaped barrel circular—(a) Hastinapur: early level of Pd. IV (200-100 B.C.). 15. Long cylinder oblate—(a) Sravasti: mid level of Pd. II (200-125 B.C.). 16. Long barrel circular—(a) Rajghat: Pd. III-VI (beginning of Christ, era—end of third cent. A.D.); (b) Tilaurakot: Layer 2 (first cent. B.C.—beginning of Christ. era); (c) Sonpur: Pd. III (200 B.C.—A.D. 200). 17. Long bicone circular—(a) Rajghat: Pd. II (300 B.C.— beginning of Christ. era); Pd. V (A.D. 700-1200). 18. Long bicone hexagonal—(a) Rajghat: Pd. V (A.D. 700-1200). 19. Long convex hexagonal—(a) Prahladpur: late phase (163-21 B.C.). 20. Conical pendant—(a) Hastinapur: un-stratified deposit. 21. Cylindrical tabular—(a) Kausambi: sub-Pd. VI (A.D. 100-175); sub-Pd. VIII (A.D. 250-325). 22. Circular—(a) Pataliputra: Pd. II (600 B.C.—A.D. 500). 23. Conical pendant—(a) Sonpur: Pd. II-III (650 B.C.—A.D. 200). 24. Amlaka shaped—(a) Ahichchhatra: un-stratified; (b) Kausambi: sub-Pd. IV-VIII (50 B.C.—A.D. 325); (c) Rajghat: Pd. I-IV (800 B.C.—A.D. 700); Pd. VI (A.D. 1200—British time). 25. Arecanut—(a) Kausambi sub-Pd. IA (350-275 B.C.); sub-Pd. VII (175 A.D.—250 A.D.); (b) Rajghat: Pd. I-VI (800 B.C.—British time). (c) Tilaurakot: rampart filling (third second cent. B.C.). 26. Plano-convex circular with wheel straitions—(a) Ahichchhatra: un-stratified. 27. Globular—(a) Rajghat: Pd. I-VI (800 B.C. British time); (b) Sonpur: Pd. II (650 B.C.—200 B.C.). 28. Crescented—(a) Sonpur: Pd. III (200 B.C.—A.D. 200). 29. Reel—(a) Sonpur: Pd. III (200 B.C.—A.D. 200). 30. Twinklet—(a) Sonpur: Pd. III (200 B.C.—A.D. 200). 31. Tortoise shaped square amulet—(a) Sonpur: Pd. III (200 B.C.—A.D. 200). 32. Rectangular amulet—(a) Sonpur: Pd. III (200 B.C.—A.D. 200. 33. Fluted ball—(a) Sonpur: Pd. II (650-200 B.C.). 34. Plano convex—(a) Vaisali: Pd. II (150 B.C.—A.D. 100). 35. Un bored long cylinder circular—(a) Hastinapur: late level of Pd. V (14th-15th cent. A.D.).

DISCUSSION: The foregoing data clearly establish the diversity of raw materials and types of beads in the archaeological sequence of the Gangetic Valley. The sources of these raw materials (particularly the sources of the semi-precious stones) should be the subject of a separate study. What is obvious, however, is the steady supply of different types of semi-precious stones to the Gahgetic Valley throughout the historic period. The materials which seem to dominate are glass, agate and carnelian. The types cited here have been taken from the relevant reports. It is perhaps possible to reduce this void (and occasionally confusing) range of types to certain basic types. This, again, may be the subject of a separate study.

Secondly, most of the types are restricted to single material or period. However, certain designs on the etched beads seem to be restricted only to the early historic period (*circa* 600-200 B.C.). It is however, worth noting that at Rajghat, Ahichchhatra and Kumrahar etched beads continue till a late period. The leech-shaped beads occur in the early historic period alone without a single exception. At Kausambi the terracotta ghata-shaped beads occur till C. 325 A.D. and at Rajghat these have been reported from British time but by and large this type tends to be associated with the early historic levels. The leech-shaped type can safely be used as a chronological marker of early historic occupation and somewhat tentatively the same status may be given to the etched and ghata-shaped varieties.

Acknowledgement

This paper was prepared under steady guidance of Dr. Dilip K. Chakrabarti.

Archaeological Survey of India,
New Delhi

S. JAMAL HASAN

REFERENCES

Altekar, A.S. and V.K. Misra *Report on Kumrahar excavation 1951-52,* Patna.

Chakrabarti, Dilip K. and S. Jamal Hasan, 1982. The sequence at Bahiri (Chandra Hazrar Danga) Distt. Birbhum, West Bengal, *Man & Environment* VI, Pune.

Dikshit, M.G. 1952 Beads from Ahichchhatra, *Ancient India* 8, New Delhi.

Deva, K. and V. Misra, 1961 *Vaisali excavations* 1950, Allahabad.

Lal, B.B. 1973 Excavations at Hastinapur another exploration in the upper Ganga and sutlej basin 1950-52, *Ancient India* 10-11, New Delhi.

Narain, A.K. and T.N. Roy 1968 *The excavations at Prahladpur 1963,* Varanasi.

Narain, A.K. and P. Singh, 1977 *Excavations at Rajghat* 1957-58; 1960-65, Varanasi.

Sinha, K.K. 1967 *Excavations at Sravasti-1959,* Varanasi.

Sinha, B.P. and L.A. Narain, 1970 *Pataliputra excavation* 1955-56, Patna.

Sinha, B.P. and V.S. Verma 1977 *Sonpur excavations* 1946 and 1959-1962, Patna.

Sharma, G.R. 1969 Excavations at Kausambi 1949-50, *Memoirs of the Archaeological Survey of India* 74, New Delhi.

Mitra, D. 1972 *Excavations at Tilaurakot and Kodan exploration in the Nepalese Tarai,* Calcutta.

The Indus Valley Civilization-An Aryan Culture ?

Are the Aryans autochthonous to India and, if so, what is their relationship with the Indus Valley Civilization? These are questions still agitating the minds of Indologists which have been answered by K.D. Sethna after a painstaking examination of all the available evidence to present an engrossing thesis. Sethna marshalls his arguments around four crucial questions:—

1. Is there any evidence for an Aryan invasion of India in 1500 BC?
2. Do the Mitanni documents of Boghazkeui (1360 BC) suggest an archaic Indo-Iranian dialect spoken by a people living outside India who separated later into Iranians and Indo-Aryans?
3. Can the *Rigveda* be dated beyond 1500 BC?
4. Is the Harappa Culture non-Aryan, anterior to the *Rigveda* and a victim of invading Aryan hordes?

The Massacre Hypothesis

The conventional opinion, represented by Wheeler, is that the Harappan Civilization was founded by non-Aryans (Dasas/Dasyus/Panis) who were massacred by invading Aryans (vide the skeletal remains at Mohenjo-daro) as described in the *Rigveda* where Indra assaults the fortresses of noseless, black-skinned aborogines, possibily of Proto-Australoid stock.

However, G.F. Dales pointed out that this massacre theory is mythical: there is no evidence of mutilation of bodies of armoured warriors or weapons, or of burning of any occupation or even defence of the most important part of the city of Mohenjo-daro in Sind—the fortified citadel. Even Wheeler admits this and feebly tries to explain away this major flaw in his theory by suggesting that the absence of skeletons from the citadel implies that it was occupied and cleared by the invaders for their own use. Unfortunately, there are also no signs of any such occupation.

'In any case', Sethna points out, nothing calls in the least for so grandiose an event as an Aryan invasion.'

Moreover, Harappa in Punjab, which was more directly in the path of these allegedly invading Aryans, streaming in from the north-west, than Sind's Mohenjo-daro, shows absolutely no signs of any massacre nor even of any decline in prosperity before abandonment which must have occurred if invaders had entered from the north-west. If we cannot accuse the Aryans of having destroyed Harappa, there is no justification for attributing Mohenjo-daro's skeletons to them. Actually, even elsewhere in Sind, as Chanhudaro, no such scene as at Mohenjo-daro is found.

The problem which remains is that of the parallel drawn between the Rigvedic account of attacks on forts of Dasas and Dasyus and archaeological finds at Mohenjo-daro, leading to the conclusion that the Rigveda records an Aryan invasion of India. Sethna proceeds to demonstrate that the current chronology for the *Rigveda* as well as the Aryan-invasion hypothesis are gross errors.

Harappans and Rigvedic Dasa-Dasyus

It is significant that the Dasa princes named, Sambara, Duni, Chumuri, Pipru, Varchin, Sushna and Ilibisa are found by Indra himself, and not by him while assisting Aryan chiefs. 'Dasa' and 'Dasyu' are epithets applied to demoniac and superhuman enemies, as noted by Mac Donell & Keith.

The *Rigveda*, X, 22,8 clearly states their non-human character. Giving of particular names to Dasas confers no humanness; afterall the gods are also given individual names. Both belong to the same universe of discourse and the very individuals specifically named emerge devoid of definite human concreteness and loom as superhuman. The *Pani* is equally ambiguous. Mac Donell & Keith note that they appear often as mythological figures and invariably in religious contexts withholding the cows or waters of heaven and are non-worshippers of the gods, which puts them, like the Dasas and Dasyus, in the same realm as the gods, quite apart from racial identification with Dravidians. In the *Rigveda* we find no anthropological or ethnic particulars about Aryans, and the word *Arya,* in it, has a cultural, not a racial, significance.

The epithets *anas, krishna-tvach* and *mridhra vach* have to be understood together. The Dasyus, Panis, Dasas, are destroyers, spoilers, of the divine word which the Aryan seeks when sacrificing to the gods. These anti-gods are *an-asah,* unable to speak the word, and belong to darkness just as the gods bring bright-hued thoughts to their worshippers. The fact that in post-Vedic ages actual tribes were termed Dasas or Dasyus should not prejudice our reading of the *Rigveda.*

The non-racial connotation of these epithets is undoubted, from yet another source of information. The Dasyus of the *Aitereya Brahmana* were descendants of the fifty sons of Viswamitra, a Vedic sage, cursed by him, i.e., degraded Aryans. The *Manusmriti* refers to them as of Kshatriya origin, branded dasyus because of their neglecting Vedic rites, i.e. again degraded Aryans. There is absolutely no evidence in the *Rigveda* warranting introduction of Dravidians into the Aryan-Dasyu conflict.

Finally, even granting that the references are to a flat-nosed, black-skinned (Dravidian?) physical type of Proto-Australoid stock, there is no evidence for identifying them with the Harappans. There is no archaeological evidence of *anas* and *krishna-tvach* Harappan population. Sankalia states that the latest report on the Harappa skeletons from cemetery R 37 shows that its population was long-headed, tall, rugged and sturdily built, with pronounced eye-brow ridges, receding forehead, broad nose with depressed root, (Type A) while the other type was gracile, shorter, finer and weaker (Type AI). The latter is the Mediterranean, but the former is not pure Proto-Australoid as that stock is of small stature, while the average height of Class A males, according to Wheeler, is 5 ft. 8-9 ins. with Class AI a few inches shorter. The latest findings from Harappa's Area G show a majority of A1 type skulls with Type A completely absent. So, the predominance of Type A cannot be beyond doubt. Further, the eight skulls found at Lothal, a site belonging to the mature Harappan Phase, are of three types: long-headed, broad-headed and extremely long-headed, representing the proto-Nordic, Alpine-Armenoid and Australoid groups respectively. The Aryans, according to S.K. Chatterji, a proponent of the invasion theory, represented a cultural union of the long-headed, straight-nosed Nordics and the shorter and dark, short-headed Alpines. Both stocks are in evidence at Lothal before the supposed migration into India. Wheeler also states that at Harappa and Lothal the population appears to have remained stable from Hrappan times till now, implying that the alleged Aryan invasion around 1500 BC resulted in no noticeable changes in physical types in these areas. Aryans are no more or less prominent there now than in Harappan times. From the racial view point, this distinction between Aryan and non-Aryan appears completely arbitrary. Sethna argues that "A single multi-charactered race, with a large linguistic and cultural diversity based on a flexible yet persistent unity of civilization, appears to have continued from prehistory to our own period."

Even granting an Aryan invasion of a Dasa-Dasyu India dominated by proto-Australoids, the Harappan stage of culture cannot be equated with that of the people invaded. Pigott points out Aryan barbarians invaded a highly urbanised culture of the Industry valley. But Mac Donell and Keith have found that in civilization there is no evidence that the Dasas equalled the invaders. Moreover, the Dasas are mountain-dwellers, Sambara being a chief of mountain people. But Wheeler makes Sambara a Harappan leader and characterises them as lowlanders, as befits a civilized folk', not realising the contradiction! Moreover, the Dasas and Dasyus seem to have been a pastoral people, possessing large herds captured by Aryans. How can these mountaineers and herdsmen represent Piggott's description of the Indus Valley Civilization as 'an empire based on a long-established tradition of literate urban culture'?

It is highly significant that cows, which are a major feature of the *Rigveda*, are never represented in this civilization. Wheeler himself notes the predominance of bulls alone among cattle in the terracottas, seals and painted potteries. Unlike the Dasas and Dasyus, the Harappans do not at all seem to have been deeply concerned with cows.

As for the forts, *purah,* the references are predominantly metaphorical, being synonyms for clouds, variously described as moving, autumnal and made of iron or stone, encompassing cows set free by Indra. Significantly, only Indra is described as destroying them, and never any human being, which reinforces the spiritual interpretation Sri Aurobindo gives to these passages. Mac Donell cautions us that there is no evidence that *pura* ever meant a town or city, as it did later, or that these forts were ever inhabited. Apte feels that it means an earthwork fortification protected by a palisade or stone wall, resorted to during emergencies which usual took the form of raids during autumn (hence called autumnal) at the end of the monsoons, or in the shape of flooding of the plains, and they possibly had a series of concentric walls. But such fortresses are hardly the elaborate, highly organised cities of the Harappans which have been found.

Various passages in the *Rigveda* (I. 11,5; VIII. 32,5; II. 24,3) indicate that the *puras* are pens of cows and horses, particularly of the former, and are referred to as 'like a city', 'firm places', 'fortified places'. Walled cities of the Harappan kind are quite foreign to the Rigvedics. To take the Rigvedic phrases about the 'hundred walls' and 'walls of iron and stone' of the *purah* literally would suggest fortifications surpassing even ancient Pataliputra, let alone Sutkagendor, Harappa, Lothal and Kalibangan: it is still not certain if Mohenjo-daro was fortified.

Above all, how do we find Indra fighting in the *Rigveda?* It is never with physical weapons but with words, religious utterances, that Indra breaks Vala, casting out the Dasyu, 'attacking those who can think not the Truth by those who think' (II. 24.3).

It has been suggested that the Rigvedic Hariyupuya where the Vrichivants are routed by Abhyavartin Chayamana (VI. xxvii. 5) is modern

Harappa and that the Vrichivants are the same as Varchin, a foe of Indra, located near river Parushni or Yavyavati, the modern Ravi on which Harappa stands. Sethna shows in an Appendix that the Turvasus and Vrichivants were settled between the Saraswati and Yamuna and opposed Sudas located near the Ravi. The attack is very clearly one from inside India, east of Harappa, on kings west of the Ravi and by no means one which might represent Indra's foes undergoing an Aryan invasion from outside India. Further, the Vrichivants, like the Turvasas and other peoples listed in the many encounters, are *never* described as non-Aryan. They also figure as opponents of Sudas and the Bharatas, never as foes of Indra. Even if they are identified with the anti-god Varchin, this would not make them non-Aryan. The epithets 'non-sacrificing', 'not worshipping Vedic gods', 'follower of strange ordinances' which are applied to Dasas-Dasyus are also flung at Aryan leaders such as the ten kings who fought Sudas.

The Rigveda and Aryan Invasion

The question remains whether the *Rigveda* speaks of Aryans as foreigners entering a country. Srikanta Sastri and the Cambridge History of India unequivocally state that Vedic and later literature afford no such evidence, but rather that Vedic Aryans regarded Sapta-Sindhu as their original home. Unlike the cases of the Egyptians, Phoenicians, Parsis, there is no looking back to the land of origin. The Cambridge History also says that the location indicated in the Rigveda is the country round the Sarasvati river, much further east than the Indus valley. Thus the Rigveda shows Aryans looking towards the main Harappan sites as inlanders rather than as invaders. This lack of evidence is admitted by such prominent invasion-theorists as S.K. Chatterjee, B.K. Ghosh and A.L. Basham. Further, Basham does not mention a single central Asian geographical allusion in the Vedas to substantiate his assertion that such allusions point to an Aryan migration from central Asia. The very verse he quotes, the river-panegyric (X.x. 75) lists ten streams all within India from east to west instead of *vice-versa* as would be natural of people who had travelled from the west to the east.

The *Rigveda* does not tell a straight tale of Aryans conquering Dasa foes, but there are many references to Aryan foes as well. Ghosh has noted from the fact that Indra combats the Dasa princess, that the first encounters, if any, with the aboriginal races were no longer a living memory, as contrasted with the battle of ten kings where Indra is invoked only to render aid. The invasion, if any must have been long before the Rigveda's time.

The Vedic speech itself shows profound influence of Dravidian languages through the use of cerebrals (second series of dental letters) as S.K. Chatterjee has observed the link between Dravidian and Aryan tongues is far closer than realised: over 100 Dravidian verbal forms occurring in ordinary speech have been found to be derived from Indo-Aryan roots, as also the majority of grammatical structures in Dravidian (vide R. Swaminathan Aiyar's *Dravidian Theories*, Madras, 1975). This is an index to socio-cultural exchange in India over a long period anterior to the *Rigveda* between Aryans and Dravidians. Sri Aurobindo has pointed out how Tamil vocables provided him with missing links in a family of words from Sanskrit, Greek and Latin, and suggests that the Dravidian and Aryan tongues may be divergent families originating from a lost tongue.

Archaeological Evidence of Aryan Invasion

The question now arises of Indian archaeology providing evidence of Vedic Aryan settlements in India long before the supposed invasion c. 1500 BC. The domesticated horse offers a clue.

Aryans have been associated with the domesticated horse, for which Zeuner has proposed c. 3000 BC as the beginning of the domestication in Turkestan. Wheeler mentions finding bones of a horse at a high level at Mohenjo-daro and from pre-Harappan layers at Rana Ghundai, as also a terracotta representing a horse from a late level at Mohenjo-daro. Lothal, dated c. 2582 BC, has revealed a terracotta figurine of a horse. J.P. Joshi's excavations 1965-68 at Surkotada in Kutch have revealed evidence of the domesticated horse within the 2455-1860 B.C. time span (re-calibrated readings), well-within the Harappan period. And now it is gathered that at Kalibangan also domesticated horse existed during the Harappan times.

Spoked wheels are also in evidence in seals frequently found at Mohenjo-daro, Kalibangan and Surkotada. Nowhere in the world before 2500 BC do we find any evidence of spoked wheels in any ideograms except those of the Indus Valley. The Finnish scholars who tried to decipher the Indus script pointed out that in seal no. 3357 a man's figure is shown standing with feet on two wheels. This is also found on a potsherd from Lothal. And in both cases the wheels are spoked. There is, thus, clear evidence of Aryan presence before the Harappan civilization.

That spoked wheels were quite possible for Harappans is proved by their advanced metallurgy. It is a unique culture for devising a saw with undulating teeth and a twisted copper or bronze drill. Sethna points out, 'If it did not care to use much the spoked-wheel chariot or even the domesticated horse, both of them most suited to war, the reason is simply the rut of conservatism and the long lulling peace.'

Sankalia had pointed out to Sethna in 1963 that although there is hardly any archaeological evidence that Harappan culture is non-Vedic, there is also no evidence of Vedic Aryanism in the 4000-2000 B.C. period in Sind and Punjab. Sethna points out that such evidence has not been found even for the post-2000 BC period when the Aryans are alleged to have invaded India. Wheeler himself admits the lack of any proto-Aryan material in India.

Sethna argues that since the earliest Indo-Aryan culture is the Rigveda's, the pre-Harappan civilization must be partly Vedic Aryan, with the Rigveda itself going further back in time.

Linguistic Evidence and date of the Rigveda

Bloomfield has pointed out, after extensive research on Vedic repetitions, that the Vedic hymns depend on a long anterior activity and represent the mixed final precipitate of a later time.

Paul Thieme's analysis of the Mittani treaty of Boghaz-Kieu has shown it to be Rigvedic, not proto-Aryan. For instance, the proto-Aryan form would have been 'Mitra-Asura', not 'Mitra-Varuna'. Again, there are 2 Nasatyas as in the Vedas, instead of only 1 as known to the Avesta. Since just after 2000 BC the Mittani moved out of the Rigvedic area to start a dynasty in West Asia, this Rigvedic culture must have flourished before 2000 BC.

Even more conclusive, observes Sethna, is the fact that the Rigveda does not know cotton, which has been found in Mohenjo-daro and Lothal. If the Rigveda is placed after Harappan culture, how can one explain that use of cotton cloth disappeared, which had been in use for 1000 years in the Indus Valley Civilization? Even in the Sutras we find no mention of cotton. It could be argued that the *Rigveda* is also silent about the banyan tree, rice and salt although these are typical of India. But the later texts do mention all three. On the other hand, none of the four Vedas, early Brahmanas, Aryanyakas and Upanishads refer to *karpasa.* Hence Harappa, with its cotton period of 2500 to 1000 BC, must succeed the Sutra period. It could be argued that in that case Harappa should have known silk, mentioned in the *Rigveda.* This would be incorrect, for the epithet 'tarpaya' does not mean silk but a linen thrice soaked in water or ghee. It is 'kauseya' which refers to silk, and occurs in the later work, *Vasistha Dharmasutra,* c. 1000 BC. Non-mention of silk both in the *Rigveda* and lack of its evidence in Harappan culture, with its occurrence only in the late sutras, bolsters the argument for the antiquity of the *Rigveda.*

From the point of view of religion Harappan religion is supposed to differ in three respects from the Rigvedic: worship of mother goddess; worship of icons; worship of bull, instead of cow. In the Rigveda we have five prominent goddesses: Mehi/Bharati, Ila, Saraswati, Sarama, Dakshina and Usha. There is also Prithvi and the seven river goddesses. Above all, there is Aditi, mother of all gods and one of the greatest conceptions of Vedic religion, who could easily lead to the development of worship of the Mother Goddess.

As for bull worship, Indra is often conceived of as a bull, the triple bull, while the divine Purusha is spoken of as the four-horned bull.

Further, excavations at Lothal Amri and Kalibankan have revealed fire-altars which are peculiar to Indo-Germanic or Aryan culture, thus reinforcing Sethna's contention that they are Aryan civilizations. Any non-Rigvedic cultural strains need not negate the fundamental Aryanism, particularly keeping in mind that Vedic Aryanism is principally a matter of culture, not of race.

In a valuable Appendix Sethna discusses T. Burrow's interpretation of the significance of the

Rigvedic term *armaka as* 'ruined settlement'. Burrow's deduction is based on the invasion hypothesis which Sethna has conclusively demolished. Sethna (1980: 150) analyses Burrow's interpretation of the Rigvedic verses to expose the 'slant' he invests them with and shows that *armaka* is not only non-Harappan but also non-material and has nothing to do with any battle or invasion.

Sethna has also discussed with the famous Assyriologist S.N. Kramer the misconception regarding the word *sindhu* and proved that it does not occur at all in Assurbanipal's library and has no links with the Hebrew *sadin* and the Greek *sindon,* as has been mistakenly assumed. The word is *sintu,* which has nothing to do with India or the Indus, and *sindon/sadin* have no integral links with *sindhu* either (Sethna 1981). The books of Sethna on which this review is based are undoubtedly outstanding contributions to Indological studies during the last decade.

Lal Bahadur Shastri,
National Academy of Administration,
Mussorie.

P. B. BHATTACHARYA

REFERENCES

Sethna, K.D. 1980 *The Problem of Aryan Origins,* S & S Publishers, Calcutta.
1981 *Karpasa in Prehistoric India: A New Chronological and Cultural Clue,* Impex India, Delhi.

New Evidence From Kolhua Pillar

Kolhua formed part of the ancient city of Vaishali (present Basarh, Lat 25° 59′ N., Long 85° 07′ E) located about 36 km south-east of Muzaffarpur. Near the village stands the uninscribed Mauryan pillar facing the remains of an ancient brick-built stupa (pl. I). Hieun-Tsang details in his itinerary about the remains.

The site was referred to by Princep as early as 1784. But first descriptive account on the site was published by J. Stephenson who visited the site in 1805. He mentions that the stupa was excavated about 1805 by a doctor from Muzaffarpur and nothing was found inside. Later Cunningham made a detailed survey of the area in 1860 and 1880. He carried out an excavation around the pillar to reach its base. However, due to high level of the sub-soil water he could not proceed beyond 4.25 m below the level of the field. The polished portion was still continuing below.

The tank close to the pillar is described by Bloch in 1903. Excavation by Cunningham to the south of the tank brought to light traces of some large structures (brick sizes 39.5x24x5 cm) including small brick stupa. Cunningham tried to identify these brick structures with *kutagara* hall and aforesaid tank with *markata-harda* or Monkey tank described by Hieun-Tsang.

Since then no further attempt was made to excavate the site till now. The main objective of the present excavation was; (i) to determine the base of pillar: (ii) find out the relationship between the pillar and the brick stupa and (iii) get a cultural sequence of the site.

Limited excavation near the lion pillar yielded the base of the pillar resting on a sandstone slab at the depth of 5.50 m from the present ground level. The underpinning stone was placed over a greenish grey sandy deposit. The entire shaft a length of 1.68 m from the base was polished. Now the exact height of the pillar including its capping members is 14.6 m.

Further excavations in between the pillar and the stupa revealed that the original stupa was built by square size bricks (30x30x8 cm). It was plastered with kānkar lime and subsequently reconstructed or repaired at least three times. The site seemed to have gained importance during the second phase (size of bricks 35x24x6 cm). Several brick built stupa bearing traces of lime plaster were contemporary to it. Corresponding with different reconstructional phases of the stupa relaying of the *Pradakshinapathas* was also traced (pl. II). Excavation towards south of the pillar yielded successive floors made of brick-bats and *surkhi.*

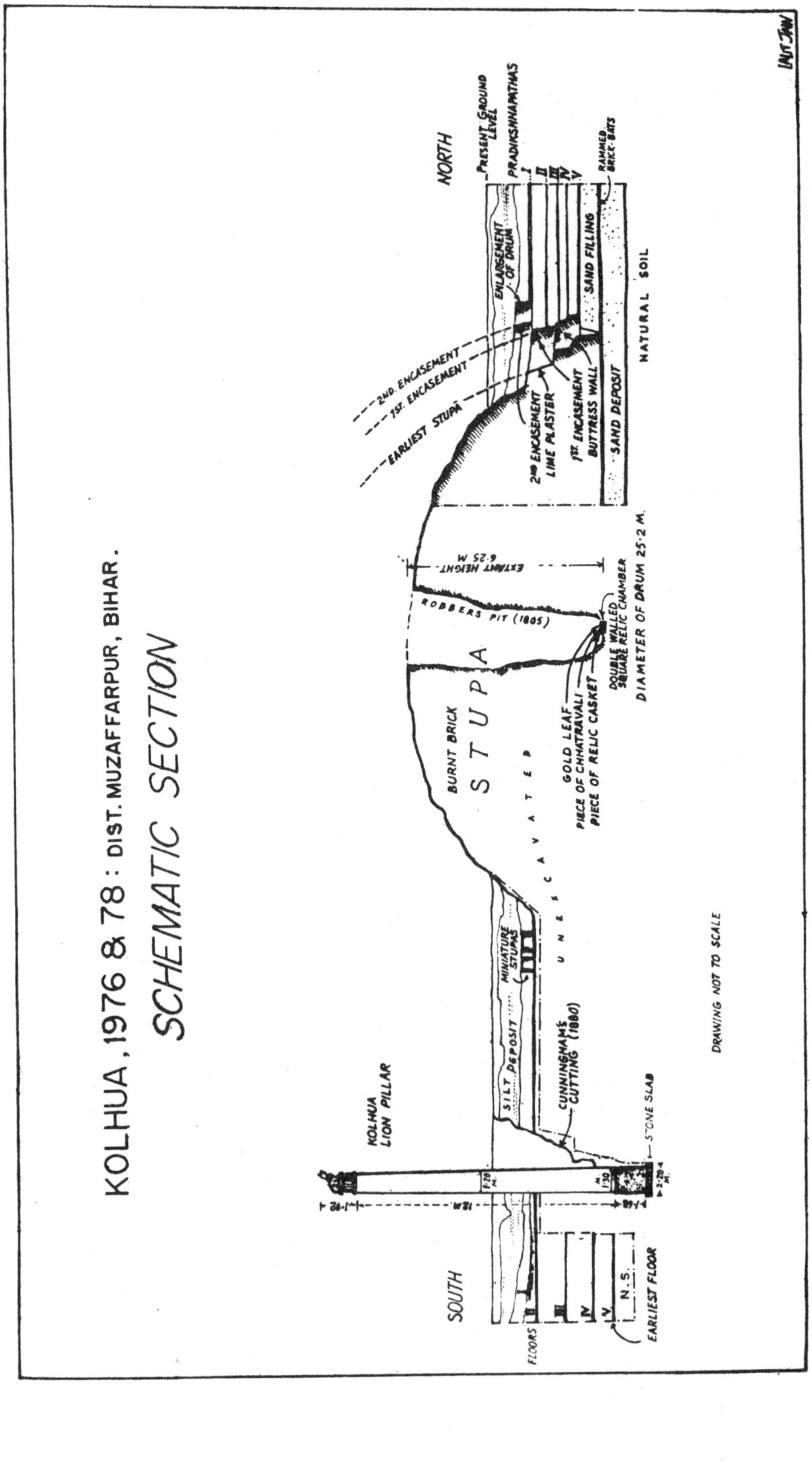
KOLHUA, 1976 & 78 : DIST. MUZAFFARPUR, BIHAR.
SCHEMATIC SECTION
SOUTH
NORTH
KOLHUA LION PILLAR
SILT DEPOSIT
MINIATURE STUPAS
CUNNINGHAM'S CUTTING (1880)
STONE SLAB
FLOORS
EARLIEST FLOOR
N.S.
BURNT BRICK
STUPA
UNEXCAVATED
ROBBERS PIT (1805)
EXTANT HEIGHT 6.25 M
GOLD LEAF
PIECE OF CHHATRAVALI
PIECE OF RELIC CASKET
DOUBLE WALLED SQUARE RELIC CHAMBER
DIAMETER OF DRUM 25.2 M.
2ND. ENCASEMENT
1ST. ENCASEMENT
EARLIEST STUPA
2ND ENCASEMENT LIME PLASTER
1ST ENCASEMENT BUTTRESS WALL
SAND DEPOSIT
SAND FILLING
ENLARGEMENT OF DRUM
NATURAL SOIL
PRESENT GROUND LEVEL
PRADIKSHNAPATHAS
RAMMED BRICK-BATS
DRAWING NOT TO SCALE

Fig 1

Simultaneous clearance of debris from the centre of the stupa resulted in the discovery of the remains of a double-walled square relic chamber (brick size; 30x30x8 cm) (Fig. 1). It was destroyed by the so-called excavator from Muzaffarpur as early of 1805, who had penetrated deep into the natural soil. However, during clearance some important antiquities, such as a fragment of *chhatravali* and pieces of broken relic casket—both bearing typical Mauryan polish, gold leaves, semi-precious stones, some of which embedded in bricks have been found. Besides a headless seated figure of Buddha and a crowned head of Buddha have also been found.

On the basis of stratigraphical evidence both the stupa and the pillar were contemporary. The earliest occupation of the site is characterised by Northen Black Polished Ware comparable with late phase of this ware found at Raja-Vishal-Ka-Garh, Vaishali (period I b). The square size bricks of the stupa are similar to square size bricks (30x30x8 cm) from I b period at Raja-Vishal-Ka-Garh. Bricks of the same dimensions were also reported from Chankigarh, a fort belonging possibly to Mauryan period, about 20 km to the north of Lauriya Nandangarh. But it may not be out of place to mention here that no such brick was reported from relic stupa (originally a mud stupa) near Kharanua tank at Vaishali which had undergone several enlargements. It is considered as one of the earliest stupas built immediately after the death of Buddha. However, the discovery of a polished fragment of a *chhatravali* (pl. III) along with pieces of relic casket definitely put the Kolhua stupa including the pillar to the Mauryan period.

No datable object belonging to Sunga-Kushan period has been found. A terracotta archaic human head found from the mid-level may be assigned to the Kushan period. The site might have lost its importance during the early centuries of the Christian era. However, it regained its importance during the post-Gupta period (sixth century). The stupa was enlarged and the facade of the drum portion was embellished with carved bricks. A number of votive stupas around the *pradakshinapatha* found to have been constructed. A niche of one of the votive stupas yielded a beautiful stucco head of Buddha assignable to sixth-seventh century (pl. IV). A few broken inscribed terracotta plaques, impressed from the same mould are important discovery from the same level (pl. V). These plaques depict the figure of Buddha in standing posture in mendicant's garb with a parasol held over his hallowed head by a small standing figure to his right, down below. His left hand seems to indicate *varada-murda* bestowing *Karuna* to kneeling human figure, probably representing Amrapali the famous courtesan of Vaisali. Though defaced it recalls similar representation in stone from Cave 19 at Ajanta. These are unique terracotta plaques, so far, not reported from any excavations carried out at Vaishali earlier.

The site seems to have been deserted due to heavy floods in the river Gandak as evident from the deposit of a fine silt (average thickness 1.20 m) which acted as a sealing layer to all the votive stupas described above. However, due to its religious sanctity the site was revived during the Pala period as number of late structures including a few Pala sculptures were found in and around the site.

Archaeological Survey of India
New Delhi.

KALYAN PRIYA GUPTA

A Burnt Brick Structure At Hulas

The site at Hulas (Lat. 29° 15′ N, Long. 78° 40′ E), located in Nakur tahsil of district Saharanpur, U.P. is about 8 km west from Nanauta, on Delhi-Saharanpur State-Highway. The excavations by the Archaeological Survey of India since 1978-79 revealed five cultural periods. Period I is represented by Harappapn, Period II, Painted Grey Ware, Period III, Northern Black Polished Ware, Period IV, Sunga-Kushan and Period V Gupta and Early Medieval. The structure in question belongs to Period IV (Dikshit 1981).

The massive structure, constructed in the centre of the mound has two arms running in east-west and north-south directions (*IAR* 1978-79, pl. XXXVI-B). Burnt-bricks measuring 52x28x8 cm and 51x26x8 cm were arranged in English bond. The junction of the arms is roundish externally, whereas internally it has a rectangular projection of 1.78 m x 1.46 m size (*IAR* 1978-79: 60-61). The east-west arm of the structure has two drains. In the construction, mud has been exclusively used as mortar. Walls, under reference were also found plastered with mud as noticed at a few places.

DETAILS OF STRUCTURE NO. 1

The east-west arm is 52 m in length and 2.10 m in width. The thickness of the extant wall at its maximum is 1.80 m i.e. eighteen courses of burnt-bricks. In the southern section of this arm starting from the round corner, mud-bricks were found used occasionally in the bottom courses. The east-west arm which terminated in the eastern side, a thin curved line further east, indicating the fallen debris of the wall, was noticed. A 2.50 m wide opening at a distance of 43 m from the roundish corner was also seen. Inner projections of bricks having five courses on either side were noticed. A few round depressions on the top of the wall, indicating brick robbery at a later date were observed.

Two drains running north-south, discharging sullage into the rain-gulley were met with. The depth and width of one of the drains, close to the roundish corner was 1.10 m and 0.35 m respectively. The rain is built across the wall. It has thirteen courses of brick masonry at the moment having a pavement of two courses of bricks at its base. The other drain 0.29 m wide is a covered one. This can be seen in the section. The bricks capping the drain are quite visible. The other end of this drain is still to be ascertained. It has sufficient projection employing about eight courses but not of complete bricks.

The north-south arm, 30 m in length and 2.10 m in width has four courses of burnt-bricks and one course of mud-bricks below it. Further excavation is necessary to know about other courses. The size of the mud-bricks at the northern end of the arm were 50x26x8 cm and 49x27.5x8 cm.

CROSS-WALL OF THE STRUCTURE

A 6.45 m long burnt-brick wall running north-south, starting from the eastern end of the east-west arm was noticed. This wall was having a small 0.85 m wide wicket-gate. The maximum width of the wall was 0.80 m and maximum extant courses were six. Again towards the west, a sharp turn 3.60 m long was noticed in the same wall with ten maximum extant courses.

DETAILS OF STRUCTURE NO. 2

The massive structure was noticed striking against a 0.80 m thick platform made of mud and mud-bricks. In the centre another structure consisting of wedge-shaped burnt-bricks was found constructed over the platform. The east-west arms of this structure were 5.96 m and 6.10 m long respectively. The north-south arm on the western side was 5.02 m in length. The width of the wall was 0.50 m, except in the north-east corner where the width of the wall was 0.80 m. The maximum extant height of the north-south wall was 0.70 m with eleven brick courses while in the east-west wall the maximum number of courses were ten. The size of the wedge-shaped bricks used in the structure was 36 cm and 36.5 cm in length, 20.5 cm and 20.7 cm width at the wider end, 13.6 cm and 13.7 cm width at the narrow end and thickness 6/6.5 cm. The east-west arm in the northern side was probably having a 1.05 m wide entrance, paved with wedge-shaped burnt bricks. The main entrance was from the eastern side. A rectangular pillar was encountered in the centre. A semi-circular niche (?) having a diameter of 0.90 m, was noticed in the centre of the inner side of western wall.

The massive structure (structure number 1) was found sealed by layer (5). The layers (5) and (6) constitute the Sunga-Kushan (Period IV) Period. The structure number 2 was sealed by layer (4). The dating of this structure is still to be ascertained.

Archaeological Survey of India
New Delhi.

V. C. SHARMA

REFERENCES

Dikshit, K.N. 1981 Excavations at Hulas and further explorations of the upper Ganga-Yamuna *doab*; *Man and Environment* V, 70-76.
Indian Archaeology—A Review 1978-79.

Rotary Quern Mining Industry at Kakachia, District, Panchmahals Gujarat

Rotary querns have been reported from various excavated and explored sites extending from second cent. B.C. to sixteenth cent. A.D. but no attention has been paid to the mines from where the stone blanks used in their manufacture have been obtained. Stone mining sites from Gujarat have been reported at Nathakua (district Panchmahals), Kadia-dungar (district Broach) etc.

The site is in the vicinity of Kakachia (23° 06′ N., 73° 34′ E.), a small village situated on the left bank of the river Mahi at a distance of about 10 km to the southwest of Lunawada in the district Panchmahals of Gujarat. It is a famous holy place having 'Triveni Sangam' (sacred confluence of three rivers) of Mahi, Panam and Veri.

About half kilometre up-stream from this confluence the left bank of the river Mahi shows an exposer of a rocky bed along the side of the bank. On the basis of lithology and bed laminations this rock of sandstones appears to originate from sand deposits laid down in the past by the running water of the river Mahi. The concave cross-stratification surface of these sandstone beds have been taken advantage of by these early miners of Kakachia by splitting and chipping the sandstone blocks along their natural curvatures. It is not improbable that the miners of this site removed circular blocks instead of the usual rectangular ones, because of the naturally carved cross stratification surface of the sandstone beds. Field examination of the rocks shows it to be well suited for manufacture of rotary querns. This bed rock measures 100 x 25 m and shows evidence of stone mining activities. The site of Kakachia reveals negative impressions of several thick circular blocks of stone removed from a sandstone out crop. The diameter of these circular negative blocks range from 40 to 70 cm with thickness varying from 10 to 20 cm. The typical size and shape of these removed blocks indicate that they have been cut out for some specific use. This feature of the industry sharply distinguishes it from other known stone mining centres excepting that of Luhar-nala exposure of Pedhamli where evidence of removal of circular blocks have been noted.

A closer observation of this mining area reveals little step like cuttings developed as a result of the working technique. The technique of separating or detaching of circular blocks from the parent rock could be determined from the traces of chisel marks left on the periphery of the deep circles. The method of separating these circular blocks seems to be identical to the process of detaching rectangular blocks as reported at other sites - such as Nathakua, Kadia-dungar and the present day Lime-stone mining industries of Barda Hills near Porbandar in Saurashtra. Generally the rectangular blocks are separated from the bed rock first by loosening them from three sides by cutting narrow slit and finally detaching them from the rock by cutting a series of rectangular slits at the base of the forth open side along the ditch. The same method seems to have been used at Kakachia. The only difference is that instead of rectangular, circular blocks of required size were detached. This appears to have been accomplished, by first of all, cutting a sufficient wide and deep ditch into the rock along one of its side. Then a series of circular blocks were cut along the side of the ditch. The circular blocks were then detached from the parent rock by skilfully chiselling horizontally into the rock along its plane of cleavage through the opening provided by the ditch. In this way, fresh, six circular blocks of stone were separated from the parent rock along the ditch. In the second stage, the adjacent series of circular blocks were cut and detached and the work progressively continued further to the right.

After removing the circular blocks, the stone cutters may have worked further on the site itself to produce the querns. In this second stage of manufacturing they might have reduced the original diameter and thickness of the blocks by further neat chiselling to convert them into a pair of hopper (upper stone) and nether (lower stone) as parts of rotary quern. Rotary querns are also prepared either square or rectangular stone blocks by shaping them into circular forms. But the noteworthy feature of the Kakachia industry is that circular blocks of required size and shape were directly removed from the rock to save extra labour.

The mining industry by itself did not reveal any evidence which would allow determination of the antiquity of the mining activity. These rotating querns had entirely different tradition technologically as well as functionally, than those of saddle querns and mullers, though they could be described as proto-types of rotary querns. Rotary querns can be described as mechanical devices based on the rotation of the hopper stone having vertical or horizontal handle and a feeding rocket. Sanskrit, Pali and Prakrit words for the hand rotary querns are *Yantrkam, Yantam* and *Jantam* respectively. All these words also designate it as a machine.

Variation in diameter and thickness of the blocks used for making rotary querns indicated that small as well as big and light as well as heavy querns might have been manufactured here for specific purposes.

Acknowledgements

The author is grateful to Profs. R.N. Mehta and K.T.M. Hegde for their valuable guidance.

M.S. University of Baroda
Vadodara

V.H. SONAWANE

Newly Discovered Gupta Sculptures From Madhya Pradesh

Two sculptures alongwith the remains of a brick temple were discovered by the author in 1964 at Dithwara which lies about 15 km north-east of Katni on Bijairaghogarh road in District Jabalpur under the Village-to-Village Survey Scheme of antiquarian remains of Archaeological Survey of India. After the discovery, the Department of Archaeology and Museums, M,P, cleared the site during 1978-79, and exposed the *adhisthana* of a brick-temple measuring 21m x 15m with a *sopana (IAR* 1978-79:97). The plan of the *adhishthana* as revealed by excavations is on the box-pattern. These sculptures lay on a brick-platform locally called Jogia Baba to the east of the village in a mango-grove. It is interesting to note that Gupta Rock cut sculptures noticed earlier by the author at Sindursi near Bahoriband in the same district are called Jogini Mai (Trivedi 1976: 42-46). The sculptures under reference are as detailed below:—

1. VISHNU: Vishnu stands in *sampada,* wears *kirita-mukuta* emitting the *mukta (pearls)* and vegetal creepers marked by flowers secured by *simanta* fillet. The circular *prabhamanadala* in contrast to usual decoration is plain. The face is roundish marked by wide eye-lashes, half-closed eyes *(ardha-unmilita netra),* flat nose, fleshy cheeks with and double strands of spiral locks falling on the shoulders. He puts on *kundala* of *nagendra* variety and flat *graiveyaka.* Of the four arms show *keyuras, yajna-Suvarna-Sutra* (a double-chain sacred thread) covering left shoulder

dangling in the knee region. The diaphanous undergarment is secured by a *kati-sutra* with conspicuous knot below the navel. The upper garment, also diaphanous, gathers on the lower arm and reminds one of Mathura Buddha. Folds of the undergarment hang vertically between the legs while the plain drapery gives the effect of wetness, thus transforming whole body into a complete transparent sheath. The navel is marked by a socket. Shoulders, arms, fingers, elbow, wrist and legs are modelled as if turned on a lathe *(tanu-vritta-madhya)*. The God as usual does not wear *Vaijayanti-mala*. The image is comparable to that of Jhushi Vishnu (Harle 1974: 20, pl. 62) now displayed in the Allahabad Museum and also Mathura Museum No. E 6 now housed in the National Museum, New Delhi (Agrawala 1977: 106). Legs below knees are missing.

2. GARUDA: Garuda is two-armed (pl .II). From the orientation of the arms though damaged, it appears that these might have been held in the *namaskar-mudra*. The head-gear consists of *Chhatrakarsirah* with locks of hair radiating from the centre simulating the form of a parasol. The curly spiral shaped hair are arranged in parallel tiers with locks falling on both the shoulders. The arrangement of hair show parallelism with the Rajghat terracotta figurines (Narain and Agarwala 1978: pl. XXXV, XXXVI, fig. 1-6). Eyes are half-closed *(ardha-unmilita-netra)*. On the neck is depicted *triavali*. Ornaments are restricted and comprise of beaded *graiveyaka, nivita, kati-sutra* with a tassel of chain pattern falling on the left thigh. It is perceived through the diaphanous drapery. The face though blissful is badly bruised. To the right are remnants of wings. Because of the enormous damage to the sculpture it is difficult to say whether it adorned the *garuda-dhavaja* as at Eran or was an independent image fixed in front of the main deity e.g. Vishnu.

The discovery is significant, for not only it adds to our information regarding existence of one more Gupta brick temple of Vishnu but also shows that the main artery connecting Pataliputra (Patna) in Magadha to Ujjayini (Ujjain) in Malwa through the river Son and its feeder Johila (ancient Jyotiratha) passed through this region from Kausambi, Nachna through Eran and Vidisha. One notices through the whole route, temples of the classical period at regular interval, through the Chedi country which was known *Atavika-rajya* under the rule of Samudragupta (A.D. 335-76 and subsequently ruled directly by his successors Buddhagupta, Harivarma (Jain 1977: 62-66) and by their feudatories the *Parivrajaka Maharajas* (c. 475-528 A.D.) of Uchchakalpa (modern Ucheraha) in district Satna, M.P.

Both sculptures are inspired by the Sarnath school which filtered in this region through Kausambi with regional variations. The traits viz., the beauty of the body, hair-do, restraint ornaments, blissful attitude depicting sprituality, treatment of drapery may date both of these to the first quarter of sixth century A.D.

Archaeological Survey of India
New Delhi

C. B. TRIVEDI

REFERENCES

Agrawala, Vasudeva S. 1977 *Gupta Art*, Varanasi.
Harle, J.C. 1974 *Gupta Sculptures*, Oxford.
Indian Archaeology—A Review 1978-79, New Delhi.
Jain, B.C. 1977 Shankerpur Plate of Buddhagupta and Harivariman Gupta Year 166, *Journal of Epigraphical Society of India*, IV.
Narain A.K. and Prithivi Kumar Agrawala 1978 *Excavations at Rajghat (1957-58; 1960-65)*, IV A & B, Varanasi.
Trivedi C.B. 1976 Rock-cut Sculptures at Sindursi, District Jabalpur, Madhya Pradesh, *Prachya Pratibha*, IV, Bhopal.

The Historical Urbanization—A Suggestive Date

Much has been discussed on different aspects of the historical urbanization of India in recent decade (Thakur 1981: 1-36). The analyses of the surveyed data attempted in the present paper revealed that in India the historical urbanization can not be placed as early as sixth/fifth centuries B.C. as suggested by several workers. D.K. Chakrabarti, while discussing the urbanization in some other context observes three distinct phases of the early historical urban growth (Chakrabarti 1974: 89). The first phase, extending from Champa and Rajgriha to Ujjayini through Kausambi including upper-Gangetic valley and the Indo-Gangetic divide is assignable to *circa* sixth-fifth centuries B.C. In the second phase, third-second centuries B.C., he includes Punjab plains, Sind, lower Gangetic Valley, Rajasthan, Gujarat, Maharashtra and Orissa besides further growth of settlements already appended in the first phase. Present States of Karnataka, Kerala, Tamilnadu and Andhra have been considered to have got urbanized only in the last chronological bracket i.e. early centuries A.D., apart from a general prosperity in the entire subcontinent. Dr. S.P. Gupta too, not differing much with Chakrabarti's thesis assigns the beginning of the early historical urbanization to 600 B.C. Of course, he viewed the historical urbanization into two developmental stages i.e. formative (600-400 B.C.) and mature (400 B.C.—A.D. 100). Other scholars, not examining this aspect in length have assigned a date of *circa* 600 B.C. for the emergence of cities in historical period.

The present paper is intended to examine the chronological issue of the dawn of the historical urban centres on the basis of present archaeological data.

Perhaps, not one but many factors may have collectively been responsible for this phenomenal growth. While discussing the problem, the following variables, surplus food economy, political base, fortification, monumental architecture, metallurgical advancement, script, trade, artistic activities and currency, advanced by Childe (1950: 3-17) and disscussed by Ghosh (1973: 23-28) in the Indian context have been considered.

It has been advocated by scholars that surplus food production played the role of prime mover in creating a favourable environment for the emergence of urban centres. It may be assessed from the fact that how the army, officials, artisans and others, who were engaged in other business and thus not in a position to cultivate themselves were fed, unless and until there was a surplus production. Lumbini Pillar Inscription of Asoka refers to the reduction in the royal share out of total agricultural yield from 1/6 to 1/8. Practice of storing food grains at the time of famine and other calamities, is also referred to in Sohgaura Bronze Plate and Mahasthan Fragmentary Stone Plaque Inscriptions.

It may be of interest to note that storage-jars were very common in Harappan Period, but they almost disappear from the subsequent cultures till the advent of NBPW in *doab*. A circular barn (?), built of wedge-shaped burnt bricks encountered from the sub-Period 2 of Period III at Hastinapura (Lal 1954-55 : 25) perhaps is indicative of the means of storing the grains.

The ancient Buddhist and Jain texts mention that earlier to Buddha there were several *janapadas* in form of primary political units. Some of them grew into *mahajanapadas,* a more powerful unit controlling relatively larger areas. Later on, of the *mahajanapadas,* Vatsa, Kosala, Magadha and Avanti expanded, consolidated their territory and attained super political status. But it was only under the Nandas and Mauryas extensive expansion of territory was carried out enabling the control of one authority from Magadha over a vast area.

The consolidation of political system provided a common technological base and favourable environment for the growth of urban centres in different regions. The uniform development of agriculture, transport and metal, stone and ceramic technologies became possible perhaps through a strong political set-up (Chakrabarti 1974: 88).

Ancient literature is replete with references of fortification wherein they have been regarded as defensive measures besides being administrative units. Evidence of fortifications have come from Vaisali, Champa, Rajgir, Balirajgarh, Kausambi, Sravasti, Mathura, Ahicchatra, Ujjain, Eran, Sisupalgarh and Tilaurakot etc. At most of these sites the fortifications were initially built of mud but during later periods they were further strengthened besides the usual repairs, indicating further consolidation of the historical urbanization. The excavations have revealed that most of these were not built earlier to the beginning of fourth century B.C. However, the fortifications at Kausambi, Ujjain and Eran have been assigned a much earlier date, not coeval with majority of sites although, the high antiquity of the fortifications at above three sites has been questioned by a many scholars (Ghosh 1973 : 62-64; Sinha

No significant structure, representing monumental buildings have so far been encountered from the NBPW levels of the early historical sites except Taxila, Kausambi, Kumrahar and Rajgir. The pillared-hall built within the house-complex at Taxila (Bhir Mound, Stratum II), stone and brick palace and Ghoshitaram Vihar of Kausambi, wooden pillared hall at Kumrahar and series of elliptical structures interpreted as the earliest form of Buddhist monastries at Rajgir are the only structures which may be viewed as the structures of monumental nature. The buildings under reference from Taxila and Kumrahar, as evidenced from the excavations, clearly indicate that they were not constructed earlier to Mauryan Period. As far as the date of elliptical structures, encountered from Rajgir is concerned, proper datable evidences are lacking. Ghoshitaram Vihar of Kausambi, thus remains the only structure which was constructed prior to the fourth century B.C.

The Northern Black Polished Ware people were perhaps the first to use baked bricks after the Harappans in their structures, apart from less durable materials i.e. wood, mud and mud bricks. But a study has revealed that it was only during the fourth-third centuries B.C., later levels of NBPW, that the people employed baked-bricks in a considerable extent.

The first urbanization during the Harappan Period is well known for the high sense of sanitary arrangement. In the early historical period too, we find remains of pottery ring-wells, soakage pits, pottery pipes and brick drains which speak of the then way of sanitation. The ring-wells constructed by putting a number of pottery rings one above the other in a vertically dug pit, were a very common feature of the period under study. These were used most likely to refuse the sewage of the houses as evidenced by their association with residential units. Ramains of the large earthen jars placed one above the other in vertical fashion, lowest having a perforation at its base, were also perhaps meant for the disposal of house refuse. Pottery Pipes and brick drains have also been encountered from the early historical levels at a number of sites i.e. Kausambi (Sharma 1969 : 34), Hastinapura (Lal 1954-55 : 25), Pataliputra (Sinha and Narain 1970 : 15) and Rajghat (Narain and Singh 1977 : 10-11). It is significant to mention that all the above means of sanitation which require certain bye-laws pertaining most likely to some civic authority have not been dated prior to about 400 B.C.

The introduction of iron-technology played an initial and primary role in the emergence of urban settlements (Sharma 1965 : 61) and had thus directly or indirectly helped in giving the society a new impetus. Of course, the PGW using people were the first to acquire the knowledge of the new metal iron in *doab* but it was only in the succeeding NBPW period that their large scale use has been attested. Now the metallurgical quality of iron was not only utilized for preparing weapons—arrowheads, spearheads, etc. but was also extended for forging other tools and implements such as axes, chisels, sickels, knives, plough-shares. The iron implements would have been very much instrumental in clearing off the dense forests for making available more land to produce the necessary surplus. A study has revealed the use of larger number and variety of iron objects during the later levels of NBPW *(circa* fourth-third centuries B.C.) than the earlier.

Knowledge of script has been considered as one of the main causative factors in the emergence of cities. But so far no written record in the form of seals and sealings and inscriptions has come from the levels earlier to Mauryan Period.

Trade always plays a crucial role in the economic growth of the society but to gear up trade certain facilities such as transport and efficient distribution are essential. The cities in most of the cases also acted as important marts and it would be observed that the majority of the urban centres were located on the banks of navigable rivers and were also connected with main trade routes providing water and land transport facilities, enabling smooth trade with far off places. The nearby villages must be exchanging their surplus with the items produced in the cities/towns. Specialized craftsmenship and the availability of raw materials in a particular region may also have been instrumental in the large scale external trade. Although direct archaeological evidence of trade does not come from the sites but the occurrence of identical artefacts such as semi-precious and terracotta beads, etched carnelian, and *ghat*-shaped ivory plaques depicting stylized female figure, iron arrow-heads, copper antimony-rods, ceramics, terracotta objects—mainly human and animal figurines, besides several other objects from the early historical levels having a wide distribution, certainly indicate towards an efficient communication system and extensive trading activities.

Several scholars have attached significance (Gupta 1980 : 8-11) to the indulgence of people in artistic activities as a contributory factor in way of the villages acquiring the status of cities/towns. As far as archaeological evidences are concerned the earliest evidence of plastic art and objects of high artistic value in the historical period have come from the levels dated later to *circa* fourth century B.C. Beautifully done terracotta human figurines adorned with ornaments and drapery have been obtained from Mauryan level onwards. Asokan pillar-capitals, Didarganj Yakshi and other objects, carved in stone and other media all were the creation of the sculptors of about fourth-third centuries B.C., which positively indicate towards the high artistic sense of the contemporary society.

The existence of a monetary exchange has been attributed by Joshi (Joshi 1972-73 : 36 B) as one of the major deciding factors in the emergence of urban centres. The system of barter prevalent in earlier times, was not practicable for the long distance trade. The earliest currency in form of punch-marked coins associated with NBPW were perhaps issued by rulers, individual merchants and guilds as indicated by one or more symbols. Their find from the excavations at several early historical sites has revealed that they were not issued earlier to *circa* 500 B.C. (Ray 1959).

Of course, from the available archaeological data it is difficult to assess the large scale drift of the population from the villages to the towns, a relevant point raised by A. Ghosh (1972-73 : 34) for the identification of a stage of urbanization in the context of early historical India, but the growth of the settlements in space do indicate despite its own limitations, that during the early historical period the size of the urban settlements grew considerably than the preceding period. The political activities, security, facilities of market, appreciation of craftsmanship and several other factors may have been behind the growth of population at the urban centres. The development of the settlement of Mathura, may be taken as a case-study. Here, the earliest settlement in the sixth century B.C. (Period I) was restricted only to a certain area and was most likely in form of a small hamlet. But somewhere during the last quarter of the fourth century B.C. and the early half of third century (mid/late phase of Period II), represented by NBPW the habitation enclosed within an earthen rampart, occupying an area of about 3.9 sq km expanded enormously (Joshi 1979). As far as the size of the settlements at other sites are concerned only sketchy data is available. At Rajghat a general prosperity was observed in Period II *(circa* 300 B.C. to the beginning of Christian-era) as evidenced from the material culture to which the excavator has assigned the stage of urbanization. The habitation during this Period was also found enlarged considerably, occupying relatively a larger area (Narain & Singh 1977 : 9-10). A major change in the details of the material equipment in Period II *(circa* 275-50 B.C.) at Sravasti has been noticed too. The cause has been attributed by the excavator to the control of a central authority and the contacts with foreigners besides extensive use of metal.

The foregoing suggests that the emergence of urban settlements in early historical period did not take place as early as sixth century B.C. However, we admit that foundations for the emergence of future towns may have laid in sixth-fifth century B.C. But the urban embryos could attain the status of cities/towns only around fourth-third centuries B.C., roughly synchronizing with mid/late NBPW levels and the Mauryan rule.

Archaeological Survey of
India, New Delhi.

A.K. SINHA

REFERENCES

Chakrabarti, Dilip K. 1972-73 Concept of Urban Revolution and the Indian Context, *Puratattva* 6, New Delhi.
1974 Some Theoretical Aspects of Early Indian Urban Growth, *Puratattva* 7 New Delhi.

Childe, V. Gordon 1950 The Urban Revolution, *The Town Planning Jorunal* XXI 1, Liverpoole.

Ghosh, A. 1972-73 Comments on the paper Concept of Urban Revolution and the Indian Context, *Puratattva* 6, New Delhi.
1973 *The City in Early Historical India,* Simla.

Gupta, S.P. 1974 Two Urbanizations in India A Side Study in their Social Structure, *Puratattva* 7 New Delhi.
1980 *The Roots of Indian Art,* Delhi.

Joshi, M.C. 1972-73 Comments on the paper, Concept of Urban Revolution and the Indian Context, *Puratattva* 6, New Delhi.
1979 Mathura As an Ancient Settlement. (Cyclostyled copy), a paper read on Mathura Seminar, New Delhi.

Lal, B.B. 1954-55 Excavations at Hastinapura and Other Explorations in the Upper Ganga and Sutlej Basins, *Ancient India* 10 & 11, New Delhi.

Narain, A.K. & P. Singh 1977 *Excavations at Rajghat-1957-58, 1960-65* III, Varanasi.

Ray, S.C. 1959 *Stratigraphic Evidence of Coins in Indian Excavations and Some allied Issues,* Numismatic Notes and Monographs 8, Numismatic Society of India, Varanasi.

Sharma, G.R. 1969 Excavations at Kausambi 1949-50, *Memoirs of the Archaeological Survey of India.* Delhi

Sharma, R.S. 1965 Material background of the Origin of Buddhism, *Das-Kapital Centenary Volume —a Sympostum,* Delhi-Ahmedabad-Bombay (ed) Mohit Sen and M.B. Rao.

Sinha, B.P. & Lala Aditya Narain 1970 *Pataliputra Excavations-1955-46,* Patna.

Sinha, K.K. 1973 Stratigraphy and Chronology of Early Kasambi—a Reappraisal, *Radiocarbon and Indian Archaeology* (ed) D.P. Agrawal and A. Ghosh, Bombay.

Thakur, Vijay Kumar 1981 *Urbanization in Ancient India,* New Delhi.

On Tughluq Architecture Of Gujarat

Gujarat seems to have received continued attention of the Tughluq rulers owing to its rich trade and commerce. They appointed trusted noblemen as governors of this region, as is evidenced from the large number of Arabic and Persian inscriptions noticed and published in recent years (Hoag 1977) The Tughluqs started brisk building activities not only at Delhi and its neighbourhood but also in Gujarat of which some of the imposing monuments in the forms of mosques and tombs at Broach, Cambay, Dholka and Mangrol testify to their deep interest and resources in building art. These remarkable monuments not only rival but certainly excel in their architectural merits and lavish ornamentation to their proto-types in Delhi and in other parts of Northern India. I have therefore tried to examine and illustrate the unique position of Tughluq architecture of Gujarat which played a significant role in balancing the Islamic and Indian styles successfully.

Most of the Khalji and early Tughluq buildings in Gujarat represented the phase of improvisation. However under Ghiyathu'd-Din Tughluq (A.D. 1320-25) and Muhammad bin Tughluq (A.D. 1325-1351) original buildings began to take the place of extemporaneous compositions as is first represented by the Jami Masjid at Broach, a seaport town of Gujarat which very early came under Muslim rule. Although it has forty-eight richly carved temple pillars and brackets reused to support the domed roofs of the prayer hall, it is not an improvisation since it was planned and constructed according to the conventional mosque design, consisting of a *sahn* with gateways on three sides and the *maqsura* at its western end. The *maqsura* is of the open pillared variety being merely an elaborated verandas, as distinct from those in which an arched facade is erected. This style is evidently deeply rooted in the Prophet Muhammad's house at Madina. The richly carved pillars of the open facade of Broach Jami mosque are so arranged as to divide the interior into three compartments. This arrangement continued to be preferred in many small mosques of stone during the rules of the sultans of Gujarat (A.D. 1411-1573). The walls enclosing the sanctuary have been constructed of dressed blocks of stone constituting the earliest example of original masonry of Indo-Islamic style in Gujarat.

The interior of the western wall is provided with three *mihrabs* and a series of arched windows filled with stone tracery, Islamic in purpose but apparently designed in Western Indian temple pattern. The *mihrabs* are virtually copies of the niches of the Jain temples of Gujarat of tenth-eleventh centuries. But the artisans had carefully avoided the didactic sculptural symbolism associated with Jain religion. It seems the niches of early mosques in Islamic countries had derived inspiration from the niches of Jain and Hindu temples of Western India.

The exquisitely fine treatment of the square sunk coffered ceilings of the *maqsura* of this mosque are the unique examples of Gujarati artisan's attempt to copy the Islamic geometric and floral ceiling ornamentation. Inscriptions appearing over the northern entrance gateway and the central *mihrab* of the Jami Masjid assign its construction in A.D. 1321-22 to Daulat Shah Muhammad al-Buthari who was a distinguished nobleman of Ghiyathu'd-Din Tughluq and Muhammad bin Tughluq (*EIM* 1939-40:25).

The next most impressive monument is the Jami Masjid at Cambay. It is the masterpiece of the Tughluqs in India (pl. I). The Tughluq mosques at Delhi including the great Begampuri Masjid of Jahan Panah cannot be its equal in any respect. From its appearance, setting and technical details it is clear that the local artisans were reinforced by the master architects and masons of the imperial capital of Delhi. Most probably they were the same persons or trained by them who had produced the masterpieces of the Khaljis and whose genius is adequately represented by the celebrated 'Ala' i Darwaza of the Qutb mosque at Mehrauli. The Jami Masjid at Cambay is a monument of considerable size and height and follows the conventional open courtyard pattern. Remarkable for its spaciousness and fine proportions its elegant facade, consisting of three lofty and shapely arches, in front of the prayerhall, having inspirations from the Quwwatu'l-Islam mosque of Delhi and Arhai-Din-ka Jhonpra mosque of Ajmer sets an ideal for the design of the later mosques built under the patronage of the sultans of Gujarat and Malwa. The imposing Jammaat Khana Masjid at the Dargah of Hazrat Nizamud'-Din Auliya whose date of construction has been a subject of controversy, bears a strong 'family likeness' to the Gujarat example. Another striking feature of this mosque are the shape and position of arches and the technical character of its masonry work, consisting of alternate broad and narrow courses, and the architectural treatment of the building as a whole, which endow it with balance, symmetry and rythm. The interior arrangement of pillars and design of its mihrab has close resemblance to that of the Ajmer mosque, mentioned above. The areas at the end of the floor in line with the corridors, have each two additional rows of pillars crossing the mosque, but these are interrupted at half the height to support two closed galleries filled with stone grilles, constituting the *muluk-khana* that are covered each by two domes of conical shape of Ajmer variety (Hoag 1977). There are only three *mihrabs* in the west wall, corresponding the three large entrances. Semicircular in plan with pointed arch resting on two engaged pillars, set within marble architraves for frames of floral pattern also contain Quranic verses inscribed in *Naskh* characters. Behind each *mihrab* in the rear wall is a semicircular buttress ornamented with carved string-courses in the form of the sikharas of Hindu temples. This pattern was invariably provided in all the Sultanate mosques at Ahmedabad and Champaner. The pulpit or *mimbar* of this mosque is also notable for it is conceptually Islamic but predominantly indigenous in execution. It assumed an independent domed structure with steps in later mosque of Gujarat, which had more direct Islamic influence of Middle eastern countries. A domed chhatri or kiosk in the centre of the *sahn* of this Jami Masjid is one of the earliest representation of a *mukabbar* in an Indian mosque. Its reservoir *(haud)* for *wazu* has undergone subsequent repairs as is evident from an inscription.

This celebrated mosque was built in A.D. 1325 in the first year of Muhammad bin Tughluq as is evident from the inscription on its northern entrance (Desai 1957:58). It is also evident that the construction must have started during the reign of Ghiyathu'd Din Tughluq since it could not have been possible to erect such a massive building within few months. Adjoining the mosque on the southern side is a remarkable double storeyed tomb of the open-pillared hall variety, originally surmounted with a dome (pl. II). The dome has fallen but its carved surfaces and exquisitely fine epitaphs represent rare specimens of *kufi* and *naskh* calligraphy beside containing one of the finest relief work on marble tablets having plant motifs of Jain paintings of twelfth and thirteenth centuries (Husain 1953:172). On these grounds this tomb (pl. III) is of sufficient artistic value and architecturally it is an example of one of the very few surviving early monuments of this class in Gujarat. Ibn Battuta visited Cambay in A.D. 1345 and found it a very fine city, remarkable for the elegance and solidity of its mosques, and houses built by wealthy foreign merchants, which formed a chief part of its population.[1]

Of almost the same character as the Cambay Jami mosque of the time of Muhammad bin Tughluq is the remarkable Masjid of Hilal Khan Qazi at Dholka a town of sufficient antiquarian interest.[2] It is a small but elegant building notable for its pair of tall ornamental turrets on each side of the central archway of the facade. In design these turrets are indigenous but they definitely anticipated the later minarets of Gujarat mosques. The *maqsura* consists of five bays, covered by five low, plain, conical domes, the central one being raised higher than the side ones. The north end is screened off inside to serve as Muluk Khana having a separate entrance from the north wall. The treatment of the central portion of the facade of his mosque is significant in as much as it finally evolved into the elaborate sculptured buttresses flanking the central arched opening in later mosques of Gujarat. Beside the rich carvings of its ceilings and finely sculptured marble mihrabs its exquisitely executed pulpit is one of the prettiest of its kind in India. The face of the rise of every step is sculptured in a different pattern. The sides of the stairs are covered with small square panelling of geometric designs in deep relief. It is surmounted by a neat canopy standing out separate from the wall, with a pyramidal roof of Indian pattern. Having close affinity with Egyptian pulpit structure it introduced purely Islamic component in Indian mosques. A marble square platform provided in front of the pulpit in the maqsura for the use of Imam is an entirely new addition since no such platform are noticed in other mosques of India or abroad. It was later followed in the mosques of Ahmedabad.

The mosque is entered through entrance porches on the south and east. The main entrance has an elegant portico supported on thirty two pillars with flight of steps. It is roofed by the corbelled dome having perforated screens of attractive designs. This monument is also notable for its fine ashlar masonry in shining red and buff sandstone.

Another Tughluq mosque at Dholka popularly called Tanka Masjid, is of the open variety. Its maqsura consists of over a hundred exceptionally sculptured pillars of temple origin. The *mihrabs* are built in deep recesses having semi-circular buttresses behind. It is also provided with a screened Muluk Khana on the northern side. In its small mihrab there is a Quranic verse inscribed in *Naskh* script (Surah LXXI, V. 18): 'It is unto Allah that the mosques are set apart; call not then on any other therein with Allah'. Its northern and southern porticos are also indigenous in character having broad projecting eaves and lion-headed drain spouts of artistic value.

According to the three versified Persian inscriptions the Jami Masjid was built in A.H. 762 (A.D. 1361) in the reign of Firuz Shah Tughluq (A.D. 1351-88) by Malik Ikhtiyaru'd Daulat Wa'd-Din Mufarrah Sultani, the royal *Dawidar (Dawat dar*/ ink bearer). One of the epigraphs composed by one Yaqub gives poetic description of building material viz. brick, clay, and lime mortar *(gach)* used in the construction. (Desai 1962:10-11).

Firuz Shah Tughluq is celebrated in history for building of new cities and public works. 'Afif and Firishta paid lavish tribute to him in their histories. (Afif 1982: 273; 1890: 127). Gujarat received due attention of Firuz Shah whose scores of stone inscriptions recording the construction of fortresses, mosques, tombs, stepwells, gardens and sarais have been discovered and published recently. During his reign Zafar Khan, governor of Gujarat, made a notable contribution by erecting the Jami Masjid at Kapadwanj (District Kaira) in A.H. 772 (A.D. 1370-71) Haig 1928:175). The epigraph written in beautiful Naskh script of Bihar variety of this mosque also mentions the names of the calligraphist and supervisor of the construction as Uthman, son of Kamal Khattat, Husain, son of 'Imad respectively. The mosque itself follows the conventional plan with *sahn* having entrances on the east and north sides. The *maqsura* is roofed by six domes in two rows of three each. In the northwest corner is the screened apartment of Muluk-khana of sufficient interest. The mihrabs in the qibla wall are alternated by narrow windows filled with artistic stone grilles. The beautiful pulpit is of the raised type of old variety representing indigenous workmanship.

Among the other surviving buildings of Firuz Shah, the Jami Masjid at Mangrol (District Junagadh) is one of the largest and best of its class in India. It represents the conventional courtyard-cum-cloisters plan of mosques having spacious *sahn* with stone flooring and double storeyed colonnade on three sides. It consists of tall columns in a most impressive manner. In the northwest corner is a fine stone step-well having elegant sculptures of *kirtimukhas* and other divinities. Its corbelled ceiling also represents a superb sculptural composition. The tank must have belonged to an earlier period but incorporated in the mosque complex for serving as a *haud* for ablution.

The monumental prayer hall is of closed variety, covered with ten conical domes of Ajmer and Cambay design. The treatment of its facade is quite interesting. The northern and southern corner are raised higher from the main roof and are balanced by corner turrets and crowned with pillared kiosks a feature which is generally found in the Tughluq and Lodi monuments of Delhi. The plain surface of ashlar wall is pierced by arched entrances and canopied projecting balconied windows below the parapet walls as well as on the ground floor. This feature later developed more and adorned several mosques at Ahmedabad. The rows of numerous sculptured pillars and beams in the *maqsura* add to the beauty of its interior. A marble tablet fixed near the pulpit bears beautiful inscription assigning the construction to the mosque to Izzu'd-Din, son of Aramshah in A.H. 785 (A.D. 1383-84).

Among other notable buildings of this period mention may be made of two smaller but beautiful mosques of Mangrol, namely Ravali Masjid and Rahmat Masjid which are built in trabeate style with open pillared facades, approached by large pretentious proches. The *mihrabs,* pulpits and their inscriptions in ornamental pattern represent the finest specimens of Indo-Islamic calligraphy in India (Desai 1962:28-31). During the later Tughluqs the central authority became feeble and marked a definite pause in the progress of building activity in this region. But this phase of Indo-Islamic building art was remarkable for it inspired all later developments both in Gujarat and elsewhere in India.

Acknowledgements:

I am grateful to Shri P. K. Trivedi for his help in the preparation of this article and Shri M. M. Srivastava for photographs.

NOTES

1. One of the epitaphs records that this is the tomb of the exalted chief, prince of Wazirs, pillar of the state and religion 'Umar son of Ahmad al-Kazruni who died on 21st October 1333 A.D. Another epitaph of similar variety registers the demise of his wife. It may be of interest to note that low relief floral surface ornamentation in Mughal buildings including Taj Mahal seem to have received definite inspiration from these beautiful epitaphs.

2. An inscription appearing on the central *mihrab* assigns the construction of this mosque to Mafkharu'l-Umara Muqarrabu'd-Daulat wad-Din Hilal Maliki on 8th September 1333 A.D. It also records the name of the architect as Abdul Karim, son of Latif.

Archaeological Survey of India
New Delhi

W. H. SIDDIQUI

REFERENCES

Afif, 1832 *Tarikh-i-Firishta,* I, 273, Bombay.
1890 Tarikh-i-Firuz Shahi, 127, Calcutta.
Desai, Z.A. 1957-58 *Epigraphia Indica Arabic and Persian Supplement,* 29.
1962 *Epigraphia Indica Arabic and Persian Supplement.*
Epigraphia Indo-Moslemica 1939-40.
Haig, Wolsely 1928 *Cambridge History of India* III, Cambridge.
Hoag, John D. 1977 *Islamic Architecture,* New York.
Husain, A.M. 1953 *Rehla: The Rehla of Ibn Battuta* (translated ino English with notes), Gaekwad Oriental series CXXII, Baroda.

A Note on the Treatment of an Excavated Iron Object

A curious looking large size iron object was discovered by the U.P. Archaeological Organisation during excavations at Hulaskhera, District Lucknow. The object belonged to Period III deposit, i.e. *circa* third century to fifth century A.D. It was received in the NRLC for treatment. The object, oval in shape, measured 56 cms x 41 cms (Fig. 1). The width of the rim ranged between 2.0 to 2.5 cms. Thickness of the rim was about 1 cm. There were 17 bars fitted to the rim. The length of the longest bar in the centre was 39 cms and that of the shortest one at the end was 25.5 cms. The bars were of varying widths, ranging between 0.8 cm to 1.75 cms. The thickness of the bars was about 0.65 cm.

CONDITION OF THE OBJECT

The iron object when received for conservation treatment, had on it thick corrosion layers and freshly formed brown droplets of ferric chloride. The brown rust droplets found present on the object were tested for chlorides. A high percentage of chlorides, in comparison to the chlorides normally present in the ordinary rust, was indicated. Small quantities of sulphates were also detected but not in any appreciable amount.

TREATMENT

For the treatment of the Hulaskhera object, in the beginning, 5% sodium sesquicarbonate solution, i.e. the extracting solution was frequently changed but less so afterwards. The idea was to provide the maximum concentration gradient for the diffusion of salts from the capillaries of the object to the treatment bath. In the initial stages the extraction of salts was rapid but later on it dropped appreciably.

At this stage, because it was discovered that metal core was present, the thick upper layers of rust were also removed except in a few places where the iron core was not present, for instance at the periphery of the object. A dental drilling machine was used for the removal of hard encrustations. Wherever the rust was completely removed, the object attained a very good shape and appeared to be sturdy. If this thick crust of rust was not removed, chlorides and sulphates would not have been extracted completely. The removal of the upper layers of rust greatly facilitated the extraction of the soluble salts.

Inspite of this treatment, it was observed that the soluble salts were still present in the rust which was retained. Treatment with sodium sesquicarbonate takes a very long time. The object was already under treatment for nearly six months and yet chlorides were present in the rust.

Recent experiments in our Laboratory indicate that the use of anion exchange resins succeeds in the quick removal of the soluble salts present in the objects. There is another advantage in the technique as happens while using sodium sesquicarbonate that there is no blocking of the fine capillaries present in the object and salts come out quickly without any hinderance. It took only 15 days using this method for the complete elimination of the soluble salts. The object, after the elimination of chlorides, was washed in several changes of hot water, for a few days. In the NRLC we have got constructed a stainless steel bath, with arrangement for electric heating. It becomes very convenient to heat the water whenever required.

The question now was concerning a protective coating on the object. It is well-known that iron in the presence of humidity is very susceptible to corrosion. It rusts even at 45% R.H. and in the absence of any impermeable and inert coating on the object, it is likely to start corroding within a short period after the treatment, if the humidity is high. A very thin coating of iron phosphate was obtained by dipping the iron object in a 2% solution of sodium dihydrogen phosphate. The process is known as 'phosphatization.' (Shrier 1978: 16-25). In industry, iron phosphate is obtained by various drastic means (Gorta 1972: 190). It was hoped that the formation of a layer of iron phosphate on the metal will protect it from further corrosion.

After the phosphate treatment, the object was rinsed in 20.05% solution of chromic acid. (Shrier: 16-27). The function of this treatment is to block the micro holes still remaining in the passive iron phosphate layer, by the formation of iron oxide, Fe_2O_3. Thereafter the object was again rinsed in distilled water and dried to 110°C, and while it was still hot it was coated with a high melting micro-crystalline wax.

Micro-crystallin wax is an impermeable coating and works well on iron objects. (ICCROM 1963: 42) Micro-crystalline waxes are semi-synthetic waxes prepared as by-products from the refining of petroleum. Because of their micro-crystalline

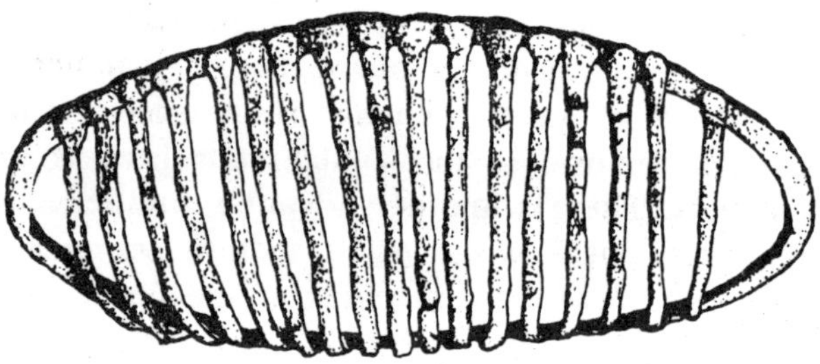

Fig 1

structure, they have a plasticity, in contrast to the paraffin wax which is brittle. Beeswax is also plastic and can be used as a protective coating but has a low melting point (55°-60°C), as compared to micro-crystalline waxes which are available in a wide range of melting points. The micro-crystalline wax used by us was with a melting point range of 89°-91°C.

After conservation work, the object was tested in a closed cabinet with high humidity for a few days. Its behaviour was also noted during the rainy season when the R.H. is qutie high. So far there is no outbreak of corrosion except in two or three small points. These points were further blocked with a protective coating to stop their outbreak. Because the object was fragile a supporting tray of wood has been prepared to keep this item. If the object is lifted at the periphery, there can be a likelihood of its breaking because of the pressure exerted.

Acknowledgements:

The authors are grateful to Mr. Pawan Kumar for help in the conservation work. The line drawing incorporated is done by Shri Prem Chand Sharma.

National Research Laboratory
for Conservation of Cultural
Property, Lucknow.

O. P. AGRAWAL
V. C. SHARMA

REFERENCES

ICCROM 1963 *Synthetic Materials Used in the conservation of Cultural Property,* Rome.

Shrier, L.L. (ed) 1978 corrosion control, corrosion 2, Newnes Butterworths, London.

Wranglen, Gorta 1972 *An Introduction of corrosion and Protection of Metals,* Institut for Metallskydd, Fack 10041, Stockholm 26.

Environmental Protection for Taj Mahal, Agra and Other Monuments

The main objective of this comprehensive research programme was to study the effects of gaseous pollutants on the various varieties of stones as well as to study the deposit cum reaction of the particulate matter leading to physical damage of abrasive action of wind borne particles.

In Agra there are about 260 Iron foundries which are also responsible for adding to the level of pollution in addition to thermal power plants, coal based engines and now Mathura Refinery which is to cater to refining of 6 million tonne of crude having sulphur content to the tune of 2%. In this region several monuments of international fame like Taj, Sikandra, Itmad-ud-daula, Fort etc. are located.

The chemical composition of marble is:

	I	II	III
1. Loss of ignition	42.00%	39.20%	40.80%
2. Acid insoluble	.82%	2.60%	1.00%
3. R_2O_3	5.40%	0.67%	0.31%
4. MgO	3.50%	1.43%	0.75%
5. CaO	47.30%	55.83%	56.23%
6. Alkalies	0.98%	—	—
	100.00	99.73	99.39
Density	2.33	2.37	2.47
Porosity	from 5 to 9% in volume		
Colour	white slightly dark		

Marble of Taj consists of calcite, has low porosity and water aborption. Sandstone is principally quartz and alkaline felspars with layered structure facilitating flaking which are running parallel-having high porosity/absorption. Several factors have been found to be responsible for the deterioration of marble and sandstone. These factors combine together to act or act alone alongwith the humidity and climatic changes. Now industiialization is also producing its own impact in the form of gaseous pollutants and particulate matters, both of which act either physically or chemically with the calcareasous part resulting in weakening of stone fabrics in compressive or mechnical strengths. Use of different types of building materials in proximity to one another has also to be watched.

The commonest air-pollutants are sulphur-dioxide and other oxides which are major source of worry to all conservators of monuments. Sulphur dioxide is an extremely strong and corrosive chemical, which once deposited on materials, cannot be cleaned easily. Further the process is catalysed by metallic constitues of suspended ash. The sulfation rate measured by the Survey's laboratory by lead-candle methods is as following:

		Taj	Sikandra
		(Unit-Mg/100 sq. cm/day (S^o3)	
1. 24.10.81 to 24.11.81	=	0.5763318	1.6070236
2. January, 82	=	0.1103735	0.1133227
4. April to May 82	=	0.0532728	0.0414346

The value clearly shows a regular pattern i.e. 1. during winter the value is higher and quite reactive because of long-duration of the stay of sulphur containing gases. 2. During January, the value is lower than winter value. 3. After and during monsoon the value comes down as indicated in charts available with the Archaeological Survey of India Science Laboratory, Dehra Dun.

BY PARAROSANITINE METHOD:

(1) November,	99 Mg/m^3
(2) January,	60 Mg/M^3
(3) May	36 Mg/m^3

The presence of elemental sulphur was confirmed by scanning electron-microscope as well as micro-chemical analysis.

Particulate matter analysis was also attempted to measure the air pollution caused by settleable particles in the air by collecting the dust in a dust fall jar. Total particulate matter suspended in the atmosphere revealed: physical weathering of stones, wind directions, wind speed, rain fall, relative humidity, temperature measurements along with the complete analysis of the rain water.

Now the particle size determination has been initiated.

Accelerated weathering tests were also carried out in the Laboratory with different quantities of sulphur-dioxide on the slabs of marble as well as marble at different altitudes. This has been done in order to test the physico-chemical behaviours of the stone. A complete data is available.

The cleaning of a marble by non-ionic detergent along with liq-ammonia and other organic solvents produced good results. The following preservatives have been used as experimental measures on a small area and these results are being watched.

EFFICACY OF DIFFERENT PRESERVATIVES

Archaeological Survey of India has used a number of preservatives based on different formulations. The most important being the vinyl resins, acrylic resins, silances, Dynaglazes, plyconates, waxes etc. After a thorough study of the preservatives, it has been noted that the product BSM-40 alongwith vinyl resins are giving the best results. The study has clearly revealed that the permeability, the reversibility, the binding power, the abrasive resistence, the film forming property are quite good in the case of BSM-dynasilan 40

+ PVA mixture. The different technical and chemical properties of these film forming synthetic coatings are given below :

1. *Poly-Vinyl Acetate*

It is a mobile, non-toxic colourless liquid in the cold, and does not show a tendency to polymerize in the absence of light. It is reversible and thermosetting in nature. In this case two techniques were employed.

(i) Brushing

(ii) Spray

Brushing technique did not produce the desired results while spray technique showed appreciable results. The permeability was such as to allow the vapour gas phase to enter the pores and thus allow the stone to breathe.

2. *Polymethyl Methacylate :* This has a good stability and is stable up to 250°C. There is a danger in this case of cross linking due to the action of light without any change in appearance. This was not found to be suitable.

3. *Dynaglaze and Dynaglaze Special* : A special British formulation intended for marbles but in this case the results were not good as translucency and whiteness were noted.

4. *Dynaglaze Special* : It has a slight improvement over the previous one but still not so good as the BSM and PVA mixture.

5. *Waxes* : Initially it was good but due to deposition of silica and carbonaceous matter it was apparent that it became quite dirty and requires periodic cleaning at much shorter frequency.

6. *Polyconates* : Polyconate which is a sodium methyl siliconate has been reported to be water repellent, as during application moisture evaporates and the polyconate reacts with the moisture and the carbon dioxide of the atmosphere to form insoluble, invisible water repellent film, of Polymethyl Silicic Acid, this was agin found to be not good.

7. *Dynasilan BSM-40* : This preservative is a Dynamic Noble product and has given excellent results; the surface is free from scratches and from carbonaceous matter. It is entirely transparent. In this case it is not the physical bond but chemical bonding which is much stronger. This is silane, the silicon atom is bonded to a water repellent alkyl group on one side and with inorganophilic ester-group on the other side. In the presence of moisture the alcohol groups are lost producing a silonal. The reaction is catalyzed by alcohol the hydroxyl group from the building takes part in the reaction.

8. *Mixture of PVA and Dynaslan BSM-40* This has given excellent results and is free from any scratch, translucency etc. It has an additional advantage of having an extremly good bonding and is reversible also. However, researches are continuing at different quantum of concentration of SO_2 which the film will withstand with and without preservatives in the accelearated testing chamber. Some flucro carbons are also being imported for a test check on the different pieces.

9. *Fomblin* - a perfluoro-nated polyether fluid-i also being tried.

Further researches are continuing in this respect.

Archaeological Survey of India
Dehradun

B. N. TANDON

The Archaeological Material from West Bengal in the Zoological Survey of India

On behalf of the Palaeozoology Division of the Zoological Survey of India, the present author has studied the archaeozoological material from a number of localities and excavated sites in West Bengal. This material is still basically unpublished but the present report sums up the basic evidence.

I. SUSUNIA (district Bankura)

Some of the fossil remains found in this locality rich in lower palaeolithic artifacts have been studied by the Palaeontology Division of the Geological Survey of India. The collection in the Zoological Survey of India comprises the following material.

1. *Equus* (family Equuidae, class Mammalia) : teeth— 8 + 1 of upper and lower jaws; limb-bones —2.

2. *Tragocerus* (sub-family Boselaphine, family Bovidae, class Mammalia): a ramus of mandible with 4 teeth. *Tragocerus* belongs to the present sub-family to which *Boselaphus tragocamelus* belongs. This animal is known as *nilgai*. *Tragocerus* is an extinct species and reported for the first time from Susunia.

3. *Cervus duvauceli* Cuv. *(Barasingha)* : antler portion—2; broken limb bones—5.

4. *Axis axis* Erxl *(Chital)* : teeth—2; antler portion—4; broken limb bones—1.

5. *Sus scrofa* Linn. (pig) : broken limb bones —2.

6. *Bos namadicus* Falc. (the ancestral stock of the "cow" group) : teeth—3 and a broken mandible with 3 teeth attached; limb-bones—1.

7. *Bos indicus* Linn (cattle) : teeth—1; limb-bones—6.

8. *Bubalus bubalis* var. *palaeindicus* Falc. and Caut. : teeth— mandible with 4 teeth + 5 teeth; limb-bones—4. This is an extinct buffalo.

9. *Bubalus bubalis* Linn, (present buffalo) : teeth— 3 and a portion of mandible; limb-bones —10.

10. *Ovis orientalis vignei* Blyth (sheep) : limb-bones—3.

11. *Capra hircus aegagrus* Erxl. (goat) : broken right maxilla with 2 teeth and 1 teeth separate.

12. *Boselaphus tragocamelus* Pallas (present *nilgai)* : teeth—2.

13. *Antilope cervicapra* Linn. (black buck) : a large number of remains—teeth = 35 + two broken maxilla with 3 teeth attached to each one of them. Five broken mandibles with 2 to 3 teeth attached with each of the mandibles. Broken vertebrae-2; antler portions-5; limb-bones—27.

14. *Giraffa* cf. *camelopardalis* Brisson (giraffe): broken limb-bones—3. This type has been reported from the Siwaliks.

II. MOCHPAL (24 Parganas district)
The material was recovered from a tank, locally known as Kaipukur, at Mochpal village near Barasat in July 1973. The identified specimens are : *Bos namadicus* Falc., *Bubalus bubalis* Linn. (the remains are much larger than those of the recent buffalo and a bit different in structure also), *Bos indicus* Linn. (cattle), present buffalo and pig. Mention should also be made of the presence of river turtle *(trionyx gangeticus,* class *reptilia,* order *Chelonia,* family *Trichnidae)*. The cultural context of this occurrence is uncertain.

III. AMGHATA (Bankura district)
The material found in March 1982 from the Silavati cliff section at Amghata 3 m below the top of the cliff was supplied by Dilip K Chakrabarti of Delhi University. It was embedded in a compact greyish soil in a semi-fossilized condition and resembled the Susunia material. There are 7 bovid teeth out of which some are broken and all belong to the class Mammalia, order *Artiodactyla* and family Bovidae. The geological era is probably late pleistocene.

IV. MAHISDAL (Birbhum district)
The site was excavated by the Archaeological Survey of India in 1964 (*IAR*. The "chalcolithic" phase of the site consists of the following material: *Felis chaus* Guld (family *Felidae,* jungle cat, tooth-1, broken limb-bone—1), *Canis lupus* Linn. (family *Canidae,* wolf, claw-1), *Sus scrofa* Linn, (family *Suidae,* pig tooth-1), *Cervus duvauceli* Cuv. (family *Cervidae, Barasingha,* antler portion-1), *Cervus unicolor* Kerr. (Sambar, antler portion—1), *Axix axis* Erxl. (*chital,* antler portion—4), *Bos indicus* Linn. (cattle, teeth—broken charred mandible with a tooth and 3 more teeth, vertebrae—1, broken limb-bone-1) and *Capra hircus aegagrus* Erxl. (goat, tooth-1). The "Iron Age" level comprises the following material : *Canis lupus* Linn. (tooth-1), *Cervus unicolor* Kerr. (antler portion—1), *Axis axis* Erxl. (antler portion—1), *Bos indicus* Linn. (broken limb-bone—1) and *Capra hircus aegagrus* Erxl. (horn core—1).

V. BHARATPUR (Burdwan district)
The site was excavated by the Burdwan university and the Archaeological Survey of India in early 1970s. The 'chalcolithic' phase of the site consists of fish remains (portion of mandible, rib and vertebrae fragments—37, from the structure of the vertebrae these appear to belong to some species of carp), *Trionyx gangeticus* Cuvier (a remain of carapace, soft shelled turtle), *Gallus* sp. (a single fragment, domestic fowl), *Canis fami-*

liaris Linn. (limb-bone—1, pariah dog), *Equus caballus* Linn. (limb-bone—1, horse), *Cervus duvauceli* Cuv. (limb-bones-6), *Axix axis* Erxl. (antler—4), limb-bones—4), *Muntiacus muntjak* Zimm. (barking deer, limb-bones—2), *Sus scrofa* Linn. (teeth and limb-bones—13), *Boselaphus tragocamelus* Pallas (teeth, vertebrae and limb-bones—15, *nilgai), Bos indicus* Linn. (broken vertebrae, limb-bones, teeth and broken ribs—168), *Bubalus bubalis* Linn. (teeth, portion of mandible and limb-bones—19), *Ovis orientalis vignei* Blyth (sheep, teeth—1, limb-bone—1), *Capra hircus* Linn. (portion of mandible with 2 molars, broken limb-bone—1, broken rib—1) and most interesting of all, *Bos? namadicus* Falc. The 'Iron Age' level at the site possesses 2 broken vertebrae of Teleotean fish remains, 2 broken limb-bones of *Equus caballus* Linn., 1 tooth of *Sus scrofa* Linn., 1 tooth of *Camelus dromadarius* Linn. (camel), 4 teeth and broken limb-bones of *Boselaphus tragocamelus* Pallas, 1 horn core and 19 limb-bones of *Bos indicus* Linn., 5 limb-bones of *Bubalus bubalis* Linn. and 1 molar tooth of *Ovis orientalis vignei* Blyth.

It may be noted that both the "chalcolithic" and "Iron Age" levels of Bharatpur yielded human remains—42 fragmentary remains in the "chalcolithic" and 46 similar pieces in the "Iron Age". These comprise maxilla, teeth, ribs, pelvic girdle and limb-bones.

VI. BAHIRI (Birbhum district)

This site was investigated by the Archaeology and Museum unit of the Department of History, Delhi University in 1982. The report has been published in *Man & Environment* VI (1982). The study of the archaeozoological material is not yet complete but the preliminary analysis of the material indicates the following remains : *Canis familiaris* Linn. (1 bone fragment), *Cervus* sp. (2 specimens), *Axix axis* Erxl. (1 specimen), *Sus scrofa* Linn. (2 specimens), *Bos indicus* Linn. (7 specimens and *Bubalus bubalis* Linn. (6 specimens). The Bahiri material spans the 'chalcolithic —Iron Age' phase.

VII. TAMLUK

The material related to this early historic site came from the Eastern Circle's excavations in 1975 and comprises *Canis familiaris* Linn., *Equus caballus* Linn. *Cervus duvauceli* Cuv., *Sus scrofa* Linn., *Bos indicus* linn, and *Capra hircus* Linn.

Acknowledgement

The present paper has been written at the request of Dr Dilip K Chakrabarti

Zoological Survey of India
Calcutta

S. BANERJEE

Slip on Pottery-A Case Study

Slip is a pre-firing surface treatment for pots, ultimately resulting in polish, lustre, and bright hue after firing. Other than enhancing the appearence of the pot, slip increases its longevity by nullifying the porosity of pot-surface against moisture. The application of slip or wash depends on the purpose for which the particular pot is made. The surface treatment of Lustrous Red Ware (Rangpur IIC) is an example of perfect slip in true sense. Prior to this, the majority of the ancient Indian potters knowingly or unknowingly were following a technique akin to that of polychrome ware of Iran. The finest specimen of slip in ancient Indian potteries can be seen in the Northern Black Polished Ware.

The author made a detailed study of present day potters using their traditional methods. He went to Shri Binod Behari Pal, Kumbhakar belonging to the village of Krishnanarampur, district Hooghly, West Bengal. Out of fifteen potter-families in this area only Shri Binod prepares fine red slipped wares.

It was gathered from Shri Binod that in this region the pot-surface is treated before firing in two ways i.e. by application of: (i) wash, (ii) slip. Wash, a single thin coating prepared of readymade colour like yellow ochre or red ochre, easily available in the market produces only a red hue after firing. But to obtain polish, and bright hue with lustre, a minimum of four coatings of four different grades of prepared slip material namely *gad, satta, mazar* and *ubharani* are required to be applied one above the other on bone-dry surface of the pots. The slip-material of different grades are prepared separately from a single clay-body which consumes more than three months of time.

The essential materials and equipment required for preparing the slip material are: (i) clay, (ii) water, (iii) earthen pots like storage jars, lid-cum-bowls, basins, wooden stick etc. The clay is obtained by digging pits in nearby areas and choosing earth from levels at least a metre and half below the ground level. The clay used is sorted, cut into small pieces and left in the sun to dry. Rain water, already collected in storage jars during rains is poured in a large basin and dried clay pieces are dropped in it. The clay is then slaked for a day or two in water by constant shaking with a wooden stick and then kept at a secure place. After ten days, this clay-solution is gently transferred to a second basin leaving the residue i.e. sand, kankar, rootlets etc. at the bottom. The process of transferring the clay solution from one basin to the other is repeated thrice after an interval of about ten to fifteen days. The sediments collected from third, fourth, and fifth basins are known respectively as *gad, satta, mazar*. The clay solution obtained from the fifth basin is now kept at a secure place to dry. When the water gets fully evaporated, the accumulated clay sediment turns into flakes with fine lustrous surface. These flakes are used as fourth and the final coating over the earlier three and is known among the potters as *ubharani.* The four grades of slip materials i.e. *gad, satta, mazar*, and *ubharani* are preserved in small basins separately with proper lids for future use.

Dried *gad,* the first coating material, is now diluted with water in a bowl and applied on bone dry pot-surface by smearing with waste cloth or cotton dipped in the solution. For drying, the pot is left under the sun. In the same manner the coatings of *satta on* dried up *gad, mazar* on dried up *satta and ubhrani* on dried up mazar are applied. *Ubharani* can be applied more than once to make the surface more lustrous. The potters don't mix any pigment alongwith slip material. After application of coatings of four different slip-materials, the colour of the pot surface looks darkish brown.

The firing is done in an ordinary up-draft kiln, built in a most traditional style. Wood and coal are normally used as fuel.

Archaeological Survey of India
New Delhi

D. K. MALIK

BOOK REVIEWS

M.S. Randhawa, *A History of Agriculture in India*, Vol. I, Indian Council of Agricultural Research, Delhi 1981, pp. xxxv & 541. Price Rs. 50

Here is a book written by the eminent scientist-administrator Dr. M. S. Randhawa, which deals not only with the history of agriculture but also with domestication of animals and other associated cultural remains, covering a period from *circa* eighth millennium to the fourteenth century A.D. As such it is a reference material alike to students of archaeology and history. In an ample measures the book is a reflection of the multi-disciplinary approach to the subject. According to the author, the history of agriculture can only be properly understood in the light of evolution of life and the material culture of man. Realizing the importance and relevance of ecological factors, the author has devoted four chapters on the Birth of the Indian sub-continent, Soils, Climate and Agricultural Regions and Vegetation which serve to furnish the reader with useful data relating to these subjects and equip him for understanding the growth and development of agriculture in India. The next five Chapters, dealing with the Tertiary and Quaternary Periods, The Hunters and Food Gatherers of the Mesolithic Period, The Neolithic Agricultural Revolution in Western Asia and The Chalcolithic Culture in Mesopotamia, provide a suitable background for understanding the antecedent stages of the neolithic way of life. Considering the importance of the recent field-work in Thailand and South-east Asia it would have certainly added to the value of the book if a small Chapter had been included on similar findings in South-east Asia. The author, however, lists for the information of the reader the cultivated plants introduced in India from South-east Asia under an Appendix. Having thus set the scene, the author proceeds to deal with the evidence in the Indian sub-continent in a most objective manner, characteristic of his writings.

The author discusses the Indian evidence in an almost chronological order, starting with the pre-Harappan village-farming peasant communities of Baluchistan, proceeding to the fully urbanized Indus Civilization. From the archaeological evidence garnered by the author, it has been shown that the domestication of goat, sheep and Zebra cattle took place in Baluchistan. A separate chapter is devoted to Harappan agriculture dealing first with the basic tools of an agriculturist viz. the plough, the wheeled cart, the protection of crops, storage in granaries and later with food crops, cotton and use of wood and deforestation. The evidence is fully illustrated with photographs and maps. Of the causative factors for the decline of the Indus Civilization, the author seems to agree with Wheeler's views, viz. widespread deforestation and Aryan invasion. While the former seems to be one of the plausible factors, the postulate of the Aryan invasion has been questioned by many scholars and does not hold validity. In fact Wheeler himself in his later writings had stated that he was recording 'this causative factor as *jeu d' espirit* without any emphasis since it is sustained by no positive evidence. It is offered as a complement to the geomorphological evidence'. On the domestic animals of the Harappans, the author makes up a case for the identification of the variety of humpless bull or aurochs *(Bos Primigenous)* with what has all along been described as unicorn and also traces the origin of the species. This is indeed a fresh bit of research. The illustrations to accompany these chapters have been very thoughtfully selected.

The next three chapters deal with the neolithic cultures in the various geographical regions, and the author has striven hard to discuss all the available evidence. Relevant to the subject of the book are cultivation of millets, pulses, rice and discovery of silk. In the regions discussed, however, the evidence for the transition from the wild to the domesticated variety is unfortunately lacking. More field-work is, therefore, called for in this direction. He has very rightly referred to the recently-excavated site of Mehrgarh in Pakistan where remains of a neolithic settlement ascribable to the sixth millennium B.C. have been uncovered. Summing up, the author rightly observes 'our Civilization still rests on the discoveries made by the Neolithic people. Historic man has added no plant or animal of major importance to the domesticated forms on which he depends.'

Proceeding further Dr. Randhawa discusses the coming of Aryans and the importance of the horse, basing his conclusions on philology, archaeology and ethnology. For the archaeological evidence he has pointed the remarkable discoveries made by (a) the soviet archaeologists on the banks of the Sintashta river in the south of Trans-Urals region and (b) the Pakistani archaeologists in the Gandhara region. One of the whodunits of Indian archaeology is the identification of the cultural remains of the Aryans. The accruing knowledge on the subject still remains inconclusive. The author brings to our notice the domestic animals and crops of the vedic and later vedic periods taking the evidence both from the vedic literature and archaeological excavations.

The rest of the book deals with the historical period ranging from the sixth century B.C. through Mauryan, Sunga, Kushan, Gupta, Rajput to the Kingdoms of south India of the eleventh-twelfth century A.D. Under these Chapters the author discusses various subjects related to agriculture, viz. the impact of iron, irrigation system, tenure, land revenue, economic conditions, including observations of foreign travellers, like Hiuen Tsang, Alberuni. In these chapters the author has carried his conviction that agriculture should not be considered in isolation from the life of the people and the political scene.

The book, beautifully produced, is written in a readable style marked with scientific objectivity.

D-II-258, Chanakyapuri
New Delhi

B. K. THAPAR

P.C. Pant, *Prehistoric Uttar Pradesh,* Agam Kala Prakashan, Delhi, 1980, pp. 183, plates 7, figures 46. Price Rs. 160

The Indian Archaeology owes its gratitude to the Banaras Hindu University for contributing two books in recent years in Indian prehistory. The title of the present book raises a number of hopes, atleast in the hearts of lay-readers, but inside one finds a drab techno-typological description of the tools collected by the author during his surface explorations. One looked for some richer and general interpretation when the title claimed to be dealing with total prehistory.

Most of the recent books on Indian archaeology, are modified versions of Ph. D. thesis. This considerably restrict their utility for the general reader, as they deal with a very narrow aspect of the problems which have little general relevance. Some set formulae for chapterization are used which have no coherance on convergenece.

The book presents a detailed account of the explorations of the author and therefore is a welcome addition to the literature on Indian Stone Age. However, it appears little unfair to use the present title, whereas the stone tools are confined to the southernmost fringe of the Uttar Pradesh. Even there the author did not have access to the huge collection of the pre-historic artifacts made by the large teams of the Allahabad University. Nor had the author cared to examine the Garhwal collection of Palaeoliths made by K.P. Nautiyal. Thus the book is reduced to the work done by the author and his student Vidula Jaiswal alone. Both being advocates of the outmoded techno-typological approach, the book becomes a technical treatise without shedding much light on the prehistory of U.P. Even for a reliable techno-typological analyses one needs a stratified, well excavated collection. Techno-typological analysis of surface tools circumscribes its utility considerably. As the author's approach is technical and not synthetic, he enjoys giving histograms and graphs and adds further technological confusion by introducing a number of new German and French terms. In the present stage of synthetic models and multivariant analysis, to analyse only a small segment of the artifact attributes appears to be same conservatism. Surprisingly, to justify his narrow and sectarian approach the author criticises new archaeology and its models.

His chapter on stratigraphy deals with some Quaternary problems also. He has criticised G.R. Sharma as also Dassarma and Biswas for giving climatic interpretation of the Belan sediments without any adequate evidence. But the author himself rules out tectonic or eustatic causes for the different deposits except the climatic ones. One has to believe the word of the author, but one is not allowed to ask for the proof.

Some statements sound very confusing. For example, he says that Ganga never meets the ocean directly. All the major rivers have to meet the ocean and therefore eustatic changes cannot be ruled out. The author simply ignores the significant palaeoenvironmental studies carried out in Rajasthan, Maharashtra, and Kashmir by various multi-disciplinary groups. The Pleistocene pollen evidence from Kashmir is known from the thirties. Most of the recent work is published in a number of articles.

It is good to see that the author does not agree with Dassarma and Biswas's views on the glacial identification of the Belan gravels but he seems to be blissfully ignorant of the global implications of bringing down the glaciers upto Rajasthan and Madhya Pradesh.

Despite the claim of blurb that the author was trained in soil analysis the author says that a particular soil was rich in humus and this identification was supported by its being nonacidic (35). A humus-rich horizon should be acidic and not alkaline.

The concluding chapter makes a good reading and it presents a comprehensive survey of the Paleolithic cultures of the world. It would have been nice if the author could also discuss the implications the chopper-chopping industry of Central Asia which is only 2.5 lac years old.

The book does not include the figures in the main text and gives graphs and sections separately. Similarly the plates hardly *illustrate* any thing; except the plate 4A, all others are either illegible or have no information value. Captions to the figures have not been given and one has to wade through the text to find out their description. The graphs give a hanging scale which is most confusing.

Still, the present volume is a useful addition to the very limited corpus of prehistoric literature in India. It would have been better to label it as Paleolithic culture in the valleys of the south on tributaries of the Yamuna.

The book is remarkably free of errors and has been written in a very lucid style.

Physical Research Laboratory, Ahmedabad — **D. P. AGRAWAL**

A.H. Dani, *Indus Civilization, New Perspectives* Centre for the study of the Civilization of Central Asia, Quaid-i-Azam University, Islamabad, Pakistan, 1981, pp. 133, Price Rs. 100, $ 12.00.

This volume is the proceedings of an International seminar organised at Islamabad in January 1979. There are eleven papers in it. A.H. Dani in his review paper traced the history of the researches on the Indus Civilization and examined 'in the clash of ideas and views' its changing perspectives. For the origin of the Indus civilization he discussed at length the views of Fairservis and Dales and about the latest work done by Mughal in Bahawalpur region. Regarding post-Indus he says it is no longer a guess. The areas like Gomal Valley, Swat and Dir (Bahawalpur, Gujarat and East Panjab have produced data to understand the inherent continuity and change. A new look at Jhukar and Jhangar has given some new ideas on the Indus survivals. Regarding the matters related to chronology he has rightly observed that in view of the great extent of the Indus civilization in different geographic zones, it has now become necessary to get at local chronologies region-wise and then assess the overall picture.

In second paper 'Kot Diji culture—Its greatness' F.A. Khan reviewed the consequences of this Pre-Indus culture having a stratigraphic break with the succeeding Indus civilization in the wider setting of the cultural wealth known in this region. He thus disagrees with Mughal on the question of terminology—he prefers pre-Harappan to early Harappan.

The third paper is on Balakot by G.F. Dales. The lower or earlier material is termed as Balakotian whereas the upper levels belonging to the

Indus civilization starts after a long break. He is of the view that Balakotia a wares are the regional variations of basic motifs common to fourth and early third millennium B.C. pottery of the adjoining regions in southern Baluchistan, for example Nal. The presence of non-Harappan pottery such as Kulli in the Harappan levels is of considerable importance for the western trade of the Harappans.

Mughal's paper on 'New Archaeological Evidence from Bahawalpur' reveals nearly 400 sites ranging from the pre-Indus to the post-Indus periods. His early Harappan period is preceded by Hakra ware in this region which he placed around the fourth millennium B.C. He is of the opinion that all Kot Diji related sites together constitute an Early Harappan or Early Urban Formative Phase of the Indus Civilization.

In next paper by A.R. Khan reports on 'Kot Kori-A site of Indus Civilization in the lower Sind. He suggested the study of palaeogeography and other natural processes operating in this area. B.B. Lal's paper on the structural remains at Kalibangan suggested a re-thinking about calling the western wing of the settlement as the 'Citadel'. According to him the so-called 'Citadel was used by priests. In next paper 'The Mosaic of the Indus Civilization beyond the Indus valley', B.K. Thapar looks at the dynamics of expansion of Indus Civilization in two different environmental zones, hilly in the north, and coastal in the south.

Jim G. Shaffer's 'The Protohistoric Period in the Eastern Panjab : A Preliminary Assessment' is a comprehensive reassessment of the large number of excavations carried out in Punjab and Haryana in the last three decades, under Siswal A,B,C, and D. Louis Dupree contributed a note on Shortugai. It was a trading out-post of Harappans for Lapislazuli. Period I is Harappan, Period II Late Harapppan, Period III is Post-Harappan with Bactrian elements and Period IV represents late Bronze Age Bactrian.

'Interpreting the Indus Script' by Asko Parpola is the outcome of a work where computer was used for counting the signs and their variables in the script. The last paper of F.A. Durrani, Indus Civilization : Evidence West of Indus' deals with the excavations of Lewan and Tarakai Qila in Bannu Basin and Rahman Dheri, the latter provides a continuity from proto-kot Dijian (I) — typical Kot Dijian (II) to evolved Kot Dijian (III). A number of ^{14}C dates provide a chronology to the site. Lewan represents period II and III of Rahman Dheri.

It is a timely presented volume of great value edited by Dr. A.H. Dani who is well known to the scholarly world.

Archaeological Survey of India **K. N. DIKSHIT**
New Delhi

D.P. Agrawal, *The Archaeology of India,* Curzon Press, London 1982, Institute of Asian Studies Monograph Series no. 46. Price £ 8.50

There is a considerable gap between the amount of work that is being done in Indian archaeology and the level of its dissemination to the informed public. Remarkable progress has been made in Indian prehistoric and protohistoric studies in recent years but in the Indian historical consciousness this has hardly made an impact. One of its major reasons is the scarcity of suitable books which will go beyond the fellow professionals and try to synthesise in clear terms the available knowledge of prehistoric and protohistoric India. In the present volume D.P. Agrawal, a leading professional in his own right, has attempted such a synthesis, and we are all thankful to him. From the point of view of a classroom teacher this book has an added importance. The study of prehistory and protohistory still occupies only a marginal part of our university curricula and those of us who have to teach a course in the subject have to do so within a highly restricted time schedule.

On close reading it appears that the most striking thing about the book is its sense of balance. It is characterized throughout by a basic scholarship which can not merely take in smoothly all the necessary details but also has the ability to judge these details in the context of the subcontinent as a whole. No undue importance has been given to a single issue, however important. On the other hand not a single important issue has been neglected or completely passed over. This book is a true reflection of the reality of Indian archaeology today. In a synthesis of this kind there is always scope of disagreement with the author's opinion on various issues but even here

Professor Agrawal has remarkably restrained himself from being too firm in his support of any particular point of view in a particular issue.

Dependable textbooks are a crying necessity and there is no doubt that this book by D.P. Agrawal will be a major textbook in our university syllabi.

Delhi University **DILIP K. CHAKRABARTI**
Delhi

Jean-Francois Jarrige - Mariecle, *Fouilles De Pirak,* Publication of the French Archaeological Mission to Pakistan, No. 2 Paris 1979 Vol I, pp. 347, Vol II, 35, figures 121, plates 56 Price-not mentioned.

It is the report of archaeological excavations conducted at Pirak in French, Vol. I contains text with summary in English, and Vol. II has illustrations of architecture and, plates and figures. The Vol. I is divided into three parts. Part I is having four chapters dealing with general introduction and respective period of the site. The last chapter IV deals with conclusion and origin of Pirak culture. The Part II of the report, divided into 4 chapters, deals with the general character of pot-forms, and designs, and at the end with the ceramics of the 3rd millennium. The last part of the report deals with the antiquities of different materials including objects of the 3rd millennium B.C. There are also five appendices—dealing with lithic industry, plant and faunal remains, radio-carbon dates and chemical analysis of metal objects. The site, which is located at the feet of the Bolan Pass in the Kachhi plains of Baluchistan, has provided a continous sequence starting from 1800 B.C. to the 8th century B.C. The site has a total occupation of 12 metre, divisible into 14 building phases. Period I, divided into two sub-phases, is datable around 1800 B.C. Period II from 1300 B.C. to 1200 B.C. and Period III again divisible into three sub-phases A to C with a knowledge of iron working and is datable to 11th century B.C.

The post-Indus phases, 2nd millennium and the beginning of the 1st millennium, was not well documented in Baluchistan. At Amri in Period III C, Casal noticed definite changes in Harappan pottery. New pot-forms with thicker and more stylized decoration in III D were termed as 'forerunners of Jhukar ware'. So Pirak, being very close to Pre-Harappan Mehargarh and Harappan Nowsharo, forms part of a much larger study of the settlement pattern between the 7th millennium and 1st millennium. However, the authors feel that there was decline of urbanism towards 1800 B.C., the Indus cities disappeared and Mesopotamian texts cease to mention the trade with eastern regions, notably Meluhha. He compared the conditions with the breaking up of urban settlements in southern Turkmenia due to pressure of population. The towns were replaced by a large number of villages.

The two Volumes thus add a lot of new informations to our knowledge of cultures in the piedmont region of the Bolan river which bridges the hilly tracts of northern Baluchistan and the flood-plains of the Indus.

Archaeological Survey of India **K. N. DIKSHIT**
New Delhi.

H.N. Singh, *History and Archaeology of Black-and-Red Ware* (Chalcolithic Period), Sandeep Prakashan, New Delhi. 1982 pp. IL + 517, plates 15, Price Rs. 400.

The present book is the first of its kind—what is just a technique of firing earthen pots has been picked up for comprehensive treatment, in the context of the Chalcolithic cultures, running through 600 pages. It has been divided into four chapters: Historical background, Sites, Stratigraphy and Chronology; Technological and typological make-up and associated materials. It is prefixed by a long chapter of discussion (Introduction) and suffixed by a short chapter called Conclusion.

In the *magnum opus* the author passes through a great dilemma when on the one hand he takes pains to find out the origin of this technique in Egyptian Black Topped Ware of 4000 B.C. and on the other he presents details of Harappa Culture through its various periods and phases at sites like Lothal just because black-and-red ware was in use at this site. This dilemma persists when the author tries to discover the 'Migration' of this technique in time and space since once again he gives details of culture-complexes of the Banas of the Malwa, of the Painted Grey Ware, of the Pandu-Rajar-Dhibi, with site-wise treatment. Thus, although the author again and again makes it clear that what he is dealing with is basically a technique and not culture yet the entire treatment is culture'-oriented as if all antiquities, both movable and immovable, found in levels where black-and-red ware is found belong to a complex whose basic ethos is represented by this pottery. This inner contradiction does not minimise the importance of this work. By all counts it is a source-book on black-and-red ware of the third and second millennia B.C.

National Museum **S. P. GUPTA**
New Delhi

K.M. Srivastava, *Community Movements in Protohistoric India,* Agam Kala Prakashan, Delhi. Price. Rs'. 200

Shri K.M. Srivastava by his work at Bakraur (the place of Buddha's Sujata) and Piprahwa (ancient Kapilavastu) has opened a new vista in Indian archaeology especially of mid-eastern India. The work at Piprahwa has drawn universal attention but the work at Bakraur may not be so well-known. As one brought up on the images of Buddhist India in Rabindranath Tagore's poems and Abanindranath Tagore's paintings the present reviewer was delighted to learn from Shri Srivastava that Sujata of the legend was a historic reality and that in the ninth century A.D. a Pala king remembered the house of Sujata.

This book, however, is in a different context and marks the author's mature interest in the protohistoric period. In *JOIB*, 1971, he published a lengthy article in which he underlined the elements of cultural diversity associated with the Black-and-red ware in different regions of India. That was the first exercise of its kind in the context of the Black-and-red ware. In this book the author elaborates his argument and domonstrates the absurdity of identifying this ware with any linguistic or ethnic group.

The present reviewer agrees with all the major conclusions of the book and he is happy with the author's anti-diffusionist approach to the problem. Shri Srivastava has substantiated his argument with a great amount of carefully considered detail and this has greatly increased the value of his work. One of the best chapters is the one on the technique of manufacture of this ware. The chapter on the comparative study of shapes is a major contribution by itself. A coherent approach, careful archaeological documentation and analysis and a wealth of drawings and photographs have turned this book into an important reference manual in Indian archaeology.

Delhi University **DILIP K. CHAKRABARTI**
Delhi

Ratan Parimoo, *Life of Buddha in Indian Sculpture,* Kanak Publication, New Delhi 1982, pp 140, .plates 126. Price Rs. 150.

It is a book written on a subject so very popular yet so much complex that one rarely realizes. Since it is written by a university professor of art with more than two decades of teaching experience it has the rare qualities of clarity of presentation, simiplicity of langauge and penetrating insight of an artist. The Buddhist art of India, performed, which established his Greatness in the author rightly points out, has eight popular themes—four connected with the life-cycle of the Lord (Birth, Enlightenment, First Sermon and Mahaparinivana) and four with the 'miracles' He performed, which established his Greatness in the eyes of his followers (the 'miracle of Sravasti, the Descent from Tushita heaven, the subjugation of Nalagiri, and the receipt of honey-bowl offered by the Monkey). Each one is narrative, and they were actually shown in narrative form from the first century through the sixth, most graphically. But then with the popularity of Buddhism from the 9th through the 12th century in Bengal and Bihar, it was felt that instead of using eight panels, involving a lot of money and a lot of space, why not use one and symbolically represent all the eight which were otherwise commonly known. The author rightly points out that more than the texts, these necessities of the artist, including compositional necessity, were responsible for the birth of certain iconographic forms. "Iconography", he writes, "is the result of the process of summarization of the narrative and the active role of the artists in this process." (Preface). In the pre-Kushan period some of these eight themes were also represented by symbols, such as the elephant, throne and turban. Significantly, although they did not form part of 'iconography' as such, they too, in a sense, represent 'summary of narrative'.

The author, with the help of a large number of plates, has convincingly proved his points since the examples have been chosen from different parts of the country and from different periods.

National Museum
New Delhi

S. P. GUPTA

Seiichi Mizuno and Takayasu Hignchi (ed.), *Thareli,* Dohosha, Kyoto 1978, pp. XIII + 164, plates 144, plans 31.

It is the archaeological report of the excavations of a Buddhist monastery conducted by the Kyoto University Scientific Mission to Iranian Plateau and Hindukush between 1963 and 1967. The site is located in the hills of the Swat, now in northern Pakistan. It is dated to the Kushan period, from the first to the third century A.D. The report is in Japanese but accompanied with 23 pages of detailed summary in English. It is a large sized book with very beautiful paper and printing. The stone and stucco sculptures, coins, pottery, iron implements have been incorporated completely in very beautiful plates. Besides the narration of explorations conducted in Gandhara region by the same mission earlier, we have here the details of architectural remains divided into several regions. Chapter V goes into thorough discussion on the chronology of the site and peculiarities of the location of the monastery.

The importance of the excavations lies in the fact that it throws a flood of light on the Gandhara art and architecture as practised not in the plains of the Kabul river, near Peshawar, but as practised in the remote hills, far away from the township and devoted exclusively to the monks. The presence of domes show that what was done in rock-cut caves of Western India was done here structurally. The sculptures in local schist enlarge enormously our understanding of the content and character of the Gandhara art. As far as dating of the sculptures is concerned, it is indirect—from the coins, the majority of which belong to Kanishka and Huvishka, pottery which can be dated to first century A.D. and the tribolate type of iron arrowheads which also belong to the early centuries of the Christian era. All put together, we have in this report a mass of extremely useful data.

National Museum,
New Delhi

S. P. GUPTA

Ananda Krishna (ed.), *Chhavi,* Bharat Kala Bhavan, Varanasi 1981, pp. XIV + 323, plate figures 655, Colour A—W + 52.

It is No. 2 of the Rai Krishna Das's Felicitation Volume, as lavishly produced as No. 1, but with many more thought-provoking articles. In all, there are 53 articles covering Indian architecture, sculpture, painting, embriodery, coins, beads, inscriptions, etc., mostly written by well-known Indian and foreign scholars, like C. Sivaramamurti, Krishna Deva, Basil bray, Joanna Williams, Kapila Vatsyayan. Doughs Barrett, D.C. Bhattacharaya, Frederick Asher and Walter Spink.

Some of the articles which bring to light new source material are by Edwin Binney on Sultanate paintings; by Martin Lerner on Early Chola bronzes; by Anand Krishna on a Laur-Chanda manuscript, etc. Some of the articles which offer fresh interpretations of older collections are by Susan Huntington on Gyaraspura stupa; by Doris Chatham on Western Chalukyan sculptures; by Mary-Ann Lutzker on a Mamallapuram panel; by Jennine Auboyer on an early terricotta plaque with winged standing figure; by Michel Meister on Early Gupta tradition; by Ajaya Kumar Singh on paintings in Alchi monastery, etc. There are a few papers dealing with concepts also, such as the one by Ananda Krishna on Chatura and Vichitra in Indian art and Culture and the other by D. C. Bhattacharaya on some Buddhist Asanas.

The Volume is, therefore, undoubtedly of lasting value for the historians of Indian art, although in bulk and heaviness it is extremely difficult to manage it.

National Museum
New Delhi

S. P. GUPTA

Chandra Bhushan Trivedi, *Dashpur* (Hindi), Madhya Pradesh Hindi Granth Academy, Bhopal 1979, pp. XVI + 152, plates 76. Price Rs. 30.

It is the first comprehensive book on the history, culture and archaeology of the Mandsor region of Madhya Pradesh, anciently known as Dasapur Janapad of north-western Malawa. The author begins with the Stone Age cultures, moves through the Chalcolithic, Early Historical and Late Historical periods to unfold the well-stratified history of the region. He utilizes practically every source of information: literary, epigraphical, numismatic, architectural, sculptural, pottery, lithics, and the rest. It is, therefore, a perfect text-book on the subject for advanced courses as well as for interested readers. Since archaeological finds also find a suitable place in it, cataloguing all important sites with their artefactual wealth, it becomes a good source book for excavators. The importance of this knowledge multiplies when we note that a large number of sites, such as Manoti, Sujanapura and Kamalapur Kohla, have been completely submerged in a hydro-electric dam recently constructed on the Chambal and all our future references to them will be drawing exclusively on this book and a few short reports. But one wishes the plates, thoughtfully chosen, were also beautifully printed, they are all below standard and the blame for this lies squarely on the shoulders of the publishers, that is Hindi Grantha Academy of the Govt. of Madhya Pradesh. We hope, in future, the Academy will pay proper attention to this most important aspect of their publications which include archaeological finds.

National Museum **S. P. GUPTA**
New Delhi

I. K. Sarma, *The Development of early Saiva Art Architecture with special reference to Andhradesh,* Sandeep Prakashan, New Delhi 1982, pp. xxvi + 223, illustrations 180. Price Rs. 350.

It is the one art history book on the most popular of Indian gods in sculpture, Siva, which has laid down the firm foundation of future studies in the field. Most of the Indian art history books are being unfortunately written by those who have neither any knowledge of field archaeology nor any appreciation of the verdict of the excavated earth—for them the world of literature can explain every thing, even the beginning of art and architecture, i.e. the objects of plastic art, even though they are conscious of the fact that the dating of early Indian literary-works is far from satisfactory. That is preciously the reason why absurd terms like 'ageless' were coined and used by no less a distinguished scholar than Stella Kramrisch. If history without firm chronology is grandmother's tale, are we not constantly fed on these tales in the name of art history? The only judicious approach to Indian art history can be the *ardhanarisvara* model—the inseparable consideration of archaeology, literature, epigraphy, numismatics and living traditions. Judging from this point of view Sarma's contribution through this book to the art history of Siva is a model to be followed, further refined and applied.

The book has been divided into ten chapters although I and II; III and IV; and IX and X could be combined in single units without losing the unity of composition of the book designing.

The book highlights, besides the controversial prehistory presentation and protohistory of Saivism, the author's meticulous presentation of the results of his own excavations of the temples of Gudimallam, Amaravati and Nagarjunakonda, all known so far through fragmentatary reports. The book also collects at one place all the known post-Ikshvaku Saiva art objects from Andhra Pradesh. At every stage he uses the evidence of literary texts, epigraphs and coins and, therefore, it is a total treatment of the subject.

However, one wishes the half-tone reproductions could be more telling, and the price of the book only half of what is charged.

National Museum **S. P. GUPTA**
New Delhi

Bridget and Raymond Allchin, *The Rise of Civilization in India and Pakistan*, Cambridge University Press, Cambridge 1982, pp. 379, tables 4, figures 217.

We are delighted to see the publication of this book which was expected for sometime. This is in a sense a revised version of their *The Birth of Indian Civilization,* 1968, but more accurately this is a new book having plates and maps of field works conducted afterwards. A lot has been achieved in the sub-continental archaeology since last publication and the authors, the foremost 'Indian' archaeologists in the West, had to change substantially the scope of their discussion. More significant discoveries have taken place in the areas of prehistory including paleo-climatic investigations and Harappan studies and one notes that a great amount of space has been devoted to these issues, although a few of the sites have been dealt summarily and their chrono-cultural position inclu ing pattern of settlement remained unexplained. The recent works at Sothi, Nohar and Sherpura also did not find place in the general survey. In their last publication, prehistory occupied a marginal part although it covered all the developmental stages. Considerable emphasis has been put on the ecological approach and the present reviewer feels that the geographical analysis is one of the best sections of the book. The conclusions drawn on the outstanding problems show their brilliant handling in synthesising the data and presenting it in clear terms. It would have been excellent had the authors given more elaborate treatment in the matter of discussion and the review of the issues as far as India-east of the Indus system upto Bengal and other sub-Indus cultures are concerned. The problems of South India also required detailed analysis. The postulated link between iron and the secondary spread of the Indo-Aryans may not appeal to all. It must, however, be pointed out that the idea of an indigenous development of Indian iron technology has been generally acknowledged. The bibliography would have been fuller and one does miss some recently excavated sites (cf. Hulas, Manda, Bhagwanpura, Sringaverapura etc.). The interlocking of the Harappa culture with the Painted Grey Ware, a cultural stage noticed in recent years in Panjab and Haryana also deserved attention. But these are only some of the minor points that can be said in criticism. We have no doubt that this handsomely illustrated volume with its profound scholarship will be a great source of pleasure for years to come.

Archaeological Survey of India
New Delhi. **K. N. DIKSHIT**

Amarnath Khanna : *Archaeology of India,* Clarion Books, New Delhi, 1982, pp. 144, illustrations, 57; Price Rs. 155/-.

After a very long time a good, authentic and beautifully produced book on Indian archaeology for interested laymen as well as senior students has been produced by one who has spent quarter of a century in the service of the Archaeological Survey of India, both as an official and as a student of its prestigeous institution, School of Archaeology. The book has been thoughtfully designed with four major chapters—History of Archaeological pursuits, Highlights of Indian Archaeology, Important Excavated Sites and Present undertakings and Future Prospects. The approach is cultural and the framework is historical —the British legacy left behind by the late Sir Mortimer Wheeler. It is a straightforward presentation of facts and figures free from American jargon and models based on anthropological approach to growth of culture and change in culture. One therefore finds a very useful narration of the directional changes through which the history of Indian archaeology passed from 1784 to 1980. The aims, objectives and passions of such great antiquarians as Sir William Jones, who founded the 'Asiatic Society' in January 1784 at Calcutta, and thus laid the foundation of Indological studies in India, of Charles Wilkins who unlocked the mystery of the Gupta and Kutila scripts, or James Princep who deciphered the Brahmi and Kharoshthi scripts, of Cunningham who explored the Buddhist sites mentioned by the Chinese pilgrims Fahien and Hiuen Tsang, Sir John Marshall who excavated Mohenjo-daro and Taxila, Sir Mortimer Wheeler who introduced scientific methods of excavations in India, A. Ghosh who started *Indian Archaeology - A Review* and standardized archaeological publications, B.B. Lal who took up the cause of correlating literary data with archaeological finds, and B.K. Thapar who expanded the bureaucratic net-work of the Archaeological Survey of India beyond comprehension, can be seen like the constantly rolling scenes on the large canvas of three centuries of generally unremembered story. Similarly, brief reviews of works done at the Indus sites like Harappa, Lothal, and Kalibangan; Chalcolithic sites like Ahar, Maski, Navdatoli and Inamgaon, and historical sites like Brahmagiri, Hastinapur, Kausambi and Ratnagiri add to the usefulness of the book. However, while telling the story of present undertakings, research and training the author made the unpardonable mistake of omitting completely the role of non-governmental professional bodies like the Indian Archaeological Society and Indian Society for Prehistoric and Quaternary Studies which through their regular publications of *Puratattva* and *Man & Environment,* respectively, have not only kept the torch of Indian archaeology alive when the Archaeological Survey and National Museum practically stopped the publications of their bulletins but also kept up the enthusiasm of young archaeologists of the post-partition period, within the Archaeological Survey and Museums, and the Universities and research institutes. The credit for this goes to Prof. A.K. Narain who was then heading the Department of Ancient History & Archaeology, the Banaras Hindu University; he founded the former organizations.

M.D. KHARE

Archaeological Survey of India
New Delhi

I. V.N. Misra *et al.* : Didwana, handaxes.

II. V.N. Misra *et al.* : Didwana, handaxes.

III. V.N. Misra *et al.* : Didwana, Choppers (1-2) Chopping tools (3-5).

IV. V.N. Misra *et al.* : Didwana, Polyhedrons.

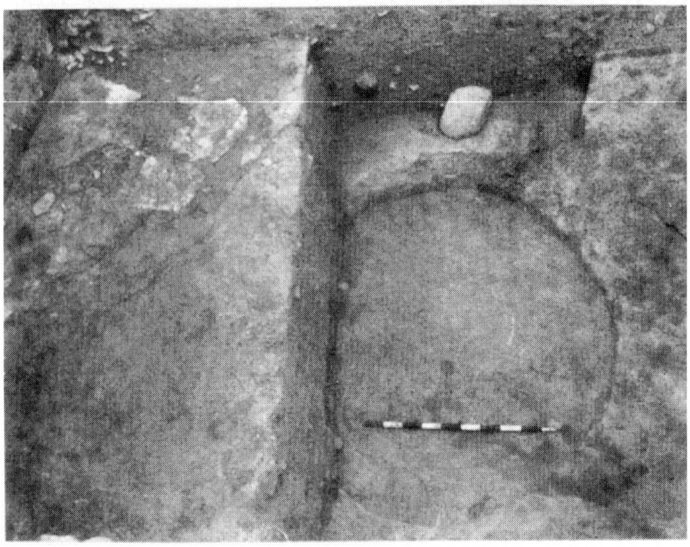

I. A.K. Sharma : Gufkral, Dwelling pit and floor level.

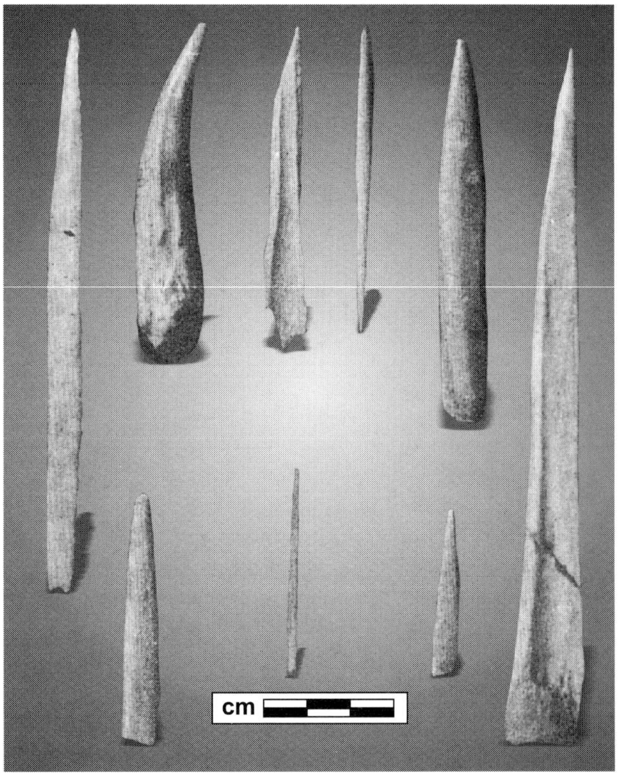

II. A.K. Sharma : Gufkral, Pottery, Period IB.

III. A.K. Sharma : Gufkral, Bone tools, Period IA.

IV. A.K. Sharma : Gufkral, Wheelmade, black burnished pottery.

V. A.K. Sharma : Gufkral, Stone harvesters and points.

VI. A.K. Sharma : Gufkral, 1-3 celts, 4 Ringstone — Period I, 5-7 Ringstone — Period II.

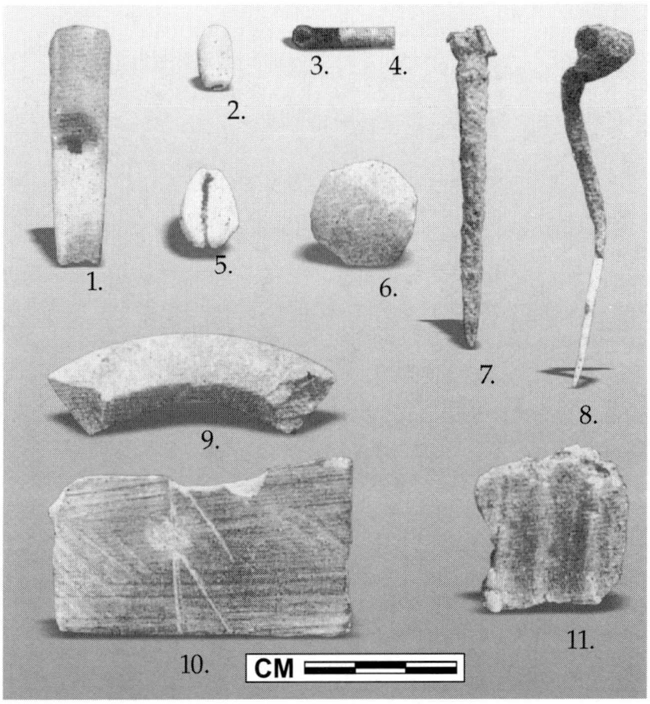

VII. A.K. Sharma : Gufkral, 1 Bone bead, 2 and 4 paste bead, 6 Marble, 11 clay with reed impression — Period IA; 8 Copper hairpin, 9 Terracotta bangle, 10 Potsherd with graffiti — Period IC; 3 Wooden bead, 5 Cowrie, 7 Copper pin — Period II.

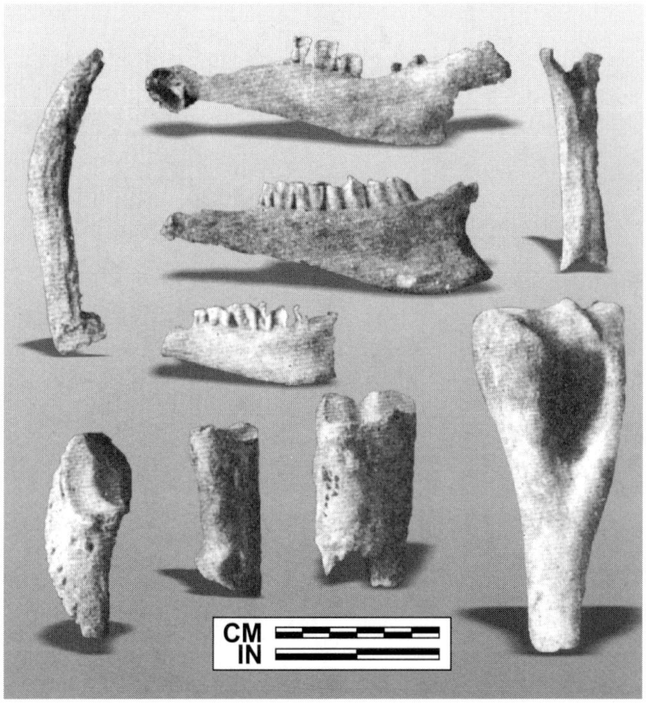

VIII. A.K. Sharma : Gufkral, Animal bones.

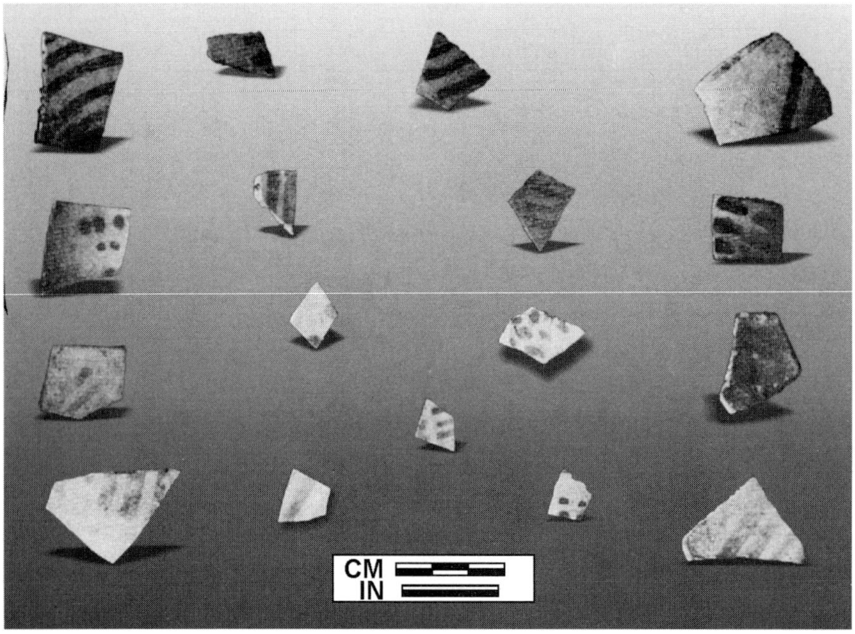

I. B.B. Lal & K.N. Dikshit : Pariar, Painted Grey Ware sherds.

I. Y.D. Sharma : Rohira, Clay sealing.

I. D.P. Sharma : Triangular celts.

II. D.P. Sharma : Surya with seven wives.

III. D.P. Sharma : Rectangular ***argha.***

IV. D.P. Sharma : Reh inscription.

V. D.P. Sharma : Korari, brick temple.

I A. Shashi Asthana : Patravahaka Yaksha (front).

I B. Shashi Asthana : Patravahaka Yaksha.

II. Shashi Asthana : Aghapur Yaksha.

III. Shashi Asthana : Head, Patravahaka Yaksha.

I. M.C. Joshi : National Museum, Vasudeva Kamalaja.

II. M.C. Joshi : National Museum, Vasudeva Kamalaja showing details of the lower garments with fine decorative patterns

III. M.C. Joshi : National Museum, head Vasudeva Kamalaja.

IV. M.C. Joshi : Baijnath, H.P., Vaikuntha Vasudeva Kamalaja.

I. P.K. Trivedi : Kayavarohana, Doorjamb.

II. P.K. Trivedi : Kayavarohana, Harihara.

I. B.B. Lal : Sringaverapura, U.P., A view of a recent retaining wall of kiln fired bricks, partly fallen and partly intact. This was onstructed to prevent erosion of natural soil behind it on which stands a temple complex.

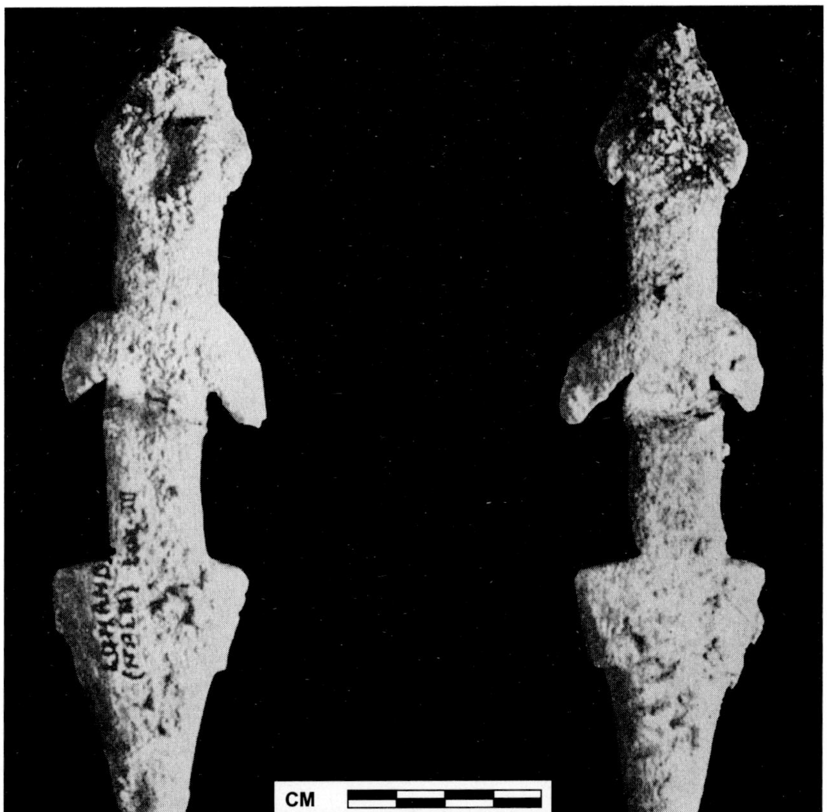

I. S.P. Gupta : Belan, the alleged bone mother-goddess.

I. Mahadevan : Hulas, U.P., Indus sealing.

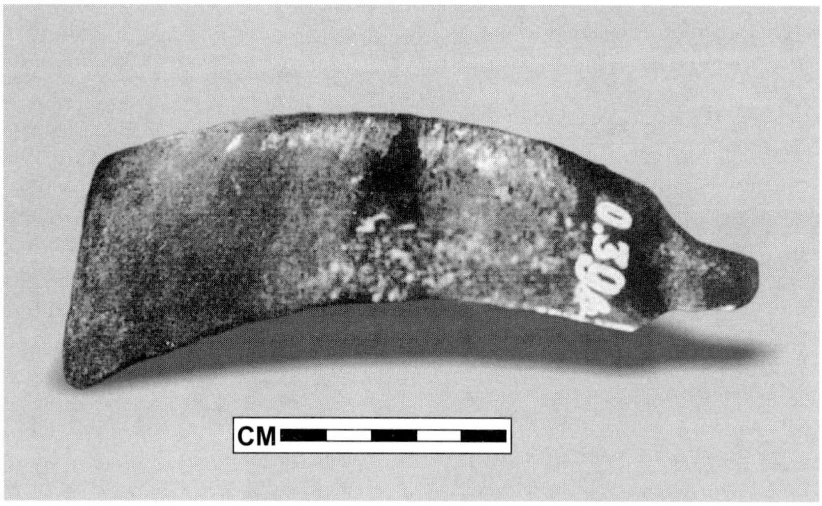

I. S.P. Gupta : Khurapi, a new copper Hoard tool type.

I. S.A. Sali : Daimabad, a unique terracotta.

I. K.P. Gupta : Kolhua, a general view, stupa and the pillar.

II. K.P. Gupta : Kolhua, showing lime plaster over the stupa alongwith brickedged pradakshinapath.

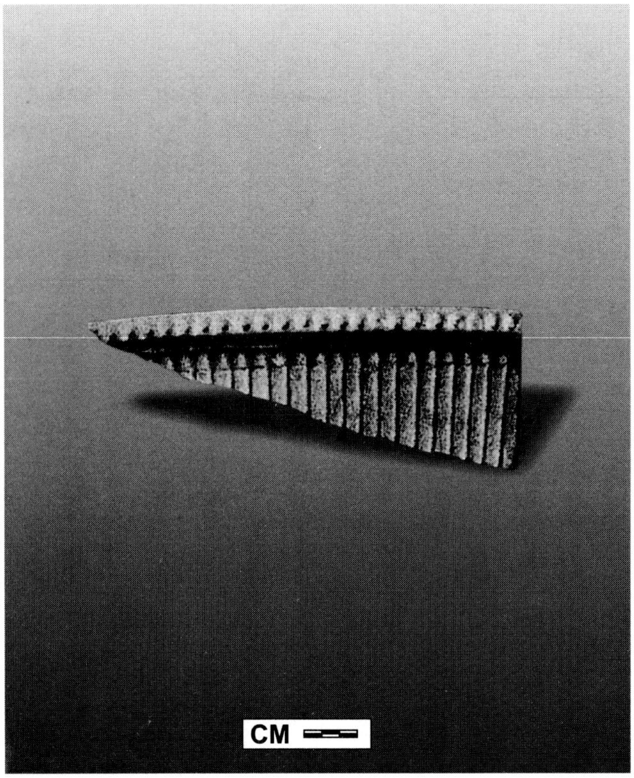

III. K.P. Gupta : Fragment of chattravali.

IV. K.P. Gupta : Kolhua, stucco head.

V. K.P. Gupta : Kolhua, inscribed plaques.

VI. K.P. Gupta : Kolhua, stupa showing treasure hunters cutting after the debris clearance.

I. C.B. Trivedi : Dithwara, Vishnu.

II. C.B. Trivedi : Dithwara, Garuda.

I. W.H. Siddiqui : Cambay, Jami Masjid.

II. W.H. Siddiqui : Cambay, tomb of Umar al-Kazruni.

III. W.H. Siddiqui : Cambay, Cambay, carved panel in relief on marble sarcophagus of the tomb of Umar al-Kazruni.